The South's Best
Bed & Breakfasts

Delightful Places to Stay

Great Things to Do When You Get There

4th Edition

FODOR'S TRAVEL PUBLICATIONS, INC.
NEW YORK • TORONTO • LONDON • SYDNEY • AUCKLAND

THE SOUTH'S BEST BED & BREAKFASTS

EDITOR: Anastasia Redmond Mills

Editorial Contributors: Daniel Drummond, Lynn Grisard Fullman, Mitzi Gammon, Jane Garvey, Sylvia Higganbotham, Mickey Ingalls, Mary Sue Lawrence, Henrietta MacGuire, Honey Naylor, Katherine Price, Susan Spano, Carol Timblin, Lisa H. Towle, John Webb.

Production Editor: Stacey Kulig

Production/Manufacturing: Mike Costa

Maps: David Lindroth, *cartographer*; Robert Blake, *map editor*

Design: Guido Caroti

Illustrations: Kayley LeFaiver

Cover Photograph: Kelley/Mooney

Fourth Edition

ISBN 0–679–00179–4

SPECIAL SALES

Fodor's Travel Publications are available at special discounts for bulk purchases for sales promotions or premiums. Special editions, including personalized covers, excerpts of existing guides, and corporate imprints, can be created in large quantities for special needs. For more information contact your local bookseller or write to Special Markets, Fodor's Travel Publications, 201 East 50th Street, New York, NY 10022. Inquiries from Canada should be directed to your local Canadian bookseller or sent to Random House of Canada, Ltd., Marketing Department, 2775 Matheson Boulevard East, Mississauga, Ontario L4W 4P7. Inquiries from the United Kingdom should be sent to Fodor's Travel Publications, 20 Vauxhall Bridge Road, London, England SW1V 2SA.

PRINTED IN THE UNITED STATES OF AMERICA

10 9 8 7 6 5 4 3 2 1

CONTENTS

Foreword *iv*

Introduction *v*

Virginia 1

Northern Virginia *4*

The Eastern Shore *13*

Williamsburg and
Southeast Virginia *21*

Piedmont *30*

The Blue Ridge/
Shenandoah Valley and
Virginia Highlands *39*

North Carolina 49

The Carolina Coast *51*

The Piedmont *64*

The Mountains *73*

South Carolina 83

Myrtle Beach
and the Grand Strand *86*

Charleston and the
Lowcountry *94*

Thoroughbred Country and
the Old Ninety Six *108*

Georgia 115

North Georgia
and Atlanta *118*

Middle Georgia *132*

Coastal Georgia *139*

Southwest Georgia *153*

Alabama 161

North Alabama *163*

Central Alabama *169*

Gulf Coast Delta *176*

Mississippi 181

North Mississippi
Hill Country *183*

Near the Natchez Trace
and the Mississippi Delta
193

Mississippi Gulf Coast
Region *212*

Louisiana 219

Greater New Orleans *222*

Plantation Country *234*

Cajun Country *241*

North-Central Louisiana
250

Tennessee 257

East Tennessee *259*

Middle Tennessee *269*

West Tennessee *277*

Maps and Charts

The South *viii–ix*

Special Features at a Glance
x–xxxi

Virginia *2–3*

North Carolina *50*

South Carolina *84–85*

Georgia *116–117*

Alabama *162*

Mississippi *182*

Louisiana *220–221*

Tennessee *258*

Alphabetical Directory 283

FOREWORD

While every care has been taken to ensure the accuracy of the information in this guide, the passage of time will always bring change, and consequently, the publisher cannot accept responsibility for errors that may occur.

All prices and listings are based on information supplied to us at press time. Details may change, however, and the prudent traveler will avoid inconvenience by calling ahead.

Fodor's wants to hear about your travel experiences, both pleasant and unpleasant. When an inn or B&B fails to live up to its billing, let us know and we will investigate the complaint and revise our entries where the facts warrant it.

Send your thoughts to us via e-mail at editors@fodors.com (specifying the name of the book on the subject line) or on paper in care of The South's Best Bed & Breakfasts *editor at Fodor's Travel Publications, 201 East 50th Street, New York, NY 10022.*

INTRODUCTION

YOUR GUIDES

You'll find bed-and-breakfasts in big houses with turrets and little houses with decks, in mansions by the water and cabins in the forest, not to mention structures of many sizes and shapes in between. B&Bs are run by people who were once lawyers and writers, homemakers and artists, nurses and architects, singers and businesspeople. Some B&Bs are just a room or two in a hospitable local's home; others are more like small inns. So there's an element of serendipity to every stay in an inn or B&B. But while that's part of the pleasure of visiting these establishments, it's also an excellent reason to plan your travels with a good B&B guide. The one you hold in your hands serves the purpose neatly. We think it's the best of its kind.

All the establishments we've included promise a unique experience, a distinctive sense of time and place; each is a destination in itself, not just a place to rest your head at night but an integral part of a weekend escape. For that reason, we tell you not only about places to stay but also about what's up in the area and what you should and shouldn't miss—everything from historic sites and parks to antiques shops, boutiques, restaurants, and nightspots.

FODOR'S B&B CRITICS

Native Virginian **Daniel Drummond** *finds reviewing B&Bs a relaxing change from the daily deadline pressure of his job as a newspaper reporter in southwest Virginia.* **Lynn Grisard Fullman,** *updater of the Alabama chapter, is a member of the Society of American Travel Writers and winner of numerous writing awards. A Chattanooga native, she has written five books, coauthored another, and is a regular contributor to magazines and newspapers. Our Georgia update is the work of* **Jane Garvey,** *who writes regularly about food and wine, art and architecture, interior design, history and culture, and travel for the* Atlanta Journal & Constitution *and other Georgia publications. Jane stays at bed-and-breakfast inns wherever she travels.* **Mary Sue Lawrence,** *who updated the South Carolina chapter, is a freelance writer and editor whose features on travel, entertainment, health, and business* *have appeared in national and British magazines. A Charlestonian, she lives on the nearby Isle of Palms. Real-live southerner* **Honey Naylor,** *author of our Louisiana chapter, is a freelance writer whose features have appeared in* Travel & Leisure, New Orleans Magazine, USA Today, *and other national publications. A member of the Society of American Travel Writers, she is a contributor to a dozen Fodor's books.* **Katherine Price** *had a blast exploring every nook and cranny of the B&Bs in her adopted state of Tennessee. She once toured a property that the innkeeper raved had an apple orchard and a babbling brook only to find a dilapidated barn; rotten fruit used for chicken fodder; and a stagnant puddle surrounded by weeds. Needless to say, this "B&B" cannot be found on the pages of this book. The former Frugal Traveler columnist for the* New York Times, **Susan Spano** *wrote the original chapter on Virginia.* **Lisa H. Towle,** *the revisor of the North Carolina chapter, is an award-winning writer and native North Carolinian living in the Raleigh-Durham area. Hailing from Jackson, Mississippi,* **John Webb** *updated his home-state chapter. A former lifestyle columnist for the* New York Daily News, *John has written for* Travel & Leisure, Art & Antiques, *and the* Washington Post.

SOME NOTES ON HOW TO USE THIS BOOK

Reviews are organized by state, and, within each state, by region. At the beginning of every review is the address and telephone; if pictures of an inn can be found on a Web site, we list URLs of Web sites where you can find out more about the inn, and the e-mail address when there's no Web site. A pineapple highlights properties that are especially recommended. At the end of the review, in italicized service information, what we describe as a double room is for two people, regardless of the size or type of its beds. Unless otherwise noted, rooms don't have phones or TVs. Note that even the most stunning homes, farmhouses, and mansions may not provide a private bathroom for each individual. Rates are for two, excluding tax, in the high season, and include breakfast unless otherwise noted. Ask about special packages and midweek or off-season discounts.

What we call a restaurant serves meals other than breakfast and is usually open to the general public. At inns listed as operating on the Modified American Plan (MAP), rates include two meals, generally breakfast and dinner.

The following credit card abbreviations are used throughout this guide: AE, American Express; D, Discover; DC, Diners Club; MC, MasterCard; V, Visa.

Where applicable, we note seasonal and other restrictions. Although we abhor discrimination, we have conveyed information about innkeepers' restrictive practices so that you will be aware of the prevailing attitudes. Such discriminatory practices are most often applied to parents who are traveling with small children and who may not, in any case, feel comfortable having their offspring toddle amid breakable bric-a-brac and near precipitous stairways.

In case you're inspired to seek out additional properties on your own, we also include names and addresses of B&B reservation services (and their URLs as well, if they have an on-line presence).

OUR BEST TIP

When traveling the B&B way, always call ahead. If you're traveling to an inn because of a specific feature, make sure that it will be available when you get there and not closed for renovation. The same goes if you're making a detour to take advantage of specific sights or attractions. And if you are traveling with children, if you prefer a private bath or a certain type of bed, or if you have mobility problems, or if you have specific dietary needs, or any other concerns, discuss them with the innkeeper.

A POINT OF PRIDE

It's a sad commentary on other B&B guides today that we feel obliged to tell you that our writers did, in fact, visit every property in person, and that it is they, not the innkeepers, who wrote the reviews. No one paid a fee or promised to sell or promote the book in order to be included in it. (In fact, one of the most challenging parts of the work of a Fodor's writer is to persuade innkeepers and B&B owners that he or she wants nothing more than a tour of the premises and the answers to a few questions!) Fodor's has no stake in anything but the truth. So trust us, the way you'd trust a knowledgeable, well-traveled friend. Let us hear from you about your travels, whether you found that the B&Bs you visited surpassed their descriptions or the other way around. And have a wonderful trip!

Karen Cure
Editorial Director

The South

Gulf of Mexico

Special Features at a Glance ↵

	Antiques	Car Not Necessary	Conference Facilities	Full Meal Service	Good for Families	Historic Building	Luxurious	No Smoking Indoors	
ALABAMA									
Bay Breeze	✸				✸			✸	
The Beach House, A Bed & Breakfast by the Sea	✸	✸					✸	✸	
Capps Cove	✸		✸					✸	
Church Street Inn	✸	✸				✸	✸	✸	
Grace Hall	✸	✸	✸		✸	✸	✸	✸	
Jemison Inn	✸				✸	✸	✸	✸	
Kendall Manor Inn	✸	✸	✸	✸		✸	✸	✸	
Lattice Inn	✸					✸		✸	
Lodge on Gorham's Bluff	✸			✸			✸	✸	
Mentone Inn	✸				✸	✸		✸	
Orangevale Plantation	✸				✸	✸		✸	
The Original Romar House	✸					✸		✸	
Raven Haven					✸			✸	
Red Bluff Cottage	✸				✸		✸	✸	
St. James Hotel	✸		✸	✸	✸	✸	✸		
Winston Place—An Antebellum Mansion	✸		✸		✸	✸	✸	✸	
Wood Avenue Inn	✸			✸	✸	✸	✸	✸	
GEORGIA									
Ballastone	✸	✸				✸	✸	✸	
The Bed & Breakfast Inn	✸	✸				✸	✸	✸	
The Beechwood Inn	✸					✸		✸	
Brasstown Valley Resort			✸	✸	✸		✸		
Carmichael House	✸					✸		✸	
Coleman House	✸			✸		✸		✸	
Crockett House	✸					✸		✸	

	On the Water	Pets Allowed	Romantic Hideaway	Beach Nearby	Boating Nearby	Cross-Country Skiing Nearby	Fishing Nearby	Golf Nearby	Hiking Nearby	Horseback Riding Nearby	Skiing Nearby	Swimming	Tennis Court	Wineries Nearby	Fitness Facilities
	❀		❀	❀	❀		❀	❀		❀		❀			
	❀		❀	❀	❀		❀	❀	❀			❀			
			❀		❀		❀	❀	❀						
				❀				❀			❀				
		❀	❀					❀							❀
			❀					❀		❀		❀	❀		
			❀					❀		❀			❀		
			❀					❀				❀			
			❀						❀						
			❀					❀	❀	❀	❀				
			❀		❀		❀	❀	❀					❀	
	❀		❀	❀	❀		❀	❀	❀	❀		❀	❀		
			❀					❀	❀	❀	❀				
								❀							
	❀						❀	❀	❀			❀	❀		❀
			❀					❀	❀		❀				
			❀				❀	❀	❀	❀		❀			
			❀	❀	❀		❀	❀	❀			❀	❀		❀
			❀	❀	❀		❀	❀	❀			❀	❀		❀
			❀		❀		❀	❀	❀	❀	❀	❀	❀	❀	
			❀	❀	❀		❀	❀	❀	❀		❀	❀	❀	❀
					❀		❀	❀	❀	❀		❀	❀		
			❀		❀		❀	❀	❀						
			❀	❀	❀		❀	❀	❀	❀		❀	❀	❀	

Special Features at a Glance ←

	Antiques	Car Not Necessary	Conference Facilities	Full Meal Service	Good for Families	Historic Building	Luxurious	No Smoking Indoors
Dunlap House		✽			✽	✽		
1884 Paxton House	✽	✽				✽		✽
1842 Inn	✽	✽				✽	✽	✽
1870 Rothschild-Pound House	✽	✽				✽		✽
Eliza Thompson House	✽	✽	✽			✽	✽	✽
Farmhouse Inn	✽				✽			✽
Foley House	✽	✽	✽		✽	✽	✽	
Four Chimneys	✽				✽	✽		✽
The Gastonian	✽	✽				✽	✽	✽
Glen-Ella Springs Country Inn & Conference Center	✽		✽	✽	✽	✽		✽
Gordon-Lee Mansion	✽		✽	✽	✽	✽		✽
Grand Hotel	✽					✽		✽
Greyfield Inn	✽			✽		✽		
Henderson Village	✽			✽	✽	✽	✽	
Inn at Folkston	✽					✽		✽
Jekyll Island Club Hotel			✽	✽	✽	✽	✽	
Kehoe House	✽	✽	✽		✽	✽	✽	✽
Lodging at Little St. Simons Island	✽	✽	✽	✽	✽	✽		✽
Magnolia Hall	✽					✽		✽
Manor House	✽	✽	✽			✽	✽	
Melhana Plantation	✽					✽		✽
Mountain Memories		✽			✽			✽
Nicholson House	✽		✽			✽		✽
1906 Pathway Inn	✽				✽	✽		✽
Open Gates	✽					✽		
Perrin Guest House	✽							✽

Georgia

On the Water	Pets Allowed	Romantic Hideaway	Beach Nearby	Boating Nearby	Cross-Country Skiing Nearby	Fishing Nearby	Golf Nearby	Hiking Nearby	Horseback Riding Nearby	Skiing Nearby	Swimming	Tennis Court	Wineries Nearby	Fitness Facilities
			✽					✽	✽		✽	✽	✽	✽
							✽	✽	✽		✽	✽		✽
		✽					✽	✽				✽		✽
							✽				✽	✽		✽
		✽	✽	✽		✽	✽	✽			✽	✽		✽
		✽	✽	✽		✽	✽	✽	✽		✽	✽		
		✽	✽	✽		✽	✽	✽			✽	✽		✽
	✽			✽		✽	✽	✽			✽	✽		
		✽	✽	✽		✽	✽	✽			✽	✽		✽
		✽		✽		✽	✽	✽	✽	✽	✽	✽	✽	
	✽	✽				✽	✽	✽	✽			✽	✽	
	✽	✽		✽		✽	✽		✽					
✽		✽	✽	✽		✽	✽	✽			✽	✽		✽
		✽				✽	✽		✽		✽			
		✽		✽		✽	✽	✽				✽		✽
✽		✽	✽	✽		✽	✽	✽	✽		✽	✽		✽
		✽	✽	✽		✽	✽	✽			✽	✽		
✽		✽	✽	✽		✽	✽	✽	✽		✽			
		✽				✽	✽	✽			✽	✽		
	✽	✽	✽	✽		✽	✽	✽			✽	✽		✽
	✽	✽				✽	✽		✽		✽	✽		✽
		✽		✽		✽	✽	✽	✽		✽		✽	✽
		✽					✽	✽				✽	✽	
	✽	✽					✽				✽			
		✽	✽	✽		✽			✽		✽			
		✽		✽		✽	✽	✽	✽		✽	✽		✽

Special Features at a Glance ←

	Antiques	Car Not Necessary	Conference Facilities	Full Meal Service	Good for Families	Historic Building	Luxurious	No Smoking Indoors
President's Quarters	❋	❋				❋	❋	
Serenbe	❋		❋		❋	❋		❋
Shellmont Bed & Breakfast	❋	❋				❋		❋
Skelton House	❋				❋	❋		❋
Whitlock Inn	❋	❋	❋			❋		❋
Whitworth Inn					❋			❋
Windsor Hotel	❋	❋	❋	❋		❋		
Woodbridge Inn				❋	❋	❋		❋
LOUISIANA								
B&W Courtyards		❋						
Beau Fort Plantation	❋					❋	❋	❋
Bois des Chênes	❋				❋	❋		❋
Butler Greenwood	❋		❋		❋	❋	❋	❋
Camellia Cove								❋
The Chimes		❋						❋
Chrétien Point Plantation	❋					❋		❋
Claiborne Mansion	❋	❋				❋	❋	❋
Cloutier Townhouse and Petit Tarn	❋	❋						❋
Cook's Cottage at Rip Van Winkle Gardens	❋		❋	❋				❋
Cottage Plantation	❋							❋
Degas House	❋		❋			❋	❋	❋
Duvigneaud House					❋			❋
Elter House Inn								❋
Estorge House	❋					❋		❋
Fleur-de-Lis		❋						❋
Garden Gate Manor								❋

On the Water	Pets Allowed	Romantic Hideaway	Beach Nearby	Boating Nearby	Cross-Country Skiing Nearby	Fishing Nearby	Golf Nearby	Hiking Nearby	Horseback Riding Nearby	Skiing Nearby	Swimming	Tennis Court	Wineries Nearby	Fitness Facilities
		❋	❋	❋		❋	❋					❋		❋
		❋				❋	❋	❋	❋		❋			❋
		❋					❋							❋
		❋	❋	❋		❋	❋	❋				❋	❋		❋
		❋					❋					❋	❋	❋
			❋	❋		❋	❋	❋	❋		❋	❋	❋	
		❋					❋				❋			
	❋	❋				❋	❋	❋						
		❋		❋		❋	❋	❋	❋					
				❋		❋		❋						
	❋			❋		❋	❋	❋	❋					
		❋				❋	❋	❋						
				❋		❋								
		❋		❋		❋	❋	❋	❋					
												❋	❋	
		❋		❋		❋	❋	❋	❋		❋			
❋		❋		❋		❋		❋						
		❋					❋							
							❋	❋						
		❋		❋		❋	❋	❋	❋					
		❋		❋		❋	❋	❋	❋					
				❋		❋		❋						
		❋					❋							
				❋		❋		❋						
		❋		❋		❋								

Special Features at a Glance ←

	Antiques	Car Not Necessary	Conference Facilities	Full Meal Service	Good for Families	Historic Building	Luxurious	No Smoking Indoors
Green Springs Plantation					✸			✸
House on Bayou Road	✸					✸	✸	✸
Jefferson House	✸	✸					✸	✸
Josephine Guest House	✸	✸					✸	✸
Lanaux Mansion	✸	✸				✸	✸	✸
Levy-East House	✸	✸					✸	✸
Lloyd Hall	✸		✸		✸	✸	✸	✸
Madewood Plantation	✸					✸	✸	✸
Magnolia Plantation	✸					✸	✸	✸
La Maison de Campagne	✸							✸
McKendrick-Breaux House	✸	✸					✸	✸
Melrose Mansion	✸	✸						
Nottoway	✸		✸	✸		✸	✸	✸
Old Castillo Hotel/Place d'Evangeline				✸	✸	✸		✸
Riverside Hills Farm					✸			✸
Salmen-Fritchie House	✸					✸	✸	✸
Sully Mansion		✸			✸			✸
T' Frère's House	✸							✸
Tante Huppé House	✸	✸				✸	✸	✸
Tezcuco Plantation	✸		✸	✸		✸		✸
Woods Hole Inn	✸						✸	
MISSISSIPPI								
Alexander House	✸			✸		✸		✸
Amzi Love House	✸			✸		✸		✸
Anchuca	✸					✸	✸	✸
Annabelle	✸					✸		✸

Louisiana/Mississippi

On the Water	Pets Allowed	Romantic Hideaway	Beach Nearby	Boating Nearby	Cross-Country Skiing Nearby	Fishing Nearby	Golf Nearby	Hiking Nearby	Horseback Riding Nearby	Skiing Nearby	Swimming	Tennis Court	Wineries Nearby	Fitness Facilities
		❋		❋		❋	❋	❋	❋		❋			
❋				❋		❋		❋						
				❋		❋	❋	❋	❋					
		❋		❋		❋	❋	❋	❋					
		❋		❋		❋		❋						
		❋						❋			❋			
		❋		❋		❋		❋						
		❋		❋		❋	❋				❋			
				❋		❋	❋	❋	❋					
		❋		❋		❋	❋	❋	❋		❋			
											❋			
❋				❋		❋		❋						
❋		❋		❋		❋	❋	❋					❋	
				❋		❋	❋	❋	❋				❋	
				❋		❋	❋	❋	❋					
		❋					❋							
		❋		❋		❋		❋						
		❋												
		❋		❋		❋	❋	❋	❋				❋	
				❋		❋	❋							
		❋				❋	❋	❋			❋			
						❋	❋	❋			❋			

Special Features at a Glance ↵

	Antiques	Car Not Necessary	Conference Facilities	Full Meal Service	Good for Families	Historic Building	Luxurious	No Smoking Indoors	
Arbor House	✻					✻	✻	✻	
Backstrom Bed & Breakfast	✻							✻	
The Bailey House	✻				✻	✻		✻	
The Balfour House	✻				✻	✻		✻	
Barksdale-Isom House	✻			✻		✻	✻	✻	
Bay Town Inn	✻	✻				✻	✻	✻	
Belle of the Bends	✻				✻	✻		✻	
The Burn									
Canemount Plantation	✻		✻	✻		✻	✻	✻	
The Caragen House	✻		✻	✻		✻	✻	✻	
Carpenter Place	✻					✻		✻	
Cartney-Hunt House	✻					✻		✻	
Cedar Grove	✻		✻	✻	✻	✻	✻	✻	
Cedar Grove Plantation	✻				✻	✻		✻	
Cedars Plantation	✻					✻	✻	✻	
The Corners	✻			✻		✻		✻	
Dunleith	✻		✻			✻	✻	✻	
Fairview	✻		✻	✻	✻	✻	✻	✻	
Father Ryan House	✻		✻		✻	✻	✻	✻	
French Camp Bed and Breakfast Inn	✻				✻	✻		✻	
Governor Holmes House	✻					✻			
Green Oaks	✻		✻	✻		✻	✻	✻	
Guest House Historic Inn	✻				✻	✻	✻	✻	
Highland House	✻			✻		✻	✻	✻	
Inn at the Pass	✻	✻			✻	✻		✻	
Liberty Hall	✻			✻		✻		✻	

Mississippi

On the Water	Pets Allowed	Romantic Hideaway	Beach Nearby	Boating Nearby	Cross-Country Skiing Nearby	Fishing Nearby	Golf Nearby	Hiking Nearby	Horseback Riding Nearby	Skiing Nearby	Swimming	Tennis Court	Wineries Nearby	Fitness Facilities
							✽							
						✽								
						✽	✽	✽					✽	
	✽					✽	✽	✽						
														✽
✽			✽	✽		✽	✽							
						✽	✽	✽						
		✽				✽		✽			✽			
						✽	✽							
						✽	✽	✽			✽	✽		✽
		✽				✽	✽	✽			✽		✽	
		✽				✽	✽	✽					✽	
✽		✽				✽	✽	✽						
		✽				✽	✽	✽					✽	
							✽							
✽		✽	✽	✽		✽	✽				✽			
						✽		✽	✽			✽		
		✽				✽	✽	✽					✽	
✽		✽	✽	✽		✽	✽							
	✽	✽				✽	✽	✽					✽	
		✽					✽				✽			
✽	✽	✽	✽	✽		✽	✽							
		✽									✽			

Special Features at a Glance ←

	Antiques	Car Not Necessary	Conference Facilities	Full Meal Service	Good for Families	Historic Building	Luxurious	No Smoking Indoors
Lincoln, Ltd., Bed & Breakfast Mississippi Reservation Service	✳							✳
Linden	✳				✳	✳		
Linden-on-the-Lake	✳				✳	✳		✳
Millsaps Buie House	✳				✳	✳		✳
Mistletoe Plantation	✳					✳		✳
Mockingbird Inn	✳							✳
Molly's	✳							✳
Monmouth	✳		✳			✳	✳	✳
Oak Square	✳					✳	✳	✳
Puddin Place	✳					✳		✳
Rambling Rose						✳		✳
Ravenna	✳				✳	✳		✳
Redbud Inn	✳			✳				✳
Sassafras Inn	✳							✳
Shadowlawn	✳				✳	✳		✳
Spahn House	✳			✳		✳		✳
Stained Glass Manor	✳		✳		✳	✳		
Tally House	✳		✳		✳	✳		✳
Wensel House	✳				✳	✳		✳
Weymouth Hall	✳					✳		✳
Who's Inn?		✳			✳	✳		✳
NORTH CAROLINA								
Arrowhead Inn	✳					✳		✳
Balsam Mountain Inn	✳		✳		✳	✳		✳
Blooming Garden Inn	✳					✳		✳
Catherine's Inn	✳					✳		✳

Mississippi/North Carolina

On the Water	Pets Allowed	Romantic Hideaway	Beach Nearby	Boating Nearby	Cross-Country Skiing Nearby	Fishing Nearby	Golf Nearby	Hiking Nearby	Horseback Riding Nearby	Skiing Nearby	Swimming	Tennis Court	Wineries Nearby	Fitness Facilities
		❁				❁	❁	❁	❁					
		❁				❁	❁	❁					❁	
❁	❁	❁		❁		❁	❁	❁						
							❁							
		❁				❁	❁	❁					❁	
						❁	❁							
						❁	❁	❁					❁	
		❁						❁						
							❁							
		❁				❁	❁						❁	
		❁				❁	❁							
		❁									❁			
❁		❁	❁	❁		❁	❁				❁			
						❁	❁	❁						
						❁	❁	❁						
		❁				❁	❁						❁	
						❁	❁						❁	
		❁	❁	❁		❁	❁							
		❁					❁	❁						
		❁				❁	❁	❁	❁	❁				
							❁							
❁		❁	❁	❁		❁	❁				❁	❁	❁	

Special Features at a Glance

	Antiques	*Car Not Necessary*	*Conference Facilities*	*Full Meal Service*	*Good for Families*	*Historic Building*	*Luxurious*	*No Smoking Indoors*
Cedar Crest Inn	❊	❊	❊			❊	❊	❊
Cedars by the Sea	❊	❊	❊			❊	❊	❊
Fearrington House		❊	❊	❊			❊	
First Colony Inn	❊		❊		❊	❊	❊	❊
Granville Queen Inn	❊					❊	❊	❊
Greystone Inn	❊	❊	❊	❊	❊	❊	❊	❊
Harmony House Inn	❊	❊	❊		❊	❊		❊
Henry F. Shaffner House	❊					❊	❊	❊
Homeplace	❊				❊	❊		❊
Inn at Celebrity Dairy	❊				❊	❊		❊
Inn at Taylor House	❊					❊	❊	❊
Island Inn	❊	❊		❊	❊	❊		❊
King's Arms Inn	❊	❊			❊	❊		❊
Langdon House	❊	❊				❊		❊
Lodge on Lake Lure	❊		❊		❊	❊		❊
Magnolia Inn	❊		❊	❊		❊		❊
Maple Lodge Bed & Breakfast	❊	❊	❊					❊
Mast Farm Inn	❊		❊	❊	❊	❊		❊
Pecan Tree Inn	❊	❊				❊		❊
Pilot Knob Inn	❊		❊			❊		
Richmond Hill Inn	❊		❊		❊	❊	❊	❊
Roanoke Island Inn	❊	❊				❊		
Tranquil House Inn					❊			
Waverly Inn	❊	❊			❊	❊		❊
White Doe Inn	❊		❊			❊	❊	❊
William Thomas House B&B	❊	❊	❊			❊	❊	❊

North Carolina

	On the Water	Pets Allowed	Romantic Hideaway	Beach Nearby	Boating Nearby	Cross-Country Skiing Nearby	Fishing Nearby	Golf Nearby	Hiking Nearby	Horseback Riding Nearby	Skiing Nearby	Swimming	Tennis Court	Wineries Nearby	Fitness Facilities
			✽			✽	✽	✽	✽	✽	✽		✽	✽	✽
			✽	✽	✽		✽								
			✽									✽	✽		✽
	✽		✽	✽	✽		✽	✽	✽			✽	✽		
			✽		✽		✽	✽	✽	✽			✽		
	✽		✽		✽		✽	✽	✽	✽	✽	✽	✽		
			✽		✽		✽	✽	✽			✽			✽
			✽				✽								✽
			✽					✽	✽						
									✽						
			✽			✽	✽	✽	✽	✽	✽				
				✽	✽		✽						✽	✽	✽
			✽		✽		✽	✽	✽						
				✽	✽		✽	✽							
	✽		✽		✽		✽	✽	✽	✽		✽	✽		
								✽	✽			✽	✽		✽
			✽			✽	✽	✽	✽	✽	✽				
			✽			✽	✽	✽	✽	✽	✽	✽	✽		✽
			✽	✽	✽		✽	✽	✽			✽			
			✽				✽	✽	✽	✽		✽		✽	
			✽			✽	✽	✽	✽	✽	✽		✽	✽	✽
	✽	✽	✽	✽	✽		✽	✽							
	✽		✽	✽	✽		✽	✽				✽	✽		✽
							✽	✽	✽				✽		✽
			✽	✽	✽		✽	✽				✽	✽		
								✽	✽						

Special Features at a Glance ←

	Antiques	Car Not Necessary	Conference Facilities	Full Meal Service	Good for Families	Historic Building	Luxurious	No Smoking Indoors
Worth House	✻					✻	✻	✻
SOUTH CAROLINA								
Annie's Inn	✻				✻	✻		
Battery Carriage House Inn	✻	✻				✻	✻	✻
Beaufort Inn			✻	✻	✻	✻		✻
Belmont Inn					✻	✻		✻
Brodie Residence						✻		✻
Cassina Point Plantation	✻					✻	✻	✻
Chesterfield Inn		✻		✻	✻	✻		
Cuthbert House Inn	✻					✻	✻	✻
Cypress Inn	✻		✻					✻
East Bay Bed and Breakfast	✻	✻			✻	✻	✻	✻
1837 Bed & Breakfast and Tearoom	✻	✻			✻	✻		✻
Fulton Lane Inn		✻	✻			✻	✻	✻
Greenleaf Inn	✻			✻		✻	✻	✻
Hayne House Bed and Breakfast	✻	✻			✻	✻		✻
Jasmine House Inn	✻	✻				✻	✻	✻
John Rutledge House Inn	✻	✻				✻		✻
Kings Courtyard Inn		✻	✻			✻		
King's Inn at Georgetown	✻					✻	✻	✻
Laurel Hill Plantation	✻							✻
Litchfield Plantation	✻		✻	✻		✻	✻	✻
Mansfield Plantation	✻					✻		✻
Middleton Inn			✻				✻	✻
Rhett House Inn	✻					✻	✻	✻
Rosemary Hall	✻		✻			✻	✻	✻

	On the Water	Pets Allowed	Romantic Hideaway	Beach Nearby	Boating Nearby	Cross-Country Skiing Nearby	Fishing Nearby	Golf Nearby	Hiking Nearby	Horseback Riding Nearby	Skiing Nearby	Swimming	Tennis Court	Wineries Nearby	Fitness Facilities
			❋	❋	❋		❋	❋				❋	❋	❋	❋
			❋					❋	❋	❋		❋		❋	
	❋		❋	❋	❋		❋	❋							
			❋		❋										
			❋				❋		❋						
								❋	❋	❋		❋			
	❋		❋	❋	❋		❋	❋				❋			
	❋			❋	❋		❋	❋				❋			
	❋		❋		❋										
	❋		❋		❋		❋	❋					❋		
			❋	❋	❋		❋	❋							
			❋	❋	❋		❋	❋							
			❋	❋	❋		❋	❋							
		❋	❋					❋	❋	❋					❋
			❋	❋	❋		❋	❋							
			❋	❋	❋		❋	❋							
			❋	❋	❋		❋	❋							
			❋	❋	❋		❋	❋							
			❋		❋		❋	❋				❋			
	❋		❋		❋		❋		❋						
			❋	❋	❋		❋	❋				❋	❋		
	❋	❋	❋		❋		❋	❋							
	❋	❋	❋		❋		❋	❋				❋	❋		
			❋		❋										
			❋					❋	❋						

Special Features at a Glance ↵

	Antiques	Car Not Necessary	Conference Facilities	Full Meal Service	Good for Families	Historic Building	Luxurious	No Smoking Indoors
Sea View Inn				✽	✽	✽		✽
Serendipity, An Inn		✽			✽			
1790 House	✽				✽	✽		✽
Town & Country Inn	✽				✽			✽
Twenty-Seven State Street Bed & Breakfast	✽	✽				✽	✽	✽
Two Meeting Street	✽	✽				✽	✽	✽
Vintage Inn	✽					✽		✽
Wentworth Mansion	✽	✽			✽	✽	✽	
Willcox Inn				✽		✽		
TENNESSEE								
Adams Edgeworth Inn	✽		✽	✽	✽	✽		✽
Adams Hilborne	✽		✽	✽	✽	✽	✽	✽
Big Spring Inn	✽					✽		✽
Blueberry Hill Bed and Breakfast	✽				✽			✽
Blue Mountain Mist Country Inn	✽		✽					✽
Bluff View Inn	✽	✽	✽	✽	✽	✽	✽	✽
Bonne Terre Country Inn & Cafe	✽		✽	✽	✽		✽	✽
Bridgewater House	✽							✽
Buckhorn Inn	✽		✽	✽				✽
Chigger Ridge	✽		✽		✽			✽
Falcon Manor Bed and Breakfast	✽		✽	✽		✽		✽
Hachland Hill Dining Inn	✽		✽	✽	✽	✽		
Hale Springs Inn	✽		✽	✽	✽	✽		
Highland Place Bed and Breakfast	✽							✽
Hippensteal's Mountain View Inn	✽		✽		✽			✽
Inn at Blackberry Farm	✽		✽	✽			✽	✽

SouthCarolina/Tennessee

On the Water	Pets Allowed	Romantic Hideaway	Beach Nearby	Boating Nearby	Cross-Country Skiing Nearby	Fishing Nearby	Golf Nearby	Hiking Nearby	Horseback Riding Nearby	Skiing Nearby	Swimming	Tennis Court	Wineries Nearby	Fitness Facilities
✸		✸	✸	✸		✸	✸				✸			
			✸	✸		✸	✸				✸			
		✸												
	✸					✸	✸	✸			✸			
		✸		✸		✸	✸							✸
✸		✸		✸		✸	✸							
						✸		✸						
		✸	✸	✸		✸	✸							
		✸					✸	✸	✸					✸
		✸		✸		✸	✸	✸	✸		✸	✸	✸	
				✸		✸	✸	✸	✸		✸			
						✸	✸		✸					
		✸				✸	✸	✸	✸				✸	
✸		✸												
✸	✸	✸		✸		✸	✸	✸			✸			
				✸		✸	✸	✸	✸				✸	
				✸		✸	✸	✸	✸	✸			✸	
				✸		✸	✸	✸	✸					
				✸		✸	✸	✸						
	✸	✸		✸		✸	✸	✸	✸				✸	
				✸		✸	✸							
						✸	✸	✸						
		✸				✸	✸	✸	✸	✸			✸	
✸		✸		✸		✸	✸	✸	✸		✸	✸		✸

Special Features at a Glance ←

	Antiques	Car Not Necessary	Conference Facilities	Full Meal Service	Good for Families	Historic Building	Luxurious	No Smoking Indoors	
Inn at Evins Mill			✻	✻	✻	✻			
Lynchburg Bed and Breakfast	✻					✻		✻	
Magnolia Manor	✻	✻				✻	✻	✻	
Old Cowan Plantation	✻					✻		✻	
Peacock Hill Country Inn	✻			✻	✻		✻	✻	
Richmont Inn	✻			✻				✻	
Simply Southern	✻					✻		✻	
Tennessee Ridge Inn								✻	
Von-Bryan Inn			✻		✻			✻	
White Elephant B & B Inn	✻					✻		✻	
Wayside Manor	✻		✻	✻	✻			✻	
VIRGINIA									
Ashby Inn & Restaurant	✻			✻			✻	✻	
L'Auberge Provençale				✻		✻	✻		
Bailiwick Inn	✻			✻			✻	✻	
Belle Grae Inn	✻			✻		✻			
Bleu Rock Inn				✻					
Cape Charles House	✻		✻			✻	✻	✻	
Channel Bass Inn									
Clifton	✻		✻	✻	✻	✻	✻	✻	
Colonial Capital					✻				
Edgewood	✻		✻			✻			
The Evergreen	✻				✻	✻		✻	
Fassifern	✻					✻		✻	
The Garden and the Sea Inn	✻			✻			✻		
High Meadows and Mountain Sunset									

On the Water	Pets Allowed	Romantic Hideaway	Beach Nearby	Boating Nearby	Cross-Country Skiing Nearby	Fishing Nearby	Golf Nearby	Hiking Nearby	Horseback Riding Nearby	Skiing Nearby	Swimming	Tennis Court	Wineries Nearby	Fitness Facilities
✳		✳		✳		✳	✳	✳	✳					
				✳		✳								
				✳		✳	✳	✳	✳					
				✳		✳								
	✳	✳					✳							✳
		✳		✳		✳	✳	✳	✳					
				✳		✳	✳	✳	✳					
		✳				✳	✳	✳	✳	✳	✳		✳	
		✳		✳		✳	✳	✳	✳		✳		✳	
			✳	✳		✳	✳	✳						
✳				✳		✳	✳	✳			✳	✳		
		✳												
		✳												
		✳											✳	
							✳							
✳		✳				✳								
			✳				✳	✳						
		✳	✳				✳							
✳		✳				✳	✳		✳		✳	✳	✳	✳
							✳				✳	✳	✳	
		✳					✳				✳		✳	
							✳	✳	✳		✳		✳	
		✳	✳											

Special Features at a Glance ←

	Antiques	Car Not Necessary	Conference Facilities	Full Meal Service	Good for Families	Historic Building	Luxurious	No Smoking Indoors
Inn at Gristmill Square				❋	❋			
Inn at Little Washington	❋			❋		❋	❋	❋
Inn at Meander Plantation	❋		❋		❋	❋	❋	
Inn at Monticello	❋		❋	❋	❋	❋	❋	
Inn at Narrow Passage					❋	❋		
Island Manor House	❋		❋			❋		❋
Jordan Hollow Farm Inn			❋	❋	❋	❋		
Joshua Wilton House			❋	❋		❋		
Keswick Hall			❋	❋	❋		❋	❋
Liberty Rose	❋							❋
Miss Molly's Inn	❋					❋		❋
North Bend Plantation	❋				❋	❋		❋
The Owl and the Pussycat	❋				❋	❋	❋	❋
Pickett's Harbor	❋							❋
Prospect Hill	❋			❋		❋		
Richard Johnston Inn	❋	❋				❋		❋
Seven Hills Inn			❋					
The Shadows								
Silversmith Inn	❋					❋		❋
Silver Thatch Inn								
Sleepy Hollow Farm								
Spinning Wheel Bed and Breakfast	❋					❋		❋
Sycamore Hill								❋
Trillium House			❋					
War Hill Inn					❋			❋
Welbourne	❋					❋		

On the Water	Pets Allowed	Romantic Hideaway	Beach Nearby	Boating Nearby	Cross-Country Skiing Nearby	Fishing Nearby	Golf Nearby	Hiking Nearby	Horseback Riding Nearby	Skiing Nearby	Swimming	Tennis Court	Wineries Nearby	Fitness Facilities
					✱		✱				✱	✱		✱
		✱											✱	
		✱			✱	✱	✱	✱	✱	✱				
		✱			✱	✱	✱	✱	✱	✱	✱	✱	✱	✱
✱		✱			✱					✱				
			✱											
		✱			✱			✱	✱	✱				
					✱		✱			✱				
		✱					✱							
✱			✱											
✱												✱		
	✱	✱		✱				✱	✱					
✱			✱								✱			
							✱							
								✱						
		✱		✱		✱		✱	✱					✱
			✱				✱							
	✱				✱		✱	✱	✱		✱	✱	✱	✱
							✱							
	✱							✱						

Virginia

Virginia

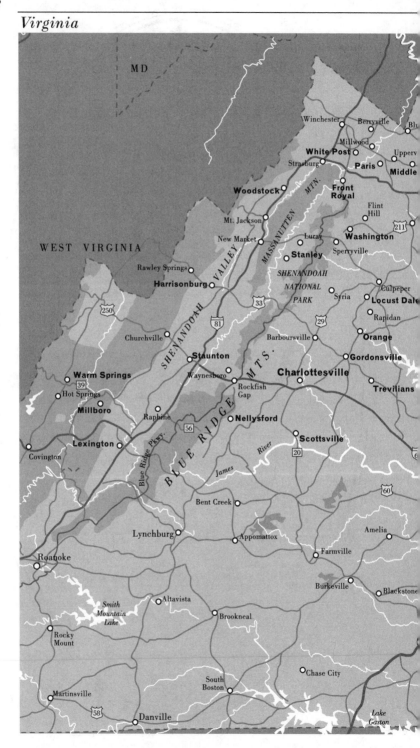

NORTHERN VIRGINIA

With a variegated landscape, intriguing hamlets, abundant antiques stores, top-notch inns, and some of the state's most lurid history, northern Virginia is an ideal getaway. Its rolling hills have nurtured great numbers of American revolutionaries. As natives will inform visitors who find their memories somehow jogged by the place-names, almost half the battles of the Civil War were waged in this countryside. Nowadays, though, refugees from Capitol Hill's partisan wars and the District's unstable city services are claiming their rewards in northern Virginia. And with defiance rivaling that of their Revolutionary forebears, some have fought to retain them. It was here, for instance, that residents helped quash Disney's bid for an historic theme park. Development, the area's only enemy, is being tenuously held at bay.

The fast track to this Eden west of Washington, D.C., is I–66 (except on Friday and Sunday afternoons), but the well-versed may opt for U.S. 50, which in an easy hour of driving puts you in Middleburg, the capital of hunt country. This subdued town breathes—and caters to—old money, with a collection of upscale galleries, antiques stores, and gun shops. Hunt season in Loudoun, Fauquier, Clarke, and Rappahannock counties begins in late October with an opening meet, peaks around Thanksgiving, and continues into March, provided the ground doesn't freeze.

Frankly, most hunt-country visitors prefer to spend their time window-shopping at Middleburg real estate offices and driving Loudoun County's back roads. (Routes 622, 626, 710, 713, and 734 are highly recommended, provided you're on the alert for careering Maseratis and BMWs.) These back roads lead to many country pleasures. Hamlets such as Hillsboro, Hamilton, Delaplane, Aldie, Purcellville, and Millwood offer plenty of opportunities for collectibles shoppers. Wineries—including Naked Mountain, Meredyth, Linden, Piedmont, Oasis—abound in the area. (For a map of them, contact the Virginia Wine Marketing Program, VDACS, Division of Marketing, Box 1163, Richmond 23209, tel. 804/786–0481.) Many farms have seasonal tours, pick-your-own days, and choose-and-cut Christ-

mas trees. (For the "Farms of Loudoun Getaway Guide," contact the Loudoun County Department of Economic Development, Agricultural Development Office, 102 Heritage Way NE, Suite 303, Leesburg 22075, tel. 703/777–0426.)

Leesburg, founded about 1760, is northeast of Middleburg. It remained in Federal hands during the Civil War and thus retains much of its Colonial architecture. Leesburg's spruced-up storefronts and row houses now function as restaurants and shops.

South and west of Leesburg, a 30-mi corridor between Flint Hill and Syria makes for peak sightseeing by auto, too. Here the Blue Ridge looms on the horizon as the roads wind up into the foothills. Fauquier County offers horseback riding in Shenandoah National Park; mounts can be claimed at the Marriott Ranch.

At the southern border of the area sits Fredericksburg, boyhood stomping ground of George Washington and a hotly contested site during the Civil War. Between 1862 and 1864, four major battles were fought—at Chancellorsville, Wilderness, Spotsylvania Court House, and in Fredericksburg itself—resulting in more than 17,000 casualties. Fredericksburg's 40-block national historic district has more than 350 18th- and early 19th-century buildings. Popular here are the wares of artists, many of whom resettled from elsewhere, as well as antiques, with more than 100 dealers in a six-block area.

Established in 1749 by a group of Scottish merchants, Alexandria—a mere 10-minute drive from Washington, D.C.—has impressive historical credentials. It was an important Colonial port and a social and political center. Tobacco was shipped from here to the smoky coffeehouses of London, and dissident Scots rankled over the Act of Union with England flocked here. This may explain Alexandria's continuing fascination with things Scottish. Alexandria is considered George Washington's hometown; Light Horse Harry Lee and Robert E. Lee both lived here. Old Town has more 18th- and 19th-century architectural gems than any other city in the country. A walk along Alexandria's shady lanes takes visitors by handsome brick homes and offers peeks into labyrinthine courtyards. Shoppers will find present-day Alexandria as teeming as ever. Ethnic variety makes dining a real exercise in decisiveness; there are more than 100 restaurants within walking distance of the visitor center.

PLACES TO GO, SIGHTS TO SEE

Alexandria Archaeology (105 N. Union St., Suite 27, tel. 703/838–4399). This research facility preserves the Colonial treasures hidden beneath the paving stones of Old Town.

Carlyle House (121 N. Fairfax St., Alexandria, tel. 703/549–2997). Built in 1752–53 by Scottish merchant John Carlyle (and still the grandest house in town), it served as headquarters for General Edward Braddock in 1755, when he summoned five Colonial governors to plot the strategy for the French and Indian War.

Christ Church (118 N. Washington St., Alexandria, tel. 703/549–1450). Its parishioners have included George Washington and Robert E. Lee.

Fredericksburg/Spotsylvania National Military Park (120 Chatham La., Fredericksburg, tel. 540/373–6122) is midway between Washington, D.C., capital of the Union, and Richmond, capital of the Confederacy. Four major Civil War battles were fought in and around Fredericksburg, a region that saw the most intense fighting of the war, with casualties exceeding 100,000.

Gadsby's Tavern Museum (134 N. Royal St., Alexandria, tel. 703/838–4242). The rooms have been restored to their 18th-century appearance; of particular note is the hanging musicians gallery in the ballroom. George Washington socialized here. Nearby **Gadsby's Tavern** (138 N. Royal St., tel. 703/548–1288) has been dispensing spirits and victuals off and on since 1793.

Gunston Hall (10709 Gunston Rd., Mason Neck, tel. 703/550–9220), 15 mi south of Alexandria, was the Georgian mansion of George Mason, author of the first Virginia constitution and the Virginia Declaration of Rights. Built around 1755, it has a Palladian parlor and a Chinese-inspired dining room.

Historic Fredericksburg. Sights include the *Mary Washington House* (1200 Charles St., tel. 540/373–1569), bought by a dutiful son for his retired mother; the *James Monroe Museum and Memorial Library* (908 Charles St., tel. 540/654–1043); the *Hugh Mercer Apothecary* (1020 Caroline St., tel. 540/373–3362); and *Rising Sun Tavern* (1304 Caroline St., tel. 540/371–1494). The Fredericksburg Visitors Center (*see* Visitor Information, *below*) has maps for several walking tours.

Kenmore (1201 Washington Ave., Fredericksburg, tel. 540/373–3381). This Colonial mansion, famous for its decorative plaster moldings, was the home of George Washington's sister, Betty. Its dining room has been called one of the 100 most beautiful rooms in America.

Manassas National Battlefield Park (12521 Lee Hwy., tel. 703/754–1861) was the scene of the First and Second Battles of Manassas (Bull Run), during which the Confederacy lost 11,456 men and the Union 17,170.

Mount Vernon (8 mi south of Alexandria, tel. 703/780–2000) is George Washington's home and burial place. The museum holds Jean-Antoine Houdon's bust of Washington, as well as the first president's sunglasses and sword.

Oatlands (20850 Oatlands Plantation La., near Leesburg, tel. 703/777–3174), a classical-revival mansion, was built in 1803 by George Carter, grandson of the Williamsburg planter "King" Carter. Its terraced formal gardens are considered some of the most distinguished in the state.

The **Saturday Morning Market at Market Square** (Alexandria), by City Hall, is the country's oldest operating farmers' market. Vendors offer baked goods, fresh produce, plants, flowers, and high-quality crafts. Come early; the market opens at 5 AM, and by 9:30 AM it's all packed up.

Torpedo Factory (105 N. Union St., Alexandria, tel. 703/838–4565). It's just that: Naval torpedo shell casings were produced here during World War I and II. The waterfront building is now a complex of studios where 160 artists produce and sell their works.

Trinity Church (Rte. 50, Upperville, tel. 540/592–3343) is one of the most beautiful Episcopal churches in America. The style was adapted from French country stone churches of the 12th and 13th centuries.

Waterford, a village north of Leesburg, evokes rural England so dramatically that it could tug at the heart of any Anglophile. From one end to the other, it is now a National Historic Site.

Woodlawn Plantation (9000 Richmond Hwy., Mt. Vernon, tel. 703/780–4000) is the estate bequeathed by George Washington to his adopted daughter, Eleanor Parke Custis, and his nephew Lawrence Lewis. The impressive brick mansion was designed by Dr. William Thornton, architect of the U.S. Capitol. Also on the grounds is Frank Lloyd Wright's Pope-Leighey House.

RESTAURANTS

Many of northern Virginia's top inns offer outstanding meals. Not to be missed are the extraordinary dinners at the **Inn at Little Washington** (*see below*). In Flint Hill, **Four and Twenty Blackbirds** (650 Zachary Taylor Hwy., tel. 540/675–1111) cooks with local ingredients. Leesburg's favorites are **Lightfoot Cafe** (2 W. Market St., tel. 703/771–2233), which has a bistrolike atmosphere, and **Tuscarola Mills** (203 Harrison St., tel. 703/771–9300), known for its varied menu and fine wine list. For local color, reasonably priced sandwiches, and a fantastic selection of baked goodies, try the **Upper Crust** (4 N. Pendleton St., tel. 540/687–5666), across the street from Safeway in Middleburg. In Fredericksburg, recommended spots are **Sammy T's** (801 Caroline St., tel. 540/371–2008) and **Merriman's** (715 Caroline St., tel. 540/371–7723) for casual dining, **Le Lafayette** (623 Caroline St., tel. 540/373–6895) for French fare, and **Ristorante Renato** (422 William St., tel. 540/371–8228) for Italian cuisine. In Alexandria, **Le Refuge** (127 N. Washington St., tel. 703/548–4661) and **Le Gaulois** (1106 King St., tel. 703/739–9494) are comfortable French bistros, **Landini Brothers** (115 King St., tel. 703/836–8404) and **Geranio Ristorante** (722 King St., tel. 703/548–0088) are the spots for fine Italian dining, and **Bilbo Baggins** (208 Queen St., tel. 703/683–0300) is a cozy café with imaginative fare. **King Street Blues** (112 N. Saint Asphah St., tel. 703/836–8800) has a funky-southern menu in a funky setting.

VISITOR INFORMATION

Alexandria Convention and Visitors Bureau (221 King St., Alexandria 22314, tel. 703/838–4200). **Fairfax County Visitors Center** (7764 Armistead Rd., Suite 160, Lorton 22079, tel. 800/732–4732). **Fredericksburg Visitors Center** (706 Caroline St., Fredericksburg 22401, tel. 540/373–1776 or 800/678–4748). **Loudoun County Tourist Information Center** (108-D S St. SE, Market Station, Leesburg 22075, tel. 800/752–6118). **Virginia Division of Tourism** (901 E. Byrd St., Richmond 23219, tel. 804/786–4484).

RESERVATION SERVICES

Blue Ridge Bed & Breakfast Reservation Service (Rocks & Rills Farm, Rte. 2, Box 3895, Berryville 22611, tel. 540/955–1246). **Princely Bed & Breakfast Reservation Service** (819 Prince St., Alexandria 22314, tel. 703/683–2159). For a copy of the Bed and Breakfast Association of Virginia's directory, describing more than 100 establishments, call the **Virginia Division of Tourism's B&B line** (tel. 800/262–1293). The Division of Tourism's Washington, D.C., office also operates a B&B and small-inn booking service (tel. 202/659–5523 or 800/934–9184 outside D.C.).

ASHBY INN & RESTAURANT 🍽
692 Federal St., Paris 22130, tel. 540/592–3900, fax 540/592–3781

West of Middleburg and Upperville along U.S. 50, the turnoff for minuscule Paris may surprise unwary motorists; half the travelers looking for this hamlet in a hollow below the road probably miss it completely and end up crossing Ashby Gap or the Shenandoah River. At the Ashby's restaurant, visitors are treated to some of rural Virginia's most sophisticated food, masterminded by innkeepers Roma and John Sherman. The menu changes seasonally; crab cakes and New England mussel chowder with pumpkin-smoked bacon and spicy oil reign as favorites. Dinner runs about $70 for two.

Perhaps the only danger in staying at the inn is that dinners leave many guests too blissfully comatose to appreciate their rooms. There are six in the main building, all furnished with a spareness that is a calming contrast to the rich food. Quilts, blanket chests, rag rugs, and the occasional cannonball bed set the country tone, though in every case, the views are the chief enhancement. As morning light shines through the windows, some guests may feast anew upon the garden, Blue Ridge foothills, lowing cows, and other pastoral delights. The coveted Fan Room has two skylights and a glorious fan window opening onto a balcony.

The four expansive rooms in Paris's former one-room schoolhouse are top-of-the-line and excellent values. Each has a private porch that opens onto those splendid countryside views. The Glascock Room has deep red walls, a canopy four-poster bed, and an antique trunk with extra towels. Oriental rugs cover the hardwood floors, and there are two sinks in the large bathroom. Two wing chairs facing the fireplace and a window seat are inviting places for curling up with a book.

Roma, an avid equestrian, and John are generally too busy during dinner to chat, but at breakfast—featuring fresh eggs cooked to order and succulent muffins—guests might get to know their hosts. Roma left advertising for innkeeping, and John, once a House Ways and Means Committee staffer, still writes speeches for politicians and CEOs between stints as the Ashby Inn's maître d'. △ *8 double rooms with baths, 2 doubles with sinks share 1½ baths. Restaurant, air-conditioning; TVs, phones, and fireplaces in schoolhouse rooms. $100–$220; full breakfast. MC, V. Restricted smoking, closed Jan. 1, July 4, Dec. 25.*

BAILIWICK INN 🍽
4023 Chain Bridge Rd., Fairfax 22030, tel. 703/691–2266 or 800/366–7666, fax 703/934–2112

As visitors to the Bailiwick, Annette and Bob Bradley fell in love with the inn; when it went on the market they spontaneously bought it. They've given the dining room a French-American flair but retained the Bailiwick's historic theme, befitting its location on one of the nation's first toll roads, across the street from the courthouse where George Washington's will is filed.

Each room in the 19th-century house honors a famous Virginian in portraits, accessories, and biographies. The window treatment and red-and-gold scheme in the Thomas Jefferson room mimic the decor of his bedroom in Monticello. The sumptuous Antonia Ford suite, named for a Confederate spy, has dormer windows, a Chippendale sitting room, and a bath with whirlpool tub. All rooms have plump feather beds and goose-down pillows.

There are two elegant parlors for lounging by the fire or taking afternoon tea. Guests staying here can head west to the countryside or hop the Metro going into the capital. ♙ *13 double rooms with baths, 1 suite. Restaurant, air-conditioning, phone jacks in rooms, fireplaces in parlors and 4 rooms, turndown service, whirlpool baths in 2 rooms, TV in sitting room. $130–$295; full breakfast, afternoon tea. AE, MC, V. No smoking.*

BLEU ROCK INN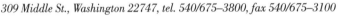

12567 Lee Hwy., Washington 22747, tel. 540/987–3190 or 800/537–3652, fax 540/987–3193

On 80 acres of the former Bleu Rock Farm, the Bleu Rock Inn enjoys a bucolic setting. While the Blue Ridge Mountains form the backdrop, a pond with ducks and geese, rolling pastures, and 7½ acres of vineyards lie in the foreground. Guests can fish for bass and bluegill in the pond and pluck peaches and apples in the farm's orchards.

The pretty guest rooms are simply furnished in pastels, light woods, and lace curtains. The four upstairs rooms have private balconies. Number 2 has a mountain view, and the room's French windows overlook the serene pond. Room 3's balcony is also delightful, providing a western view of the mountains.

The food is the star here. Owners Bernard and Jean Campagne operate the successful La Bergerie Restaurant in Alexandria and may be seen around the inn on weekends. Chefs Richard and Lynn Mahan's eclectic menu features Mediterranean and Asian favorites, including lamb chops with chanterelle mashed potatoes and red wine sauce, as well as a series of delicious seasonal desserts— in the fall, expect dark chocolate and hazelnut mousse cake; in the summer, key lime cake with fresh strawberry sauce. ♙ *5 double rooms with baths. Restaurant, air-conditioning, fireplaces in dining rooms and lounge. $125–$195; Continental or full breakfast. AE, MC, V. Restricted smoking, closed Mon.–Tues. and Dec. 24–25.*

INN AT LITTLE WASHINGTON

309 Middle St., Washington 22747, tel. 540/675–3800, fax 540/675–3100

In a village of 160, 1½ hours west of Washington, D.C., master chef Patrick O'Connell and his partner, Reinhardt Lynch, opened a restaurant that grew into a legend. In the eastern foothills of the Blue Ridge, this inn began serving in 1978 and has been attracting guests from all over the world ever since. From the outside, the three-story white-frame building looks like any other quiet southern hotel; only the Chinese Chippendale balustrade on the second-floor porch suggests the decorative fantasy within. The rich interior is the work of British designer Joyce Conwy-Evans, who has designed theatrical sets and rooms in English royal houses. The settees in the inn bear as many as 13 elegantly mismatched pillows each; the garden, with crab-apple trees, fountain, and fishpond, cries out to be used as a stage backdrop. One bedroom has a bed with a bold plaid spread, shaded by a floral-print half-canopy—and, amazingly, the mélange works. In the slate-floor dining room with William Morris wallpaper, a fabric-swathed ceiling makes guests feel like pashas romantically sequestered in a tent. (A room and a suite in the Guest House, across the street, are good for two couples traveling together, but they lack the sumptuousness of the main building.)

Chef O'Connell's food appears to have cast a spell over almost all of those who have sampled it, as the abundant positive reviews testify. Now, with plans to expand the kitchen, the proprietors seem intent on adding to the ranks of the bewitched. The menu, which changes nightly, makes compelling reading itself, and the six-course dinner costs $98 per person on Saturday, $88 Friday, and

$78 Sunday and weekdays, not including beverages. Some rare vintages rest in the 10,000-bottle wine cellar.

Breakfast, served overlooking the courtyard garden, is far above the usual Continental fare. Miniature pastries and muffins are tucked in a basket alongside tasty croissants; raspberries glisten in large goblets. Those still not sated from dinner can order, at extra cost, a full breakfast—a lobster omelet with rainbow salsa or a bourbon-pecan waffle.

Clearly the inn, with its staff of 50, is a place for indulgence, and anyone unwilling to succumb to it—both psychologically and financially—should opt for humbler digs. But the waiting list alone suggests there are plenty of hedonists out there. ⚱ *9 double rooms with baths, 3 suites. Room service, air-conditioning and phone in rooms, robes, turndown service, whirlpool baths and separate double showers in suites, fireplace in entrance lobby; bicycles. $270–$675; Continental breakfast, afternoon tea. MC, V. No smoking in dining room, closed Dec. 25 and Tues. except in May and Oct.*

L'AUBERGE PROVENÇALE 🕊

Rte. 340 (Box 190), White Post 22663, tel. 540/837–1375 or 800/638–1702, fax 540/837–2004

Fourth-generation chef Alain Borel and his wife, Celeste, have brought the romance, personal touches, and fine dining of a French country inn to tiny White Post, an hour and a half west of the Beltway. The 1753 stone house is on 8½ acres of rolling pastureland. Inside are the Borels' special accents: Alain's great-grandmother's copper pots in the dining room, provincial prints in the guest rooms, whimsical carved carousel animals, painted tiles, and art by Picasso, Buffet, and Dufy.

Visitors might be advised not to fill up on the plate of fresh fruit, chocolate, and homemade cookies that welcomes them to their rooms, saving their appetites instead for the five-course prix-fixe dinner ($62). The meal may commence with tempura-style shrimp and saffron sauce or fried plantains, continue with Bahamian conch chowder, then culminate with rack of lamb and black beans, roasted garlic, and rosemary or pompano in parchment and citrus with papaya and tarragon. Celeste, who handles the wine, has assembled a 250-selection list, plus the Captain's List, with rare vintages for the connoisseur. Breakfast in the sunny, peach-color dining room with bay windows starts with a mix of tangerine and orange juice and is followed by such temptations as fresh fruit, rich croissants, poached egg in phyllo cups, applewood smoked bacon, and house-cured smoked salmon.

For guests who request it, a bit of Borel magic can accompany them in the form of a picnic basket (tablecloth, fruit, cheese, sandwiches, salads, chocolates, and wine) to be savored in some nook along Skyline Drive or at one of the local wineries. Alain's particularity extends to his gardens, where he fusses over herbs and vegetables grown from seeds imported from France or one of the 54 fruit trees, including such exotics as Asian pears, persimmons, and kiwis.

Celeste is as deft a decorator as she is a wine selector. The three rooms in the newer wing are furnished with the fabrics and colors of Provence, accented by hand-painted Spanish tiles; they have fireplaces and private entrances opening onto the gardens. Room 9, the Chambre des Amis, has a canopy bed, cheery yellow and blue prints, and windows facing two directions. For lazy hours with a book or just for views of the countryside, the large private deck off Room 7 in the main house is perfect. ⚱ *8 double rooms with baths, 3 suites. Restaurant, air-conditioning, TV in suite, phone jacks (phones on request) in 3 rooms, fireplaces in 6 rooms,* *living room, and dining room. $145–$250; full breakfast. AE, D, DC, MC, V. No children under 10, restaurant closed Mon.– Tues., inn closed Dec. 25 and 2 wks in Jan. and Aug.*

RICHARD JOHNSTON INN ☙
711 Caroline St., Fredericksburg 22401, tel./fax 540/899–7606

In a prime Caroline Street location, just above the Rappahannock River and across from the visitor center, is this diminutive-looking 18th-century brick row house. Visible on the outside are a dormer on the third floor and a pleasant patio adjoining the parking lot in the rear, shaded by magnolia trees. Inside, restoration work has been top-drawer, and owner Susan Williams, married on site in September 1996, has lavished loving care on the immaculate inn.

In the common rooms downstairs, board floors are polished to a rich luster and covered with Oriental rugs. The furnishings are Chippendale- and Empire-style antiques. Of the guest rooms, Room 5 has an imposing, queen-size, 19th-century mahogany plantation bed, and Room 2 has a dormer, a king-size brass bed, and Victorian furnishings. Two commodious suites, with living rooms, wet bars, and wall-to-wall carpeting, have private entrances opening onto the patio.

Susan serves her freshly baked breads and muffins in the vast dining room, set with fine china, crystal, and silver. With such amenities, it's little wonder the inn has become a major destination, especially during the Renaissance festivals that have sprung up in town over weekends in May and June. ♨ *7 double rooms with baths, 2 suites. Air-conditioning, cable TV in 3 rooms. $95–$145; Continental breakfast. AE, MC, V. No smoking.*

SYCAMORE HILL ☙
110 Menafee Mountain La., Washington 22747, tel. 540/675–3046,
www.bnb-n-va.com/sycamore.htm

Cameras should be poised for the serious photo opportunities available at Sycamore Hill, a ranch-style house seemingly dropped from the sky onto the crest of Menefee Mountain. Winding through the mile-long approach from town, many a visitor may doubt there could be a lodging at road's end. But eventually the forest gives way to Kerri Wagner's extensive gardens, including a vast perennial bed featuring peonies in spring and mums in fall, and the Virginia fieldstone house, wrapped by a 65-ft veranda.

The view from this spot is the raison d'être of Sycamore Hill—there's Old Rag to the right, Tiger Valley, and Red Oak Mountain. The 52-acre lot is a certified wildlife sanctuary. With its views and gardens, this is a spot for the nature lover. The best view is from the 6-ft picture window in the master bedroom, which has a queen-size four-poster bed. Kerri Wagner is an energetic hostess who treats her guests like friends, aided by her husband, Steve, an artist whose fascinating magazine covers line the walls, and by a shaggy white mop of a dog named Molly Bean. ♨ *3 double rooms with baths. Air-conditioning, TV in living room and 1 room, fireplace in living room, turndown service. $115–$165; full breakfast. MC, V. No smoking, 2-night minimum holiday and May weekends and Oct.*

WELBOURNE ☙
22314 Welbourne Rd., Middleburg 20117, tel. 540/687–3201

There are so many stories attached to this 1775 mansion that it may make a guest's head spin. Thomas Wolfe visited. F. Scott Fitzgerald came often and set his short story "The Last Case" here. During the Civil War a Dulany of Welbourne served J. E. B. Stuart breakfast on horseback outside the front door. And however poorly the inn may at times seem to wear its age, it remains a singular site in Virginia with a host of repeat guests, some drawn back to the area for horse shows and auctions.

Welbourne is the genuine, blue-blooded hunt-country article, a sweeping, stately yellow home fronted by six columns and surrounded by 550 acres. It's been in the same family for seven generations, though as owner Sherry Morison says, "We have the acreage, but not the bank account." Recognizing that the old homestead isn't in peak condition, Sherry, who operates the inn with her husband, Nat, describes it as "definitely faded elegance, shabbily genteel, homey. The chairs are wobbly because they've been sat in for 150 years." There are no pretensions here, only peeling paint and faded upholstery, countless family artifacts and antiques, and an unequaled wealth of history. ♘ *5 double rooms with baths, 3 cottages. Air-conditioning in rooms, TV in living room, fireplaces in 4 rooms and 2 cottages. $99–$120; full breakfast, evening cocktails. No credit cards. No cigars, no cats, 2-night minimum spring, fall, and holiday weekends.*

THE EASTERN SHORE

Most people think of the long peninsula east of the Chesapeake Bay as territory claimed by the states of Maryland and Delaware. Indeed, the most developed and touristy parts of DelMarVa are. Yet those who look closely at a map may see a boundary line and a beguiling strip of land tapering off to the south bearing the name of Virginia. This cusp of land is the Old Dominion's Eastern Shore, encompassing two counties—Northampton and Accomack—with a combined population close to that of Charlottesville. The area was settled in the 1600s by English colonists; visited by vacationers (who made the trip by ferryboat) in the 19th century; and surveyed by the railroad, which reached the peninsular terminus, at Cape Charles, in about 1885. Several decades ago the peninsula was bisected by a highway, U.S. 13, which brought some—but not many—1950s-style motels and drive-in restaurants. Off U.S. 13, however, the Eastern Shore lives and looks the way it did around the turn of the century—no quaint restored villages or tony resorts. True back-roaders will like it immensely—providing they understand a few basic facts in advance.

Above all, Virginia's Eastern Shore is not a beach haven, except for the stellar sandy stretches at its northeast corner lying within the Chincoteague National Wildlife Refuge. On the bay side, tidal creeks and marshes predominate. Seaside, a string of barrier islands has kept beaches from forming at the shoreline. The islands themselves are either privately owned or, like the islands of Cobb, Smith, and Hog, provinces of the Nature Conservancy's Virginia Coast Reserve (VCR). Reaching them requires chartering a boat or signing up for one of the VCR's infrequent island trips. There are spring and fall boat tours and three-day photography weekends (tel. 757/442–3049) led by trained naturalists.

There are no cities of note on Virginia's Eastern Shore, with the possible exceptions of Chincoteague, whose meager population swells in peak summer months but otherwise figures at about 3,500, and Cape Charles, which thrived during ferry and railroad days but now has only a cranking cement factory to keep it from succumbing to the sand. County maps show many other towns (with colorful names such as Temperanceville, Birds Nest, and Oyster), but these are really only crossroads with, perhaps, a general store. East of U.S. 13, skinny local arteries such as Routes 679 and 600 reach such villages and the architectural contradictions that surround them. The Virginia peninsula has its own unique building style, followed for hundreds of years: "chain" houses made of frame, consisting, when the pattern holds, of big house, little house, colonnade, and kitchen linked in a row. A good example is the privately owned Holly Brook Plantation, on the west side of U.S. 13, some 8 mi south of Nassawadox.

The town of Chincoteague lies on 8-mi-long Chincoteague Island (not to be confused with the island holding the wildlife refuge, Assateague Island, to which it provides access via a bridge) and exists almost wholly to cater to visitors, with motels, restaurants, and shops. In atmosphere, it is more subdued than other, more developed Atlantic beach resorts in Maryland and Delaware; the area's low-lying, marshy location, which brings occasional septic and mosquito problems, may in part explain the difference. Still, it has one attraction that will probably never cease drawing crowds: the legendary Pony Penning event, held in late July. The wild ponies swim the channel between Assateague and Chincoteague and are then corralled and auctioned off, usually for prices ranging from $200 to $800 each. This roundup began in 1924, though it was made nationally famous by Marguerite Henry's Misty of Chincoteague *in 1947. Misty herself was a real pony; her descendants can be seen roaming free on Assateague throughout the year.*

PLACES TO GO, SIGHTS TO SEE

Accomac. This particularly pretty town has enough restored Colonial architecture to rival Williamsburg, and it is one of two villages on the Eastern Shore (the other is Eastville) with an 18th-century debtors' prison. The Victorian clerk's office on the west side of the courthouse green holds records dating from 1663.

Cape Charles, a place decidedly in the slow lane, was by 1953 abandoned by the passenger railroad and ferry service that allowed the town to flourish briefly around the turn of the century. Today most of its 136 acres are a historic district. A walking tour takes visitors past two Sears-catalog homes built in the mid-1920s, the pleasant bayside boardwalk, and a wonderful art-deco movie house. Some may argue that the industrial works to the south mar the townscape, though the process of loading freight trains onto barges for passage to Norfolk makes for interesting viewing. Yet it is just this slow, elemental way of life and the reasonably priced property that have begun to lure more and more refugees from northern metropolises to the area.

Chesapeake Bay Bridge-Tunnel (tel. 757/787–2960). This 17½-mi, $200 million engineering marvel links the peninsula with Norfolk and Virginia Beach.

Completed in 1964, it has brought the Eastern Shore into the Virginia fold only to a degree, largely due to the hefty $10 toll each way—which, as some peninsula dwellers see it, keeps the navy riffraff out. To support its mammoth span, four islands were built; one has a scenic stopping place, a fishing area, a snack bar, and a gift shop. To accommodate Chesapeake Bay ship traffic, the two-lane bridge gives way to 2 mi-long tunnels. The trip is either awesome, unsettling, or soporific, depending on the soundness of motorists' stomachs and nerves.

Chincoteague National Wildlife Refuge (8231 Beach Rd., tel. 757/336–6122). Despite the surfboarders and sun worshipers headed toward its long stretch of Atlantic beach, the refuge exists first and foremost for the benefit of birds, snakes, ponies, rare DelMarVa gray squirrels, and Sika deer. Many of the species preserved in this veritable Noah's Ark are visible from a 6-mi loop drive that winds through forests and marshes. There are, as well, a visitor center, lighthouse (built in 1866), crabbing ridge, and fishing area—but no restaurants, camping, or bonfires. In season the refuge sponsors a wildlife safari (tel. 757/336–3141), which takes nature lovers along back roads to observe the intimate habits of the famed Chincoteague feral ponies.

Eastern Shore of Virginia National Wildlife Refuge (5003 Hallett Circle, Cape Charles, tel. 757/331–2760). This 651-acre refuge provides good birding year-round. Each fall, migrating birds gather in large groups until favorable conditions permit an easy crossing of Chesapeake Bay.

Eyre Hall (Turn right 3 mi south of the Eastville bank [from the north] or turn left 3 mi above the Cheriton stoplight [from the south] onto Eyre Hall Rd., a private dirt lane, opposite Rte. 636, and drive about 1 mi to the house). The peninsula's most handsome and historic plantation was built in 1733, on land granted to the owners in 1662. The privately owned brick frame house near the bay is open only during Historic Garden Week in April, but its grounds, with ancient plantings, flowering shrubs, and venerable trees, can be visited year-round.

Kerr Place (69 Market St., Onancock, tel. 757/787–8012). The distinguished brick mansion on the outskirts of town was built in 1799. Housed within are the collections of the Eastern Shore of Virginia Historical Society, including costumes, portraits, and furnishings.

Kiptopeke State Park (tel. 757/331–2267). Three miles north of the Bay Bridge Tunnel on Route 704, the park has a wide swimming beach, biking and hiking trails, and a lighted fishing pier. Its Atlantic Flyway location has made it a bird-banding site for several decades.

NASA Goddard Flight Center and Wallops Flight Facility Visitor Center (Wallops Island and areas surrounding Chincoteague, tel. 757/824–2298). The first rocket at this 6,000-acre NASA enclave was launched in 1945. The visitor center, which is the only part of the complex open to visitors, displays space suits, moon rocks, and scale models of satellites and space probes. On the first Saturday of every month NASA conducts model-rocket launches on the grounds.

Pear Valley (near Johnsontown). Constructed in the early 1700s, this is in all likelihood the peninsula's oldest house. The one-room cottage with a chimney and loft is owned by the Association for the Preservation of Virginia Antiquities and is currently unrestored. It can be seen from Route 689.

Refuge Waterfowl and Oyster Museums (7059 Maddox Blvd. and 7125 Maddox Blvd., Piney Island, tel. 757/336–5800 and 757/336–6117, respectively). These two tiny museums are neighbors on Piney Island (barely an island really, as it's only tenuously separated from Chincoteague by skinny Eel Creek). The Waterfowl Museum has a collection of handcrafted decoys, and the Oyster Museum tells the life story of the bivalve (mollusk) and how generations of watermen have pursued it.

Tangier Island. Made popular by the 1980s PBS television series *The Story of English,* this tiny island is stuck like a buoy in the middle of Chesapeake Bay. To reach it, catch the *Captain Eulice* at Onancock harbor (tel. 757/787–8220). The boat sails June–September at 10 and returns at 3. A livestock-grazing range before the Revolution, Tangier is now home to approximately 900 souls—most of them named Crockett, Parkes, Pruitt, and Shores—whose speech rings with an English West Country dialect barely changed since the first settlers moved in. (It was this linguistic insularity that secured the island its spot in the documentary.) Today, residents, who have been known to turn away from less than tactful attempts to observe their speech patterns, remain devotees of seafood harvesting and Methodism. There is one main street, too narrow for cars.

Wachapreague. This sleepy village on the Atlantic side of the peninsula once held a 30-room hotel and attracted vacationers from as far away as New York City. But the hotel burned down, leaving only the 340-odd permanent residents, along with a carnival ground that still lights up in late July. The village remains a fishing mecca, especially for those seeking flounder.

RESTAURANTS

Virginia's Eastern Shore has two culinary stars. The first is the **Garden and the Sea** (Turn west off Rte. 13 at Rte. 710 [First Virginia Bank] and go ¼ mi; New Church, tel. 757/824–0672) where chef Tom Baker takes advantage of the fine seafood market across the street to whip up delights from a broad American Continental repertoire, including his signature dish, a shrimp, scallop, and oyster special in chardonnay sauce. The menu (entrées $18–$24) features seasonal desserts and changes every three weeks. The second is **Eastville Manor** (6058 Willow Oak Rd., Eastville, tel. 757/678–7378), where chef Bill Scalley, formerly of Washington's Four Seasons and Mayflower hotels, serves entrées ($9–$14) garnished with herbs from his and his wife Melody's own garden along with crab cakes that even the locals have declared heavenly. Prospective patrons may want to call ahead to secure space at evening seatings, since even in these sparsely populated surroundings, Scalley's galley is fast becoming a major draw.

Hopkins and Bro. General Store (2 Market St., Onancock, tel. 757/787–4478) isn't what it seems to be. This Virginia Historic Landmark, which was built in 1842, is a restaurant to be reckoned with. On a wharf on Chesapeake Bay, the restaurant promises to serve up the freshest seafood on the Eastern Shore. Chef David Tweedie notes that the catch of the day is "just a few feet away."

For casual dining, guests should not be put off by the truck-stop appearance of the **Stingray's Restaurant at Cape Center** (26507 Langford Hwy., Cape Charles, tel. 757/331–2505). Locals call it "Chez Exxon" (for its proximity to the gas station) and praise the sophisticated dinner entrées and reasonable prices. Other casual options include **Ray's Shanty** (Rte. 175, Wattsville, tel. 757/824–3429), the **Village** (6576 Maddox Blvd., Chincoteague, tel. 757/336–5120), and **AJ's on the Creek** (6585 Maddox Blvd., Chincoteague, tel. 757/336–9770). In Onancock, trendy **Armando's** (10 North St., tel. 757/787–8044) has a bistro atmosphere. The casual **Formy's Pit Barbecue** (Rte. 13, Painter, tel. 757/442–2426) is the Eastern Shore's only barbecue restaurant.

A fixture of Tangier Island is the **Chesapeake House** (Main St., tel. 757/891–2331), whose reputation for family-style shellfish feasts has spread far and wide. Slightly less renowned is **Double-Six** (Main St., tel. 757/891–2410), a local haunt once featured in *National Geographic* because it serves hot oyster sandwiches.

VISITOR INFORMATION

Chincoteague Chamber of Commerce (Box 258, Chincoteague 23336, tel. 757/336–6161). **Virginia Division of Tourism** (901 E. Byrd St., Richmond 23219, tel. 804/786–4484). **Virginia's Eastern Shore Chamber of Commerce/Tourism Commission** (Drawer R, Melfa 23410, tel. 757/787–2460).

RESERVATION SERVICES

Amanda's Bed & Breakfast Reservation Service (1428 Park Ave., Baltimore, MD 21217, tel. 410/225–0001). **Bed & Breakfast of Tidewater Virginia Reservation Service** (Box 6226, Norfolk 23508, tel. 804/627–1983). **Inns of the Eastern Shore** (1500 Hambrooks Blvd., Cambridge, MD 21613, tel. 800/373–7890). For a copy of the Bed and Breakfast Association of Virginia's directory, describing more than 100 establishments, call the **Virginia Division of Tourism's B&B line** (tel. 800/262–1293). The Division of Tourism's Washington, D.C., office also operates a B&B and small-inn booking service (tel. 202/659–5523 or 800/934–9184 outside D.C.).

CAPE CHARLES HOUSE 🐚

645 Tazewell Ave., Cape Charles 23310, tel. 757/331–4920, fax 757/331–4960, www.capecharleshouse.com

This 1912 Colonial-revival frame house, with its spacious wraparound front porch, is one of Cape Charles's largest and most opulent inns. Innkeepers Carol and Bruce Evans, who took over in 1994, quickly learned how to make their guests feel pampered, from the soft classical music in the parlor to gourmet, heart-healthy breakfasts. Carol credits a fellow innkeeper with persuading the Evanses to move from Chesapeake to join the reawakening of what she calls "this jewel of a town."

Rooms, named after prominent people in Cape Charles's history, are furnished with antiques, unusual collectibles, and family items, such as furniture painted by Carol's mother. The tiniest room is named after Alexander Cassat, president of the local railroad and brother of artist Mary Cassat, whose works are featured here. The Julia Wilkins Room has a whirlpool and private balcony.

Carol teaches cooking classes and serves five-course dinners (about $100 per couple). ♨ *5 double rooms with baths. Air-conditioning, ceiling fans in rooms, whirlpool tub in 1 room, cable TV in parlor; beach chairs, bicycles. $80–$105; full breakfast, afternoon refreshments. AE, D, MC, V. No smoking.*

CHANNEL BASS INN 🐚

6228 Church St., Chincoteague 23336, tel. 757/336–6148 or 800/249-0818, fax 757/336–6599

The Channel Bass Inn occupies a lovely peach and green building with white trim that was constructed in the 1880s. One of Chincoteague's oldest structures, it was added to in the 1920s. The inn remains a welcoming destination just off Main Street in the sleepy village, where taking a stroll down to the seashore is probably the most activity anyone will accomplish.

The Channel Bass has come under the command of David Wiedenheft and his wife, Barbara, who hope their success at Miss Molly's (*see below*), just a "scone's" throw away, rubs off on this distinguished residence. The six guest rooms, on the second and third floors, are extremely large and open onto airy seating areas.

Rooms and halls are hung with original artwork, there are triple-sheeted beds and ceramic tile baths, and an English garden is a reminder of Barbara's heritage. One self-contained suite offers all the space more privacy-conscious guests could seek, along with its own mini-refrigerator. Both the comfortable front sitting rooms downstairs and the courtyard make pleasant space for reading or enjoying full breakfast and afternoon tea. ⌂ *8 double rooms with baths, 2 suites. Air-conditioning. $89–$175; full breakfast. No smoking, 2-night minimum weekends, 4-night minimum during holidays and Pony Penning.*

THE GARDEN AND THE SEA INN ✿

4188 Nelson Rd., New Church 23415, tel. 757/824–0672 or 800/824–0672 outside VA, www.bbonline.com/va/gardensea.htm

The Garden and the Sea Inn sits on a quiet lane near Route 13, the main thoroughfare along the Eastern Shore, in tiny New Church, just 1½ mi south of the Maryland border and 15 minutes from Chincoteague. The main house of the inn is composed of the 1802-built Bloxom's Tavern and its 1901 addition. New Church's oldest farmhouse, dating from the mid-19th century, has been moved onto the property. It's now the Garden House, with a parlor where guests can relax with sherry, apples, and brownies, an inviting wide porch, and three guest rooms.

In 1994 Sara and Tom Baker bought the inn because they wanted to be in business together. After looking at properties from Pennsylvania to Florida, the newly married couple visited this property, and Sara said, "Let's do it."

Sophisticated and inviting, the inn mixes antique furnishings, French wicker, Oriental rugs, ballooning fabrics, Victorian moldings and detail, and bay windows. From the multicolored gingerbread trim on the wide front porch to the sunny, rose-hued dining room, it's exceptionally appealing. Guest rooms are spacious. In the main house, the Chantilly Room, with a wicker sleigh bed and painted dresser, and the Giverny Room, with floral prints and dark-green lacquered wrought-iron furniture, have large baths with double sinks and bidets. The large, private Champagne Room in the Garden House has a two-person whirlpool tub and shower and a wrought-iron canopy bed.

Tom, who has been the chef at top Washington hotels, creates dinners featuring produce from local farms and fresh fish from nearby waters in menus that change every three weeks. There are two fixed-price menus, as well as à la carte choices (entrées run about $18–$24). Specialties include a sea scallop, shrimp, and oyster dish and Tom's outstanding soups. The buffet breakfast, a bit of a letdown after the excellent dinner, is available in the dining room or—when weather permits—in the garden patio beside the lily pond and fountain. Afternoon refreshments are available for guests who wish to loaf around at the inn. ⌂ *6 double rooms with baths. Restaurant, air-conditioning, ceiling fans in rooms, robes, whirlpool bath in 4 rooms; sheltered outdoor area for small pets. $75–$165; Continental breakfast. AE, D, MC, V. No smoking, 2-night minimum weekends, closed Dec.–Mar.*

ISLAND MANOR HOUSE ✿

4160 Main St., Chincoteague 23336, tel. 757/336–5436 or 800/852–1505, www.chincoteague.com/b-b/imh.html

In this 1848 three-story, T-shape, white-frame house on Main Street, Charles and Carol Kalmykow, married on site in September 1995, have created a special destination. The house is furnished in Federal style with an impressive collection of antiques. Classical music plays quietly in the impeccable, rose-color Garden Room, a serene retreat with fireplace, big windows, and French doors opening onto a brick courtyard with roses and a fountain. The large Nathaniel Smith Room has a sloped ceiling, a sitting area, and four dormer windows, each with a window seat. The premier room is the Mark Twain, which has a king-size bed.

Carol prepares lavish breakfasts that include homemade bread each morning, and Charles helps attend to maintenance and guests' needs. Afternoon tea is available also. For those eager to visit nearby Assateague Island but avoid the $4 park admission, ask the innkeepers about passes they may have.

Since Miss Molly's (*see below*) is just across the street, travelers can choose from two distinct personalities—the more casual Miss Molly's or the more formal, well-appointed Island Manor House. ♤ *6 double rooms with baths, 2 doubles share 1 bath. Air-conditioning; bicycles. $70–$120; full breakfast. AE, MC, V. No smoking, no children under 10, 2-night minimum weekends, 3-night minimum holidays.*

MISS MOLLY'S INN 🖙
4141 Main St., Chincoteague 23336, tel. 757/336–6686 or 800/221–5620

In stark contrast to the high-priced, high-rise resorts up the coast, Chincoteague's Miss Molly's Inn instills visitors with a sense of place that for some may prove indelible. Like the small island on which it sits, whose isolation and thin soil have prevailed despite the various booms that have threatened to consume it, the inn conveys an old-fashioned perseverance. It lies on the island's main drag, which is orderly and navigable even on holiday weekends, just over the causeway bridge from the wisp of the mainland. Just listening to the seagulls fly by and the soft hum of the Atlantic gives visitors a peaceful feeling. While the island as a whole may once again be undergoing something of a rediscovery, Miss Molly's is a quiet retreat, an enclave of simple hospitality and respectful company.

A chief reason is innkeeper Barbara Wiedenheft, who makes the most of this low, unobtrusive 1886 Victorian whose wooden frame is painted in four colors—green, deep purple, mauve, and cream—that blend with the seacoast's rustic sky on a clear evening just as the sun is setting. Flanked by a series of porches and sitting just off Main Street, it is named after builder J. T. Rowley's daughter, who lived there until she was 84. In a previous incarnation as a rooming house, the inn played host to Marguerite Henry, author of *Misty of Chincoteague*. Barbara will point out the second-floor room where Henry stayed in 1946 while writing the book, which has helped produce a constant stream of guests since its publication in 1947. The upstairs rooms, which have reading lights and copies of the text, are cozy, and guests may wander onto the inn's various porches to enjoy the Atlantic breeze. Antiques and Victorian furnishings lend an air of elegance to the cozy retreat.

However versed they may happen to be with the island's habits, Barbara, who still calls Yorkshire, England, home, and her husband, David, a native of Chicago, will strike up a conversation with a visitor on whatever the news of the day may be. Weather permitting, Barbara may be found out back serving tea in the screened-in gazebo, which faces the channel and its fishing traffic, or just around the corner at the Channel Bass Inn, which the Wiedenhefts also operate and where guests of both inns mingle with the public over Barbara's scrumptious scones. ♤ *5 double rooms with baths, 2 doubles share 1 bath. Air-conditioning, clock radios in rooms, woodstove in dining room, beach towels; bikes. $59–$155; full break-*

fast, afternoon tea. D, MC, V. No smoking, 2-night minimum weekends, 3-night minimum holiday weekends, closed Jan. 1–mid-Mar.

PICKETT'S HARBOR ☙

*28288 Nottingham Ridge La. (Box 97AA), Cape Charles 23310, tel. 757/331–2212,
www.bbonline.com/va/pickharb.html*

Sara and Cooke Goffigan's beige frame-and-brick house sits off an isolated country lane 4 mi north of the Chesapeake Bay Bridge-Tunnel and 2 mi west of U.S. 13. The front yard is a vast stretch of private beach frequented by deer and horseshoe crabs and, since 1983, adventurous guests of Pickett's Harbor.

Sara's warmth and the high-ceiling rooms furnished with antiques and family photographs immediately make guests feel as if they were sharing an immensely cozy home with friends. The one downstairs bedroom has a four-poster bed, easy chairs, and an exceptional water view. The upstairs rooms have quilt-covered beds and water views that lighten them and give them an airy feel.

Sara serves a country breakfast that routinely features sweet-potato biscuits, Virginia ham, and popovers. Before she heads off to teach school, guests may want to ask her about her family, a clan that came to the Eastern Shore in the 1600s, not long after Captain John Smith explored the peninsula. ♨ *2 double rooms with baths, 4 doubles share 2 baths. Air-conditioning, TV/VCR in family room, fireplaces in family and dining rooms; bicycles. $75–$125; full breakfast. No credit cards. No smoking, 2-night minimum holiday weekends.*

SPINNING WHEEL BED AND BREAKFAST ☙

*31 North St., Onancock 23417, tel. 757/787–7311,
www.esvanet\~evergreen\spinningwheel.html*

For five years, this 1890s Victorian home in the heart of Onancock was Karen and David Tweedie's summer home. Then in 1993, they jump-started their plans to open a B&B by converting the house, a job Karen declares was "more fun than we ever expected." Karen, a spinner, displays her collection of antique spinning wheels throughout the house. David serves elaborate morning meals in the dining rooms, indulging guests with breads, meats, and other goodies that leave them full throughout the day. The Tweedie's huge sheepdog, Nelly, is a third host. When not at the Spinning Wheel, which is open late spring to fall, the Tweedies operate an antiques shop, art gallery, and a mail-order jewelry business, which, as Karen proudly says, sells items "culled from the landscape of the Eastern Shore." The Tweedies are also the proud owners of the Hopkins and Bro. General Store, which specializes in seafood. Additionally, David works with students with hearing impairments at Gallaudet University in Washington, D.C.; Karen tends to the inn while he's away.

Of the guest rooms, a favorite is Room 2, decorated with oil lamps, an oak dresser, crocheted pillow covers, and a wedding-ring quilt on the brass bed. Closet space was sacrificed throughout to make room for the private baths. There are just rods or racks with hangers and little drawer space, but who needs a lot of clothes for casual Onancock? ♨ *5 double rooms with baths. Air-conditioning, wood-burning stove in living room, turndown service; bicycles. $75–$95; full breakfast. MC, V. No smoking, closed Thanksgiving–Apr.*

WILLIAMSBURG AND
SOUTHEAST VIRGINIA

"Down in Virginia there is a little old-fashioned city called Williamsburg. It stands on the ridge of the peninsula that separates the James and York rivers." So begins The City of Once Upon a Time, *a children's book written by Gilchrist Waring in 1946. That book and the Official Guide to Colonial Williamsburg are two of the best introductions to the legendary city, which more than a million people visit every year.*

Williamsburg was the capital of Virginia between 1699 and 1780, when the colony was immense, extending west to the Mississippi River. A planned city like Annapolis, Maryland, and a thriving commercial hub serving the farms and tobacco plantations between the rivers, it was an alluring place then and remains so to this day, even if its legislative chambers and trading floors have fallen silent. In 1926 the rector at Williamsburg's Bruton Parish Church persuaded John D. Rockefeller Jr. to restore the town. The continuing project has resulted in a living-history museum of 173 acres, a mile long and a half-mile wide, holding 88 restored and 50 major reconstructed buildings and surrounded by a 3,000-acre "greenbelt." The restoration has become a pattern for similar endeavors nationwide. Outlying discount malls and commercial strips woo travelers to bargain emporiums like the Williamsburg Pottery Factory and Berkeley Commons. The attractive Merchants Square, adjoining the historic district, houses a movie theater, restaurants, and some 40 shops.

Having located Colonial Williamsburg proper, visitors can simply wander in and soak up the atmosphere, perhaps slaking their thirst on cups of cider, peddled streetside. Others may opt to stop at the visitor center (102 Information Center Dr., tel. 804/220–7645, open daily 8:30–5), which lies off Colonial Parkway (the National Park artery that connects Jamestown, Williamsburg, and Yorktown), to view a 35-minute film and buy passes that enable entrance to buildings and quick access to shuttle buses that link the top sights. The outlet stores in neighboring Lightfoot are a shoppers' delight. There are more than 100 stores selling everything from Ralph Lauren clothing to Waterford crystal. Call the information center in Williamsburg for more information.

Williamsburg is not the oldest continuous English settlement in the United States. That title is held by nearby Jamestown, where a sea-weary party of 104 men and boys aboard the Susan Constant, Godspeed, *and* Discovery *landed in 1607 and clung to survival, despite hostile relations with Native Americans, disease bred in nearby swamps, and chaos fueled by the fear that they'd been forgotten by suppliers across the Atlantic. Today Jamestown Island, the site of a national park, is a much more rustic place than civil Williamsburg. One singular enjoyment wrought of its earthiness, however, is the glassblowing shop.*

It is entirely understandable that visitors to the area should feel overwhelmed. Several different paths of the nation's history converge. Those mindful of the roles of African and Native American people in the nation's heritage will note that Williamsburg is where the first slaves entered the colonies in 1619 and that Jamestown marks the starting point for a long, often brutal push westward of the continent's native inhabitants by English-speaking settlers. Besides Jamestown and Williamsburg, there's nearby Yorktown to explore (the scene of the last Revolutionary War battle and the surrender of General Cornwallis) and a half dozen plantations along the James River, which are formidable attractions in their own right. Charles City County, which hugs the river between Richmond and Williamsburg, is truly a place apart. The same handful of families have owned and farmed its plantations since the 17th century and have stoically kept development out, as a drive along Route 5 will reveal. The high-traffic shipping channel lying just beyond the mouth of the James was the site of the Civil War battle between the ironclads Monitor *and* Merrimack, *which made military and maritime history. More recently, the region has played a crucial role in the development of the nation's space program.*

The key thing to keep in mind about Williamsburg's bed-and-breakfasts is that none of them lie within the historic district; indeed, none of them occupy a historic home, though several are exceedingly fine places to stay. Those intent on booking accommodations in a bona fide Colonial structure with a historic pedigree should contact the **Williamsburg Inn** *(tel. 757/229–1000 or 800/447–8679). It manages 85 rooms in taverns and houses in the restored district.*

Farther down state Route 5 is the historically impressive (it celebrated its 250th anniversary in 1998) city of Petersburg, which is home to antiques shops and tiny restaurants, and Petersburg National Battlefield.

Finally, the southeast part of the state is home to an abundance of parks and natural areas such as Pochahontas State Park.

PLACES TO GO, SIGHTS TO SEE

Abby Aldrich Rockefeller Folk Art Center (307 S. England St., Williamsburg, tel. 757/220–7670). Some 3,000 pieces—furniture, paintings, carvings, textiles, and decorative useful wares—make this the nation's leading American folk-art center. Mrs. Rockefeller's 424-work collection forms the core.

Busch Gardens Williamsburg (Off U.S. 60, Williamsburg, tel. 757/253–3350). This theme park re-creates things German, French, Italian, and English and offers rides on such curiosities as the Loch Ness Monster.

Carter's Grove (Williamsburg, tel. 757/220–7453). An 18th-century plantation 8 mi east of the historic district, Carter's Grove was built in 1750 by a grandson of the Colonial tobacco tycoon Robert "King" Carter and renovated and enlarged in 1928. It's now part of the Colonial Williamsburg Foundation, and a lovely one-way country road wends its way back to the historic district. The Winthrop Rockefeller Archaeology Museum explores the discovery of the Wolstenholme Towne site here. This village had fewer than 50 inhabitants; all were massacred by Native Americans in 1622.

College of William and Mary (Williamsburg, tel. 757/221–2630). The second-oldest college in the United States (after Harvard, which dates from 1636) was founded in 1693 by charter from King William and Queen Mary of England. Its centerpiece, the Wren Building, begun in 1695, is the country's oldest academic building still in use.

Colonial Williamsburg (51 mi southeast of Richmond, tel. 800/447–8679). In the restored district, some of the most interesting historic buildings are the Capitol, where Patrick Henry delivered his famous speech; Bruton Parish Church; and the handsome Governor's Palace, with its stable, kitchen, exquisite gardens, and working wheelwright's shop. The Courthouse in Market Square, fronted by pillories and stocks, reenacts 18th-century court trials. Along Duke of Gloucester Street are the Printing Office, Shoemaker's Shop, the James Anderson Blacksmith Shop, and Golden Ball Silversmith. Crafts shops in the historic district include Prentis Store, for pottery, baskets, soaps, and pipes; the Post Office, for books, prints, maps, stationery, and sealing wax; and Raleigh Tavern Bake Shop, for ginger cakes and cider.

DeWitt Wallace Decorative Arts Gallery (325 Francis St., Williamsburg, tel. 757/220–7554). This modern museum behind the Public Hospital contains 10,000 examples of English and American furniture, ceramics, textiles, prints, metals, and costumes primarily from the 17th and 18th centuries.

Hampton. This town is the birthplace of America's space program and is home to the **Virginia Air & Space Center** (600 Settlers Landing Rd., tel. 757/727–0800), which houses some of the most dramatic artifacts from the U.S. space program. From the nearby visitor center, the *Miss Hampton II* (710 Settlers Landing Rd., tel. 757/727–1102) cruises Hampton Roads harbor and passes the world's largest naval base. Visit St. John's, the country's oldest continuous English-speaking parish, or ride the 1920-built Hampton Carousel.

Historic Air Tours (Williamsburg Airport, tel. 757/253–8185 or 800/822–9247). Narrated flights over Colonial Williamsburg, Yorktown, Jamestown, the James River Plantations, and Hampton Roads give an intriguing perspective on the area's history and growth.

James River Plantations. On Route 5, where descendants of Virginia's earliest families still live, work, and preserve a way of life spanning three centuries, these estates are open for tours. *Berkeley* (12602 Harrison Landing Rd., Charles City, tel. 804/829–6018) is a perfect Georgian. Built in 1726 and later inhabited by a signer of the Declaration of Independence and two U.S. presidents, William Henry Harrison and Benjamin Harrison, it is surrounded by 10 acres of formal boxwood gardens. Guests can dine in its *Coach House Taverns* (12604 Harrison Landing Rd., Charles City, tel. 804/829–6003). *Evelynton* (6701 John Tyler Memorial Hwy., Charles City, tel. 804/829–5075 or 800/473–5075) was the site of several fierce Civil War skirmishes. Today the 2,500-acre farm is still family-owned and -occupied, and the house brims with photographs and portraits. *Sherwood Forest* (14501 John Tyler Memorial Hwy., Charles City, tel. 804/829–5377) was purchased in 1842 by John Tyler, the 10th president of the United States, who moved here when he left the White House. The current occupants are the third generation of Tylers to live here. At 321 ft, this is the longest frame house in the country. *Shirley Plantation* (501 Shirley Plantation Rd., Charles City, tel. 804/829–5121 or 800/232–1613), a Georgian house, capped by a hand-carved pineapple finial, has been owned by 10 generations of Hills and Carters (Anne Carter was the mother of Robert E. Lee). Shirley was founded six years after the settlers arrived in Jamestown, with the house erected in 1723. Its three-story "flying" staircase, which looks unsupported, and the Queen Anne forecourt are noteworthy. *Westover* (7000 Westover Rd., Charles City, tel. 804/829–2882), seat of the Byrd family, is one of the finest Georgian plantations in the United States. Its grounds are open daily, though the house can be seen only in late April, during Virginia's Historic Garden Week.

Jamestown Colonial National Historical Park (Colonial Pkwy., Jamestown, tel. 757/229–1733). The site is an island, which is why the colonists chose it for a settlement in 1607. It was a bad choice; in one year nine-tenths of the settlers died of starvation, violence, or disease, and the capitol burned four times before it was moved to Williamsburg. Visitors will find an information center, museum, paths leading through the ruins of "James Cittie," a scenic loop drive, and the Glasshouse, where craftspeople may pique the imaginations of those still puzzling over the logistics of ships-in-a-bottle.

Jamestown Settlement (Off Jamestown Rd., next to the National Historical Park, tel. 757/229–1607). The state-operated museum depicts the Jamestown experience in its gallery and outdoors, with living-history re-creations of the colonial fort and Powhatan Indian village and replicas of the three English ships that arrived in 1607.

Mariners' Museum (100 Museum Dr., Newport News, tel. 757/596–2222). Here maritime history is documented, from the Native American dugout canoe and Chesapeake workboats to modern shipbuilding efforts at Newport News.

Pamplin Historical Park (6125 Boydton Plank Rd., Petersburg, tel. 804/861–2408) is one of the newest in southeast Virginia yet one of the most important. Chronicled here is the decisive Civil War battle of April 2, 1865, which eventually led to the end of the war. Visitors can see artifacts from the war and tour the battle ground. The National Museum of the Civil War Soldier will open here in summer 1999.

Petersburg National Battlefield (1539 Hickory Hill Rd., Petersburg, tel. 804/732–3531) is not only one of the most visited but also one of the most researched battlefields. Petersburg is one of the stops on the "Lee's Retreat" tour, which marks Lee's path to surrender at Appomattox. A guide for those driving the path can be picked up at the Battlefield's Visitor Center or ordered in advance by calling the Virginia Division of Tourism (tel. 888/248–4592).

Petersburg Visitor Center (425 Cockade Alley, tel. 804/733–2400 or 800/368–3595) is the first place guests should go before venturing to such places as the Batterseas Revolutionary War Museum, Center Hill Mansion, or the Siege Museum. Restoration of the downtown is ongoing, but most of the city's 12 different historic sites and homes are open year-round.

Pocahontas State Park (10301 State Park Rd., Chesterfield, tel. 804/796–4255) has more than 7,500 acres of sprawling woods and streams. There are hiking and biking trails and a swimming pool.

Williamsburg Winery (5800 Wessex Hundred, tel. 757/229–0999). Tours and tastings are given. Especially noteworthy are the chardonnay and the Governor's White.

Yorktown and Yorktown Battlefield Colonial National Historic Park (Colonial Pkwy. and Rte. 238, Yorktown, tel. 757/898–3400). Here Washington laid siege to Cornwallis's army, and in 1781 the British surrendered in the (restored) Moore House. English, French, and American breastworks still line the battlefield. It's a good idea to stop at the visitor center first to view the dioramas and rent a taped tour.

Yorktown Victory Center (Rte. 1020 and Colonial Pkwy., tel. 757/887–1776). This state-operated museum chronicles America's evolution from colony to nation in gallery exhibits, living-history Continental Army encampments, and an 18th-century farm site.

RESTAURANTS

Visitors can choose from a host of Colonial taverns scattered around Williamsburg's historic district, among them the **King's Arms, Shields,** and **Chownings** (tel. for all three: 757/229–1000 or 800/447–8679 for reservations). These serve such traditional fare as prime rib, game pie, Sally Lunn (slightly sweet raised bread), and peanut soup. For expensive formal dining, there's the award-winning **Regency Room** at the Williamsburg Inn (136 E. Francis St., tel. 757/229–7978). The **Trellis** (403 Duke of Gloucester St., tel. 757/229–8610), in Merchants Square, features a changing menu of regional food and decadent desserts. The **Old Chickahominy House** (1211 Jamestown Rd., tel. 757/229–4689) is noted for its Brunswick stew; **Pierce's** (Just off I–64, tel. 757/565–2955) has good barbecue. At **Indian Fields** (Rte. 5, Charles City, tel. 804/829–5004) the menu has such Tidewater delicacies as Virginia ham in pineapple-raisin sauce and scallops in puff pastry.

SHOPPING

At the **Williamsburg Outlet Mall** (6401 Richmond Rd., Lightfoot, tel. 888/746–7333), just 10 minutes from Colonial Williamsburg, shop for bargains from Farberware, Ralph Lauren, J. Crew, and other quality brand names.

VISITOR INFORMATION

Colonial National Historical Park (Jamestown-Yorktown; Superintendent, Yorktown 23690, tel. 757/898–3400). **Colonial Williamsburg Foundation** (Williamsburg 23187, tel. 757/229–1000 or 800/447–8679). **Hampton Visitor Center** (710 Settlers Landing Rd., Hampton 23669, tel. 757/727–1102 or 800/800–2202). **Jamestown-Yorktown Foundation** (Box JF, Williamsburg 23187, tel. 757/253–4838). **Petersburg Visitors Center** (Box 2107, Petersburg 23804, tel. 800/368–

3595). **Virginia Division of Tourism** (901 E. Byrd St., Richmond 23219, tel. 804/ 786–4484). **Virginia Plantation Country** (Box 1382, Hopewell 23860, tel. 804/ 541–2206). **Williamsburg Area Convention & Visitors Bureau** (Box 3585, Williamsburg 23187-3585, tel. 757/253–0192 or 800/368–6511).

RESERVATION SERVICES

Bensonhouse (2036 Monument Ave., Richmond 23220, tel. 804/353–6900). For a copy of the Bed and Breakfast Association of Virginia's directory, describing more than 100 establishments, call the **Virginia Division of Tourism's B&B line** (tel. 800/262–1293). The Division of Tourism's Washington, D.C., office also operates a B&B and small-inn booking service (tel. 202/659–5523 or 800/934–9184 outside D.C.).

COLONIAL CAPITAL 🐚

501 Richmond Rd., Williamsburg 23185, tel. 757/229–0233 or 800/776–0570, fax 757/253–7667

The Colonial Capital, a three-story frame house painted spring-mist green, is within walking distance of the historic district, Merchants Square, and the College of William and Mary. The exceedingly nice innkeepers, Barbara and Phil Craig, are respectively a retired university administrator and stockbroker who moved to Williamsburg after 25 years in North Carolina. The Colonial's five rooms are named after area rivers. The York has an enclosed, green-canopy bed. Prettiest, though, is sunny Pamlico, with window seats and a white-canopy bed. The third floor can be made into a two-bedroom suite, a plus for families. Downstairs there's a large parlor with a wood-burning fireplace and access to a sunporch, where the Craigs keep games, books, and puzzles. In the rear, near the Colonial garden, is guest parking, which solves a serious problem in teeming Williamsburg. **△** *4 double rooms with baths, 1 suite. Air-conditioning, cable TV/VCR in parlor and suite, turndown service; bicycles. $95–$135; full breakfast, welcome drink. AE, MC, V. No smoking, no children under 8, 2-night minimum during peak weekends.*

EDGEWOOD 🐚

4800 John Tyler Memorial Hwy., Charles City 23030, tel. 804/829–2962 or 800/296–3343

Says frothy innkeeper Dot Boulware in her liquid southern accent, "I have to tell you, I am a romantic." And so is Edgewood—three marriage proposals were made in one week here. But before she and her husband, Julian, bought Edgewood Plantation, on scenic Route 5 approximately half an hour from Colonial Williamsburg, in 1978, she didn't care a bit for Victoriana. Fortunately tastes change, and when she became the mistress of an 1850s Carpenter Gothic house, she began collecting Victorian antiques like a woman possessed.

Dot's eight-bedroom house, visible from Route 5, looks on the inside like Miss Havisham's dining room, minus the cobwebs. It is full to bursting with old dolls, antique corsets and lingerie, lace curtains and pillows, love seats, baby carriages, stuffed steamer trunks, mighty canopy beds, highboys, Confederate caps—the list goes on and on. At Christmastime she professionally decorates 18 trees and festoons the banister of the graceful three-story staircase with bows. Clearly, more is better at Dot Boulware's Edgewood.

In her hands, Victoriana is thoroughly feminine, even though in one chamber, the Civil War Room, she's tried to cater to the opposite sex, decorating with intimate details of men's 19th-century apparel. Large people of either sex will have a hard time moving freely in this wildly crowded bed-and-breakfast. Lizzie's Room, the favorite, has a king-size pencil-post canopy bed and a private bath with a double marble shower and claw-foot tub. The room enshrines the memory of a teenager who, Dot says, died of a broken heart when her beau failed to return from the Civil War. Prissy's Quarters, upstairs in the carriage house, has a kitchen area.

Breakfast is served in the dining room by candlelight. The brick-walled, beam-ceilinged downstairs tavern is a cozy sitting area with a fireplace, backgammon board, TV, and popcorn machine. There are also fireplaces in the dining room, a kitchen, a tearoom, and two bedrooms. Outside there's an unrestored mill house dating from 1725, an antiques shop, gazebo, swimming pool, and formal 18th-century garden (which makes a delightful wedding setting). Edgewood is centrally located for touring the James River plantations. **♿** *6 double rooms with baths, 2 suites. Tearoom, air-conditioning, turndown service; pool. $118–$178; full breakfast, light afternoon refreshments. AE, MC, V. No smoking, 2-night minimum holiday weekends.*

LIBERTY ROSE ♟

1022 Jamestown Rd., Williamsburg 23185, tel. 757/253–1260 or 800/545–1825, www.libertyrose.com

Bed-and-breakfast keepers in Williamsburg are in something of a bind. Because all the historic buildings in town are owned by either the Williamsburg Foundation or the College of William and Mary, they can't offer travelers authentic Colonial accommodations. Some innkeepers have decorated in the Colonial style anyway, but others, like Sandy and Brad Hirz, owners of the Liberty Rose, have come up with different, imaginative solutions to the dilemma.

Besides sheer ingenuity, Sandy and Brad have romance going for them. They were just friends when Sandy decided to leave the West Coast to open a B&B in Williamsburg. Brad was helping Sandy house-hunt when they looked at a 1920s white-clapboard-and-brick home a mile west of the restored district (on the road to Jamestown). Sandy bought it in five minutes. Then Brad started seriously courting her, but it was Sandy, and not the B&B, who inspired him. Now they run Williamsburg's most beguiling B&B, decorated à la nouvelle Victorian with turn-of-the-century touches.

Sandy, a former interior designer, has a special talent for fabrics and is responsible for the handsome tieback curtains, many-layered bed coverings, and plush canopies. The patterns are 19th-century reproductions. Brad has held up his end of the business by managing remodeling. The bathrooms are particularly attractive: One has a floor taken from a plantation in Gloucester, a claw-foot tub, and an amazing freestanding, glass-sided shower. The sumptuous Suite Williamsburg has an elaborate carved-ball and claw-foot four-poster bed and a fireplace. (The parlor, too, has a fireplace.) All rooms have a TV/VCR and a collection of films as well as an amenities basket bulging with everything the traveler might need, from bandages to needle and thread. The furnishings are a fetching mix of 18th- and 19th-century reproductions and antiques. Two tree swings (one a two-seater) are by the new courtyard.

Liberty Rose sits on a densely wooded hilltop, and the lake on the William and Mary campus is within easy walking distance. A stroll at dusk may be hard to resist, since romance sets the tone here all year round. ♙ *1 double room with bath, 3 suites. Air-conditioning, phone and TV/VCR in rooms, turndown service. $135–$195; full breakfast, afternoon refreshments. AE, MC, V. No smoking, no children under 12.*

NORTH BEND PLANTATION
12200 Weyanoke Rd., Charles City 23030, tel. 804/829–5176 or 800/841–1479, www.inngetaways.com/va/north.html

Routinely, a stay at this Charles City County plantation begins with a tour of the house and grounds conducted by Ridgely Copland, a farmer's wife and a nurse (once named Virginia nurse of the year). Along the way Ridgely points out Union breastworks from 1864, wild asparagus, herds of deer, a swamp, and the wide James River. Only one other Virginia bed-and-breakfast—Welbourne (*see above*), near Middleburg—is so strikingly authentic, but North Bend differs from that slightly gone-to-seed mansion in that it's a well-maintained working farm. The Coplands are salt-of-the-earth people striving to keep their 850 acres intact in the face of modern agricultural dilemmas.

North Bend, on the National Register and also a Virginia Historic Landmark, was built for Sarah Harrison, sister of William Henry Harrison, the ninth president, who died in office having served just one month. It's a fine example of the Academic Greek Revival style, a wide white-frame structure with a black-and-green roof and a slender chimney at each corner. Built in 1819 with a classic two-over-two layout, large center hall, and Federal mantels and stair carvings, it was remodeled in 1853 according to Asher Benjamin designs. But beyond its architectural distinctions, North Bend is drenched in history. The Sheridan Room, the premier guest bedroom, represents both sides of the Civil War. It contains a walnut desk used by the Union general Philip Sheridan, complete with his labels on the pigeonholes. A copy of his map was found in one of its drawers and is now laminated for guests' viewing. The room's tester bed belonged to Edmund Ruffin, the ardent Confederate who fired the first shot of the war at Ft. Sumter. The headboard is a reproduction; a Yankee cannonball in 1864 splintered its predecessor.

Above all, though, at North Bend history means family. George Copland is the great-great-nephew of Sarah Harrison and the great-great-grandson of Edmund Ruffin. Family heirlooms are everywhere, as is the amazing collection of Civil War first editions, which make fascinating bedtime reading. There's an inviting upstairs wicker-furnished sunporch and a one-of-a-kind children's area with vintage toys. ♙ *4 double rooms with baths, 1 suite. Air-conditioning, TV in rooms, robes, fireplace in 1 room; pool, tandem bicycles, croquet, horseshoes, badminton, volleyball. $105–$135; full breakfast, welcome refreshments. MC, V. No smoking, no children under 6, closed Thanksgiving.*

THE OWL AND THE PUSSYCAT
405 High St., Petersburg 23803, tel. 804/733–0505, fax 804/862–0694, www.ctg.net/owlcat

As they toured myriad bed-and-breakfasts around the country and, in fact, the world, Juliette and John Swenson found themselves wanting to open an inn of their very own. And it was in 1998 that the two worldly travelers did just that, buying one of historic Petersburg's most celebrated houses.

Planted in the middle of historic town, the 1899 Queen Anne mansion is breathtakingly beautiful yet simple. Once the house of John Gill, a well-known coffee broker, the mansion was always home to a family; the Swensons do everything they can to make their guests feel a part of their family, right down to sending you home with a jar of Juliette's homemade jams. Also part of the family are cats Twiggy and Tutu and their finned friends, goldfish Grant and Lee (John's a big Civil War buff).

While the house is filled with 18th- and 19th-century antiques, it's not stuffy; fresh flowers are placed in every room. With bay windows that open onto an overhanging porch, the Pussycat Room has the most impressive view of the city while the Owl Room's turret overlooks Juliette's garden below. The suite has a library, where its shelves are filled with the works of Shelley, Dickens, and Longfellow along with a collection of children's stories. Each bath has a claw-foot tub and bath salts are left in each room, so guests can wind down after a day of walking Petersburg's historic streets.

Breakfast is scrumptious: John usually makes a cheese and vegetable quiche and Juliette bakes scones and muffins. And for those who wish to loaf in bed, breakfast, along with mimosas, can be brought to your room. **♵** *5 double rooms with baths, 1 suite. Air-conditioning, alarm clocks in rooms, TV/VCR in living room. $75–$95; full breakfast, afternoon tea. AE, D, MC, V. No smoking, no big pets.*

WAR HILL INN ☞

4560 Longhill Rd., Williamsburg 23188, tel. 757/565–0248,
www.inngetaways.com/va/warhill

The War Hill Inn is 3 mi north of town; this is a drawback or an attraction, depending on whether visitors prefer to stay overnight in the thick of Colonial things or put some space between their lodging and the crowds. Adding to the inn's feeling of remoteness are the surrounding pastures, where owner Bill Lee's prizewinning Black Angus cows munch on the grass—though a condo development has risen on one of the property's flanks. Bill is a retired veterinarian who built the house in 1968 for his family. It's a copy of the Anderson House in Colonial Williamsburg, and a fine one at that. Inside are architectural features that came from other places—the heart-pine floors from a schoolhouse and a staircase from a Lutheran church. The decor in the guest rooms is a mélange of Colonial reproductions and family things; the downstairs chamber is notable for its size and privacy. War Hill is a good choice for families—thanks to its fenced-in grounds, a small orchard of peaches and plums, and a cottage. Two of its rooms sleep four. **♵** *5 double rooms with baths. Air-conditioning, cable TV in rooms, fireplace in parlor, whirlpool bath in cottage. $75–$120; full breakfast. MC, V. No smoking, 2-night minimum weekends.*

PIEDMONT

Few cities in this country are so deeply devoted to—one might say, so in love with—a single man as is Virginia's Piedmont capital, Charlottesville. On a farm east of town (in the present-day hamlet of Shadwell), Thomas Jefferson, the third president of the United States, was born; and on a mountaintop overlooking a countryside Jefferson himself considered Edenic, he built his home. Even the youngest of visitors has already seen Monticello, for it appears on one side of the nickel, though its minted image hardly does it justice. The exquisite edifice, constructed on architectural principles that would change the face of America, is a house that reveals volumes about the man who built it and lived there.

For instance, in the terraced vegetable gardens (restored according to Jefferson's Garden Book), he helped popularize the tomato in North American cuisine and raised 19 types of English pea, his favorite food. (Mr. Jefferson, as he is called around here, attributed his long life—he lived to be 83—to his vegetarian eating habits.) Here he built a glass-enclosed pavilion, where he went to read, write, and watch his garden grow. Most of the 20,000 letters he wrote were penned in his study in a reclining chair with revolving desk (he had rheumatism and worked from a semirecumbent position). Jefferson was also a collector; the walls of the formal parlor are lined with portraits of friends, like Washington and Monroe, and the east entrance hall displays mastodon bones and a buffalo head brought back from the West by Lewis and Clark. Still, on the estate of the man acclaimed as a leading architect of American liberty, the irony of the nearby slave quarters will not be lost on more than a few visitors.

"Architecture," wrote Jefferson, "is my delight and putting up and pulling down one of my favorite pastimes." Originally he built Monticello in 1779 as an American Palladian villa, but after seeing the work of Boullée and Ledoux in France, he returned to Monticello with a head full of new ideas, above all about its dome, and an aversion to grand staircases, which he believed took up too much room. Today the full effect is best seen from the flower gardens on the west side.

There's another reason for Charlottesville's love affair with Jefferson—the University of Virginia. If Monticello is a taste of Jeffersonian style, the school's rotunda and colonnade offer up a banquet. Jefferson began designing the university buildings at the age of 74; in 1976 the American Institute of Architects voted them the most outstanding achievement in American architecture. The rotunda was inspired by the Pantheon, in Rome, but the dual colonnade that extends from it, intended as both dwelling place and study center for students and faculty, is all Jefferson's own. Students still inhabit the colonnade rooms, amid fireplaces, porches, and rocking chairs.

Charlottesville lies in the Blue Ridge foothills, and the driving here is fun and scenic. Route 20, called the Constitution Route, takes travelers past Montpelier (James Madison's home) in Orange, 25 mi north of Charlottesville. It also takes motorists south to the village of Scottsville on the James River, once the seat of Albemarle County, rich in Revolutionary and Civil War history. It's a favorite spot for canoe and inner-tube trips. Twenty miles to the west the Blue Ridge rises, with access to the Skyline Drive or Parkway at Rockfish Gap.

PLACES TO GO, SIGHTS TO SEE

Ash Lawn–Highland (James Monroe Pkwy., Charlottesville, tel. 804/293–9539). Just down the road from Monticello, this is the restored home of James Monroe; its mountaintop site (selected by Jefferson) offers views of Monticello's dome. A tour covers the original rooms and the warming kitchen. Today it's still a working 550-acre farm where sheep and peacocks roam. Summertime brings a Festival of the Arts and Plantation Days.

Barboursville Vineyards (17655 Winery Rd., Barboursville, north of Charlottesville, tel. 540/832–3824). In addition to tasting the several varieties produced here, you can explore the ruins of Governor James Barbour's plantation home. Among the other dozen or so wineries in the area are *Oakencroft* (1486 Oakencroft La., Charlottesville, tel. 804/296–4188), *Horton/Montdomaine* (6399 Spotswood Trail, Gordonsville, tel. 540/832–7440), and *Totier Creek Vineyard* (1652 Harris Creek Rd., Charlottesville, tel. 804/979–7105). (For a map of Virginia wineries, contact the Virginia Wine Marketing Program, VDACS, Division of Marketing, Box 1163, Richmond 23218, tel. 800/828–4637.)

Exchange Hotel & Civil War Museum (Rte. 15, Gordonsville, tel. 540/832–2944). Built in 1860 as a railroad hotel, this Greek Revival structure served as a military hospital during the Civil War and is now an excellent museum devoted to the military and medical history of that conflict.

Michie Tavern (683 Thomas Jefferson Pkwy., Charlottesville, tel. 804/977–1234). This tavern, dating from 1765, was moved to its present location on the road to Monticello in 1920. This is quite a commercial operation; visitors might be advised to call ahead to request a narrated (not recorded) tour. The cafeteria-style restaurant serves such historic dishes as fried chicken, black-eyed peas, and stewed tomatoes. The *Virginia Wine Museum* is within the tavern and part of the tour.

Monticello (Rte. 53, Charlottesville, tel. 804/984–9822). Jefferson's home lies about 2 mi southeast of the intersection of I–64 and Route 20. The tour, which ascends Mr. Jefferson's "little mountain" by shuttle bus, lasts about half an hour and is extremely rewarding. Afterward visitors are free to roam the gardens, view the hidden dependencies, and make a pilgrimage to the great man's grave. Earlier arrivals make for shorter waits.

Montpelier (11407 Constitution Hwy., Montpelier Station, tel. 540/672–2728). James Madison, despite two terms as president through the War of 1812, is best known as the father of the Constitution and formulator of the Bill of Rights. Somewhat lost in Jefferson's shadow (he stood only 5'2"), Madison and his wife, Dolley, lived here from 1817 to 1836, later followed by William du Pont Sr., who bought it in 1901. Those with rocky in-law relations will savor the tale of acrimony that festered among the Madison family members. The guided tour of the estate leads visitors over the 2,700-acre grounds, through the 55-room house, past Madison's grave, and into the curious mind of his mother, who brooked no contact with the imperious Dolley. The Montpelier Hunt Race is held here on the first weekend in November.

Moormont Orchards (6530 Moormont Rd., Rapidan, tel. 540/672–2730 or 800/572–2262 in VA). In season you can pick your own apples, peaches, plums, and nectarines.

Orange. The *James Madison Museum* (129 Caroline St., tel. 540/672–1776) is filled with James's and Dolley's possessions and correspondence, and local historical and agricultural exhibits. Next door, *St. Thomas' Episcopal Church* (tel. 540/672–3761) was created with Jefferson's only known (and now demolished) ecclesiastical work in mind.

Scottsville sits on the James River and is where Lafayette made a successful stand against General Cornwallis in 1781. The village holds 32 Federal-style buildings and the locks of the James River Kanawha Canal, which were a target for 10,000 bluecoats under General Sheridan during the Civil War. The nearby *James River Runners* (10082 Hatton Ferry Rd., tel. 804/286–2338) rents tubes, rafts, and canoes.

University of Virginia (Charlottesville, tel. 804/924–7969). Visitors may wander the grounds or take one of the tours that leave the rotunda several times daily (except on school holidays, save summer, when it is open, and during exams). Inside the rotunda is Alexander Galt's statue of Jefferson, which students saved from the fire of 1895.

Walton's Mountain Museum (Rockfish River Rd., Schuyler, tel. 804/831–2000). Earl Hamner Jr., creator of the long-running TV series *The Waltons,* based the family's tales on his own experiences growing up in this small village. The simple museum re-creates the TV sets and has lots of memorabilia, videotapes, and photos of the show and cast.

RESTAURANTS

In addition to top dining at the area's inns, there's a cosmopolitan assortment of restaurants in Charlottesville. **Metropolitan** (214 Water St., tel. 804/977–1043) serves popular nouvelle American cuisine. **Memory & Company** (213 Second West St., tel. 804/296–3539) offers $27.50 prix-fixe dinners and a terrific wine list. **C & O** (515 E. Water St., tel. 804/971–7044) has a bistro downstairs and formal French dining upstairs. **Eastern Standard** (Downtown Mall, tel. 804/295–8668) has the same formal upstairs–bistro downstairs setup. For casual dining in Charlottesville, there's **Café Noelle** (20 Ellie Wood Ave., tel. 804/296–1175), on University Corner; **Court Square Tavern** (E. Jefferson and 5th Sts., tel. 804/296–6111), with a pub atmosphere and more than 120 imported beers; and **South-**

ern Culture (633 W. Main St., tel. 804/979–1990), a reasonably priced mix of Caribbean and Cajun. In Gordonsville, **Toliver House Restaurant** (209 N. Main St., tel. 540/832–3485) gets top ratings, as does the **Bavarian Chef** in Madison (Rte. 29 S, tel. 540/948–6505). **Keswick Hall** (701 Country Club Dr., Keswick, tel. 804/979–3440) serves elegant seven-course dinners, and its wine cellar is one of the most expansive in the Piedmont. Reservations are required as is proper attire (jacket and tie for men).

SHOPPING

Downtown Charlottesville has been converted into a pedestrian mall where shoppers find intriguing stores, such as **Spirit Vision**, for Native American and southwestern art; the **Signet Gallery**, for extraordinary crafts; and, for great arrays of vintages, **Market Street Wineshop & Grocery and Tastings**, which doubles as a café.

VISITOR INFORMATION

Charlottesville/Albemarle Convention & Visitors Bureau (Box 161, Charlottesville 22902, tel. 804/977–1783). **Orange County Visitors Bureau** (Box 133, Orange 22960, tel. 540/672–1653). **Virginia Division of Tourism** (901 E. Byrd St., Richmond 23219, tel. 804/786–4484).

RESERVATION SERVICES

Guesthouses Bed & Breakfast, Inc. (Box 5737, Charlottesville 22905, tel. 804/979–7264). For a copy of the Bed and Breakfast Association of Virginia's directory, describing more than 100 establishments, call the **Virginia Division of Tourism's B&B line** (tel. 800/262–1293). The Division of Tourism's Washington, D.C., office also operates a B&B and small-inn booking service (tel. 202/659–5523 or 800/934–9184 outside D.C.).

CLIFTON
1296 Clifton Inn Dr., Charlottesville 22911, tel. 804/971–1800
or 888/971–1800, fax 804/971–7098, www.clifton.com

From the warm, paneled library and the comforter-covered beds to the sunny terrace and the languid lake, there are reasons aplenty to settle in here at one of the state's top inns.

Clifton stands in quiet Shadwell, near Jefferson's birthplace. No wonder it's a National Historic Landmark—the handsome white-frame, six-columned manse was once home to Thomas Mann Randolph, governor of Virginia, member of Congress, and husband of Jefferson's daughter, Martha. It's now owned by a Washington attorney but ably administered by innkeepers Craig and Donna Hartman. As chef, Craig also oversees Clifton's wonderful meals (the applewood-smoked loin of veal with Vidalia-onion marmalade has lots of takers). Midweek dinners are $38. Saturday's six-course, prix-fixe dinners ($48) include entertainment.

There are guest rooms in the manor house, the carriage house, the livery, and Randolph's law office. All have wood-burning fireplaces, antique or canopy beds, and large baths; some also have French windows, lake views, or antique bed-coverings. Rooms in the dependencies have a fresh, cottagey feel: whitewashed walls, bright floral prints, lots of windows. Suites in the carriage house have shutters, windows, and other artifacts from the home of the explorer Meriwether Lewis.

The grounds spread through 48 acres of woods. The 20-acre lake offers good fishing (the inn provides rods and tackle boxes) and lazy floats on inner tubes. Vines and slate stonework blend the swimming pool and heated spa tub into the bucolic setting. There's also a clay tennis court, as well as croquet, volley-ball, horseshoes, and badminton. For a little quiet, there are gardens off the dependencies, wooden chairs scattered across the lawns, and a small gazebo. The extensive gardens are carefully tended: The estate grows its own flowers, lettuce, and herbs.

Clifton offers a magical combination of elegance and homeyness. Common areas, too, have fireplaces. A corner of the big butcher-block island in the kitchen is for guests, who often sit and chat with Craig as he cooks. Catch him when he's out of his kitchen and he'll be glad to show you the inn's new wine cellar. With more than 400 bottles, the cellar is a place where people may eat a late lunch, enjoy a glass of wine, and relax. A jar of cookies is always there, and sodas are in the refrigerator. ♙ *10 double rooms with baths, 4 suites. Restaurant, air-conditioning; lake, pool, spa tub, tennis court. $175–$235; full breakfast, afternoon tea. MC, V. No smoking, 2-night minimum weekends.*

HIGH MEADOWS AND MOUNTAIN SUNSET ☜
High Meadows La. (Rte. 4, Box 6), Scottsville 24590, tel. 804/286–2218 or 800/232–1832, www.highmeadows.com

High Meadows, which stands on 50 acres in Scottsville, is above all a bed-and-breakfast inn done by hand. The hands in question are those of Peter Shushka, a retired submariner, and his wife, Mary Jae Abbitt, a financial analyst.

In this unique B&B, Federal and late-Victorian architecture exist side by side, happily joined by a longitudinal hall. It wasn't always so. The Federal-style front section was built in 1832. The older house, built in 1830, was several paces behind it and was slated for demolition. For a time there was a plank between the two buildings. Today High Meadows is on the National Register.

Peter and Mary Jae have decorated the place with great originality, keeping intact the stylistic integrity of each section. They've also used fabrics on the bed hangings and windows imaginatively. Fairview, in the 1880s portion, is the quintessential bride's room, with a fireplace, flowing bed drapery, a three-window alcove, and a claw-foot tub. The Scottsville suite, upstairs in the Federal section, has stenciled walls lined with antique stuffed animals, a fireplace, and rafters across the ceiling. A two-person whirlpool sits in the middle of the Music Room.

The Carriage House, also called Glenside, is a contemporary building of cedar, glass, and slate on the site of the original; this two-room suite has a kitchen, deck, and two-person outdoor hot tub. The property also includes the Mountain Sunset (named for its view), a 1910 Queen Anne manor house with two suites, two rooms, fireplaces, decks, and plenty of privacy.

Breakfast consists of Shushka specialties like cranberry-almond muffins and ham-and-egg cups laced with tomatoes and Gruyère cheese. During the week, four-course dinners here run $25 per person and include wine. Saturday, there is a six-course dinner for $40. And to cap this all off, there are close to 2 acres of vineyards, which produce pinot noir grapes for the inn's own private-label wine. ♙ *7 double rooms with baths, 6 suites. Air-conditioning, cable TV in 1 suite, fireplace in 11 rooms and 4 common areas, robes, turndown service, whirlpool baths in 3 rooms. $79–$185; full breakfast, evening hors d'oeuvres and wine tasting. MC, V. No smoking, pets permitted in ground-level rooms by arrangement only, 2-night minimum all spring, fall, and holiday weekends, closed Dec. 24–25.*

INN AT MEANDER PLANTATION ☞
U.S. Rte. 15 (Rte. 5, Box 460A), Locust Dale 22948, tel. 540/672–4912
or 800/385–4936, fax 540/672–0405

Even those already versed in the treasures of the Piedmont region may be guilty of a gasp when they visit the Inn at Meander Plantation, just off Route 15 about 10 mi north of Orange. The simple sign and whitewashed brick markers give little hint of the architectural jewel that comes into view at the top of the driveway. On an estate settled in 1727 by Joshua Fry, a map-making partner of Thomas Jefferson's father, the inn bears faithful testament to its Colonial origins, replete with slave quarters and summer kitchen.

Innkeepers Suzanne Thomas and Suzie Blanchard, who along with Blanchard's husband, Bob, run the establishment, offer a reliably warm welcome that has kept a host of visitors coming back regularly to this historic hilltop residence.

An ample parlor and dining area, an occasional low-slung hallway, and bedrooms notable for their high, roomy beds and large windows recall the days before electric light and central air, when natural assets had to be exploited. The series of outbuildings, including a stable, recalls the role that equestrian expertise has played in the area's history, both military and economic. The owners still keep horses on the property.

Another dependency, the summer kitchen, separated from the main house by a shaded brick walkway decked out with nodding fuchsia buds in the milder months, features a two-story suite with a claw-foot tub and shower in the sunny bathroom upstairs. Here, as in any of the other spacious rooms, visitors can revel in the immense solitude this venue affords or contemplate the nearby attractions, a list of which the hosts provide on parchment-style paper at check-in. Far beyond the reach of city lights and sounds, the inn provides a wide back porch for those who want to savor dusk, and brick paths for others who want to take the property's name at face value and wander off to enjoy the pristine view of the constellations. Pets are allowed in some rooms. ⌂ *8 double rooms with baths, 5 suites. Fireplaces, piano, conference facilities, TV; hiking, fishing, tubing, pony rides, stabling for horses, lawn games. $95–$185; full breakfast. No smoking.*

INN AT MONTICELLO ☞
1188 Scottsville Rd., Charlottesville 22902, tel. 804/979–3593, fax 804/296–1344

Carol and Larry Engel forsook the plains of the upper Midwest because they were enchanted with Virginia. The Inn at Monticello, which they found and renovated, is an 1850s farmhouse south of town and just 2 mi from Jefferson's oft sought-out abode. The condos on a hill in the back hardly spoil the peacefulness for guests, who sit on the two-story front gallery, soaking up the bucolic view of a brook trickling over the long front lawn.

Downstairs there's a parlor, a twin-bedded room, and a nicely furnished honeymoon room. Of the three upstairs bedrooms, the lilac and the yellow rooms share honors with cotton balloon shades and plump rope beds. The Engels take special care with the bed linen, which is downy soft and complemented by European coverlets. Mornings begin with gourmet breakfasts (for instance, orange yogurt pancakes topped with fresh berries). The rest of the day can be spent visiting nearby Monticello or snoozing in a rocker on the wide front porch. ⌂ *5 double rooms with baths. Air-conditioning, fireplaces in 2 rooms. $115–$135; full breakfast, afternoon refreshments. MC, V. No smoking, no children under 12, 2-night minimum some high-season weekends, closed Dec. 25.*

KESWICK HALL

701 Country Club Dr. (Box 68), Keswick 22947, tel. 804/979–3440
or 800/274–5391, fax 804/977–4171, www.keswick.com

A visit to Keswick Hall is like a weekend with friends in the English countryside—
that is, if those friends are very wealthy and live in a vast house with armies of
antiques, plump chairs and couches, a butler to serve drinks, and a golf course
in the backyard. Keswick sits on 600 acres in the wooded, rolling countryside east
of Charlottesville. It's owned by Sir Bernard Ashley, who was married to the late
Laura Ashley, so fabrics and furnishings from the company are used throughout. Tiny floral prints, though, do not dominate the place. Instead, fabrics, none
of which are repeated, run the gamut from crisp stripes to elegant brocades. Sir
Bernard's personal collection of antiques, century-old books, paintings, and
silver-framed family photos gives the house the lived-in-for-generations look. Mahogany doors and gold fixtures in each of the rooms speak for Ashley's attention to detail.

Bedrooms are individually decorated in color schemes ranging from soft beige
and white to crisp blues to cozy dark green. All have comfy chairs, couches, or
cushioned window seats. Baths have extra touches, such as whirlpool tubs in
six rooms, extra-long tubs in several others, heated towel racks, hair dryers, an
abundance of thick towels, terry-cloth robes, and dishes with cotton balls. Some
rooms have private terraces with golf-course views, and several have decorative fireplaces.

Visitors may find it hard not to lounge about here, perhaps in front of a roaring
fire on chilly days, lingering over coffee and the paper in the sunny morning room,
having afternoon tea with delicate madeleines and scones in the yellow Crawford Lounge, or penning a letter at Sir Bernard's desk in the library. The all-red
snooker room is the spot for predinner drinks and canapés and a late-night brandy,
served by the friendly butler.

There's a full country breakfast with a wide range of choices in the garden room.
Dinner in the elegant white-and-pastel dining room is a seven-course affair ($58).

Guests have access to the Keswick Club, a private facility whose crowning asset
is an Arnold Palmer–designed 18-hole golf course. Also on the property are fitness facilities, an indoor-outdoor pool, tennis courts, a croquet lawn, and a
wood-paneled casual dining room. △ *43 double rooms with baths, 3 suites. Restaurants, air-conditioning, cable TV and phone in rooms, turndown service, conference
facilities; golf course, fitness facility, bicycles, pool. $195–$645; full breakfast,
afternoon tea. AE, DC, MC, V. No smoking in dining rooms.*

PROSPECT HILL

*2887 Limetrack Rd., Trevilians 23093, tel. 540/967–0844 or 800/277–0844,
fax 540/967–0102*

For elegance and luxury, Prospect Hill is one of Virginia's finest inns, lying just
east of Charlottesville in the 14-square-mi Greensprings National Historic District. It's the oldest continuously occupied frame manor house in Virginia. But
except for the obligatory dependencies and impressive boxwood hedges, Prospect
Hill doesn't look like a plantation, because it was rebuilt in the Victorian era, when
a columned facade and decorative cornices were added. The innkeepers have
painted it lemony yellow.

Fresh flowers, a basket of fruit, and just-baked cookies welcome guests to their
rooms. There are four nicely furnished rooms in the main house, but the big
treat is the six refurbished dependencies. Sanco Pansy's cottage, 100 ft from

the manor, has a sitting room and whirlpool tub for two. The Carriage House, lit by four Palladian windows, offers views of ponies in the meadow nibbling the green Virginia turf. Surrounded by such *luxe, calme, et volupté*, it's strange to consider that in the last century, the dependencies were filled with hams, ice blocks, and livestock.

Dinner at the inn is a marvelous production, not so much for the cuisine (French-inspired and well above average) as for the ceremony. This begins with complimentary wine and cider a half hour before supper—outdoors in good weather. When the dinner bell rings, guests file in to hear the menu recited by innkeeper Bill Sheehan or his son, Michael. Then come an earnest grace and five excellent courses ($50 prix-fixe).

A hot breakfast arrives on a tray for guests wishing to stay ensconced in the dependencies. Some, however, crawl out of the soothing whirlpool tub, into the dining room. As splendid as the inn is, it hasn't become too smoothly professional. Even the most low-profile guest is liable to meet the gregarious innkeepers and appreciate the way they've put their stamp on Prospect Hill. ♦ *5 double rooms with baths in manor, 5 doubles with baths and 3 suites in dependencies. Air-conditioning, TV/VCR in meeting room, fireplaces in rooms, whirlpools in 8 rooms, clock radios in rooms; pool. $240–$345; MAP. D, MC, V. 2-night minimum with Sat. stay, closed Dec. 24–25.*

THE SHADOWS ☞
14291 Constitution Hwy., Orange 22960, tel. 540/672–5057

Travelers will be hard-pressed to find a home (or guests) more lovingly tended than at the Shadows. Pat and Barbara Loffredo have filled their 1913 stone farmhouse, serenely set in a grove of old cedars on the road between Orange and Montpelier, with cheerful country Victorian antiques. Prize pieces include an impressive collection of personal trappings, including a Civil War–era hunt board, an old pump organ, numerous claw-foot tubs, and Maxfield Parrish prints wherever the eye rests. The house is what Barbara calls Gustav Stickley Craftsman style, a modified bungalow built of wood and local fieldstone. It has lustrous oak floors and windowsills around which lace curtains flutter. The four spotless guest rooms upstairs have standard Victorian trappings.

All the tangibles here are pleasant enough, but Pat and Barbara, their skills honed over one decade in the business, put the Shadows over the mark. They're refugees from New York, where Pat was a police officer, and their joy in their ex-Gotham surroundings is infectious. The two of them delight in coddling guests, overwhelming them with country gourmet breakfasts of French toast soufflé and poached pear with sherry cream. Guests may also appreciate the hiking trails that traverse the inn's 44-acre plot, especially when fall colors near their peak, and the host's extensive library. ♦ *4 double rooms with baths, 2 cottage suites. Air-conditioning, gas-log fireplace in 1 cottage, turndown service. $80–$110; full breakfast, afternoon refreshments. MC, V. No smoking, 2-night minimum some fall weekends and holidays.*

SILVER THATCH INN ☞
3001 Hollymead Dr., Charlottesville 22911, tel. 804/978–4686, fax 804/973–6156

The Silver Thatch is 7 mi north of downtown Charlottesville off U.S. 29. The oldest part of its semicircle of connected buildings is log, built by mercenary Hessian prisoners hired by the British during the Revolutionary War. The inn, decorated in a comfortable country-Colonial style, has richly colored walls and trim that look fresh yet embody the Colonial period, when a main portion of the house was constructed. The guest rooms all have quilts, down comforters, and antiques; four have fireplaces. The four cottage rooms surpass those in the main house because of their newer bathrooms.

New innkeepeers Terry and Jim Petrovits say, "Food brought us together." The restaurant menu features American–Continental fare, but Jim's experience in New York restaurants means that a Mediterranean or Thai dish may be included in the night's offerings. Vegetarian diners will also find a special for them each day, as well. For more than nine years, the wine list has received an award of excellence from *Wine Spectator* magazine. Silver Thatch guests may use a pool nearby. ♨ *7 double rooms with baths. Restaurant, air-conditioning, clock radios in rooms, cable TV in bar, turndown service. $120–$165; full breakfast. AE, DC, MC, V. No smoking, 2-night minimum weekends Apr.–May and Nov.*

SLEEPY HOLLOW FARM 🐾
16280 Blue Ridge Turnpike, Gordonsville 22942, tel. 540/832–5555 or 800/215–4804, fax 540/832–2515

North of Charlottesville, as motorists roller-coaster past cattle farms and vineyards on Route 231, they may pass the bright red roof of the barn at Sleepy Hollow Farm. This two-story brick house, begun in the 18th century, is surrounded by fields grazed by Black Angus and Tarentais cattle. The pastoral backdrop helped lure a film crew to the area, as visitors who have seen *Hush*, starring Jessica Lange and Gwyneth Paltrow, may recognize.

Sleepy Hollow is homey and eminently suited to families with children: There's a play set on the grounds, rabbits in the hedgerows, and a spring-fed pond that attracts ducks and is good for swimming. The main house has four rooms, and there are two suites, one with kitchen, dining room, and deck, in the Chestnut Wood Cottage. Sleepy Hollow's owner, Beverley Allison, came to the house as a bride, raised a family, was a news producer, served as an Episcopal missionary in Central America, then returned to open her comfortable bed-and-breakfast and tend its lush gardens. Thus, she has stories to tell, if you can persuade her; ask for the one about a ghost who frequented one of the guest rooms. ♨ *3 double rooms with baths, 1 housekeeping suite with full kitchen and whirlpool, 2 suites. Air-conditioning, TV in 3 rooms, whirlpools in 2 rooms, TV/VCR in sitting room, 3 fireplaces and 2 stoves in common rooms and suites; swimming pond, riding arranged. $95–$135; full breakfast, afternoon refreshments. MC, V. No smoking in dining room, 2-night minimum some weekends.*

THE BLUE RIDGE/
SHENANDOAH VALLEY
AND VIRGINIA HIGHLANDS

The standard way to see the Blue Ridge Mountains is to pile into a car on a weekend in October and drive south from Front Royal along the Skyline Drive. Bumper-to-bumper traffic may keep many a vexed motorist from covering the full 105-mi course in full. But even with a turnoff around Rockfish Gap (just east of Waynesboro), where the drive becomes the equally (some would claim more) splendid Blue Ridge Parkway, the trip will hardly constitute a disappointment. Above all, the landscape at Virginia's western border, with mountains, forests, and waterways smudging rectilinear boundaries, stands in marked contrast to the rest of the state's.

In geographical terms the Blue Ridge is the eastern wall of the wide Shenandoah Valley, which is framed at the other side by the Allegheny Mountains. Down the middle of the valley, bisecting it for some 50 mi, rises a mini–mountain range called Massanutten Mountain, even though it holds a pretty valley of its own. The Shenandoah River, which runs through the valley, divides north of Massanutten—to confuse the issue further—into a North and South Fork.

Basic geography aside, visitors can plot a more informed assault by crossing the ridge along such strategic and scenic routes as U.S. 211 and 33 and especially Route 56, an untrammeled two-laner that's a favorite even of view-jaded locals. These paths lead into the central and southern sections of the Shenandoah Valley.

Shenandoah National Park holds the heights of the Blue Ridge in a 100-mi strip from Front Royal to Waynesboro and provides nonpareil views of the Virginia Piedmont to the east and the splendid Shenandoah Valley to the west. To the park come anglers to catch the crafty brook trout and hikers who find meanders aplenty. Even a short stroll from a trailhead on the Skyline Drive brings visitors within viewing range of the park's abundant and varied wildlife. Spring and fall are peak seasons for nature lovers. In May the green of new foliage moves up the ridge at a rate of 100 ft a day, with clouds of wild pink azaleas providing contrast. Fall colors are at their most vivid from approximately October 10 to the 25th, when migrating hawks join the human leaf-gazers to take in the display.

Even for less lingering sightseers, there are better ways to take in the countryside than by zooming along I–81. U.S. 11 parallels the superhighway in a delightfully labyrinthine fashion, providing access to big-name sights, such as the New Market Battlefield and Luray Caverns and running through small towns, including Woodstock, Edinburg, Mt. Jackson, and Steele's Tavern, where produce stands, flea markets, and local history museums further delay many travelers' progress.

Among Shenandoah's gems, the town of Staunton, as hilly as Rome, was Woodrow Wilson's birthplace; it's also home to pretty Mary Baldwin College and the Museum of American Frontier Culture. Lexington lives and breathes for Stonewall Jackson and Robert E. Lee, who was president of Washington and Lee University after the Civil War. Nearby stands Virginia Military Institute, where Jackson taught before bedeviling Union armies as a Confederate general.

West along winding country roads from Staunton and Lexington lies a countryside often neglected by valley visitors. U.S. 33 and 250 and Route 39 lead to the Appalachian plateau and West Virginia, bordered by the thick foliage of the George Washington National Forest. The roads frequently cross rocky waterways—such as that lovely trio of rivers, the Bullpasture, Cowpasture, and Calfpasture—providing excellent spots for wading and picnicking. Most of the towns in this area are no more than crossroads, with the exception of Hot Springs, site of the Homestead, a 15,000-acre resort that's a Virginia institution. The town has a pleasant collection of arts-and-crafts shops, gourmet delis, and restaurants.

Farther south in the state is the very rural Virginia Highlands. Jefferson-Washington National Forest, Virginia Tech, and the historic Creeper Trail in Abingdon are just a few of the gems found in this part of the commonwealth. Each little town, most with antiques shops and restaurants that serve local fare, has its own flavor.

PLACES TO GO, SIGHTS TO SEE

Barter Theater (301 E. Main St., Abingdon, tel. 540/628–3991). Virginia's state theater, which celebrates its 66th anniversary in 1999, is where such great actors as Gregory Peck and Ernest Borgnine got their start. People attending a performance at the Barter will no doubt find the building as striking as the musicals and plays staged inside. Milk, chickens, or eggs were once acceptable payments for tickets.

Belle Grove (336 Belle Grove Rd., Middletown, tel. 540/869–2028). The mansion, built of local limestone in 1794, shows the architectural influence of Thomas Jefferson. It suffered greatly in 1864, when Confederate forces launched an attack on a Union Army headquartered at the mansion, but it has since been restored.

Blue Ridge Parkway (tel. 704/627–3419). One of the country's most breathtaking drives begins at the southern end of the Skyline Drive and follows the mountain crest south to North Carolina and Tennessee.

Luray Caverns (Hwy. 211 W, Luray, tel. 540/743–6551). They're famed for the "stalacpipe organ," which gets played on cave tours. The valley's underground world can also be surveyed at Grand, Shenandoah, Endless, Skyline, and Dixie caverns.

Massanutten (Rte. 644, McGaheysville, near Harrisonburg, tel. 540/289–9441). This four-season resort has downhill skiing on 11 slopes, golf, tennis, and indoor swimming.

Museum of American Frontier Culture (1250 Richmond Rd., Staunton, tel. 540/332–7850). In four farmsteads reminiscent of those the early settlers left behind in Europe, costumed workers show how families planted, harvested, and did chores.

Natural Bridge (Rtes. 11 and 130, Natural Bridge, tel. 540/291–2121 or 800/533–1410). As a young surveyor, George Washington carved his initials in the limestone walls. Thomas Jefferson was so impressed by this 215-ft-high, 90-ft-long rock span that he bought it in 1774. Visitors would be advised to focus on the spectacular rock formation and overlook commercial intrusions, such as the wax museum.

New Market Battlefield (8895 Collins Dr., New Market, tel. 540/740–3101). Of all Civil War memorials, this is one of the most affecting, for in 1864, 247 cadets from the Virginia Military Institute were sent here to a "baptism of fire." The line of VMI soldiers, some as young as 15, died that day.

Shenandoah National Park (3655 U.S. Hwy. 211 E, Luray, tel. 540/999–3500). Extending 80 mi along the Blue Ridge, the park was created to restore the scenic terrain to the condition in which the earliest settlers found it. A movie shown at the Byrd Visitors Center at Big Meadows tells the story of the park's regeneration. Information on trails, overlooks, facilities, and activities is available here and at the Dickey Ridge Visitors Center south of Luray.

Shenandoah River Floating. The wide, lazy river offers opportunities for gentle canoe and raft rides, with a little fishing, swimming, and inner-tubing thrown in. Good outfitters include the Downriver Canoe Company (884 Indian Hollow Rd., Bentonville, tel. 540/635–5526) and Shenandoah River Outfitters (6502 S. Page Valley Rd., Luray, tel. 540/743–4159).

Shenandoah Valley Folk Art and Heritage Center (Bowman Rd. and High St., Dayton, tel. 540/879–2681). The museum focuses on local history, culture, and tradition. An electronic map traces the movements of troops in Stonewall Jackson's Valley Campaign.

Skyline Drive. The spectacular 105-mi route that meanders through Shenandoah National Park passes scenic overlooks, hiking trails, restaurants, and visitor centers.

Statler Brothers Complex (501 Thornrose Ave., Staunton, tel. 540/885–7297). Even more than Woodrow Wilson, Staunton loves the Statlers, because the four country musicians are local boys who defied Nashville by cutting their records in their hometown. A converted elementary school showcases artifacts from their careers.

Stonewall Jackson House (8 E. Washington St., Lexington, tel. 540/463–2552). This trim, brick two-story is where Thomas Jonathan Jackson, a natural philosophy professor at VMI, lived with his second wife before he rode away to lead the men in gray. General Jackson died after the Battle of Chancellorsville at the age of 39.

Theater at Lime Kiln (Box office: 14 S. Randolph St., Lexington, tel. 540/463–3074). In an abandoned lime quarry, this stage for a professional company of actors has been called the most unusual theater setting in the United States. The Memorial Day–Labor Day schedule includes concerts and plays.

Virginia Horse Center (Rte. 39 W, Lexington, tel. 540/463–2194). The huge equestrian complex has 720 stalls, a 3,800-seat coliseum, regulation dressage areas, horse trails, cross-country courses, and a full calendar of shows and events.

Virginia Military Institute (Letcher Ave., Lexington, tel. 540/464–7000) has made recent headlines over its ill-fated fight to remain all-male while continuing its tradition as the nation's first state-supported military school, founded in 1839. Uniformed cadets conduct tours of the campus (an austere and blocky Gothic Revival fortress) and parade most Fridays at 4:30 PM. The *Virginia Military Institute Museum* (Letcher Ave., tel. 540/464–7232) highlights the institute's history and most famous graduates. A taxidermic Little Sorrel, Stonewall Jackson's warhorse, is here, as is the black raincoat that Jackson was wearing when he was shot in 1863. The *George C. Marshall Museum and Library* (Parade Ground, VMI, tel. 540/463–7103) is devoted to the general, a 1901 graduate of VMI. He is the only professional soldier awarded the Nobel Peace Prize (on display here), which he received for his plan to rebuild Europe's economy after World War II.

Virginia Tech (428 N. Main St., Blacksburg, tel. 540/231–3001). Virginia's largest public university has on campus the *Museum of Natural History*, which houses a collection of flora and fauna from across the state. The university was founded as an institution for farmers. Today, however, it is a leader in veterinary medicine, engineering, and Division I NCAA football.

Washington and Lee University (Washington St., Lexington, tel. 540/463–8400) was founded in 1749, subsidized by George Washington when the institution was near bankruptcy in 1796 and presided over by Robert E. Lee in the late 1860s. More recently it has served as a backdrop in the memoir *Jeb and Dash*. An extraordinary front colonnade and the Lee Chapel and Museum, where the general is buried, are its most noteworthy sights.

Wintergreen (Rte. 664, Wintergreen, tel. 804/325–2200 or 800/325–2200). This 11,000-acre, four-season resort lies on the eastern flanks of the Blue Ridge. It has golf, skiing, horseback riding, swimming, restaurants, and an acclaimed nature program.

Woodrow Wilson Birthplace and Museum (24 N. Coalter Ave., Staunton, tel. 540/885–0897). The imposing white Greek Revival home, in the prettiest section of town, has lots of Wilson memorabilia, including his Pierce Arrow limousine.

RESTAURANTS

In Staunton, there's a varied menu in the formal dining rooms or casual pub at **McCormick's** (41 N. Augusta Ave., tel. 540/885–3111) and Italian fare at **L'Italia** (23 E. Beverly St., tel. 540/885–0102). Harrisonburg's **Joshua Wilton House** (412 S. Main St., tel. 540/434–4464) and the **Osceola Mill Country Inn** (Rte. 56, tel. 540/377–6455) in Steele's Tavern get top ratings. In Front Royal, ribs, the specialty at **Dad's Restaurant** (10 Commerce Ave., tel. 540/622–2768), were once voted best ribs in the valley. **Grapevine Restaurant** (914 N. Royal Ave., tel. 540/635–6615) serves seafood, steaks, and pasta. The **Springhouse** (325 S. Main St., Woodstock, tel. 540/459–4755) produces reasonably priced food in a comfortable setting. In Lexington, **Il Palazzo** (24 N. Main St., tel. 540/464–5800) serves traditional Italian food. For casual dining there's **Harbs' Bistro** (19 W. Washington St., tel. 540/464–1900) and **The Palms** (101 W. Nelson St., tel. 540/463–7911). Fine Italian cuisine, a relaxed atmosphere, and a large wine list can be found at **Vincent's** (1200 S. Main St., Blacksburg, tel. 540/552–9000). The **Starving Artist** (134 Wall St., Depot Square, Abingdon, tel. 540/628–8445) has Emily Dickinson and Pablo Picasso sandwiches at lunch and also serves dinner.

SHOPPING

From the Heart (265 Franklin St., Rocky Mount, tel. 540/489–3887). This eclectic gift boutique sells baskets, quilts, and other odds and ends that typify the Appalachian region.

Factory Merchants Outlet Mall (I–81, Exit 80, Fort Chiswell, tel. 540/637–6214). You can find factory outlets for Corning, Van Heusen, and Black and Decker as well as unique gifts from around the region.

VISITOR INFORMATION

Abingdon Convention and Visitor's Center (325 Cummings St., Abingdon 24210, tel. 540/676–2282 or 800/435–3440). **Augusta-Staunton-Waynesboro Visitors Bureau** (Box 58, Staunton 24402, tel. 540/332–3972 or 800/332–5219). **Front Royal Chamber of Commerce** (Box 568, Front Royal 22630, tel. 540/635–3185). **Harrisonburg-Rockingham Convention and Visitors Bureau** (800 Country Club Rd., Box 1, Harrisonburg 22801, tel. 540/434–2319). **Lexington Visitor Center** (106 E. Washington St., Lexington 24450, tel. 540/463–3777). **Marion Chamber of Commerce** (124 W. Main St., Marion 24354, tel. 540/783–3161). **Shenandoah Valley Travel Association** (Box 1040, New Market 22844, tel. 540/740–3132). **Virginia Division of Tourism** (901 E. Byrd St., Richmond 23219, tel. 804/786–4484). **Winchester and Frederick County Visitors Center** (1360 S. Pleasant Valley Rd., Winchester 22601, tel. 540/662–4135).

RESERVATION SERVICES

Bed & Breakfasts of the Historic Shenandoah Valley (402 N. Main St., Woodstock 22664, tel. 540/459–4828). **Historic Country Inns of Lexington** (11 N. Main St., Lexington 24450, tel. 540/463–2044). **Virginia's Inns of the Shenandoah Valley** (Box 1387, Staunton 24401). For a copy of the Bed and Breakfast Association of Virginia's directory, describing more than 100 establishments, call the **Virginia Division of Tourism's B&B line** (tel. 800/262–1293). The Division of Tourism's Washington, D.C., office also operates a B&B and small-inn booking service (tel. 202/659–5523 or 800/934–9184 outside D.C.).

BELLE GRAE INN 🖎

515 W. Frederick St., Staunton 24401, tel. 888/541–5151 or 540/886–5151,
fax 540/886–6641, www.valley.com/bellegrae/html

The Belle Grae is a classic small-town hotel occupying an old Victorian house and several restored buildings close to Staunton's downtown. The Old Inn, built circa 1870, has a wide porch with views of Betsy Belle and Mary Grae, two of the town's many hillocks. Its six bedrooms have high ceilings and are decorated with Victorian antiques, and downstairs there are two restaurants—one elegant, in Staunton terms, the other a more casual garden room.

The suites in the 1870 Jefferson House are Belle Grae's top-of-the-line, for their spaciousness and such amenities as fireplaces, balconies, phones, and cable TV. Town-house rooms are oversize and contain fireplaces, cable TV, and four-poster or canopy beds. The Mission oak– and wicker-furnished Cottage has a kitchen, and the Bishop's Suite, with fireplace, kitchen, and garden, is extremely private. △ *9 double rooms with baths, 5 suites, 2 cottages. Air-conditioning, cable TV and phone in 11 rooms, fireplace in 13 rooms and 3 common areas, turndown service, 2 restaurants; nearby health club. $85–$150; full breakfast. AE, MC, V. No smoking.*

EVERGREEN-BELL-CAPOZZI HOUSE 🖎

201 E. Main St., Christiansburg 24703, tel. 800/905–7372 or 540/382–7372,
www.bnt.com/evergreen

Turning their home of 20 years into a bed-and-breakfast wasn't that hard of a decision for Rocco and Barbara Capozzi. With the children all moved out, the Capozzis felt the time was right to start a new life. So, in 1993 they opened their Victorian home as the Evergreen, a lavish 17-room inn that exudes elegance and comfort from every nook and cranny.

Heart-pine floors run throughout the house, and in each of the two parlors is a library filled with both classics and the latest paperbacks. A 19th-century-era grand piano is in one of the parlors, as are plush velvet love seats and chairs for loafing around. The works of local artists are throughout the house, and Barbara's VIB bears are placed around the house, giving it a cozy feel. These are Very Important Bears, collectibles that are fashioned after famous historical figures or celebrities. The wraparound veranda and gazebo are places for solitude and are perfectly set to see the sun go down on a late spring day.

The five rooms are each unique in their own way. Room 4, the *Gone With the Wind* Room, has a king-size canopy bed and original copies of Margaret Mitchell's work that are laid out on the nightstand. Room 2 has a study and is the most masculine. A room that's geared toward the child in all of us is Room 3. A large die-cast metal train set winds around the room, and a working rocking horse Barbara picked up at a local antique store sits waiting for a friend.

As if they were feeding their own children, the Capozzis serve a larger-than-life breakfast that New York native Rocco likes to call "a mix of Yankee ingenuity and southern hospitality." A typical morning finds Barbara, a native of southwest Virginia, preparing large, fluffy biscuits with gravy, grits, and jam while Rocco is in charge of pork chops, flapjacks, and coffee; all of these are part of one meal.

After a dip in the Evergreen's pool, guests may want to lounge around in the sunroom, where you can read a book, watch TV, or play with the Capozzis friendly cat, Smokey. △ *5 double rooms with baths. Air-conditioning, TV/VCR, alarm clocks* *in rooms, fireplaces in parlors; pool. $75–$125; full breakfast and afternoon tea. No smoking.*

FASSIFERN ☞

27 Gallery La., Lexington 24450, tel. 540/463–1013 or 800/782–1587

There are 96,000 horses in Virginia—and counting. For anyone wanting to buy or show one of them, the place to do so is the Virginia Horse Center, just north of Lexington. Visitors staying overnight in the area can show their horse sense by picking one of the Shenandoah Valley's prettiest bed-and-breakfasts, just a trot down the road. It's Fassifern, named after the Scottish ancestral home of its builder, who erected this three-story, smoky-lavender brick farmhouse circa 1867.

It's owned by Francis Whitsel Smith and managed by her animated daughter, Ann Carol Perry, who keeps two Welsh ponies and a horse in the pasture. There's no particular history connected to Fassifern; it's just a lovely country place with a pond, towering maple trees, and an old icehouse that's been converted into two extra guest rooms. The Colonel's Quarters, perhaps the best, has wide-plank floors and pasture views. The small Pond Room overlooks the flower-rimmed water—and the nearby road. In the main house, three more guest rooms are furnished with Victorian armoires, Oriental rugs, and crystal chandeliers. ⚓ *4 double rooms with baths. Air-conditioning, fireplace in living room. $84–$92; full breakfast. MC, V. No smoking, closed Thanksgiving, Dec. 24–25, Dec. 31.*

INN AT GRISTMILL SQUARE ☞

Rte. 619, Court House Hill Rd. (Box 359), Warm Springs 24484, tel. 540/839–2231, fax 540/839–5770, www.va.inns.com/grist.html

Bath County in western Virginia covers 540 square mi inhabited by just 5,000 souls and nary a stoplight. Warm Springs, the county seat, has a post office, courthouse, and inn—and that's about all. Still, the Inn at Gristmill Square, occupying several 19th-century buildings—a blacksmith's barn, restored mill, miller's house, and hardware store—is reason enough to visit this quintessentially peaceful spot. One of the area's best places to sup is its Waterwheel Restaurant, where one thrill is wandering down to the cool subterranean wine cellar to select a bottle. The Steel House, across the lane, has a small swimming pool, sauna, and three tennis courts. The Silo has a round living room, and the large, rustic Board Room, a favorite, is paneled with barn siding and has a claw-foot tub. Former owners of an inn in Vermont, Janice McWilliams and her son, Bruce, are the able proprietors. They serve a simple breakfast along with the *Richmond Times Dispatch* in a picnic basket at guests' doors. ⚓ *16 double rooms with baths, 1 apartment. Restaurant, bar; air-conditioning, cable TV, phone and mini-refrigerator in rooms, fireplaces in 8 rooms. $85–$100; Continental breakfast; MAP available. D, MC, V. Restricted smoking.*

INN AT NARROW PASSAGE ☞

U.S. 11 S (Box 608), Woodstock 22664, tel. 540/459–8000, fax 540/459–8001, www.innatnarrowpassage.com

Guests here may want to pack their inner tubes, swimming togs, and fishing rods; they'll all prove useful at the Inn at Narrow Passage, which sits right on the North Fork of the Shenandoah River. Ed Markel, owner of the inn, will kindly put in any crew of human waterbugs about a mile south, and from there it's a 3½-hour float to reach home. The oldest section of the inn was built as a way station on the Great Wagon Road (now U.S. 11) around 1740, and the Markels meticulously restored it.

The older guest rooms evoke Colonial times with queen-size canopy beds, wood floors, and stenciling. Newer rooms, though similar, open onto porches. The Stonewall Jackson Room, a heavily requested chamber in the older section, served as the Confederate general's headquarters during the Shenandoah Valley campaign of 1863. When the valley is blanketed in snow, the inn is a cozy place—especially the living room, with its handmade reproduction couches and big limestone fireplace (one of 10 here, seven in guest rooms). Chef John Gardner serves local fare for breakfast and at dinner Saturday nights, when his rainbow trout recipe is a favorite draw. △ *12 double rooms with baths. Air-conditioning, TV/VCR in sitting room, clock radios in rooms. $85–$145; full breakfast, afternoon refreshments. MC, V. No smoking, 2-night minimum in spring, fall, and holiday weekends, closed Dec. 24–25.*

JORDAN HOLLOW FARM INN 🖝
326 Hawksbill Park Rd., Stanley 22851, tel. 540/778–2285 or 888/418–7000, fax 540/778–1759, www.jordanhollowfarm.com

As anyone who's traveled much in rural America knows, farms aren't always the idyllic-looking places about which city folk fantasize. However, this one comes close. Jordan Hollow Farm is on 150 acres in the middle of the scenic Shenandoah Valley at the base of the Blue Ridge range, with great views of the Massanutten Mountains. It is a restored Colonial working horse farm that has been given new life as a cozy, beautiful, and serene country inn. At the heart of the farm amid maple trees sits a 200-year-old farmhouse incorporating two hand-hewn log cabins and now known as the Farmhouse Restaurant.

Proprietors Gail, Kyle, and Betsy Anderson run the place, whose reincarnation as a stopover began in 1981. Guests can choose from 16 rooms in the Arbor View Lodge, and four upscale rooms in the Mare Meadow Lodge, which is built of hand-hewn logs. The last are carpeted and have fireplaces, quilts and matching curtains, cedar furniture, and whirlpool tubs. The old carriage house and corncrib have a new life as a gathering lounge, whose antique couches and chairs and a small library put guests at ease.

Half the guests come to ride, half to savor the tranquillity. Every day, several equestrian groups (including beginners) leave the farm to wander over the foothills; youngsters go on pony rides. Guests can even bring their own horses; a stall is $15. Beautiful hiking trails crisscross the property, and folks at the farm can direct guests to even more in Shenandoah National Park or George Washington National Forest. Canoeing on the Shenandoah, caving, swimming, and golfing are also nearby.

The Farmhouse Restaurant, whose specialties are served inside and in three dining rooms, has built a considerable reputation with locally grown ingredients. Chefs Greg Scott and Julia Slye, experts at regional American recipes, also ensure that Virginia wines and local microbrews remain staples of the menu. △ *20 double rooms with baths. Restaurant, air-conditioning, phone in rooms, fireplace in guest house and 4 rooms; horseback riding. $110–$150. AE, D, DC, MC, V. Horses welcome.*

JOSHUA WILTON HOUSE 🖝
412 S. Main St., Harrisonburg 22801, tel. 540/434–4464, www.rica.net/jwhouse

In Harrisonburg's neighborhood of well-kept, handsome old homes, the Joshua Wilton House strikes the highest note. It's a lovingly renovated and luxuriously equipped mauve, lavender, and pink Victorian mansion with gingerbread trim with a turret. Throughout, owners Roberta and Craig Moore have provided a sense of polished professionalism, a put-together look of coordinated decor.

Guests enter by way of a front door surrounded by leaded glass and through a foyer with gleaming parquet floor, a chandelier, and bushy potted plants. Painted mantels and pictures displayed by the Shenandoah Valley Watercolor Association populate the first floor. The guest chambers are really lovely, particularly Room 5, with its four-poster bed and white wing chairs, and Room 4, which has a three-window alcove in the turret. △ *5 double rooms with baths. Restaurant, air-conditioning, phones in rooms, fireplace in 1 room. $95–$105; full breakfast. AE, D, DC, MC, V. Restricted smoking, 2-night minimum some weekends, closed Dec. 24–25.*

SEVEN HILLS INN ☙

408 S. Main St., Lexington 24450, tel. 540/463–4715 or 888/845–3801, fax 540/463–6526

Seven Hills Inn, a classic brick, white-columned southern Colonial dwelling in the heart of Lexington's historic Main Street district, was built in 1928 as a fraternity house for nearby Washington and Lee University. Hence the expansive living room (with fireplace), dining room, and casual downstairs chapter room (also with a fireplace as well as TV/VCR and games). It's doubtful, though, that the house had such an impeccably fresh and inviting appearance when the college crowd occupied it. Ben Grigsby, a Washington and Lee alumnus, bought the place and restored it, removing walls between the small fraternity bedrooms to create large guest rooms. When Ben's work sent him out of the country, he asked his mother, Jane Daniel, and innkeeper Shirley Ducommun to operate the bed-and-breakfast.

The pale-yellow third-floor Holly Hill Room, with a sloping ceiling, has a bath that's bigger than the bedroom. Fruit Hill has a whirlpool tub and a four-poster bed, and it can be opened into a suite with a parlor. △ *7 double rooms with baths. Air-conditioning. $80–$125; full breakfast. AE MC, V. Restricted smoking, 2-night minimum some weekends.*

SILVERSMITH INN ☙

102 E. Main St., Abingdon, 24210, tel. 540/676–3924

The Silversmith, an 1871, four-story Federal row house that is magnificently detailed and well preserved, is on Abingdon's historic Main Street. Nicknamed the Barr House after the builder of the house, a former judge, the inn is shaded by maple trees, and a cobblestone sidewalk gives guests a feeling of a time gone by.

On a warm summer evening, the high front porch is a favorite spot for guests wanting an ample view of the town. After a night on the town, many guests like to sway into the evening in one of the five oversize wicker rocking chairs on the front porch. Ceiling fans on the porch provide an extra level of comfort, as do the overhanging oak trees. In the dining room, windows that go straight to the floor are a reminder of the house's age, when the windows also served as doorways.

Owners Rick and Mary Jayne Stevens have ensured that the rooms are welcoming; all have triple-sheeted queen beds, private baths, and views of the town. The Judge's Chamber is especially impressive, with a whirlpool tub, private sitting area, and small balcony. The Cheaspeake Room has a more nautical flavor to it, decorated in light blues and whites, with paintings by Eastern Shore artist Herbert Jones.

Breakfasts at the inn are a special affair, with the Stevenses offering large portions of cheese-and-ham casserole, fresh fruit, breakfast bread, and other assorted goodies that keep guests full till mid-afternoon. △ *3 rooms with bath, one suite. Air conditioning, turndown service, TV and alarm clocks in rooms, fireplace in 2 rooms and suite, whirlpool tub in 1 room; fitness room. $85–$145; full breakfast, afternoon tea. No smoking.*

TRILLIUM HOUSE ✿

Wintergreen Dr., Wintergreen (Box 280, Nellysford 22958), tel. 804/325–9126 or 800/325–9126 (reservations only), fax 804/325–1099

Guests from near and far alike have to hand it to Ed and Betty Dinwiddie. For the pair, building a bed-and-breakfast on the grounds of Wintergreen resort may have seemed the most natural thing in the world; after all, their family had vacationed there for years. But to skiers, refugees from the Blue Ridge Parkway, wildflower enthusiasts, and all-round mountain devotees, the idea was a stroke of genius. The fact that Trillium House lies across the road from the gargantuan sports complex, with its indoor pool, tennis courts, ski slopes, hiking trails, golf course, and stables, should give prospective visitors a clue as to the activities available.

From Wintergreen's gate, a roller-coasterish road brings guests 3½ mi to the doorstep of Trillium House. The beige frame building fronted by a porch and a Palladian window, surrounded by trees and stylish condominiums owned by Wintergreen residents, was built in 1983. Entrance is through the Great Room, which is two stories high, near a staircase at the side leading to a loft library. The front sitting area has a wood-burning stove, above which hang several organ pipes; by the front door, a canister holds a collection of walking sticks. Breakfast is served in the dining rooms, with views of bird feeders and the backyard gazebo, and Friday and Saturday dinners (by reservation) are cooked by chef Ellen, who formerly worked in one of Wintergreen's restaurants. The 12 guest rooms at Trillium House lie in two wings off the Great Room. Their architectural tone is slightly motelish, but decorative touches add some personality—here a quilt or a framed picture that could have been created only by one of the Dinwiddie brood, there a writing desk from the Homestead or a bed with a lace canopy.

The odds are that guests will spend most of their stay pursuing varieties of R&R on the resort or ensconced in the Great Room, chatting with other guests or Ed and Betty, who manage to seem amazingly relaxed despite their demanding housekeeping duties. The single disappointment is that Trillium House doesn't have mountain views; those after such scenery will have to grab a stick and walk. △ *10 double rooms with baths, 2 suites. Air-conditioning, TV in rooms on request, cable TV/VCR and movie collection in sitting room, turndown service, phone in rooms. $90–$150; full buffet breakfast. MC, V. Restricted smoking, 2-night minimum weekends, 3-night minimum some holidays.*

North Carolina

North Carolina

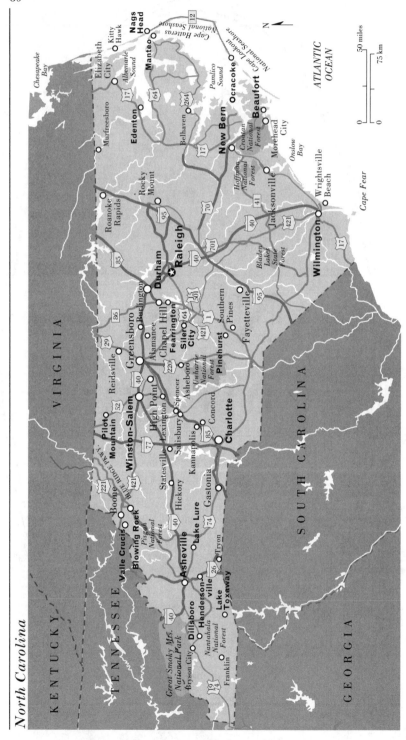

THE CAROLINA COAST

The northern part of the North Carolina coast is a region of broad bays, meandering rivers, and shallow inlets protected by a chain of barrier islands known as the Outer Banks. Long before Plymouth Rock, earlier than Jamestown, English colonists came in 1584, lived for a time on Roanoke Island, and disappeared mysteriously in 1591. For 100 years or more, the dunes were left mostly undisturbed, and the shifting shoals garnered their annual harvest of shipwrecks. A few towns were founded, a Colonial capital was established, and farming and fishing flourished. In this mild and mannerly land much remains the same.

The old character of the Outer Banks is most evident on Ocracoke Island and in fishing villages like Wanchese and Hatteras. The descendants of early settlers of these isolated places speak their own dialect of Elizabethan English, and the wild ponies that roam the Shackleford Banks are another reminder of a bygone era.

On the 130 mi of barrier islands that stretch from Cape Lookout to the Virginia line, large areas are protected as national seashores, which helps to preserve the marshes, dunes, rare plants, birds, and aquatic life. Although fishing is still the main industry in some of the small villages, tourism has taken hold in most of the region. In summer, the ferries and bridges from the mainland are loaded with cars bound for Ocracoke, Kill Devil Hills, Nags Head, and Manteo.

Visitors tour the historic houses in Edenton, flashes of bright nylon on the backs of windsurfers and hang gliders are seen in Nags Head and Kill Devil Hills, and charter boats and head boats leave daily for deep-sea fishing. In the northernmost part of the Outer Banks, where exclusive hunting clubs once flourished, posh residential communities are taking shape. Even with all the changes, though, the area still has that uncrowded, laid-back, old-sneakers feel. Though you can swim or fish, sail or dive, the Outer Banks is one of the great places on earth to do nothing.

Unlike the Outer Banks region, where the treacherous coastline and fragile barrier islands have restricted development, the sheltered southern arc of the North Carolina coast gave rise to the first commercial ports and some of its oldest cities. In the northern part of this region, at the confluence of the Trent and Neuse rivers, lies New Bern, a quiet town that served for a time as North Carolina's Colonial capital. The reconstructed Tryon Palace is one of the major tourist attractions in the state, and the town also contains a large historic district.

Beaufort was an early port and today draws sailors and yachters who tie up at the picturesque docks, which are lined with shops and restaurants. This seaside village, founded in 1713, is the state's third-oldest town and has more than 100 historic houses and a complex of restored Colonial buildings. Morehead City, just slightly south, is still a commercial port. The popular beaches of Atlantic Beach, Emerald Isle, and Pine Knoll Shores complete the area known as the Crystal Coast.

Wilmington, in the Cape Fear region, to the south, is on the peninsula between the Atlantic Ocean and the Cape Fear River. It blossomed into a commercial port when cotton was king and is still the state's largest port; despite its size, it remains picturesque and charming, with tall church spires and scores of historic homes and buildings. Most recently, it has become the movie-making center of the state, thanks to the sound stages of Screen Gems Studios.

PLACES TO GO, SIGHTS TO SEE

Beaches. Most of the Outer Banks' 130 mi of unspoiled beaches are part of the national seashores and are ideal for a variety of water sports. Recreation areas are at *Coquina Beach, Salvo, Cape Hatteras, Frisco,* and *Ocracoke* in the Cape Hatteras National Seashore. On the Crystal Coast, *Atlantic Beach* is a popular spot with young people, while families gravitate to *Salter Path, Indian Beach,* and *Emerald Isle. Hammocks Beach State Park,* just slightly south of Swansboro, is a completely undeveloped island accessible only by ferry. In the Cape Fear region, *Wrightsville Beach,* about 7 mi from Wilmington, appeals to families. *Carolina* and *Kure,* 20 mi south, are other options. *Bald Head Island,* where people gather to watch the hatching of loggerhead turtles each year, is accessible only by passenger ferry (no cars are permitted on the island).

Beaufort Historic Site (130 Turner St., tel. 252/728–5225) is a complex of 13 restored buildings, including the 1796 *Carteret County Courthouse,* 1859 *Apothecary Shop,* and 1829 *County Jail.* Nearby is the *Old Burying Ground,* listed on the National Register of Historic Places; inhabitants include a privateer with a cannon on his tomb, a sailor buried upright in his casket, and a little girl buried in a cask of rum.

Cape Hatteras Lighthouse (tel. 252/995–4474), 208 ft high, is the tallest lighthouse in America. The visitor center has exhibits on the Lifesaving Service and the USS *Monitor,* the Civil War ironclad that sank offshore.

Chandler's Wharf (Water and Ann Sts., Wilmington), a restored warehouse district on the waterfront, and the **Cotton Exchange** (321 Front St., Wilmington), in a pre–Civil War building, contain some of the city's best restaurants and most interesting shops.

Edenton. The first provincial capital of North Carolina, dating to 1685, Edenton was the site of a 1774 rebellion against the Crown known as the Edenton Tea Party. A walking tour run by *Historic Edenton* (tel. 252/482–2637) includes *St. Paul's Episcopal Church* (built between 1736 and 1760); the *Cupola House* (1725), a Jacobean wood building; the Georgian *Chowan County Courthouse,* on the village green; and the waterfront on Albemarle Sound.

Ft. Fisher State Historic Site (Kure Beach, tel. 910/458–5538), the largest earthwork fortification in the South during the Civil War, has exhibits of war relics and artifacts from sunken blockade runners. The *North Carolina Aquarium* (tel. 910/458–8257), also at Ft. Fisher, has a 20,000-gallon shark tank, a touch pool, and a whale exhibit, among other attractions.

Ft. Macon State Park (Atlantic Beach, tel. 252/726–3775) contains a Civil War fort. The five-sided fortress, still in good condition, has cannons and restored soldiers' quarters. Audio recordings describe life in the fort during the Civil War.

The **North Carolina Aquarium** (Pine Knoll Shores, tel. 252/247–4003) contains exhibits on the endangered loggerhead turtle, which nests on nearby beaches, as well as "The Living Shipwreck," a 12,000-gallon aquarium that is home to many reef fish and other marine life.

The **North Carolina Maritime Museum** (315 Front St., Beaufort, tel. 252/728–7317) explores the state's maritime history, including fishing, whaling, and wartime sinkings that took place just offshore. The *Watercraft Center,* just across the street, demonstrates traditional boatbuilding.

Ocracoke Island, ideal for walking and bicycling, is accessible only by ferry and has a quiet village of shops, inns, and restaurants.

Roanoke Island. In summer, historical interpretations and guided tours are given at the *Roanoke Island Festival Park* (tel. 252/473–1144), which includes the *Elizabeth II,* a replica of a 16th-century sailing vessel, harbored in Shallowbag Bay in downtown Manteo. *The Lost Colony* (tel. 252/473–3414), an outdoor drama, is a reenactment of the story of the first colonists, who mysteriously disappeared when some of their party returned to England for supplies. In summer, there are performances nightly, and backstage tours are given in the afternoon. Also on Roanoke Island are the *Ft. Raleigh National Historic Site* (tel. 252/473–5772), a reconstruction of what's thought to be the first colonists' fort; the *Elizabethan Gardens* (tel. 252/473–3234), with walking trails amid period plantings; and the *North Carolina Aquarium* (Airport Rd., tel. 252/473–3493), which offers exhibits, tours, and expeditions to coastal habitats. Two other aquariums are at Ft. Fisher and Pine Knoll Shores (*see above*).

Thalian Hall (102 N. 3rd St., Wilmington, tel. 910/343–3664) was built in 1858 for performances by such greats as Buffalo Bill, John Philip Sousa, General Tom Thumb, Lillian Russell, and Oscar Wilde. It's been restored and is now the site of plays and concerts.

The **Tryon Palace Restoration** complex (610 Pollock St., New Bern, tel. 252/638–1560) includes the reconstructed palace of *Governor William Tryon* (1770s), the *John Wright Stanley House* (circa 1783), the *Dixon-Stevenson House* (circa

1826), and *New Bern Academy* (circa 1764). Throughout the year many special events are staged, and costumed guides give tours of the palace.

The **USS *North Carolina* Battleship Memorial** (Wilmington Harbor, tel. 910/251–5797). The *North Carolina* took part in every major naval offensive in the Pacific during World War II and is now a museum. An orientation film prepares visitors for the two-hour, self-guided tour, and a narrated tape is available for rent.

Wilmington sightseeing tours. Bob Jenkins of *Wilmington Adventure Tours* (tel. 910/763–1785) will give you the inside story on the city during his animated walking tour. Or you can get acquainted with Wilmington through *Sightseeing Tours by Horse Drawn Carriage* (tel. 910/251–8889). River tours are conducted by Capt. Carl Marshburn aboard the paddle wheeler *Henrietta II* (tel. 910/343–1611 or 800/676–0162) and by *Capt. J. N. Maffitt Harbor Tours* (tel. 910/343–1611).

Wright Brothers National Memorial (Kill Devil Hills, tel. 252/441–7430). The visitor center has on display a replica of the plane that the two bicycle mechanics from Ohio, Wilbur and Orville Wright, used in their first successful flight, on December 17, 1903. National Park Service rangers give interpretive talks on the historic event. The aviators' four takeoffs and landings are marked on the grassy strip outside.

RESTAURANTS

The **Sanderling Inn and Restaurant** (Rte. 12, Duck, tel. 252/261–4111) serves gourmet Continental and southern regional dishes in an elegantly restored life-saving station on the oceanfront. Some of the best seafood can be found at **Queen Anne's Revenge** (Old Wharf Rd., Wanchese, tel. 252/473–5466) on Roanoke Island, and at **Café Atlantic** (Rte. 12, tel. 252/928–4861) on Ocracoke Island. In Beaufort, the best place for lunch is **Beaufort Grocery** (117 Queen St., tel. 252/729–3866); for dinner, try the seafood supreme at **Spouter's Inn** (218 Front St., tel. 252/728–5190). In New Bern, there's fine dining at the **Harvey Mansion** (221 Tryon Palace Dr., tel. 252/638–3205). Wilmington's **The Pilot House** (Chandler's Wharf, tel. 910/343–0200) serves excellent, fresh seafood.

SHOPPING

The **Cotton Exchange** (321 N. Front St., tel. 910/343–9896), a shopping-dining complex in Wilmington, is housed in eight restored buildings on the Cape Fear River that have flourished as a trading center since pre–Civil War days.

You can find nautical items at antiques shops and hand-carved wooden ducks and birds at local crafts shops in Duck, a few miles north of Nags Head, and in Wanchese, at the south end of Roanoke Island. **Kitty Hawk Kites** (U.S. 158 at Mile Marker 13, tel. 252/441–4124 or 800/334–4777) in Nags Head, is the largest kite store on the East Coast. It offers every type of kite and windsock known to man as well as toys and outdoor clothing.

VISITOR INFORMATION

Cape Fear Coast Convention and Visitors Bureau (24 N. 3rd St., Wilmington 28401, tel. 910/341–4030 or 800/222–4757). **Carteret County Tourism Bureau** (3409 Arendell St., Morehead City 28557, tel. 252/726–8148 or 800/786–6962). **Dare County Visitor Bureau** (Box 399, Manteo 27954, tel. 252/473–2138 or 800/446–6262). **Historic Albemarle Tour, Inc.** (Box 1604, Washington 27889, tel. 252/974–2950 or 800/734–1117).

RESERVATION SERVICE

North Carolina Bed & Breakfast Assn. (Box 1077, Asheville 28802, tel. 800/849–5392).

CATHERINE'S INN 🍍

410 S. Front St., Wilmington 28401, tel. 910/251–0863 or 800/476–0723,
fax 910/772–9550, www.catherinesinn.com

As a young girl, Catherine Ackiss traveled with her family to Virginia's Skyline Drive, where they stayed in primitive tourist homes. She thought then that the accommodations—and the atmosphere—could stand a little southern hospitality. At Catherine's Inn, she has created that atmosphere in a sterling setting, an 1883 Italianate mansion in Wilmington's historic district. Ackiss operated Catherine's Inn on Orange from 1988 to 1994 before buying the Forshee-Sprunt House, overlooking the Cape Fear River. The home is painted a crisp white and has a brick and wrought-iron fence. Though Catherine lost some trees in 1996's devastating Hurricane Fran, she otherwise survived unscathed.

Guests can pass the time in one of the twin parlors at the front of the house. Catherine's mother's grand piano made the move, along with many other family items that give the inn warmth and charm. If the weather is good, most guests congregate in rockers and swings on the front and back porches, where they can view the Cape Fear River and romantic sunsets. Another big attraction is a lush sunken garden. Once planted with strawberries and scuppernong grapevines, it's now a beautifully landscaped retreat where guests can watch the big ships come into port and enjoy the smell of magnolia blossoms spilling over the stone wall.

Guests of Catherine's former inn will feel right at home, since she has duplicated much of the decor. The twin room is once again painted a striking dark purple, while other rooms have four-poster and canopy beds. Crocheted bed covers and hand-tied canopies add romance to the guest rooms. Fresh flowers and glasses of sherry in the evenings give the inn a personal touch.

Walter Ackiss, a semiretired engineer, is in charge of storytelling and helps out with breakfast on weekends. Pancakes with orange or blueberry syrup are served alongside homemade sausage on family silver and china. Conveniences include a stocked refrigerator and library, and there are evening refreshments. ⌂ *5 double rooms with baths. Air-conditioning, ceiling fans, cable TV in parlors, phone in rooms, turndown service. $95–$110; full breakfast. MC, V. No smoking, children by prior arrangement.*

CEDARS BY THE SEA 🍍

305 Front St., Beaufort 28516, tel. 252/728–7036 or 800/732–7036, fax 252/728–1685,
www.cedarsinn.com

What Beaufort lacks in size it more than makes up for in history and hospitality. Sam and Linda Dark, the fourth owners of the Cedars, are doing their best to keep that tradition alive. And they're succeeding very nicely, in part because they have an eye for detail, whether it's combining contemporary and antique furnishings from their world travels for a room's decorating theme or selecting wine for the wine bar. Sweating the small stuff is a talent they honed during all their years of working as Washington lobbyists. They were homesick for North Carolina, though, and by 1996 had decided they were ready to exchange the rough-and-tumble of national politics for a more genteel pace. That's when they heard about the sale of the inn.

Actually, their inn is two historic homes. The principal one was built in 1768 and the other, right next door, in 1851. Both face Front Street, Beaufort's pedestrian-friendly main thoroughfare; both catch the breezes off the waterfront, just steps from Front Street; both are elegant, immaculately kept, multistory houses whose clean white-on-white paint stands out in contrast with the green of the landscaped lawn, cedar and magnolia trees, and the bright colors of the surrounding flower gardens. It's not surprising, then, that this is a popular place for weddings and receptions. Those celebrating honeymoons and anniversaries often request the Carolina Cottage, with its sitting room and fireplace, white wicker furniture, king canopied four-poster bed, and bathroom with whirlpool bath and hand-painted mural of a spring garden. When it comes to actual bed space, two rooms are snug, reminiscent of a boat's berth. The rest of the sleeping rooms are spacious. The Simpson, with its yellow-and-white color scheme and cottage decor, is cheery. The Bristol and the Owens are downright deluxe.

The inn has seven working fireplaces. The dining room seats 22 at antique tables covered with white linen tablecloths. Years ago, when the inn was a restaurant, the kitchen was upgraded to full commercial status. Breakfast is a big event. Generally served buffet-style, it features all manner of egg dishes, pancakes and lemon French toast, country ham, sausage and bacon, fresh fruits, a variety of juices, and that southern staple, grits. These, billed as "The Cedars Famous Grits," contain secret ingredients that among other things give them a very creamy texture.

The Darks, who live on-site, enjoy passing time with their guests, watching the sun set over Taylor's Creek from the front porch of the main house, and sipping wine on the rooftop deck of the 1851 house. ⌂ *10 double rooms with baths, 1 cottage. Air-conditioning, cable TV in rooms. $85–$165; full breakfast. MC, V. No smoking, no children under 10.*

FIRST COLONY INN ☙

6720 S. Virginia Dare Trail, Milepost 16, Nags Head 27959, tel. 252/441–2343 or 800/368–9390, fax 252/441–9234, www.firstcolonyinn.com

The last of Nags Head's old shingle-style inns was scheduled for demolition when two generations of a Lexington family pooled their resources, mortgaged their homes, and bought the First Colony Inn in 1988. Richard and Camille Lawrence had two things going for them: a piece of land where the inn could be relocated and children with expertise, including a preservation architect, an engineer, an accountant, and a designer. The whole town lined the streets the night the inn (sawed into three pieces) was moved down the road, away from the ocean's grasping fingers.

Today the inn is listed on the National Register of Historic Places and is far more luxurious than it was in 1932, when it was first constructed. In all, nine of the Lawrences own and operate the inn, and they all helped to restore it with their own hands. The exterior has been returned to its original beauty, complete with two-story, continuous wraparound porches and a brown-shingled roof. The whole interior was reconfigured; now the 26 rooms have private baths and lots of extras, such as heated towel bars, English toiletries, irons and ironing boards, refrigerators, and microwaves. Luxury rooms also have wet bars or kitchenettes, as well as whirlpool baths and private screened porches. White walls give the inn a fresh feeling, and each room is furnished differently, with cherry beds and dressers, white wicker with floral-print cushions, or canopy beds with crocheted lace.

Breakfast, which includes a hot entrée, croissants, pastries, and fruit, is served in the first-floor dining room, which contains antique buffets, enormous old mirrors, and vintage photos of Nags Head. In the afternoon tea is served. The second-floor library is a cozy enclave where guests can read or play games. One of the most delightful bits of reading is a framed letter about a classic Nags Head vacation on letterhead stationery, circa 1934, when it was called LeRoy's Seaside Inn. There's a 55-ft pool with a roomy wooden deck in back, and the ocean is a short walk across the street.

The inn is also convenient to *The Lost Colony* outdoor drama in Manteo, hang gliding at Jockey's Ridge, first-flight history at the Wright Brothers National Memorial, and the many attractions of the Cape Hatteras National Seashore. ⌂ *26 double rooms with baths. Air-conditioning, cable TV and phone in rooms. $145–$275; full breakfast. AE, D, MC, V. No smoking, 2-night minimum weekends, 3-night minimum holidays.*

GRANVILLE QUEEN INN ☙
108 S. Granville St., Edenton 27932, tel. 252/482–5296,
www.edenton.com/granvillequeen

Guests get to live out their fantasies at this bed-and-breakfast inn in the heart of Edenton. The ornate sign with its elaborate crown is the first clue to what's inside, and the peach paint on the neoclassic 1907 house hints at the romance to be found within. For Marge and Ken Dunne, it was love at first sight. After staying at the inn themselves, they sold their chain of gourmet cheese shops on Long Island, New York, and bought the inn in 1991. They've retained the unique character that has charmed guests since the inn was first created in 1989.

The first thing you encounter after entering the front door is a sculpture of a pair of cranes, their feet planted in a square white marble fountain and their heads pointed upward to a dark ceiling made of plaster squares hand-molded with Cupid faces and then gilded. There's a formal dining room with a crystal chandelier; a side porch with white wicker, glass-top tables, and ceiling fans has been enclosed as another dining area.

Each of the guest rooms provides an ambience you might find by taking a trip to a foreign country or stepping into the pages of a storybook. In the Egyptian Room, the most exotic and most requested, guests sleep under a leopard coverlet, watched over by two huge, black sphinxes flanking a pair of thronelike chairs draped with the same sheer gold fabric that's at the windows. In the Queen of Italy bathroom, the water spouts from a cherub's mouth. All the oversize tubs have waterfalls. The Queen Victorianna Room is bright and airy and has window seats, a canopy bed, and a claw-foot tub. The Captain's Quarters has dark mahogany furnishings and a decorated, lacquered dinghy suspended over the bed. The Queen of Queens Room has a massive bed with a bronze plaque of the Blessed Mother set into the headboard. Some rooms have gas-log fireplaces and private patios.

Dining at the Granville Queen is just as lavish. The five-course gourmet breakfast includes grilled chicken breast or filet mignon with eggs and potatoes. Wine and cheese are served on weekend afternoons. ⌂ *9 double rooms with baths. Air-conditioning, cable TV/VCR and phone in rooms. $95–$105; full breakfast. No credit cards. No smoking.*

HARMONY HOUSE INN ☙
215 Pollock St., New Bern 28560, tel. 252/636–3810 or 800/636–3113,
fax 252/636–3810, www.harmonyhouseinn.com

This Greek Revival house in New Bern's historic district was built in the early 1850s and enlarged three times. It was even sawed in half as part of one enlargement around the turn of the century and converted to apartments in the '70s. It was made whole again in 1985, converted to a bed-and-breakfast inn that's elegant and homey at the same time.

The double front doors and hallways are the only hint of its strange architectural past. Its history can be seen in framed photos from *Harper's Weekly* depicting the Battle of New Bern. The town fell to Union forces and served as their base of operations in eastern North Carolina for the duration of the war. The Harmony House was occupied by Company K of the 45th Massachusetts Regiment, who posed for a picture in front of the house in 1863.

Ed and Sooki Kirkpatrick, who bought the inn in 1994, have added two new suites. The romantic Eliza Ellis suite has a king-size bed and heart-shape whirlpool. The Benjamin Ellis suite has two separate rooms, a bedroom with a queen-size canopy bed and a sitting area with a queen-size pull-out sofa bed. This arrangement is ideal for families or couples who prefer more space. Harmony House is furnished with many homey touches: family photos, handcrafted local furniture, and antiques, including an 1875 pump organ. The soft pastel colors of the walls set off the canopy beds and colorful comforters. Sooki's needlepoint flowers and "HH"-crocheted coasters give the house a personal touch.

Breakfast is a time for socializing in the dining room, where the Kirkpatricks lay out a different hot dish on the Empire sideboard each day: pancakes stuffed with cottage cheese; apple, bacon and cheddar quiche; Scotch eggs, ham Strada; or bacon and eggs, plus fruit, homemade granola, and coffee cake. There's also fresh-ground coffee and an assortment of teas; complimentary beverages are available throughout the day.

The Kirkpatricks have brochures on local attractions and restaurants; many are within walking distance. Ed has mapped out suggested bike routes for visitors; the inn has long been a favorite overnight stop for bike tours from all over the country. ⌂ *8 rooms with baths, 2 suites. Air-conditioning, ceiling fan, cable TV, and phone in rooms. $89–$140; full breakfast. AE, D, DC, MC, V. No smoking.*

ISLAND INN ❧
Lighthouse Rd. (Box 9), Ocracoke 27960, tel. 252/928–4351, fax 252/928–4352, www.ocracoke-island-inn.com

This historic inn, the oldest one on the Outer Banks, has stood for nearly a century. It got its name because it sat on Ocracoke's highest point, with a creek on either side. Built in 1901 of old ship timbers, it served as an Odd Fellows Lodge, public school, and officers' club before becoming an inn in 1945. It may not be as polished as a modern hotel, but the inn has the character and atmosphere you won't find in a contemporary lodging. It even has a ghost, Mrs. Godfrey, the wife of a former innkeeper; she opens the kitchen door from time to time and leaves things out of place. People have such a good time here, they don't miss luxury; they do find good food and very caring, hospitable hosts. Bob and Cee Touhey, formerly of Winston-Salem, gave up careers in marketing and teaching respectively and are renovating the inn in stages. With basic improvements behind them, they've now added cosmetic touches such as blue-and-white striped awnings, interior doors, and carpeting.

The best rooms, with panoramic water views, are in the Crow's Nest, up some steep stairs. These rooms have light-gray natural-wood walls and ceilings, new bathrooms, and contemporary furnishings with a beach motif. The ocean breeze pours in from sliding glass doors on two sides. In the main inn, rooms have antique furnishings and vintage photographs and feel like Grandma's house. Families prefer the modern annex, where extra large rooms open onto the heated pool. In

June of 1998 villas were added. There are three two-bedroom suites and one one-bedroom suite, each with a kitchen, whirlpool bath, and private balcony.

The dining room, the oldest Outer Banks restaurant, has also gotten a face-lift, with fresh white walls, new windows, and new wood ceilings with track lighting. The prints on the walls—including one of the inn itself—were done by an Alabama artist who stays at the inn every summer. A no-smoking area is on the enclosed sunporch. Many cooks are children of people who cooked here decades ago; they use the same recipes for such trademark dishes as oyster omelets, crab cakes, clam chowder, and scrambled eggs with herring roe. A new chef has added dinner delights such as grilled shrimp with Aunt Annie's green chili cheese grits.

The village of Ocracoke is on the island of the same name, accessible only by ferry. The laid-back, casual atmosphere seems a little like that of Cape Cod. The pirate Blackbeard was killed close to where the Ocracoke Lighthouse is. At the British Cemetery, the Union Jack flies over the graves of British sailors killed offshore, and everyone loves Ocracoke's wild ponies. ♠ *35 double rooms with baths, 4 suites. Air-conditioning, cable TV in most rooms, phone in annex rooms. $45–$150; full breakfast with room only in winter. D, MC, V. No smoking, 3-night minimum holidays.*

KING'S ARMS INN ☙

212 Pollock St., New Bern 28560, tel. 252/638–4409 or 800/872–9306, fax 252/638–2191, www.bbhost.com/kingsarmsinn

New Bern was ravaged by fire in the early 1840s, and the home that is now the King's Arms Inn was constructed in the aftermath. The Federal-style frame house was built in 1848 and enlarged in 1895 to include a "bellcast" (bell-shape) mansard roof with gabled dormers. The late-Victorian stairway has a polished newel post as thick as a tree trunk. In 1980, the house became an inn, named for an old New Bern tavern frequented by members of the First Continental Congress when they visited Tryon Palace.

Richard and Pat Gulley, originally from Illinois, fell in love with bed-and-breakfasts shortly after they fell in love with each other. They spent their honeymoon touring New England, staying in B&Bs along the way. They took over the King's Arms in 1993 and have been making improvements ever since.

In one room, a Colonial-style four-poster is draped with tulip-pattern fabric that matches the comforter and draperies. The whole third-floor area, originally the attic, is now a suite with a bedroom and spacious sitting room with a view of the Neuse and Trent rivers. A downstairs bedroom was converted into a sitting room.

A morning newspaper and a full breakfast of quiche, muffins, fresh fruit, and juice are delivered to the rooms. Pat is known for her unique muffins, including peanut-butter-and-jelly muffins for kids. Adults will love the custom coffee blend, a mixture of Guatemalan and Indonesian cinnamon coffees. Refreshments are also served in the afternoon. ♠ *7 double rooms with baths, 1 suite. Air-conditioning, cable TV and phone in rooms. $100–$145; full breakfast. AE, MC, V. No smoking.*

LANGDON HOUSE ☙

135 Craven St., Beaufort 28516, tel. 252/728–5499, fax 252/728–1717

Langdon House, a block from the Beaufort waterfront and across the street from the Old Burying Ground, is just about as old as that historic cemetery. It's built of hand-hewn heart-pine timbers and put together with hand-forged nails, and owner Jimm Prest is fairly sure the ballast-stone foundation was laid in 1733. (The cemetery was deeded to the town in 1731.)

A Colonial–Federal-style house with a Bahamian roof line, Langdon House is painted white with dark green shutters and has upstairs and downstairs porches across the front. The floor plan is very simple—a central hall and stairway running down the middle, a parlor on the left side, a bedroom to the right (the largest and sunniest), and three to the rear. All the rooms have queen-size beds (with no headboards but with lots of comfy pillows) and are named for different guests. The dining room, upstairs over the parlor, resembles an 18th-century tavern; an Edwardian oak table takes up most of the room. The kitchen is also upstairs—an arrangement already in place when Prest renovated the house in 1985. Furnishings are an assortment of antiques, some on loan from local residents. The parlor contains an Estes pump organ, an 1840s Empire secretary, and other treasures—all furniture that is friendly and familiar, not museum pieces you wouldn't dare touch.

What really sets Langdon House apart is Prest himself. Having spent 365 days a year on the road for Coca-Cola before he became an innkeeper, he knows what it is to be a traveler, and he's accommodating to a remarkable degree. He'll arrange excursions, make sure guests are fishing with the right lure, and furnish beach baskets with towels and suntan lotion. Complimentary beverages are always available, as is just about anything a guest may have neglected to bring, from hip waders and clam rakes to Pepto-Bismol and Band-Aids. To top it off, he's just plain friendly, the kind of innkeeper who likes to share a glass of wine and good conversation with guests on the rocking-chair-dotted verandas.

Prest encourages his guests to sleep late and will cook a full breakfast for them anytime after 7:30 AM. He describes the food, such as too-pretty-to-eat orange-pecan waffles and omelets, as wholesome but not without sin. And he describes his business—aptly—not just as the renting of rooms but rather as the fine art of innkeeping. ♣ *4 double rooms with baths. Air-conditioning; bicycles, fishing rods, ice chests. $88–$120; full breakfast. No credit cards. No smoking, 2-night minimum summer weekends and holidays.*

PECAN TREE INN ☞
116 Queen St., Beaufort 28516, tel. 252/728–6733

On Joe and Susan Johnson's first visit to Beaufort, they sat in a waterfront restaurant and watched wild ponies graze on nearby Carrot Island. When dolphins swam up the river to complete the scene, the Johnsons took it as a sign they were where they belonged. Joe, who ran a chain of hardware stores, and Susan, who sold auto insurance, left New Jersey and bought a Victorian home less than a block from the waterfront. The home was built in 1856, and Victorian embellishments, including porches, turrets, and gingerbread trim, were added in the 1890s. Now restored to its original splendor, it's a charmer that lures 20–30 people a week just for a tour.

Rooms are bright and airy, with light floral wallpapers and bed covers. The furnishings are a mix of antiques and reproductions from different periods. The Blue Room, for example, has a queen-size pencil-post canopy bed in warm wood tones and antique tables and dresser. The Pine Room has a pine pencil-post canopy bed and an antique trunk. The Green Room was renamed the Wow Room for the response it inevitably provokes. Here, deep-green carpeting and fabrics provide a dramatic contrast to the white walls. The Bridal Suite is pure romance. The four-poster canopy bed is accented with a brocade coverlet, and the rose-and-white tile bath includes a two-person whirlpool.

A small library is outfitted with books, games, and a guest refrigerator stocked with complimentary beverages. Other favorite places for relaxing are the porches, where breakfast is often served in fair weather. The fare includes homemade muffins, cereals, fresh fruit, and, of course, pecan sticky buns.

Named for two ancient pecan trees that grow on the property, the inn is beautifully landscaped. There's a small yard in front and a huge garden in back, planted with more than 1,000 flowers, shrubs, and trees. (The local chefs also stroll back here to pluck some of Susan's herbs.) The city's best restaurants are all within walking distance, as are the historic district and the waterfront. ▲ *7 double rooms with baths. Air-conditioning. $70–$135; Continental breakfast. MC, V. No smoking.*

ROANOKE ISLAND INN ❧

305 Fernando St., Manteo 27954, tel. 252/473–5511 or 877/473–5511, fax 252/473–1019

When he was five, John Wilson vowed that one day he'd own the waterfront house originally built for his great-great-grandmother in the 1860s. Today, he shares the home with summer visitors. Set on a large lot overlooking Shallowbag Bay, the house is surrounded by gardens.

It started as a simple island house, but each generation added on. The guest rooms, in a separate wing, are individually decorated, and some have massive beds created by seamlessly crafting additions onto smaller antiques. Each room has a private outside entrance, and all rooms access a large porch filled with rockers that overlook the bay. The parlor is lined with books and decorated with explorer John White's original drawings of Roanoke. A guest kitchen provides soft drink and juice dispensers, coffeemaker, microwave, and separate refrigerators for milk and ice.

Though the busy Manteo waterfront shops and restaurants are only a block away, the inn is out of the hustle and bustle just enough to feel like a quiet retreat. ▲ *6 double rooms with baths, 2 suites, 1 two-bedroom bungalow. Air-conditioning, cable TV and phone in rooms. $88–$128; Continental breakfast. AE, MC, V. Pets allowed (dogs must be leashed), 2-night minimum weekends.*

TRANQUIL HOUSE INN ❧

405 Queen Elizabeth St. (Box 2045), Manteo 27954, tel. 252/473–1404 or 800/458–7069, fax 252/473–1526

On Manteo's waterfront in the heart of the village, this inn was built in 1988 to blend with its older neighbors. Modeled on the architecture of the old Roanoke Hotel, the inn is a three-story, gray-shingled building with a green roof overlooking Shallowbag Bay. Guests watch the comings and goings on the waterfront from long verandas and a spacious second-floor deck furnished with Adirondack chairs.

Don Just, a retired bank and advertising executive, bought the inn in 1993. His wife, Lauri, redecorated the rooms with handmade comforters, dust ruffles, and shams in designer fabrics. Bathroom mirrors in some rooms were hand-stenciled to match flowers in the wallpaper. The furnishings are all pine reproductions.

The inn's restaurant, 1587, has salmon-color sponge-painted walls and handcrafted sconce lights. A Continental buffet breakfast is served here for guests only. The dinner menu changes about eight times a year and is an adventure, including entrées ranging from lamb, ostrich, and quail to pasta and Cajun-bronzed mahimahi atop basmati rice surrounded by tequila-spiked gazpacho. Room service is also available, as are evening refreshments. △ *23 double rooms with baths, 2 suites. Air-conditioning, cable TV and phone in rooms; bicycles. $129–$169; Continental breakfast. AE, D, MC, V. 2-night minimum summer weekends, 3-night minimum holiday weekends.*

WHITE DOE INN ☞

319 Sir Walter Raleigh St., Manteo 27954, tel. 252/473–9851 or 800/473–6091, fax 252/473–4708, www.whitedoeinn.com

The white Victorian on the corner of Sir Walter Raleigh Street has been a Manteo icon for generations. The Meekins family of Rodanthe moved to the island and built the house in 1896 as a 1½-story frame structure. Years later, Rosa Meekins saw a picture in the Sears catalog and had her husband build an addition modeled on the Victorian home in 1910.

Bebe Woody grew up wondering what lay behind the lace curtains of the majestic Queen Anne. In 1993 she and husband Bob Woody bought the house, now on the National Register of Historic Places, and spent two years renovating the home into an inn. They were uniquely suited to the job: Bebe retired from 31 years with the National Park Service, specializing in historic preservation and restoration, and Bob still works in visitor services.

The study, tastefully furnished with antiques, has a fireplace with built-in bookcases on either side. A baby grand dominates the parlor, where chamber-music concerts are sometimes held. Breakfasts are three-course creations that include fruit, hot entrées, freshly baked breads, and gourmet coffees and teas. It's all served in the downstairs dining room or, weather permitting, on the veranda, where you can also enjoy afternoon refreshments.

The Garret Bedchamber, on the third floor, is one of the most unusual rooms. A two-way fireplace serves the bedroom and the bath, which has a whirlpool. The Virginia Dare room is the most romantic, with a four-poster, queen-size rice bed and a bath with whirlpool. Light pours in through the windows of the Turret Room, in the turret on the corner of the house. The Old Towne Bedchamber has two wicker double beds and a stained-glass window. The Scuppernong has 9-ft sloped ceilings and an antique cast-iron claw-foot tub.

The inn takes its name from an old Indian legend that Virginia Dare, the child who disappeared with the Lost Colony, was turned into a white doe that still roams the island today. △ *7 double rooms with baths. Air-conditioning, fireplace, ceiling fan, and phone in rooms, whirlpool tubs in 2 rooms. $120–$190; full breakfast. AE, MC, V. No smoking, no children under 12, 2-night minimum on weekends Easter–Thanksgiving.*

WORTH HOUSE ☞

412 S. 3rd St., Wilmington 28401, tel. 910/762–8562 or 800/340–8559, fax 910/763–2173, www.bbonline.com/nc/worth

This picture-perfect Queen Anne home stands out, even in a historic district full of beautiful homes. Its twin turrets, trimmed with shingles, their windows lined with lace curtains, promise an intriguing interior—and deliver. Built by merchant Charles Worth in 1893, it was a private home for many years before being converted to a boardinghouse during World War II, when shipbuilding boomed in the port city. Abandoned in the late 1970s and restored in the mid-'80s, it was purchased by Francie and John Miller in 1994.

Francie likes to say that while you might find more elegant accommodations, you won't find any more comfortable. The Worth House is, in fact, beautiful without being fussy or intimidating. It's furnished with antiques from the period, with the exception of a big-screen TV in one of the downstairs parlors. Mirrors, tables, and other pieces come from Baton Rouge, New Orleans, Atlanta, and Wilmington, North Carolina. There's a sitting room on each floor, as well as a garden with a decorative pond in back, and a porch on the second floor.

Guest rooms have antique wood beds, including four-posters. Favorite rooms include the Azalea and Rose suites, both of which have private glass-enclosed sunporches. The Azalea suite is inside the big turret and has two large bay windows. The third-floor bathrooms are not for tall people: conforming to the roof and turret lines, they have sloping ceilings and unusual shapes. But for some guests, that just adds to the charm.

Breakfast is served in one of three places: the formal dining room, the second-floor porch, or rooms. Francie will accommodate most any schedule. Special amenities include a modem line and a laundry room. ♨ *7 double rooms with baths. Air-conditioning, ceiling fans and phone in rooms, cable TV in library and third-floor lounge, fireplaces in some rooms, laundry room. $80–$120; full breakfast. AE, MC, V. No smoking, 2-night minimum on holiday and special-event weekends.*

THE PIEDMONT

Between the mountains and the coastal plain of North Carolina lies a region of rolling hills, large rivers, and lakes. In his journal (published in 1709), John Lawson called it "the finest part of Carolina." In the 1700s, the Piedmont, populated by Native American tribes and teeming with game and fish, was the western frontier. Today, with its interstate crossroads and large cities, the area, long devoted to commerce, is beginning to be recognized for its travel appeal. People riding the interstates on their way north, south, or west are likely to spend some time in the Piedmont.

The region is rich in historic attractions and museums of history, art, science, transportation, tobacco, furniture, and textiles. You can spend an entire day exploring the Moravian settlements of Old Salem and Bethabara near Winston-Salem; retrace Revolutionary War battles at Kings Mountain, Guilford Courthouse, and Alamance; or visit the Civil War site at Bentonville. You can see animals from around the world at the North Carolina Zoological Park in Asheboro; enjoy opera, Shakespeare, and concerts; and observe government at work in Raleigh, the state's capital and home to a splendid collection of free museums.

Busloads of travelers shop for clothing, furniture, and household goods at large outlet centers along the interstates in Burlington ("Outlet Capital of the World"), Greensboro, High Point, Winston-Salem, Hickory, Kannapolis, and Charlotte. Antiques are also hot; in fact, entire towns like Waxhaw and Pineville are devoted to buying and selling them. Long recognized for its handmade pottery, the sandy, pine-treed area called the Sandhills has several dozen shops where you can buy utilitarian and decorative pieces. The epicenter for the craft is Seagrove, where potters have worked at wheels for 200 years.

North Carolina prides itself on its golf courses, its tennis facilities are increasing, and croquet is making a comeback. The craze for basketball is contagious in the Tarheel State, thanks to the NBA's Charlotte Hornets and NCAA standouts Duke, UNC, Wake Forest, and NC State. The Durham

Bulls immortalized in the film Bull Durham *are also wildly popular, as is NASCAR racing. Paramount's Carowinds theme park (*see below*) on the South Carolina line has hair-raising rides, and the state's parks and lakes offer other recreation, as well as natural beauty.*

PLACES TO GO, SIGHTS TO SEE

Discovery Place (301 N. Tryon St., Charlotte, tel. 704/372–6261), one of the best science museums in the country, has hands-on and rotating exhibits as well as aquariums, a rain forest, and an Omnimax theater.

Duke Chapel (Chapel Rd., West Campus, Durham, tel. 919/681–1701), a Gothic structure patterned on a European cathedral, was built in the early 1930s. Its 210-ft bell tower is a landmark of Duke University. Free organ concerts are given regularly.

Duke Homestead and Tobacco Museum (2828 Homestead Rd., Durham, tel. 919/477–5498). At the mid-19th-century home of Washington Duke, tobacco barns, an original factory, and a museum are open for tours. The complex is a National Historic Landmark.

Furniture Discovery Center (101 W. Green Dr., High Point, tel. 336/887–3876). In a former fabric warehouse near hundreds of showrooms, this unique museum is devoted entirely to furniture production and includes an extensive miniature collection.

Golf Courses. More than three dozen golf resorts, among them *Pinehurst Resort and Country Club* (tel. 910/295–6811 or 800/487–4653), *Pine Needles* (tel. 910/692–7111 or 800/747–7272), and *Mid-Pines Resort* (tel. 910/692–2114 or 800/323–2114), are in the North Carolina Sandhills. (Some courses are open only to guests at the resort.)

The **Mint Museum of Art** (2730 Randolph Rd., Charlotte, tel. 704/337–2000), built in 1837 as a U.S. mint, has an outstanding collection of pre-Columbian pottery and attracts traveling exhibits.

North Carolina Transportation Museum (411 S. Salisbury Ave., Spencer, tel. 704/636–2889), in the old railroad repair shops, traces the history of transportation from pre-settler days through the heyday of railroading to the present. A steam train takes visitors on a short loop tour.

Old Salem (600 S. Main St., Winston-Salem, tel. 336/721–7300), a restored Moravian village dating to the 1700s, comprises 60 buildings where visitors can see Colonial cooking, gardening, and the making of pewter, candles, furniture, and cloth. At Christmas there are candlelight teas and worship services. The *Museum of Early Southern Decorative Arts* (tel. 336/721–7360) has 21 rooms reconstructed from southern houses and six galleries.

Paramount's Carowinds (14523 Carowinds Blvd., off I–77, tel. 704/588–2600 or 800/888–4386) is a 100-acre amusement park on the South Carolina state line that's owned by the Paramount movie studio. There are costumed movie and TV characters and movie-themed attractions, from heart-stopping rides to a water entertainment complex. It's open daily June to August and weekends only mid-March to May and September to mid-October.

Reed Gold Mine (off U.S. 601 at Rte. 200, 10 mi east of Charlotte, tel. 704/786–8337) is where America's first gold, a 17-pound nugget, was found, in 1799. In the museum, you can explore the mine, pan for gold, and learn about mining.

The **State Capitol** (Capitol Sq., Raleigh, tel. 919/733–4994), completed in 1840 and restored in 1976, once housed all the functions of state government. The *Capital Area Visitor Center* (301 N. Blount St., tel. 919/733–3456) conducts free guided tours daily, which include the contemporary State Legislative Building and the executive mansion.

RESTAURANTS

North Carolina's best hickory-smoked pork barbecue is served with red slaw and hush puppies at **Lexington Barbecue** (I–85 Business, tel. 336/249–9814) in Lexington. The **Lamplighter** (1065 E. Morehead St., tel. 704/372–5343) in Charlotte serves gourmet cuisine in the elegant atmosphere of a house in the old Dilworth neighborhood. Authentic food of the 18th century is offered at the **Salem Tavern** (736 S. Main St., tel. 336/748–8585) in Old Salem. The **Angus Barn, Ltd.** (U.S. 70, tel. 919/781–2444) in Raleigh is famous for its steaks, ribs, and extensive wine list. At the **Colmant House** (Main St., Pilot Mountain, tel. 336/368–2823), John and Sue Colmant, formerly of New Orleans, serve wonderful Cajun fare at dinner Thursday–Sunday.

SHOPPING

The towns of **Waxhaw, Pineville, and Matthews** near Charlotte are havens for antiques hunters. Waxhaw sponsors an annual antiques fair each February. On the first and third weekends of the month you can also find a good selection of antiques at the **Metrolina Expo** (Off I–77N at 7100 N. Statesville Rd., tel. 704/596–4643 or 800/824–3770) in Charlotte.

Reynolda Village (2250 Reynolda Rd., tel. 336/725–5325) is a collection of shops and restaurants that fill what were the outbuildings of an estate near Winston-Salem. In Winston-Salem, at 6th and Trade streets (just behind the Winston-Salem Visitor Center), are several galleries and arts-and-crafts shops.

Replacements, Ltd. (I–85/40 at Mt. Hope Church Rd., Exit 132 between Burlington and Greensboro, tel. 800/737–5223) is the world's largest retailer of discontinued and active china, crystal, flatware, and collectibles. There are more than 3 million pieces of inventory and 65,000 patterns.

Raleigh's **City Market** (Martin St. at Moore Sq., tel. 919/828–4555) is a revitalized shopping area with cobblestone streets and an array of shops and art galleries. **Artspace** (201 E. Davie St., Raleigh, tel. 919/821–2787) is a visual arts center where you can visit and interact with more than 40 artists working in open studios with a variety of media. Almost everything you see can be purchased. Durham's **9th Street** has funky shops and restaurants that cater to the hip crowd. Not far away is **Brightleaf Square** (905 W. Main St.), an upscale shopping-entertainment complex housed in old tobacco warehouses in the heart of downtown.

VISITOR INFORMATION

Chapel Hill/Orange County Visitors Bureau (501 W. Franklin St., Suite 104, Chapel Hill 27516, tel. 919/968–2060). **Durham Convention & Visitors Bureau** (101 E. Morgan St., Durham 27701, tel. 919/687–0288 or 800/446–8604). **Greensboro Area Convention & Visitors Bureau** (312 Greene St., Greensboro 27401, tel. 336/274–2282 or 800/344–2282). **High Point Convention & Visitors Bureau** (Box 300, S. Main St., High Point 27261, tel. 336/884–5255). **INFO! Charlotte** (330 S. Tryon St., Charlotte 28202, tel. 704/331–2700 or 800/231–4636). **Pinehurst Area Convention & Visitors Bureau** (1480 Hwy. 15-501, Southern Pines 28388, tel. 910/692–3330 or 800/346–5362). **Raleigh Convention and Visitors Bureau** (NationsBank Building at 421 Fayetteville St. Mall, Suite 1505, Raleigh 27601, tel. 919/834–5900 or 800/849–8499). **Winston-Salem Convention & Visitors Bureau** (601 W. 4th St., Winston-Salem 27101, tel. 336/725–2361 or 800/331–7018).

RESERVATION SERVICE

North Carolina Bed & Breakfast Assn. (Box 1077, Asheville 28802, tel. 800/
849–5392).

ARROWHEAD INN ☙
106 Mason Rd., Durham 27712, tel. 919/477–8430 or 800/528–2207,
fax 919/471–9538

The large arrowhead monument from which this inn draws its name designates
an old Native American trading route called the Great Path, which once stretched
from eastern Virginia to the North Carolina mountains. It's a proper frame of
reference for this house, which, like the path, predates the United States. The
manor house was built about 1775 on a 2,000-acre land grant purchased from
Joseph Brittain, and for more than 100 years, slaves worked the land. The original house had four rooms—two upstairs and two down—but several were added
over the years. On 4 acres, it is a two-story Colonial-style house with brick chimneys and tall Doric columns that support the long front porch. The house is painted
white with black shutters. The boxwood, magnolias, and flower beds around it
are about 150 years old, and more than 40 species of birds live on the property.

In 1985 the inn was turned into a bed-and-breakfast, winning an award from
the Durham Historic Preservation Society for adaptive reuse. The new innkeepers, Phil and Gloria Teber, are both gourmet cooks. Phil owned a remodeling company and is a master carpenter and restorer; Gloria is a former medical sales
consultant and teacher.

Guest rooms are decorated with an assortment of antiques and collectibles from
the Colonial through the Victorian period. The front rooms of the house look out
on the flower beds, while the back view is dominated by an enormous magnolia. For those wanting more privacy, there are two rooms in an adjacent carriage
house. The Land Grant Cabin, which has a downstairs sitting room and a loft
bedroom, is a favorite. In addition to being a favorite with families and couples,
the inn is quite popular with business travelers who desire flexible check-in
and check-out policies as well as private phones and modems.

The Tebers greet arriving guests with complimentary refreshments, serve afternoon tea, and are always available in the evening when everyone gathers in the
keeping room to work puzzles, read, or talk. Phil promises guests a different breakfast every day, ranging from hearty country breakfasts with bacon, eggs, fruit,
and muffins to more exotic gourmet fare. ⌂ *5 double rooms with baths, 3 suites,*
1 cabin. Air-conditioning, phone, TV/VCR, coffeemaker, and ceiling fan in rooms,
whirlpool baths in suites and cabin, guest refrigerator. $98–$195; full breakfast.
AE, D, DC, MC, V. No smoking.

BLOOMING GARDEN INN ☙
513 Holloway St., Durham 27701, tel. 919/687–0801, fax 919/688–1401

Aptly named, this inn is an oasis in Durham's Holloway Historic District, where
many stately old homes still await renovation. The sunny yellow Victorian is
surrounded with flower beds and bordered with a neat white fence. It's like a
riotous garden inside, too, overflowing with floral-print fabrics, stained-glass
pieces, marbles, kaleidoscopes, and other whimsical accents. Dolly Pokrass, a
nurse by profession, ran an antiques and handicrafts shop in Hillsborough for several years before she and husband Frank, a retired medical sociologist, bought
the inn. It's largely decorated with the items she could never bear to sell. Each

guest room is named according to its colors—Ivy (dark green with cheery accents), Tiffany (stained glass), Moroccan (dark green, gold, and red), and so on. Fresh flowers from the garden adorn each one. Frank and Dolly also own another historic home across the street. The Holly House, for visitors on extended stays, includes a full kitchen and laundry area.

Breakfast begins with original juice blends and home-ground coffee and can include walnut crepes with ricotta cheese and warm raspberry sauce. ♙ *6 double rooms with baths, 2 suites. Air-conditioning, ceiling fans in rooms, cable TV in library and 1 suite, whirlpool bath in suites. $85–$160; full breakfast. AE, D, DC, MC, V. No smoking.*

FEARRINGTON HOUSE 🐚

Fearrington Village Center, U.S. 15–501, Pittsboro 27312, tel. 919/542–2121, fax 919/542–4202, www.fearrington.com

If you didn't know better, you'd think a click of the heels had transported you to the Cotswolds of England. Actually, this bucolic setting is Fearrington Village, a 200-year-old farm remade into a residential community just off U.S. 15–501 between Chapel Hill and Pittsboro. The village is the creation of R. B. and Jenny Fitch, who studied inns and restaurants in Europe before they began the 1,100-acre project in 1974. It consists of the inn and private homes, a restaurant (in the former farmhouse), a bank, pharmacy, pottery, jewelry store, bookstore, garden shop, and market café.

The inn's guest rooms are clustered around a charming courtyard with a central fountain and look out over the gardens and the pasture, where Galloway cows graze. English pine furniture matches the flooring from a London workhouse; rooms also have floral-print fabrics and fresh flower arrangements. The luxurious bathrooms have towel warmers. The Fitch children now help run the business, from decorating the rooms to overseeing the restaurant and gardens.

Breakfast is served in the restaurant, which has several rooms decorated in the elegant country style that is Fearrington's hallmark. Green ivy stenciled on the walls provides a natural complement to the real vines and boughs that peek through the many windows overlooking the gardens. Dinner draws not only inn guests but diners from Chapel Hill and Durham. Entrées include sautéed halibut with roasted fennel; yellowfin tuna with white-wine ginger sauce and fried leeks; and grilled beef tenderloin on a Parmesan disk with peppercorn sauce. Most guests eat lunch in the Market Café or go for a picnic, which can be ordered from the deli. Then they gather for afternoon tea in the Garden Room.

One of the most pleasant things about the Fearrington is its low-key country atmosphere. You won't be subjected to a schedule here, but you might try a round of croquet or ride one of the bikes to the swimming pool and tennis courts. Of course, there are plenty of diversions nearby—the Morehead Planetarium at Chapel Hill, Duke Chapel, and the Duke Homestead. ♙ *17 double rooms with baths, 12 suites. Air-conditioning, TV and phone in rooms. $165–$275; full breakfast. AE, MC, V. Restricted smoking.*

HENRY F. SHAFFNER HOUSE 🐚

150 S. Marshall St., Winston-Salem 27101, tel. 336/777–0052 or 800/952–2256, fax 336/777–1188

The Henry F. Shaffner House was built between 1907 and 1909 by Henry Fries Shaffner, one of the founders of Wachovia Bank. The house was saved twice, the first time from fire by Shaffner himself, who went onto the rooftop with buckets of water. He later replaced the cedar shingles with copper, which helped to preserve the mansion through the next 70 years, even after it was abandoned and neglected. The house was saved again in 1990 by Henry and Betty Falls, who spent two years renovating it. Henry, who owns the insurance agency across the street, initially had designs on the overgrown back lot, which he needed for parking. But once he stepped inside the home, he saw past the layers of paint and dirt to the treasure underneath.

The house was built using the finest materials and workmanship. Tiger-oak paneling covers the walls of the entry hall and adorns the doors, windows, and exposed ceiling beams. Many of the brass fixtures remain, as do the tile fireplaces and a huge ornate radiator in the library. The Queen Anne detailing on the exterior, with large wraparound porches and a wrought-iron fence, is stunning enough to stop traffic, even on the busy main thoroughfare that now runs past it. It was the coming of the interstate, which cuts alongside the house, that moved Shaffner's widow to sell it in 1949. For today's travelers, the location provides easy access from downtown to any Winston-Salem attraction.

Rooms are beautifully appointed with rich fabrics, comfortable sofas and chairs, and gleaming reproduction furniture. Each room is different. The Winston Room is decorated in English Regency—deep sapphire-blue carpet, stucco walls, and a queen-size sleigh bed. The Reynolda is bright and feminine, the Bethabara darkly masculine. The Piedmont Room is a remarkable penthouse suite, with whirlpool bath and wet bar, in the 18th-century Biedermeier style. The king-size canopy bed is covered with a leopard-print comforter, and leopard-print accents are echoed tastefully in the wallpaper and bolster pillows. Throughout, the inn combines the charm of the past with modern amenities. Special touches such as chocolates, turndown service, afternoon wine and cheese, and gift baskets for special occasions make the inn a popular spot for weddings, honeymoons, and anniversaries. ♣ *6 double rooms with baths, 3 suites. Air-conditioning, cable TV and phone in rooms; passes to nearby fitness center. $99–$219; Continental breakfast. AE, MC, V. No smoking.*

THE HOMEPLACE ☜
5901 Sardis Rd., Charlotte 28270, tel. 704/365–1936, fax 704/366–2729

The Homeplace, a well-preserved remnant of the past, has somehow survived modern development in the bustling Sunbelt city of Charlotte. The buff-colored house, on 2½ wooded acres with profuse plantings of flowers, is at the corner of a busy residential intersection but is so quiet inside, you might just as well be at the top of Walton's Mountain.

Frank and Peggy Dearien had admired the 1902 country Victorian farmhouse for several years before the chance arose in 1984 for them to buy it and turn it into a bed-and-breakfast. Frank took early retirement from his accounting job, and the inn is now their full-time occupation. They furnished the house in Victorian period pieces, quilts, cross-stitch pictures, and family memorabilia. Peggy made all the curtains. The most cherished artwork in the house is a collection of primitive paintings reminiscent of Grandma Moses's work that Peggy's father did during the last years of his life.

The Victorian Lady Room, done in mauve and green, was planned around a cross-stitch picture made by the Dearien's daughter Debra Moye. The largest room in the inn, it has a four-poster rice bed. The blue-and-white English Country Room overlooks the garden and the gazebo. The Pewter Rose Suite is great for families or honeymooners. The bedroom is particularly romantic; it has a queen-size canopy bed with a rose-print comforter. The adjoining TV room has a twin bed. All the rooms have little personal touches, such as a purse or hand mirror that belonged to Frank's mother.

The Deariens, who live on the property, are great believers in practicing southern hospitality. There's always hot water for tea or coffee, as well as ice and soft drinks. Breakfast, served in the dining room, might be poached pears with raspberry sauce, scrambled dill eggs with cheese sauce, or waffles and cinnamon cream. ⚑ *2 double rooms with baths, 1 suite. Air-conditioning, ceiling fans, irons and ironing boards in rooms, cable TV in common areas and the suite. $108–$135; full breakfast. AE, MC, V. No smoking, 2- or 3-night minimum holiday and special-event weekends.*

INN AT CELEBRITY DAIRY 🐾

2106 Mt. Vernon–Hickory Mountain Rd., Siler City 27344, tel. 919/742–5176, fax 919/742–1432

The Inn at Celebrity Dairy is one hour from Raleigh, one hour from Greensboro, and a world away from either of those urban centers. And that suits Fleming and Brit Pfann, their guests, and their goats just fine.

The couple—she a weaver of clothes and wall hangings, he an engineer—were weary of their transitory lifestyle. When Fleming inherited a 200-acre oak-shaded farm (circa 1820) from her father they decided to take the opportunity to return to her native state. They moved in 1987.

First came the goats, who were brought in to help clear the overgrown grounds. Goats begat more goats and eventually the Pfanns were licensed to run a dairy, where now a variety of award-winning goat cheeses are produced for gourmet grocers, restaurants, and farm markets. The animals, who are affectionate, intelligent, and docile, are named after celebrities such as Katharine Hepburn, Lauren Bacall, and Tina Louise—thus the name of the dairy and inn.

The second part of the plan, creating a bed-and-breakfast, took a bit longer, as the Pfanns designed and constructed the inn, which is actually two buildings. The heart of the inn, the Old House Suite, is the original settler's cabin. It has rough-hewn walls, heart-of-pine floors, stone fireplace, and hanging quilts made by local craftspeople. The new, three-story, Greek Revival-style farmhouse has wide porches. The rooms, named for goats past and present, are simply but comfortably and artfully decorated. All beds have feather padding atop firm mattresses. The uncarpeted ground-floor rooms with their extra-wide doorways are wheelchair accessible. Upstairs, Lauren's Room has a mirrored armoire and two-person whirlpool tub; Lynan's Room, with its four-poster bed, has walls of periwinkle blue stenciled with a lace-pattern border; and Benjamin's Room has teal tones and an ornate Victorian headboard.

Connecting the two buildings is a sunlight-filled atrium. This huge space, dominated at one end by a Jacobean chest, has hand-painted floors courtesy of Fleming. Breakfast, consisting of goat cheese (of course), freshly baked breads, and dishes made from the eggs of the chickens who roam the property, is eaten here. Guests are then invited to read in the inn's small library, hike in the nearby woods, try their hand at a spinning wheel or loom, or join in the chores and help with the milking of the goats. ⚑ *5 double rooms with baths, 1 single room with adjacent shower, 1 suite. Air-conditioning, ceiling fans in rooms, TV in common area, whirlpool tub in one room, therapeutic massage available by appointment. $60–$130; Continental breakfast weekdays, full breakfast on weekends. MC, V. No smoking, children by prior arrangement.*

MAGNOLIA INN ❦
Magnolia St. and Chinquapin Rd. (Box 818), Pinehurst 28374, tel. 910/295–6900
or 800/526–5562, fax 910/215–0858

Pinehurst has been a favorite vacation spot for more than a century, as this historic inn attests. Built in 1896, it is now on the National Register of Historic Places. Owners Jan and Ned Darby cater to golfers, who come in droves to enjoy the many courses of the Sandhills. The inn has package arrangements with several clubs, including the prestigious Pinehurst Resort and Country Club. The outdoor pool and wraparound porches at Magnolia are a welcome sight after several rounds.

Guest rooms are furnished in a turn-of-the-century Victorian style, with brass beds and wicker. Original bathroom fixtures, claw-foot tubs, and accent pieces, like an old Victrola, add to the ambience.

Chefs Mark Elliott and Lucille Faulk serve unforgettable gourmet food. The dark bar has the feel of an old English pub and offers unusual brews, such as Watney's Red Barrel and Belhaven Scottish Ale. ❧ *11 double rooms with baths. Restaurant, air-conditioning, cable TV in rooms and pub. $130, including full breakfast; $170, MAP. AE, MC, V. Restricted smoking, 2-night minimum spring and fall weekends.*

PILOT KNOB INN ❦
Box 1280, Pilot Mountain 27041, tel. 336/325–2502

The two-story log tobacco barns that dot this rural landscape aren't usually the kind of places you'd consider spending the night. Here, however, they have become a one-of-a-kind B&B. The property adjoins Pilot Mountain State Park, and the knob that crowns the 1,500-ft mountain is within view. (If the names ring a bell, it's because they inspired the place names in Andy Griffith's mythical Mayberry.)

Five small barns and a slave cabin, all at least 100 years old, were moved to the 50-acre wooded site by innkeeper Jim Rouse, who enlarged the slave cabin and added decks and porches to the barns while keeping their rustic look. Jim's father, Don, who is also involved in the operation, can always find something that needs fixing or changing. Norman Ross, a silent business partner from Chicago, owns the collection of 6,000 records in the library. The barns have Oriental and dhurrie rugs and a mix of 18th-century reproductions, southern primitive, and country English antiques. Each has a whirlpool tub for two, a fireplace, bathrobes, hair dryers, fresh fruit, and flowers. Some of the barns have massive "Paul Bunyan" beds, handmade of juniper logs by a local craftsman. The common room, downstairs in the bi-level central barn—where guests gather to read and listen to music—has a 300-year-old Italian-marble fireplace, a William and Mary love seat, and a coffee table made of parquet flooring from Versailles (really!). There's a dry sauna and a pool, and a 6-acre lake and gazebo are ideal for fishing. A contemporary building overlooking the pool and the mountain beyond houses the office, kitchen, a conference room, and a gift shop that sells community crafts. Guests can also while away the evening at a gazebo that has a ceiling fan and picnic tables.

Privacy and isolation are the main attractions at Pilot Knob. It's tucked away with no signs or billboards to point the way and is the perfect place to commune with nature, slow down, and rekindle romance. Guests usually get together at breakfast, which is served in the central barn. Prepared by Jim's mother, Pat, breakfast might be chocolate-chip sour-cream coffee cake, waffles and sausage, poached pears, or a peach and cream-cheese concoction called Peach Pilot—all served with fresh berries in season. ♨ *6 cabins. Air-conditioning, TV and phone in cabins. $110–$130; full breakfast. MC, V. 2-night minimum Oct. and holidays.*

WILLIAM THOMAS HOUSE BED & BREAKFAST ℘
530 N. Blount St., Raleigh 27604, tel. 919/755–9400 or 800/653–3466, fax 919/755–3966, www.ntwrks.com/~wmthomasb+b

Every day for eight years the Loftons would drive by the Victorian house on the edge of downtown Raleigh on their way to work: Sarah to the Executive Mansion where she served as the first lady's executive assistant, Jim to the state government complex where he was first the governor's chief of staff and then a member of his cabinet. When the governor decided to reenter private life so did the Loftons—sort of. In June 1993 they bought the house, which for a decade had been functioning as an office building. By that December they had turned it into a home for themselves and a home away from home for visitors. The following year it was designated a Raleigh Historic Site.

The William Thomas House, named for the fathers of Jim and Sarah, is a spacious place, stately but not stuffy. And it's quiet, thanks to the 7-inch-thick walls and double-paned windows. The richly hued common rooms, with their oversize windows and 12-ft ceilings, are filled with heirlooms: a grand piano from 1863, antique china, a refinished 1947 television serving as an end table. The library-media room, with original wainscoting, contains a TV/VCR, videos, compact disks, books and periodicals, as well as bird-hunting trophies and menus from local restaurants.

Sleeping quarters are also named for Lofton family members, whose pictures are displayed throughout the house. The guests' rooms, with their muted tones, large beds, easy chairs, desks, ample but soft lighting, TVs, tapestries or framed art, Oriental rugs, and small but well-stocked refrigerators, are refuges. For the businessperson they can also double as an office. Front porches and a back deck with rocking chairs allow for down time and enjoyment of the afternoon wine and cheese. But if it's action you're after, the inn is within walking distance of shops, restaurants, and many state-run museums and historic sights, including the Queen Anne–style Executive Mansion. ♨ *4 double rooms with baths. Air-conditioning, ceiling fans, cable TV, mini-refrigerators and phone with fax hookups in rooms, turndown service, off-street parking. $96–$135; full breakfast. AE, MC, V. No smoking, children by prior arrangement.*

THE MOUNTAINS

Western North Carolina is blessed with two major ranges in the Southern Appalachian chain: the Blue Ridge Mountains, extending from Virginia, and the Great Smokies, called Shaconage ("place of blue smoke") by Native Americans. The gentle foothills of both ranges crest into peaks of blue and purple grandeur, many more than 5,000 ft high. Grandfather Mountain, near Linville, is said to be a billion years old. Mt. Mitchell, at 6,684 ft, is the highest point east of the Mississippi.

The Cherokees lived in these mountains for thousands of years before the arrival of Scotch-Irish farmers and enterprising lumberjacks in the mid-1800s. Later, Georgia and Carolina lowlanders, seeking to escape the scorching summer heat, established retreats at Flat Rock, Hendersonville, Highlands, Linville, and Blowing Rock. Around the turn of the century, George Vanderbilt and Edwin Wiley Grove fashioned their dreams into fabulous estates at Asheville and invited their friends to breathe the pure mountain air amid incredible beauty. In the past 25 years, the region has become a magnet for skiers and golfers, and resort communities like Linville Ridge, Elk River, Fairfield, Chetola, and Etowah Valley have sprung up.

Today there's year-round recreation, not only for the silk-stocking set but also for anyone who loves the outdoors. You can camp, hunt, and fish in the Great Smoky Mountains National Park; dig for rubies in Franklin; ride a steam train through the Nantahala Gorge; join thousands of other rubberneckers during leaf season on the Blue Ridge Parkway; and shoot the rapids on the French Broad. Many come to play golf and tennis at posh resorts like the Hound Ears Club or schuss through white powder at Ski Beech and Sugar Mountain. You can attend plays at the Flat Rock Playhouse, listen to classical music at the Brevard Music Festival, watch European folk dancers at Folkmoot, or learn to clog (the native dance) at the Stompin' Ground. If it's not a B&B you're after, you can stay in century-old log cabins at Cataloochee Ranch or live it up at the luxurious Grove Park Inn and Country Club. To complete the experience, dine on rain-

bow trout and vinegar pie at Jarrett House in Dillsboro or have a seven-course gourmet dinner at Eseeola Lodge.

Most people like the high drama of the mountains' four seasons. Many fall in love and decide to sink in deeper roots: Look at the preserved cabins, A-frames, and million-dollar second homes that dot the hillsides. When Rand McNally rated Brevard and Asheville among the most desirable places to live in America, residents were not surprised.

PLACES TO GO, SIGHTS TO SEE

Biltmore (Exit 50 off I–40 East, Asheville, tel. 828/255–1700 or 800/624–1575). The best times to see the fabulous 8,000-acre George C. Vanderbilt estate are April and May, when the gardens are in bloom, and December, when the 250-room mansion is decorated for Christmas as it would have been in 1895. There's a modern winery in the former dairy, where you can see the entire process and sample some of the products.

The Blue Ridge Mountain Frescoes (Glendale Springs and Beaver Creek, near West Jefferson, no phone). In the 1970s, North Carolina artist Ben Long painted these frescoes of New Testament scenes in two abandoned Episcopal churches that have since been restored.

Blue Ridge Parkway. Thousands of Americans travel this famous crestline highway every year from its beginning at Front Royal, Virginia, to its terminus near Great Smoky Mountains National Park and the Cherokee Indian Reservation. The way is dotted with scenic overlooks, mountain cabins, and markers that explain the history and natural phenomena of the area.

Connemara (1928 Little River Rd., Flat Rock, tel. 828/693–4178). During the final years of his life, Lincoln biographer and poet Carl Sandburg lived at this estate with his wife, Lilian, who raised goats. (The name is borrowed from the name of the western region in County Galway in Ireland; it means "country land by the sea.") The National Park Service gives daily tours.

Great Smoky Mountains National Park (tel. 423/436–1200 or 423/436–5615). The most visited park in the United States straddles the North Carolina–Tennessee border and offers a wealth of outdoor activities amid its 517,368 acres. There are more than 800 mi of hiking and riding trails and 16 summits higher than 6,000 ft.

Great Smoky Mountains Railway (Dillsboro, tel. 828/586–8811 or 800/872–4681). Excursion trains traverse the route through rock tunnels and along river gorges between Dillsboro, Bryson City, and Nantahala. Travelers can ride in coach, caboose, or "Kodak" (open) cars.

Mountains. *Grandfather Mountain* (U.S. 221, Mile Marker 305, tel. 828/733–4337 or 800/468–7325) is a must. Known for a rocky profile that resembles an old man, it stands 5,964 ft tall and has a mile-high swinging bridge, hiking trails, nature center with a restaurant and movie theater, and an "environmental habitat" for bear, deer, and other animals. *Mt. Mitchell* (Blue Ridge Pkwy., tel. 828/675–4611)—at 6,684 ft the highest point east of the Mississippi River—is surrounded by a large state park that offers camping and hiking, an observation lounge and tower, and museum. In the heart of Great Smoky Mountains National Park is *Clingmans Dome*, whose 6,643-ft peak is actually in Tennessee.

Thomas Wolfe Memorial (52 Market St., Asheville, tel. 828/253–8304). The famous writer's mother operated a boardinghouse at this downtown dwelling. Now a state historic site, it is open for tours.

RESTAURANTS

You can make an evening of dining at **Gabrielle's** (87 Richmond Hill Dr., tel. 828/252–7313), in the Richmond Hill Inn in Asheville; at the **Market Place on Wall Street** (20 Wall St., tel. 828/252–4162), also in Asheville; or at the **Eseeola Lodge** (U.S. 221, tel. 828/733–4311) in Linville. Another option is the **Green Park Inn** (U.S. 321, Blowing Rock, tel. 828/295–3141), which some critics number among the best in the mountains.

SHOPPING

Biltmore Village (Hendersonville Rd., tel. 828/274–5570) on the Biltmore Estate in Asheville is a cluster of specialty shops, restaurants, and galleries built along cobbled sidewalks. Here there's a decided turn-of-the-century English hamlet feel, and everything—from children's books to music, antiques, one-of-a-kind imports, and wearable art—can be found. **Malaprops** (55 Haywood St., tel. 828/254–6734) bookstore and café is a mainstay in downtown Asheville. There are two stories filled with the carefully chosen inventory, which includes a good-size selection of cards and books about the region.

The **Folk Art Center** (Mile Marker 382 on the Blue Ridge Parkway, tel. 828/298–7928) sells authentic mountain arts and crafts made by the 700 artisans of the Southern Highland Handicraft Guild. **Goodwin Weavers** (Off U.S. 321 Bypass, tel. 828/295–3394), near Blowing Rock, has bedspreads, afghans, and other woven goods, as well as home furnishings designed by North Carolina artist Bob Timberlake. Found at **Bolick Pottery** (Off U.S. 321, NC 8, Lenoir, tel. 828/295–3862), 20 mi southeast of Blowing Rock, are mountain crafts and pottery, handcrafted on the spot by Glenn and Lula Bolick.

Built in 1882, the **Mast General Store** (NC 194, tel. 828/963–6511) in Valle Crucis remains a gathering spot. Coffee is a nickel a cup in this store, which sells everything from cradles to coffins.

VISITOR INFORMATION

Asheville Convention and Visitors Bureau (151 Haywood St., Asheville 28801, tel. 828/258–6100 or 800/257–1300). **Blowing Rock Chamber of Commerce** (Box 406, Blowing Rock 28605, tel. 828/295–7851 or 800/295–7851). **North Carolina High Country Host** (1701 Blowing Rock Rd., Boone 28607, tel. 828/264–1299 or 800/438–7500).

RESERVATION SERVICE

North Carolina Bed & Breakfast Assn. (Box 1077, Asheville 28802, tel. 800/849–5392).

BALSAM MOUNTAIN INN

Box 40, Balsam 28707, tel. 828/456–9488 or 800/224–9498, fax 828/456–9298, www.aksi.net/~cmark/balsam.htm

On spring nights, the moon rises perfectly placed between two mountain peaks, as if a painter set it there for the benefit of the folks sitting in rocking chairs at the Balsam Mountain Inn. Actually, it wasn't the moon but the inn that was strategically placed so that the sun, which warmed the porches in the morning, would leave them in shade during hot summer afternoons and so guests could watch the moonrise year-round.

At one time, the North Carolina mountains were full of rambling wood-frame inns like this one, but the Balsam Mountain Inn is one of only a handful remaining. Built at what was then the highest elevation of the Western North Carolina Railroad, it offered a cool escape from the summer heat when it opened in 1908 as the Balsam Mountain Springs Hotel. It operated into the 1980s but was boarded up and had 125 broken windows when Merrily Teasley bought it in 1990 and began restoration. Plumbing, wiring, and heat are all new, but the inn retains virtually all of its vintage charm. Bead-board paneling covers all the walls, and the heart-pine floors have a comforting creak.

A huge mansard roof with more than 100 dormer windows covers the inn, which is fronted by a two-story porch lined with rockers and hanging plants. Everything about this inn says "relax," from the library, stocked with 2,000 volumes, to the chairs gathered around the lobby fireplaces.

Some of the guest rooms have ornate iron beds, while others have "twig" beds—headboards fashioned from boughs and twisted vines by a local craftspeople. Bathrooms have either showers or Victorian claw-foot tubs and corner-mounted sinks.

The large dining room is painted gray with lavender, green, and burgundy trim for a charming effect. The restaurant serves three meals on Sunday and two daily meals the rest of the week. Representative of the lavish breakfasts, included in room rates, is French toast with a caramelized syrup coating and topped with fresh fruit. There's help-yourself tea and hot chocolate in the lobby, and box lunches are available every day if ordered by 6 PM the day before. ⌂ *42 double rooms with baths, 8 suites. Restaurant. $90–$160; full breakfast. D, MC, V. Restricted smoking, 2-night minimum some weekends and holidays.*

CEDAR CREST INN 🐦

674 Biltmore Ave., Asheville 28803, tel. 828/252–1389 or 800/252–0310, fax 828/253–7667, www.cedarcrestvictorianinn.com

The Cedar Crest Inn, its yellow paint and high-pitched roof exuding warmth and cheer, sits on a hill overlooking Biltmore Village. The Victorian inn has close ties to Vanderbilt's 250-room French château. Built in 1891 by the craftspeople who worked on the famous mansion, Cedar Crest has the same hand-carved mantels, beveled glass, and other fine detailing found in Biltmore. On 4 acres, the inn has lovely gardens that were designed to bloom about 10 months of the year.

Innkeepers Jack and Barbara McEwan, former residents of Racine, Wisconsin, looked for a year and a half before finding Cedar Crest, which in 1930 had been converted into a tourist house. The McEwans restored it in 1984, removing 13 layers of wallpaper and adding several bathrooms. Barbara did the decorating herself, using family heirlooms, antiques, and pieces found at estate sales; Jack drew upon the management skills he had learned as a hotelier.

Dark, rich paneling and wide, ornate window frames are set off with white lace curtains in the common rooms downstairs. Each of the guest rooms has its own Victorian character, accomplished with lace and silk fabrics, soft colors, and wallpapers. The Queen Anne Room, which has shirred fabric on the ceiling, is a favorite; another is the Garden Room, with a brass bed, mosquito netting, and white linen bedding. Honeymooners and anniversary couples love the guest cottage, a 1915 bungalow furnished with Mission-style furniture in the Arts and

Crafts style. The Celebration Suite has a large bedroom, sitting room, and whirlpool. Four of the bedrooms have a gas fireplace.

Visitors enjoy gathering around the fire in the parlor; in the formal dining room, where the McEwans serve a buffet breakfast; or in the study, which has a coffee table made by Spanish ironsmiths. Depending on the season, iced tea, lemonade, pressed cider, hot chocolate, or wassail is served in the parlor or library. When the weather is warm, guests often team up for croquet; otherwise, indoor activities include reading and playing cards and board games. In addition to visiting the Biltmore estate, guests can explore the sights and shops in the village, including All Souls' Episcopal Church, which George Vanderbilt had built in 1896 for his daughter's wedding. ♙ *8 double rooms with baths, 1 suite, 1 cottage with 2 suites and a common kitchen. Air-conditioning, cable TV in study and suites, phone in rooms. $120–$210; full breakfast. AE, D, DC, MC, V. No smoking, 2-night minimum weekends and holidays.*

GREYSTONE INN ✍

Greystone La., Lake Toxaway 28747, tel. 828/966–4700 or 800/824–5766, fax 828/862–5689, www.greystoneinn.com

In the early 1900s, wealthy folks arrived in their private railcars to vacation at secluded Lake Toxaway. Modern travelers head for the Greystone Inn, a Swiss-style mansion on the National Register of Historic Places that's at the edge of the lake. Built in 1915, the house was converted to an inn in 1985 by Tim Lovelace, a retired financial consultant, who later added Hillmont, a 12-room annex.

Guests can choose between staying in the historic house, which has casement windows, glass doorknobs, and antique beds, and enjoying the modern luxury of the Hillmont Annex, whose rooms contain fireplaces with gas logs, king-size beds, and private balconies overlooking the lake. These contemporary rooms are quite spacious. There are wing-back chairs by the fireplace and leather chairs by the window, and the huge bathrooms have large whirlpool baths and separate, free-standing glass showers. The Presidential Suite, the former library, is the most impressive of the mansion rooms, highlighted by soaring 25-ft ceilings, built-in oak bookcases, a huge floor-to-ceiling stone fireplace, and a bay window overlooking the lake. The Firestone Room, formerly the kitchen, still has a wood-burning stove, a stone fireplace, and exposed beams.

In the dining facility, a separate building that seats 80 and is open only to guests, vast windows frame the mountains and the lake. Chef Chris McDonald serves southern cuisine with a modern twist, such as trout Pontchartrain and delicate baby-corn fritters. The six-course gourmet dinner and lavish breakfast are included in the room rates.

Greystone guests can play tennis and golf at the adjoining Lake Toxaway Country Club and go swimming, waterskiing, windsurfing, sailing, and canoeing on the lake from the inn's private dock. Many guests enjoy hiking. There's Mills Creek Falls or Deep Ford Falls, ideal for a picnic, and an excellent trail runs along the Toxaway River. Rainy days are devoted to playing bridge and reading or pampering oneself at the spa.

After tea, a social highlight of the day, Tim conducts animated lake tours on the *Mountain Lily II*. Everyone gathers in the library lounge for hors d'oeuvres and cocktails before dinner. ♙ *30 double rooms, 3 suites. Air-conditioning, ceiling fan, cable TV/VCR, and phone in rooms, whirlpool baths in suites, turndown service, morning newspaper; airport transportation available. $265–$525; MAP. MC, V. 2-night minimum weekends, open weekends only Jan.–Mar.*

INN AT TAYLOR HOUSE 🦚

Rte. 194 (Box 713), Valle Crucis 28691, tel. 828/963–5581, fax 828/963–5818,
www.highsouth.com/taylorhouse

In a green mountain valley dotted with grazing Charolais cattle and Christmas trees, this inn, built in 1911 and looking as fresh as the daisies, is still an attention-grabber. Passing motorists stop to ask if there is a vacancy at the white house with wraparound porches. Guests are also captivated by the chickens and pot-bellied pigs kept in a little Swiss barn on the grounds.

Chip Schwab, who used to own the Truffles Cooking School in Atlanta, runs the inn, and her sour cream pancakes—frequently one component of the two-course breakfast—are legendary. Schwab opened the inn in 1987; filled it with unusual antiques, such as the 120-year-old music box in the parlor; and turned the old springhouse into a gift shop.

Guests are offered afternoon tea, sleep under duvets in guest rooms that have fine art and antiques, and cuddle in terry-cloth robes tucked into each closet. Valle Crucis has one of the hottest attractions around—the Mast General Store, more than 100 years old and still going strong. △ *7 double rooms with baths, 3 suites. Air-conditioning on 3rd floor, ceiling fans in rooms, day spa with massage therapist. $135–$295; full breakfast. MC, V. No smoking, 2-night minimum weekends, children by prior arrangement.*

LODGE ON LAKE LURE 🦚

Charlotte Dr. (Rte. 1, Box 519), Lake Lure 28746, tel. 828/625–2789 or 800/733–2785,
www.lodgeonlakelure.com

This lakeside mountain lodge is the kind they don't build anymore: A massive millstone fireplace separates the library and great room, all of which is paneled in rare wormy chestnut. The lodge was built in the '30s, long before the chestnut blight that wiped out every tree in North America. In those days, the North Carolina highway patrol came here for R&R. Today, anyone can enjoy its rustic elegance. Texans Robin and Jack Stanier jumped at purchasing the property when they were scouting for inns in 1989; he had worked in the steel industry, she in oil.

National Geographic called Lake Lure one of the 10 most beautiful artificial lakes in the world. From the breakfast room guests have a spectacular view of the lake, from which mountains appear to rise. Robin's breakfast is served to the strains of recorded dulcimer music.

The Staniers provide books and games, but the biggest attraction is the lake itself. Guests can sunbathe on the private deck or take a boat, canoe, or sea cycle (a kind of high-tech paddleboat) from the dock below. The hosts take anyone who's game for a lake cruise just before sunset, and then it's back to the veranda for refreshments. Guest rooms overlook the lake or Robin's well-tended gardens. Quilts cover the four-poster, canopy, and iron beds. Four rooms have soaking tubs. Antiques and items from their travels—such as a Malaysian temple gong—add interest in the library, where you can watch TV or read a magazine. An addition contains a spacious two-bedroom suite. △ *12 double rooms with baths, 2 suites. Air-conditioning, ceiling fans in rooms, cable TV in library; boats, canoes, and sea cycles. $99–$200; full breakfast. AE, D, MC, V. No smoking, 2-night minimum weekends, 2- or 3-night minimum holidays.*

MAPLE LODGE BED & BREAKFAST ☙

152 Sunset Dr. (Box 1236), Blowing Rock 28605, tel. 828/295–3331,
fax 828/295–9986, www.maplelodge.net

Marilyn and David Bateman often visited the Maple Lodge Bed & Breakfast when vacationing from their own B&B in Annapolis. As luck would have it, the owner of Maple Lodge was ready to sell when the Batemans relocated to Blowing Rock in 1993.

The two-story Colonial-style inn was built in 1946. Today, with its white picket fence, Williamsburg gold exterior, and red shutters, it's a neighborhood stand-out. Pine paneling covers the walls of the foyer and twin parlors, and there are pine ceilings and woodwork throughout. The Bridal Wreath suite has eggshell-blue wallpaper and a four-poster rice bed draped with a hand-tied canopy. A few rooms are small, but most are big enough to hold comfortably a queen-size bed, antique dresser, small table with a decanter of cream sherry, and chair.

Breakfast is served in a large enclosed patio with a flagstone floor overlooking the wildflower garden. The granola and muesli cereals are homemade. Just off Main Street, it's convenient to the shops and restaurants of the quaint downtown. ♨ *10 double rooms with baths, 1 suite. Ceiling fans in rooms, cable TV in 4 rooms, and jacks for phones or modems in 2 rooms. $98–$150; full breakfast. AE, D, DC, MC, V. No smoking, 2-night minimum some weekends, no children under 12, closed Jan.–Feb.*

MAST FARM INN ☙

2543 Broadstone Rd., Valle Crucis 28691, tel. 828/963–5857 or 888/963–5857,
fax 828/963–6404, www.mastfarminn.com

There are many places in picturebook-perfect Watauga Valley that feel as though they've been frozen in time. The rambling green-and-white Mast Farm Inn, for all of its modern touches, is one of those places. You can't duplicate in newly built structures the sound feet make when hitting aged wide-plank floors, nor can you re-create the look of wooden walls mellowed to an amber sheen over the course of a century. Wanda Hinshaw and Kay Hinshaw Philipp understand peoples' desire for beauty, tradition, and nature, and that is what helps make them such ideal high-country hosts.

In the late 1700s, Joseph Mast, a German immigrant, traded his rifle, dog, and a pair of leggings for 1,000 acres of Watauga River valley land. As the family grew, so did the homestead, which has had its ups and downs since becoming an inn around the turn of the century. In 1996, Wanda, living in Texas with her husband, Lyle Schoenfeldt, a professor, and their daughter, had the opportunity to fulfill two dreams: return to her home state and buy an inn. She and her family moved to the village of Valle Crucis. Her sister Kay, who with her family had made Watauga County home for many years, agreed to help as keeper of the inn, which is listed on the National Register of Historic Places. The arrangement is similar to that struck by sisters Josie and Leona Mast, celebrated weavers, who in addition to caring for guests used the original log cabin as a loom house to make, among other things, linens for the White House of President Woodrow Wilson.

The loom house is now a suite with a wood-burning original fireplace, kitchen, and private porch. While each of the rooms and outbuildings contains turn-of-the-century antiques, quilts, and cozy comforters, and many have big-enough-for-two claw-foot tubs and fireplaces with gas logs, there are new linens, upholstery, showers, and even some mood lighting. The atticlike third floor has central air-conditioning for those few hot days in summer. One of the biggest changes has been with the restaurant, which is now open to the public. While a dinner may include artichoke and Parmesan-filled ravioli, breakfast for guests is chef's choice of three-grain pancakes, omelets, or French toast, and fresh fruit. Well before the first meal, however, freshly brewed coffee is delivered to your door, and prior to dinner there's wine and cheese. △ *9 rooms with baths, 4 cottages. Air-conditioning, ceiling fans in rooms. $96–$135; full breakfast. AE, MC, V. No smoking.*

RICHMOND HILL INN 🕊

87 Richmond Hill Dr., Asheville 28806, tel. 828/252–7313 or 800/545–9238, fax 828/252–8726, www.richmondhillinn.com

As a young man, Thomas Wolfe used to look up at the Richmond Hill mansion and wonder what kind of people lived in such a glorious place. Years later he would meet members of the Pearson family and write that they were as grand as the house itself. The Queen Anne–style mansion was built in 1889 as the home of Richmond Pearson, a diplomat and statesman, and his wife, Gabrielle. It had long since fallen into disrepair when Jake and Marge Michel of Greensboro bought the home in 1987 and invested $3 million to restore it. The Richmond Hill Inn opened in 1989, and the Michels' daughter, Susan, is now the innkeeper.

The Michels retained not only the elegant architecture but also the gracious ways of the past, from valet service at the carriage entrance to afternoon games of croquet on the manicured lawn. Afternoon tea is served in the sweeping oak-paneled entry hall, where leather and tapestry-print Victorian chairs are grouped around the fireplace under the benevolent gaze of Gabrielle herself. The restored portrait is one of many Pearson family items that the Michels have recovered. Guests can relax on the porches or in a cozy oak-paneled library.

The 12 guest rooms in the mansion are named for historic figures of the era and North Carolina writers with Asheville ties and are furnished in antiques, such as canopy beds and claw-foot tubs. The most popular is the romantic Gabrielle Pearson Room, an eight-sided room that has lace curtains and a canopy bed draped in peach-colored fabric. The Chief Justice Suite has a whirlpool bath, wet bar, and fireplace with gas logs. In a more contemporary style, the nine rooms in the Croquet Cottages also have fireplaces with gas logs as well as pencil-post beds and private porches with rocking chairs. An addition includes 15 Garden Rooms, the most spacious rooms at the inn.

Gabrielle's, inside the mansion and one of Asheville's best restaurants, serves new American cuisine with southern regional influences. Breakfast, featuring fresh fruit crepes and exotic omelets, is served near the gardens. And just to make sure you really feel pampered, the turndown service includes chocolates and a gift to take home. △ *27 rooms with baths, 9 cottages. Air-conditioning, cable TV and phone in rooms. $135–$375; full breakfast. AE, MC, V. No smoking, 2-night minimum weekends, closed 2 wks in Jan.*

WAVERLY INN 🕊

783 N. Main St., Hendersonville 28792, tel. 828/693–9193 or 800/537–8195, fax 828/692–1010, www.waverlyinn.com

Hendersonville's oldest inn, which celebrated its centennial in 1998, is on the National Register of Historic Places. The present owners, John and Diane Sheiry, have breathed new life into the old place, putting into practice all the skills and knowledge they acquired in the Atlanta hotel industry and offering murder-mystery weekends, wine tastings, and romance packages.

The three-story inn with a wraparound porch and upper balcony is on a small lot overlooking busy North Main Street, within walking distance of a variety of shops and restaurants. Waverly print wallpaper and curtains complement the antiques and other family treasures. Guest rooms are named for native plants and flowers. Some have four-poster canopy and brass beds as well as bathrooms with claw-foot tubs and pedestal sinks. There's a communal parlor on each floor and plenty of front-porch rockers. John's cooked-to-order breakfasts get rave reviews; complimentary refreshments, including Diane's Tollhouse cookies, are available around the clock. 🔔 *13 double rooms with baths, 1 suite. Air-conditioning, ceiling fans in most rooms, cable TV in parlors, TV and phone in all rooms. $89–$195; full breakfast. AE, D, MC, V. No smoking, 2-night minimum holidays, 3-night minimum for special events.*

South Carolina

South Carolina

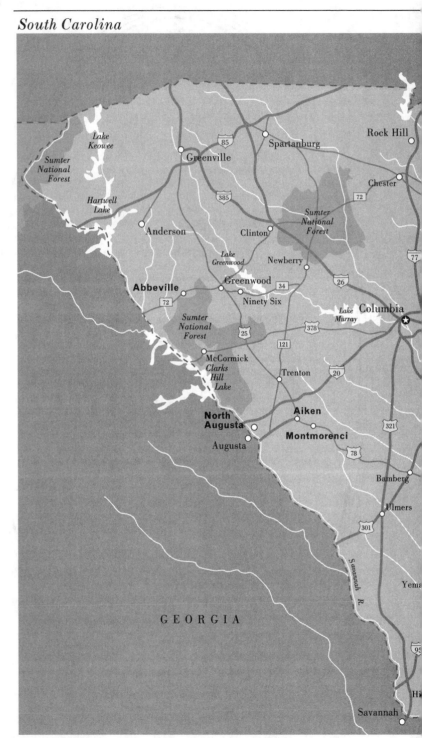

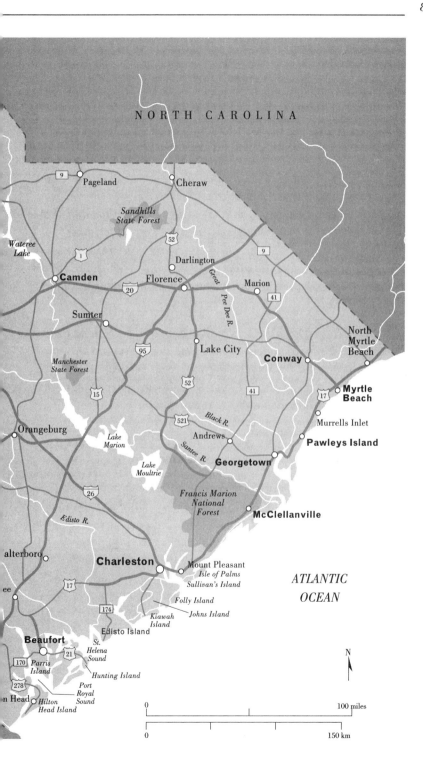

MYRTLE BEACH AND
THE GRAND STRAND

The extended necklace that is the Grand Strand begins at Little River on the North Carolina border and reaches about 60 mi south to Georgetown, a Colonial settlement of the 1500s halfway between Charleston and Myrtle Beach that entices visitors with its oak-lined avenues, waterfront shops, and 18th-century homes. The jewels dotting the Strand from end to end— glitzy, neon, and natural at the same time—are the oceanside condos and hotels, golf courses, tennis courts, water parks, amusement centers, shops, and restaurants.

Myrtle Beach, the largest town on the Strand, is comparable to Miami Beach in the '50s. It has high-rise hotels, nightclubs, upscale restaurants, and bumper-to-bumper traffic. No longer is the tide of tourism tied to the golden days between Memorial Day and Labor Day; it is a year-round flood. Though the region still draws many visitors from the Carolinas, it has become a mecca for Canadians and Midwesterners, who think nothing of a little nippy weather in November. The beach is the area's biggest attraction, with miles and miles of sugar-white sand.

The Grand Strand, also famous for golf courses (more than 90) and tennis courts (about 200), has the distinction of being the "Miniature Golf Capital of the World," with at least 50 courses, each new one more outrageous than the last. The Strand is also a great place for fishing, particularly in fall, and anglers vie for cash prizes in contests like the Arthur Smith King Mackerel Tournament, one of the world's largest. Shoppers flock to beachwear-souvenir shops, outlet centers like Waccamaw Pottery, and Barefoot Landing, an enormous shopping center built over marshland and water in North Myrtle Beach. Broadway at the Beach, a shopping, dining, and nightlife complex, has a pyramid-shape Hard Rock Cafe and an IMAX movie theater, which shows giant films on a six-story-tall screen.

PLACES TO GO, SIGHTS TO SEE

The **Bellefield Nature Center Museum** (U.S. 17, north of Georgetown, tel. 843/ 546–4623), a field station for botanical and marine research, has aquariums, terrariums, and a saltwater touch tank. It offers weekly tours of its 1,300-acre wildlife refuge and Waccamaw River (part of the Intracoastal Waterway) excursions.

The sleepy, picturesque town of **Conway** (U.S. 501, 20 minutes west of Myrtle Beach) grew up around the Waccamaw River, which is lined with beautiful old homes and churches and a riverwalk, and is the site of Rivertown Jazz Concert in May and Riverfest in July. Streets that hold 39 historic sights and the Horry County Museum (428 Main St., tel. 843/248–1542), which has exhibits on early native tribes and regional wildlife, meander around thick old oaks.

Georgetown has a historic district dating to 1729, where time has stood still; there are more than 60 early buildings and sites. The area was settled by the Spanish in 1526, claimed by the English 200 years later, and by the mid-1800s was the rice-producing capital of America. Today it is famous for ghost-busting tours of old haunts, Gullah-roots tours, and performances at the Strand Theatre on Front Street. On a trolley, carriage, or self-guided tour, you'll see the *Harbor Walk*, a boardwalk lined with shops, galleries, and restaurants; the *Rice Museum* (Front and Screven Sts., tel. 843/546–7423), for the history of rice and indigo production; the 1721 *Prince George Winyah Episcopal Church* (Broad and Highmarket Sts., tel. 843/546–4358); and the *Harold Kaminski House* (1003 Front St., tel. 843/546–7706), a restored seafarers' house (circa 1760).

At **Hampton Plantation State Park** (Off U.S. 17, 15 mi south of Georgetown, tel. 843/546–9361) you can tour the mansion, rice fields, and grounds.

Hopsewee Plantation (Off U.S. 17, 12 mi south of Georgetown, tel. 843/546– 7891), a 1740 rice plantation, has tours year-round.

Mansfield Plantation (Hwy. 701, 4 mi north of Georgetown, tel. 843/546– 6961 or 800/355–3223) offers guided tours by appointment of its 760 acres, including slave village, hand-dug canals, and the original 1812 "big house."

Murrells Inlet. At *Brookgreen Gardens* (U.S. 17, tel. 843/237–4218 or 800/ 849–1931), a sculpture garden and wildlife zoo, more than 500 works by the likes of Augustus Saint-Gaudens, Daniel Chester French, and Frederic Remington are displayed amid formal English landscaping. *Huntington Beach State Park* (U.S. 17, tel. 843/237–4440), south of town, is home to alligators and other wildlife. Besides enjoying camping, fishing, hiking, and beachcombing, you can tour Atalaya, the 30-room Moorish-style mansion.

Myrtle Beach. The *Myrtle Beach Pavilion* (9th Ave. N and Ocean Blvd., tel. 843/448–6456), a cluster of amusements, shops, and restaurants, is the heart of the Grand Strand. It has a pipe organ with figures that move, an antique merrygo-round, and Big Eli, the Ferris wheel. *Ripley's Believe It or Not Museum* (N. Ocean Blvd. at 9th Ave., tel. 843/448–2331) has more than 750 oddities. *Ripley's Aquarium* (9th Ave. N and U.S. 17 N Bypass, tel. 843/916–0888 or 800/734–8888) has an underwater tunnel, touch tanks, and exotic marine creatures.

Pawleys Island, south of Murrells Inlet, originally a summer retreat of wealthy rice planters, is one of the last vestiges of the Strand's old days. Scattered amid marsh and dunes are elegantly shabby cottages and a handful of inns—places where going barefoot is still okay. The 4-mi island, said to be haunted, is famous for its hand-tied hammocks.

RESTAURANTS

On the Strand seafood is king. At the clusters of restaurants in Calabash, just across the North Carolina line, and in Murrells Inlet, where the fishing boats come in, it is served any way you like it, but the most popular is Calabash-style, lightly battered and deep-fried. The **Sea Captain's House** (3002 N. Ocean Blvd., Myrtle Beach, tel. 843/448–8082), in a former bed-and-breakfast on the ocean, has the best fresh seafood on the Grand Strand. **Latif's Cafe & Bar** (503 61st Ave. N, Myrtle Beach, tel. 843/449–1716), a casual eatery, offers soups, light meals, and homemade desserts. At Myrtle Beach's north end, where U.S. 17 divides, is Restaurant Row. Although **Mr. Fish** (919 Broadway, Myrtle Beach, tel. 843/946–6869) is a seafood store, you can also sit down and eat the freshest fish in town; the fish sandwich is unbeatable. At **Collectors Cafe** (7726 N. Kings Hwy., Myrtle Beach, tel. 843/449–9370) the chef serves fresh seafood, pasta, and elegant desserts amid his fun, funky artwork. In Conway, the **Rivertown Bistro** (1111 Third Ave., tel. 843/248–3733) gets creative with southern food. On Pawleys Island, **Frank's** (U.S. 17, tel. 843/237–3030) serves reputedly the best southern dinners on the coast. Locals dine elegantly at **Litchfield Plantation's Carriage House Club** (River Rd., Pawleys Island, tel. 843/237–9322), where after entrées of grouper or steak they retire to the restaurant's book-lined, firelit library for after-dinner drinks. Crab cakes are a must at the **Island Country Store** (Hwy. 17, Pawleys Island, tel. 843/237–8465). At the **Rice Paddy** (819 Front St., Georgetown, tel. 843/546–2021), overlooking the Sampit River, locals settle in at lunchtime for homemade vegetable soup, garden-fresh salads, and sandwiches; dinners feature southern delicacies such as quail with ham cream grits and meaty crab cakes. Also on the waterfront, the **River Room** (801 Front St., tel. 843/527–4110) specializes in crab balls, char-grilled fish, and steaks. **Kudzu Bakery** (120 King St., tel. 843/546–1847) has some of the best desserts in town (including deep-dish pecan pie) as well as fresh bread and deli items.

NIGHTLIFE

Legends in Concert (301 U.S. 17, Surfside Beach, tel. 843/238–7827 or 800/960–7469), **Alabama** (4750 U.S. 17, Barefoot Landing, North Myrtle Beach, tel. 843/272–1111 or 800/342–2262), and the **Carolina Opry** (8901 U.S. 17, Myrtle Beach, tel. 843/449–6779) are live shows in flourishing music halls. **Dolly Parton's Dixie Stampede** (8901-B U.S. 17 Business, Myrtle Beach, tel. 843/497–9700) is a ring-side horse show with a "North-South competition" and four-course "country" dinner. **Studebaker's** (U.S. 17 at 21st Ave. N, tel. 843/448–9747) is the place in Myrtle Beach to shag and listen to beach music. In North Myrtle Beach try **Duck's** (229 Main St., tel. 843/249–3858), **Harold's** (2301 N. Ocean Blvd., tel. 843/249–5601) or the **Spanish Galleon** (100 Main St., tel. 843/249–1047). Shagging contests are popular (shagging is the state dance of South Carolina); each spring and fall thousands attend the Society of Stranders reunion in Myrtle Beach.

SHOPPING

At **Waccamaw Pottery and Outlet Park** (U.S. 501 at the Waterway, tel. 843/236–1100), more than 3 mi of shelves in several buildings are stocked with china, glassware, wicker, brass, pewter, and other items, and about 50 factory outlets sell clothing, furniture, books, jewelry, and more. **Hathaway/Olga Warner** (U.S. 501, tel. 843/236–5717), in the Factory Shops across from Waccamaw, offers menswear by Chaps, Ralph Lauren, Speedo, and Jack Nicklaus, and women's lingerie. **Barefoot Landing in North Myrtle Beach** (4898 S. Kings Hwy., tel. 843/272–8349) is built over marshland and water, with scores of shops and restaurants. **Broadway at the Beach** (U.S. 17 Bypass, tel. 843/444–3200 or 800/819–2282) has 75 shops and restaurants and nightlife venues.

At the gift shop at Brookgreen Gardens in **Murrells Inlet** (*see* Places to Go, Sights to See, *above*), shoppers can find unique gifts, books, and art works. The **Hammock Shops at Pawleys Island** (10880 Ocean Hwy., tel. 843/237–8448) is a complex of two dozen boutiques, gift shops, and restaurants built with old beams, timber, and ballast brick. Outside the Original Hammock Shop, in the Hammock Weavers' Pavilion, craftspeople demonstrate the more than 100-year-old art of weaving the famous cotton-rope Pawleys Island hammocks. In Georgetown, the **Prevost Gallery** (Front St., tel. 843/546–7423) has unique crafts, gifts, pottery, palmetto wood boxes, photos, glass, and jewelry, most made by South Carolina artisans. You can browse through the colorful display garden with more than 600 container-grown daylilies at **Roycraft Daylilies** (942 White Hall Ave., off U.S. 17, 6 mi south of Georgetown, tel. 843/527–1533), which ships award-winning modern hybrids worldwide.

VISITOR INFORMATION

Conway Area Chamber of Commerce (203 Main St., Conway 29526, tel. 843/248–2273). **Georgetown County Chamber of Commerce and Information Center** (102 Broad St., Box 1776, Georgetown 29442, tel. 843/546–8436 or 800/777–7705). **Myrtle Beach Area Chamber of Commerce and Information Center** (1200 Oak St., Box 2115, Myrtle Beach 29578–2115, tel. 843/626–7444 or 800/356–3016). **Pawleys Island Chamber of Commerce** (U.S. 17, Box 569, Pawleys Island 29585, tel. 843/237–1921 or 800/777–7705).

CHESTERFIELD INN ☞

700 N. Ocean Blvd. (Box 218), Myrtle Beach 29578, tel. 843/448–3177 or 800/392–3869, fax 843/626–4736, www.chesterfieldinnmb.com

To stay at the Chesterfield Inn, built more than half a century ago, is to get a sense of Myrtle Beach in the old days. The long, three-story brick building faces the ocean with a wide, rocking-chair-lined veranda where guests catch ocean breezes. In walking distance from the Pavilion and many other attractions and restaurants, the location is unbeatable. The lobby, with a fireplace, has changed little over the years and is a cozy spot for reading, playing board games, and working puzzles. The guest rooms are plain and motelish, with small bathrooms and new but low-quality linens, but that doesn't deter the families who have been coming here for five generations. First-floor rooms have high wood ceilings and ceiling fans; all rooms have the original louvered doors that encouraged breezes before the days of air-conditioning. The motel annex, added in 1970, has six rooms with kitchenettes; all have oceanfront balconies. The inn has been freshly repainted, recarpeted, and reupholstered.

The owners—Barry and Chong O'Leary and son Patrick—are almost always about, greeting guests at meals or overseeing operations. Many guests come just for the meals, served family-style on starched white tablecloths. Throughout your stay the same white-dinner-jacketed waiter will serve you in the paneled dining room overlooking the beach. Breakfast is all-you-care-to-eat and is cooked to order; dinner menus change daily with such choices as prime rib and crab cakes. Guests may bring their own alcoholic beverages. ⚐ *31 double rooms with baths in old section, 26 doubles with baths in new section. Restaurant, air-conditioning, cable TV and phone in rooms; pool, shuffleboard, croquet. $74–$124 (breakfast extra); $112–$150, MAP. AE, D, MC, V. Closed Dec. 13–Feb. 13.*

CYPRESS INN 🕊

16 Elm Street, Conway 29528, tel. 843/248–8199 or 800/575–5307, fax 843/248–0329,
www.bbonline.com/sc/cypress

This new inn in sleepy, old-fashioned Conway, about 20 minutes from Myrtle Beach, is a peaceful, soothing alternative to staying on the busy Strand. Built in 1997, the inn overlooks the Conway Marina on the Waccamaw River. It's clean and fresh, with shiny wood floors and spacious, airy public rooms. Yet resident innkeepers Jim and Carol Ruddick, who moved here from Atlanta, have also taken care to include the architectural details of an old house. The large public room downstairs, separated by a hall into a living room and a music room, has a fireplace and is decorated with the Ruddicks' finds from auction and estate sales. The breakfast room is sunny with many windows; guests help themselves to lemonade, tea, and juice from a small refrigerator. The long porch facing the marina is lined with rocking chairs and ferns; there are plenty of books and magazines about; stairways are hand-painted with birds and flowers of the region; and guest linens are luxurious. The place resounds with comfortable, unstuffy elegance.

Guest rooms are on the second and third floors, and each is different but has the same restful, well-thought-out style of old combined with new. Sinks and TV cabinets have been fashioned out of old armoires and buffets. Nearly all rooms have whirlpool baths and work spaces; three have gas fireplaces. The Carolina Room, decorated in soothing sage greens, has a fireplace, a rice bed, silk drapes, and a "waterfall" shower in the spacious bathroom. The Miss Marples Room, like an elegant old aunt's, with flowery wallpaper and red velvet, is filled with Agatha Christie novels.

You can stroll along the waterfront; borrow the bicycles and ride along streets lined with shady old oaks, historic houses and churches; or walk a few yards to the riverboat *Kingston Lady*, which departs most afternoons for a lazy cruise down the black river. The more adventurous might want to rent their own boat from the marina.

The professionalism of the innkeepers combines the services of a small hotel with the personal attention of a B&B. The Ruddicks provide laundry service for guests, may of whom are business travelers. Breakfast is elaborate, with bacon and cheese puff pie, crab quiche, or Belgian waffles, all with fresh fruit and a basket of homemade breads and muffins. ♠ *12 double rooms with baths. Air-conditioning, phone, cable TV and ceiling fan in rooms; bicycles. $95–$140; full breakfast, afternoon sherry and cookies. AE, D, MC, V. No smoking.*

KING'S INN AT GEORGETOWN 🕊

230 Broad St., Georgetown 29440, tel./fax 843/527–6937 or 800/251–8805,
www.bbonline.com/sc/kingsinn

This inn, in Georgetown's historic district, hardly resembles the simple four-plan Federal built in 1825. Long piazzas were added in the 1840s, elaborate French plaster molding in the 1850s, and entire rooms since. Marilyn and Jerry Burkhardt have transformed what was a dilapidated but stunning Federal home—occupied during the Civil War by a Yankee commandant and later run as a boardinghouse—into a lovely inn with formal Empire furnishings. Energetic Marilyn, who once owned a fabric and dressmaking shop, has searched for the perfect fabrics and furniture. Her handmade drapes and lace curtains bracket many windows; walls are painted in striking hues, such as lavender and lemon yellow; and many rooms are anchored by Empire antiques: credenzas, settees, and crystal tear-drop chandeliers and sconces. Off the dramatically wide staircase on the second floor (where art by local artists is available for purchase), the large bedrooms contain gilt-framed paintings, canopy beds, and Oriental rugs over authentic heart-pine floors. The Blue Room has sapphire-blue walls and accents and a private porch. Only the breakfast room, with latticework walls, a gas fireplace, and a porch overlooking the pool, is informal. Breakfast includes such treats as pineapple-ham quiche and a wine-and-cheese omelet, served with homemade scones and fresh fruit. ♧ *7 double rooms with baths. Phone in rooms, turndown service with robes, TV in lounge; lap pool, bicycles, croquet, Ping-Pong, boccie. $89–$139; full breakfast, afternoon refreshments upon request. AE, MC, V. No smoking.*

LITCHFIELD PLANTATION ☜

River Rd. (Box 290), Pawleys Island 29585, tel. 843/237–4286 or 800/869–1410, fax 843/237–8558, www.litchfieldplantation.com

One of the most photographed plantations in the state, Litchfield offers an authentic inn experience along with resort amenities. Missing are innkeepers; you show up, get your key from the nearby guest center, proceed past gnarled live oaks to this dramatic 1750 Georgian mansion, and let yourself in. The sensation that you've broken into somebody's home fades in about an hour.

Once the region was the rice capital of North America; almost half the nation's rice was produced here in the mid-19th century. The house, built with rice money, sits a couple of miles off Pawleys Island's golden seashore on the interior banks of the Waccamaw River, whose dikes and canals once cross-stitched these fields. Suites are luxurious and quite large, and all have views of the striking landscape. The Ballroom Suite has a fireplace, hot tub, long and stately living room fashioned out of the old ballroom, and compact kitchen. A few yards from the mansion, the new, 6-room Guest House has more of a corporate feel but is elegant and comfortable, with several separate sitting areas, Orient-inspired fabrics and furnishings, a grand piano, a large kitchen, and a porch with brick fireplace. Also tucked away on the property are several condos. Amenities include full use of a beach club on nearby Pawleys Island, tennis courts, a pool, cabana, and the elegant Carriage House Club restaurant a few yards away. ♧ *4 suites in the Plantation House, 5 rooms and 1 suite in the Guest House. Air-conditioning, cable TV and phone in rooms. $185–$220; Continental breakfast. AE, MC, V. No smoking.*

MANSFIELD PLANTATION ☜

U.S. 701 N (Rte. 8, Box 590), Georgetown 29440, tel. 843/546–6961 or 800/355–3223, www.bbonline.com/sc/mansfield/

As you drive up the unpaved road to the 760-acre plantation, past slave quarters and under the requisite canopy of moss-draped live oaks (of which there are 222 on the property), you sense what a plantation must have looked like 200 years ago. The original 1812 "big house," where breakfast is served, is actually rather small but still imposing, with fine Federal detailing and a tile roof. Professional historians Sally and Jim Cahalan, who inherited this former rice plantation, have filled the house with their impressive collection of 19th-century furniture, paintings, and books. Guest accommodations are spread among three historic redbrick outbuildings, all with fabulous views overlooking the Black River: the old kitchen, the former schoolhouse, and the 1930s guest house (with especially cozy rooms upstairs). Rooms have hardwood pine floors, detailed molding, and excellent reproduction period antiques. All have coal or wood-burning fireplaces and are decorated with pretty floral Ralph Lauren linens and comfortable stuffed chairs. Except for air-conditioning, the tone is rustic; there are no phones or TVs, and the bathrooms are simple and small, with 1930s fixtures. This is not the Ritz-Carlton passing itself off as a plantation, but it's as close to a real pre–Civil War experience as is possible. Kids and pets can roam freely on the plantation grounds; there's a dock for fishing, boating, and kayaking (rentals nearby). △ *8 double rooms with baths. Air-conditioning in rooms, VCR on request, video library; bicycles. $95; full breakfast, afternoon refreshments on request. No credit cards. No smoking.*

SEA VIEW INN ☞

Myrtle Ave., Pawleys Island 29585, tel. 843/237–4253, fax 843/237–7909

On clean, lye-washed hardwood floors, you can pad barefoot back and forth, coming from the beach or the big, rocking chair–lined porch as the fresh air filters through starched white curtains and the sound of the surf and ease of long, languid days release your stress. This is the seaside as it was meant to be—unadulterated by air-conditioning, neon, and wall-to-wall carpeting. Built in the 1930s and rebuilt in the 1950s after being devastated by Hurricane Hazel, the Sea View is a no-frills, two-story beachside boardinghouse with long porches. There is also a six-room air-conditioned cottage on the marsh.

Page Oberlin, who once ran a large restaurant, took over as innkeeper about 25 years ago. A stay at her "barefoot paradise," though certainly not for everyone, is a special experience. Unless you're attending one of the semiannual painting workshops or wellness retreats, the time is yours—to read, swim, collect shells, walk on the beach, or just do nothing. This is life on Pawleys Island.

In the quiet, casual living room are comfortable sitting areas, a table for game-players, and a fire on cool days. Meals, which are included in the price of the rooms and are served family style in the oceanfront dining room, are the only scheduled events. The menu is diverse: grits, avocado soup, poached salmon, Cobb salad, pecan pie, oyster pie and, on Mexican and Thai nights, enchiladas with green chilies, burritos, fried bananas. Day-trippers and picnic-lovers can opt for boxed lunches.

Each guest room has pickled cypress walls and is simply furnished with a hand-painted dresser, a double bed and a twin covered with handmade bedspreads from Guatemala, and art from the spring workshop. Each room has a half-bath; showers are down the hall (and also outside for ocean swimmers). All the rooms have a view of the ocean or the marsh, and the design of the building guarantees a cross breeze. Your program for getting your life in order won't be disturbed here; the inn has a well-stocked library, the tube is nonexistent, and there's only one phone. Guests help themselves to rafts, chairs, umbrellas, and boogie boards. Sailing, golf, tennis, and arts-and-crafts shops are nearby; meditation and massage are available at the inn. And you can always go ghost hunting among the moss-draped live oaks; you might encounter Alice, searching for her engagement ring in the marshes, or the Gray Man, who warns people about approaching storms. △ *19 doubles and 1 single share 6 showers. Ceiling fan in rooms. $184–$260; AP. No credit cards. 1-wk minimum June–Aug., closed Nov.–Apr.*

SERENDIPITY, AN INN ☞

407 71st Ave. N, Myrtle Beach 29572, tel. 843/449–5268 or 800/762–3229

This Spanish villa–style inn, about 300 yards from the beach, is a dream come true for new owners Kay and Phil Mullins, who took over in 1998 and are originally from Ohio. The pool area is a colorful, relaxing haven dotted with terra-cotta-potted and hanging flowers, a trickling fountain, chess and Ping-Pong tables, and a shuffleboard. The decor, which is full of character, includes wrought-iron birdcages and wooden statuary. Though Serendipity's layout is much like a hotel's, each guest room is tied to a particular period (e.g., the art deco Roaring '20s Room) with an eye for detail. And no, there are no plans to install those irksome contraptions known as telephones.

Guests gravitate to the airy, white-wickered Garden Room, the gathering place for breakfast and conversation. In the morning, you can help yourself to boiled eggs, fresh fruit, and homemade breads and coffee cakes before dashing off to any of the Strand's myriad amusements. ♣ *12 double rooms with baths, 2 suites. Air-conditioning, TV and refrigerator in rooms; pool, outdoor hot tub, Ping-Pong, shuffleboard. $79–$129; Continental breakfast. MC, V. No smoking in breakfast room, 2-night minimum July–Aug. 15.*

1790 HOUSE ☞

630 Highmarket St., Georgetown 29440, tel. 843/546–4821 or 800/890–7432, www.1790house.com

Transplanted Californians Patricia and John Wiley bought this restored house in the historic district in 1992. Built just after the Revolutionary War, it suits those who appreciate the feel of staying with old friends and those seeking privacy. For the latter, the detached cottage has a brick floor and private patio, Oriental rugs, a small refrigerator and dry bar, and a huge bathroom with a hot tub. In the main house, the Rice Planters Room has a canopied rice bed, heavy drapes, wingback chairs, and a cozy window seat. One room has a working fireplace, and several have nonworking ones. Fine artisanry is apparent throughout, from heart-pine floors to hand-carved dentil work and moldings. Furniture is a mix of Victorian and Colonial antiques and reproductions. Boots the cat is the inn's official greeter; now retired, John was a printing executive and Patricia was a legal administrator. They will happily offer ideas for local jaunts or leave you alone. From the open kitchen door, the aroma of apple coffee cake, oven-baked French toast, or afternoon cookies entices. ♣ *4 double rooms, 1 suite, 1 cottage. Air-conditioning, TV in rooms on request; bicycles, Ping-Pong. $85–$135; full breakfast, afternoon refreshments. AE, D, DC, MC, V. No smoking, 2-night minimum holiday weekends.*

CHARLESTON AND
THE LOWCOUNTRY

At first glimpse, historic Charleston and Beaufort (the state's second-oldest town), in South Carolina's storied Lowcountry, appear stopped in time. But make no mistake: Both cities bustle with 20th-century purpose, past and present meshing gently.

Founded in 1670 by eight English lord-proprietors and named for Charles II, Charleston has over the centuries endured the Civil War, fires, earthquakes, and hurricanes. Mariners still use Charleston's church spires to find their way to port. Along the Battery (pronounced Bah-tree in Charlestonese), handsome balconied mansions line the point of a narrow peninsula bounded by the Ashley and Cooper rivers. Here one of the nation's largest historic districts preserves scores of house museums, churches, private houses, and commercial and municipal buildings. During the spring and fall historic-house tours, you can get a glimpse into private homes and gardens, many still belonging to sixth- or seventh-generation descendants of the original owners. In late May and early June, Charleston hosts the international Spoleto Festival USA, founded in 1977 by Gian Carlo Menotti, featuring concerts, dance, theater, and the visual arts.

In this mild climate, you can play golf virtually year-round at public courses like Oak Point, Charleston Municipal, and Shadowmoss, and at some resort courses on a space-available basis, including Wild Dunes and Kiawah Island. Public-beach parks are open from mid-April through most of October; there's surf fishing at most of them and deep-sea fishing charters at Charleston Marina and Wild Dunes.

From Charleston, U.S. 17 winds south through the heart of the Lowcountry, where seaside islands are separated from the mainland by extensive salt marshes and meandering estuaries. Rivers with lyrical Indian names like Edisto, Ashepoo, Combahee, Coosaw, and Coosawatchie flow through the coastal plains and empty into the Atlantic Ocean. Indigo and rice were once the mainstays of this region; then came Sea Island cotton, fol-

lowed by produce crops. Now Beaufort (pronounced Bew-*furt*) and nearby towns are centers of the oyster, shrimp, and crab industry.

Once called *"the wealthiest, most aristocratic, and cultivated town of its size in America,"* Beaufort was established in about 1710. The handsome mansions of wealthy planters and merchants still line its streets, contributing to a 19th-century ambience. Scenes from several well-known movies *(*The Big Chill, Forrest Gump, Prince of Tides, G.I. Jane*) have been shot here. As word has spread, increasing numbers of vacationers have begun to visit serene, sunny Beaufort, and many of them have chosen to settle here, as have personnel from nearby military bases. Each year the city celebrates the Gullah Festival in May and the Water Festival in July.

PLACES TO GO, SIGHTS TO SEE

Beaches. There are public beaches at Beachwalker Park on Kiawah Island, Folly Beach on Folly Island, Sullivan's Island, the Isle of Palms, Edisto Beach, and Hunting Island State Park.

Beaufort Museum (713 Craven St., tel. 843/525–7077). Housed in a 1795 neo-Gothic arsenal, the museum displays prehistoric relics, Indian pottery, Revolutionary War and Civil War artifacts, and regional decorative arts.

Charleston Museum (360 Meeting St., tel. 843/722–2996). The nation's oldest municipal museum (1773), now in a handsome, contemporary $6 million building, features South Carolina decorative arts, along with natural history, archaeology, and ornithology exhibits.

Charleston's formal gardens explode with azaleas, camellias, daffodils, wisteria, and dogwood from late March into April. *Cypress Gardens* (U.S. 52, 24 mi north of Charleston, tel. 843/553–0515) was created as a freshwater reserve for Dean Hall, a 160-acre rice plantation with moss-draped cypress trees. *Magnolia Plantation and Gardens* (Ashley River Rd., 10 mi west of Charleston, tel. 843/571–1266) was acquired in 1676 by the Draytons, whose 10th-generation descendants still occupy it. The manor house depicts plantation life after the Civil War. The landscaped gardens at *Middleton Place* (Ashley River Rd., 14 mi west of Charleston, tel. 843/556–6020) date to 1741, and the manor house has collections of family silver, furniture, paintings, and historic documents. In the plantation stable yards, Lowcountry rural life is depicted through displays of tools, artifacts, and crafts demonstrations.

Charleston's historic houses date from the early 1700s and represent a variety of architectural styles. The *Aiken-Rhett House* (48 Elizabeth St., tel. 843/723–1159), with kitchen, slave quarters and work yard, is one of the most complete examples of African-American urban life of the 1800s; *Drayton Hall* (Ashley River Rd., 9 mi west of Charleston, tel. 843/766–0188), built between 1738 and 1742, is considered the nation's finest example of Georgian Palladian architecture; the *Heyward-Washington House* (87 Church St., tel. 843/722–0354), a 1772 building, has the city's only restored 18th-century kitchen that's open to visitors. The *Joseph Manigault House* (350 Meeting St., tel. 843/723–2926) is the city's first Federal residence. The *Nathaniel Russell House* (51 Meeting St., tel. 843/724–8481) is headquarters of the Historic Charleston Foundation.

Charles Towne Landing State Park (1500 Old Towne Rd., Charleston, tel. 843/852–4200). The idyllic 663-acre site of the original "Charles Towne" settlement has replicas of fortifications, a reconstructed village, beautiful English gardens with bicycle trails and walkways, a large animal park, a hands-on museum about the coastal region, and a replica of a 17th-century trading vessel.

The **Dock Street Theatre** (135 Church St., Charleston, tel. 843/720–3968) combines a reconstructed early Georgian playhouse and the Old Planter's Hotel (circa 1809), built around the ruins of the nation's first theater building.

Fort Sumter National Monument (Charleston Harbor; boat tours from Patriots Point, Mount Pleasant [L.O. Bud Darby Blvd., tel. 843/881–2805] and City Marina [17 Lockwood Blvd., Charleston, tel. 843/722–1691]). Confederate forces captured this massive fort on April 13, 1861, after a 34-hour siege, and its occupation became a symbol of Southern resistance until the end of the Civil War in 1865. The magnificently restored National Park Service site has historic displays, dioramas, and guided tours.

Gibbes Museum of Art (135 Meeting St., Charleston, tel. 843/722–2706). The notable American art collection includes 18th- and 19th-century portraits of Carolinians and more than 400 exquisitely detailed miniature portraits.

Market Hall (188 Meeting St., Charleston, tel. 843/723–1541). Home of a Confederate museum run by the Daughters of the Confederacy, this 1841 building was modeled after the Temple of Nike in Athens. The adjacent Old City Market contains restaurants and shops, along with old-time vegetable and fruit vendors, a bustling flea market, and the Mount Pleasant craftswomen who are so famous for their handmade sweetgrass baskets.

Old Exchange Building/Provost Dungeon (122 E. Bay St., Charleston, tel. 843/727–2165) was originally a customs house that the British used as a prison during the Revolutionary War. Today a tableau of lifelike mannequins recalls this era.

Old Powder Magazine (79 Cumberland St., Charleston, tel. 843/805–6730), built in 1713 and used during the Revolutionary War, is now a museum with costumes, armor, and other artifacts from 18th-century Charleston. Newly restored, it offers a fascinating audiovisual tour.

Old Point, part of Beaufort's 304-acre historic district, is a National Historic Landmark. Some of its many private antebellum houses are open during the spring and fall house-and-garden tours. Two outstanding ones are the *George Elliott House* (1001 Bay St., tel. 843/524–8450), a Greek Revival mansion of 1840, and the *John Mark Verdier House* (801 Bay St., tel. 843/524–6334), a Federal mansion of 1790, where the Marquis de Lafayette was entertained in 1825.

Patriots Point Naval and Maritime Museum (U.S. 17, Mount Pleasant, tel. 843/884–2727). Board the aircraft carrier *Yorktown,* the World War II submarine *Clamagore,* the cutter *Ingham,* and the destroyer *Laffey.*

The **War Memorial Building Museum** (Parris Island U.S. Marine Corps Recruit Depot, tel. 843/525–2951) has collections of vintage uniforms, photographs, and weapons. Visitors may watch actual recruit training on guided or self-guided tours.

RESTAURANTS

Charleston is known for its great restaurants. At **Carolina's** (10 Exchange St., tel. 843/724–3800), a local favorite, you might try the Carolina quail with goat cheese and sun-dried tomatoes. **Anson** (12 Anson St., tel. 843/577–0551), just across from the Old City Market, serves old South foods with a contemporary twist in a dining room framed by about a dozen magnificent French windows. For fresh, Mediterranean-inspired fare, eat at **Sermet's Corner** (276 King St., tel. 843/853–7775) surrounded by the chef's artwork. **Slightly North of Broad** (192 E. Bay St., tel. 843/723–3424) is a high-ceiling haunt with some seats looking directly into the exposed kitchen, which serves inventive Lowcountry dishes. Wonderful meals are also had at **Louis's Restaurant & Bar** (200 Meeting St., tel. 843/853–2550), where Louis Osteen prepares a variety of grilled meat and fish fillets with exotic sauces. For fried or baked chicken, okra gumbo, red rice, and macaroni cheese pie, stop at **Alice's Fine Foods** (468–470 King St., tel. 843/853–9366). For great southern food that blends old-style with new, try **Hominy Grill** (207 Rutledge Ave., tel. 843/937–0903). **Gaulart and Maliclet Cafe Restaurant** (98 Broad St., tel. 843/577–9797) is a quick-serve French eatery featuring soups, salads, and sandwiches. The **Wreck** (106 Haddrell St., tel. 843/884–0052), on Shem Creek across the Cooper River in Mount Pleasant, is a no-frills place where you can sample shrimp, crab, and oysters straight off the docks out back.

The **Old Post Office** on Edisto Island (Hwy. 174 at Store Creek, tel. 843/869–2339) is worth the scenic drive—just ask Charlestonians about their creamy grits, roast duck, and pecan chicken with blueberry sauce. The best drink with a view is at the **Library Rooftop at Vendue Inn** (19 Vendue Range, Charleston, tel. 843/577–7970). In Beaufort, the **Beaufort Inn Restaurant** (809 Port Republic St., tel. 843/521–9000) offers dining on the veranda and serves innovative dishes including spinach salad with port-soaked figs and crisp flounder with gazpacho sauce. **11th Street Dockside** (11th St. W, Port Royal, tel. 843/521–7433) is supreme at fried fish and oysters, which come with a view overlooking the docks. The **Shrimp Shack** (Hwy. 21, St. Helena Island, tel. 843/838–2962) is another great place for seafood on the way to or from the beach.

SHOPPING

In Beaufort, **Den of Antiquity** (SC 170 W, tel. 843/521–9990), the area's largest antiques shop, carries a wide assortment of Lowcountry and nautical pieces. On canvas and sculpture as well as on bits of tin roofing, rugs, frames, and furniture, the colorful, whimsical designs of Suzanne and Eric Longo decorate the **Longo Gallery** (407 Carteret St. and 103 Charles St., tel. 843/522–8933 for both). The **Rhett Gallery** (901 Bay St., tel. 843/524–3339) sells Lowcountry art by members of the Rhett family and antique maps and prints, including Audubons. On nearby St. Helena Island, the **Red Piano Too Art Gallery** (853 Sea Island Pkwy., tel. 843/838–2241), in a huge old wooden building, is filled with quirky folk and southern art, beads, and pottery.

In Charleston, **Petterson Antiques** (201 King St., tel. 843/723–5714) offers curious objets d'art, books, furniture, porcelain, and glass. **Livingston & Sons Antiques**, dealers in 18th- and 19th-century English and Continental furniture, clocks, and bric-a-brac, has a large shop west of the Ashley (2137 Savannah Hwy., tel.843/556–6162) and a smaller one on King (163 King St., tel. 843/723–9697). **Birlant & Co.** (191 King St., tel. 843/722–3842) sells fine 18th- and 19th-century English antiques, as well as the famous Charleston Battery bench. **Blink** (62B Queen St., tel. 843/577–5688) has regionally and locally produced paintings, photos, pottery, jewelry, and garden art. **Charleston Crafts** (38 Queen St., tel. 843/723–2938) has a fine selection of pottery, quilts, weavings, sculptures, and jewelry fashioned mostly by local artists. Prints of Elizabeth O'Neill Verner's pastels and etchings are on sale at the **Tradd Street Press** (38 Tradd St., tel. 843/722–4246). The **Marty Whaley Adams Gallery** (120 Meeting St., tel. 843/853–8512) has original vivid watercolors and monotypes, plus prints and posters by this Charleston artist. **Nina Liu and Friends** (24 State St., tel. 843/722–2724) has contemporary art objects including handblown glass, pottery, jewelry, and photographs. Famous for his Lowcountry beach scenes, watercolorist Stephen Jordan displays his best at **Stephen Jordan Gallery** (192 King St., tel. 843/722–8808). The **Virginia Fouché Bolton Art Gallery** (127 Meeting

St., tel. 843/577–9351) sells original paintings and limited-edition lithographs of Charleston and Lowcountry scenes.

Olde Colony Bakery (280 King St., tel. 843/722–2147) has Charleston's famous benne seed wafers and Bubba brand items, including Grit Chips, Y'alsa Salsa, and Charleston hot pepper sauce.

The Market in Charleston is a complex of specialty shops and restaurants, including the three-block **Old City Market** (E. Bay and Market Sts.) and, adjacent to it, the open-air flea market, with crafts, antiques, sweetgrass baskets, and memorabilia. Other such complexes in the historic district are the **Shops at Charleston Place** (130 Market St.) with Gucci, Gap, and Brookstone. **Rainbow Market** (40 N. Market St.) is in two interconnected 150-year-old buildings. King Street has some of Charleston's oldest and finest shops, along with **Saks Fifth Avenue** (211 King St., tel. 843/853–9888). From May until September, the festive farmer' market takes place each Saturday morning in Marion Square.

VISITOR INFORMATION

Beaufort County Chamber of Commerce (1006 Bay St., Box 910, Beaufort 29901, tel. 843/524–3163). The **Charleston Area Convention and Visitors Bureau** (Box 975, Charleston 29402, tel. 843/853–8000 or 800/868–8118).

RESERVATION SERVICES

Historic Charleston B & B (60 Broad St., Charleston 29401, tel. 843/722–6606 or 800/743–3583). **Southern Hospitality B&B Reservations** (110 Amelia Dr., Lexington 29464, tel. 843/356–6238 or 800/374–7422). **RSVP Reservation Service** (9489 Whitefield Ave., Box 49, Savannah, GA 31406, tel. 800/729–7787).

BATTERY CARRIAGE HOUSE INN 🐚
20 South Battery, Charleston 29401, tel. 843/727–3100 or 800/775–5575, fax 843/727–3130, www.charleston-inns.com

Wander down the old carriageway that leads to this B&B, and you might think you've wandered off to Europe. The walkway is bordered by a brick and stucco wall that ends in an English-style garden with rose arbor and fountain. Breakfast is served here or in your room. Rooms are in the carriage house and on the ground floor of the 1843 home (where owners Kat and Drayton Hastie live) that looks out over Charleston's waterfront Battery. A glass-paneled sitting area has a fireplace and board games. Rooms are intimate, each with a private entrance; those on the top floor have high ceilings, several windows, garden views, and steam showers. Dusky florals and warm colors blend with antiques, hand-painted desks, and area rugs on wood floors. The suite is in the old cistern of the main house; though not for everyone, its coved, adobelike ceiling and cavelike coolness create an escape from summer's heat. ⚓ *10 double rooms with baths, 1 suite. Air-conditioning, cable TV, phone and robes in rooms, turndown service, complimentary newspaper. $99–$225; Continental breakfast, evening wine and snacks. AE, D, MC, V. No smoking, 2-night minimum on weekends.*

BEAUFORT INN 🐚
809 Port Republic St., Beaufort 29902, tel. 843/521–9000, fax 843/521–9500

An attorney built this peach-color, dollhouselike Victorian, with its many gables and porches, in 1897. In the 1930s the three-story building, one block from Beaufort's waterfront park, became the Beaufort Inn; it reopened in 1996 after being closed for more than 30 years. For Beaufortonian Debbie Fielden it was a chance to come home; her contractor husband, Rusty, oversaw the extensive remodeling and expansion. Bubbly Debbie and laid-back Rusty (whom famous guest Julia Roberts mistook for the handyman) infuse the inn, which has the feel of a small hotel, with their warmth and hometown friendliness.

A mahogany staircase curls its way up a 50-ft atrium leading to a sunroom and to the guest rooms, named after Lowcountry plantations and decorated with handsome English and French reproductions, tasteful florals and plaids, and overstuffed chairs. All have pine floors; several have fireplaces, private verandas, and four-poster beds; and a few have wet bars and whirlpools. Two additional rooms in a rear carriage house overlook a private garden; there is also a two-bedroom cottage with a kitchen, living room, and two porches. The inn offers unique Lowcountry specialties at its gourmet restaurant. Breakfast is an extra decadent affair here or on the porch, with pecan and peach pancakes, eggs Benedict with crab cakes, or waffles stuffed with dried fruits. ♠ *11 double rooms with baths; 1 cottage. Restaurant, wine bar; air-conditioning, ceiling fan, TV, phone, refrigerator, and honor bar in rooms, small conference room. $125–$195; full breakfast, afternoon tea upon request. AE, D, MC, V. No smoking.*

CRAVEN STREET INN ♟

1103 Craven St., Beaufort 29902, tel. 888/522–0250, tel./fax 843/522–1668, www.virtualcities.com/ons/sc/s/scs7701.htm

Southern Californians Donalee and Ray Dittenhoefer renovated this 1870 double-piazzed home in the historic district in 1997. The fresh paint and clean lines work well with the style of Donalee, who has decorated the inn in contemporary Pottery Barn style, with velvet and pinstripe drapes, olive and neutral tones, wreaths, baskets, black iron beds and curtain rods, Martha Stewart linens, and her own fish paintings. Ray has crafted most of the TV cabinets and some of the other furniture in the rooms.

There are three guest rooms on the top floor of the main house; two of these share a kitchen and all have 10-ft ceilings, pine floors, private entrances, wood-burning fireplaces, and piazzas. The four guest rooms in the renovated 1920s garden house are small but cozy, with pine floors and light colors; two also have separate sitting areas. A one-bedroom cottage out back (with living area, full kitchen, and patio area) has touches of blue and red gingham and plaids and is great for families and those wanting extra privacy.

Breakfast arrives in a basket warm with croissants, homemade blueberry muffins, cinnamon pecan coffeecake, and juice delivered to your room. There are fresh flowers and coffeemakers in each room. ♠ *4 double rooms, 3 suites, 1 cottage. Air-conditioning, ceiling fan, phone, cable TV, refrigerator in room. $95–$175; Continental breakfast. AE, MC, V. No smoking indoors.*

CUTHBERT HOUSE INN ♟

1203 Bay St., Beaufort 29902, tel. 843/521–1315 or 800/327–9275, fax 843/521–1314, www.cuthbert-bb-beaufort.com

From the front rooms of this grand, white, pillared 1790 home, long windows and wide piazzas overlook the bay (across a street) through moss-draped trees. This is how it feels to live in a grand old southern house—amid detailed crown and rope molding, original Federal fireplaces (one scratched with the signatures of Union soldiers), and tasteful antiques, on a section of a street called

General's Row. This is real but comfortable elegance. In the morning, awakening from your high, antique four-poster or rope bed, you might bathe in a cast-iron soaking tub (one room has a shower but no tub), then walk out on one of the nearby balconies to check out the weather. Owners and hosts Sharon and Gary Groves, Florida natives who spent most of their career years in Washington, D.C., live on the first floor; this inn, in Beaufort's historic district, is their way of returning to the South.

The Groves have filled their B&B with 18th- and 19th-century heirlooms as well as their own collection of American Empire and Eastlake Victorian antiques, and Venetian reproductions. Rooms are large (most with 12-ft ceilings), elegant, and livable, with Oriental rugs on pine floors, commanding beds, dreamy linens, quilts, and books.

Late afternoon, there are snacks and Gary's homemade cookies served in the bay-front parlor or on the double-gazebo porch as the sun sets. Breakfast in the lime sherbert–color breakfast room will likely include Gary's homemade scones, fresh juice and fruit, and eggs Benedict. ♙ *7 double rooms, 1 suite. Air-conditioning, cable TV, phone, robes and refrigerator with sodas in rooms; bicycles, croquet, business services. $145–$170; full breakfast, afternoon refreshments. AE, D, MC, V.*

EAST BAY BED & BREAKFAST ❦
301 East Bay St., Charleston 29401, tel. 843/722–4186, fax 843/720–8528

The Adam woodwork and dentil detailing throughout this Federal-style single house are incredible, accenting rooms, walls, doors, windows—even the porch. Built by a wealthy merchant in 1807, the mansion still has its separate kitchen house and slaves quarters, both of which now have two guest rooms upstairs and an open downstairs area including living room, dining room, kitchenette, and private garden.

The house was divided into several apartments when Carolyn Rivers, who is in the publishing business, bought it; she restored it and opened it as a B&B in the mid-'90s. Her bedroom and office are on the second floor; on your way up to a third-floor guest room, you're likely to find her doors slightly ajar. She's decorated and hand-picked most of the furniture in the house. In the bright yellow sitting room and black-and-white dining room, she's mixed antiques and reproductions with contemporary and African touches, including cream linen sofas and zebra prints. Colors and fabrics in guest rooms are cheerful yet refined; artwork is by Charleston artists.

The inn is off a busy street, but the piazza is cocooned by a palmetto-shaded walled garden that overlooks Charleston's port. A Continental breakfast of croissants and fruit is delivered to your room or is available on the porch. ♙ *6 double rooms with baths. Air-conditioning, cable TV, phone. $105–$185; Continental breakfast. MC, V. No smoking.*

1837 BED & BREAKFAST AND TEAROOM ❦
126 Wentworth St., Charleston 29401, tel. 843/723–7166

Though not as fancy as some of the other B&Bs in town, this inn, near the College of Charleston downtown, is long on hospitality: You'll get a sense of what it's really like to live in one of Charleston's beloved homes. The gathering point is the dining room, with its open kitchen partitioned by two massive reproduction sideboards. Guests enjoy an afternoon tea of homemade muffins and lemon curd, chicken salad canapés and benne wafers. Creamy pastels and dark blue floral drapes accent wide-plank floors and lovely fireplaces here and in the parlor.

Restored and operated by artists and teachers Sherri Weaver and Richard Dunn, the home and carriage house have rooms furnished with their artwork, antiques, and reproductions, including romantic canopy beds. Since the inn is off a rather busy street, rooms have window louvers insulated with soundproofing material. All rooms have their own entrance, two have claw-foot tubs, and those in the carriage house have beamed ceilings and brick walls.

A gourmet breakfast of fruit, homemade breads, coffee cakes, and hot entrées such as sausage pie or French toast is served in the dining room or on the porch, under ceiling fans. ♨ *7 double rooms with bath, 1 suite. Air-conditioning, TV, refrigerators in rooms; parking. $109–$135; full breakfast, afternoon tea. AE, MC, V. No smoking.*

FULTON LANE INN 🐚
202 King St., Charleston 29401, tel. 843/720–2600 or 800/720–2688, fax 843/720–2940, www.charminginns.com

The entrance to this brick-and-stucco inn, built in the late 1890s as shops and living quarters by a Confederate blockade runner, is down a small lane just off King Street. It opened as an inn in 1994. Airy and contemporary in feel, Fulton Lane Inn evokes the summer plantation style with its light muslin fabrics, sisal carpeting, and wooden shutters. It has a small but elegant sitting area accessorized in cool, soothing shades; wine and sherry are always available here. All rooms are decorated in soft, cheerful tones, with natural wicker and canopy beds hung with hand-tied netting. A few have cathedral ceilings, and several have fireplaces and whirlpool baths. One suite has five windows overlooking historic King Street, a bath area with whirlpool tub and shutters that open onto the room, and a sitting area. All have one king-size or two queen beds, honor bars, and modern bathrooms. Continental breakfast is delivered to your bedside by your chambermaid. ♨ *22 double rooms with baths, 5 suites. Air-conditioning, cable TV, phone, refrigerator, and honor bar in rooms, turndown service. $165–$285; Continental breakfast. MC, V. No smoking.*

HAYNE HOUSE BED AND BREAKFAST 🐚
30 King St., Charleston 29401, tel. 843/577–2633, fax 843/577–5906, www.haynehouse.com

Stepping off a tranquil street lined with 18th- and 19th- century homes into the peaceful, lemon sorbet–color drawing room of this inn, you'll feel you've come home. In Charleston's prestigious South of Broad neighborhood, one block from the Battery, the Hayne House was built in 1755 by a Revolutionary War hero. Freshly painted and decorated, with a brick courtyard garden shaded by trees, the inn has the quirkiness of an old house but the easy, unintimidating style of Jane and Brian McGreevy, who purchased and reconfigured it in 1997 after moving from Atlanta with their three children. Rooms are dominated by heirlooms from both of their families—mostly Federal antiques. Two of the guest rooms are in the main portion of the house; the other four are in the kitchen house, with its narrow stairway and colonial brickwork. Brian grew up in Charleston and worked with the Historic Charleston Foundation and Drayton Hall. He'll gladly point out the city's hidden charms and favorite restaurants.

Work by Charleston artists, books, family portraits, teacup collections, cotton sheets, gas fireplaces, and warm, bright colors bring rooms alive. Rooms in the kitchen house are truly historic, with leaning walls from the earthquake of 1886. The Plantation Suite has a sleigh bed and other furniture from Brian's family plantation; it also has a small sitting room. The Cypress Suite has a four-poster bed, sitting room with original fireplace, kitchen, whirlpool tub, and a private balcony nestled in the trees.

A breakfast of homemade breads, muffins, fruit, yogurt, and cheese-grits casserole or sausage-and-egg casserole is served in the formal dining room with linens, silver, and crystal. ♠ *4 double rooms with baths, 2 suites. Air-conditioning in rooms, turndown service with sherry, chocolates, robes; bicycles. $120–$295; full breakfast. MC, V.*

JASMINE HOUSE INN 🍃

64 Hasell St., Charleston 29401, tel. 843/577–5900 or 800/845–7639, fax 843/577–0378, www.aesir.com/Indigoinn

The decor in each guest room is different in this double-piazza, Greek Revival (circa 1874) mansion on a quiet residential street off Meeting Street in the historic district. This inn, within walking distance of all the sights, is the smallest of three owned by Frankie Limehouse, who lives on the third floor when she's in town. The adjacent Indigo Inn oversees this B&B, so it offers seclusion but with the benefits of a large hotel. Rooms in the main house are large, with 14-ft ceilings and large Italian marble bathrooms; the two rooms on the second floor open onto a long veranda with cushioned wicker sofas and faux rugs painted on the floor. The Commodore Suite has fantastic original woodwork and an African safari feel, with animal prints and a bamboo armoire. Blue walls and Asian decor in the Canton Suite are cool and inviting. Rooms in the carriage house out back overlook a patio garden area and are more cozy; most are decorated in an English country–Pottery Barn style with pine antiques and reproductions. Guests help themselves to a buffet of fruit, ham biscuits, Danish, and muffins set out on a table in the large foyer each morning. ♠ *10 double rooms with baths. Air-conditioning, cable TV, phone, and ceiling fan in rooms; outdoor whirlpool. $180–$250; Continental breakfast. AE, D, DC, MC, V.*

JOHN RUTLEDGE HOUSE INN 🍃

116 Broad St., Charleston 29401, tel. 843/723–7999 or 800/476–9741, fax 843/720–2615, www.charminginns.com

This commanding Georgian Colonial town house, built in 1763 by prominent statesman and signer of the Constitution John Rutledge, sparkles in the historic Broad Street district. It is one of only 15 houses still remaining that belonged to one of the 55 signers of the Constitution. The attention to 18th- and 19th-century architectural details—original woodwork, plaster moldings, inlaid parquet floors, hand-carved Italian marble fireplaces, 14-ft ceilings—is impressive. The ornate ironwork was added in the 1850s. The most popular rooms are in the main inn, including three 850-square-ft suites, two with whirlpools and one opening onto a balcony. Although decor in the carriage houses (one authentic, the other built recently to match it) resembles that of the main house, the historic ambience is comparatively lacking. A Continental breakfast with choices including biscuits with sherried fruit and grits is delivered to your room or enjoyed outside on the patio; more substantial fare costs extra. Afternoon tea, held in the dramatic second-floor ballroom—where George Washington is said to have met with Rutledge—includes homemade sweets, tea sandwiches, and cheese and crackers. ♨ *16 double rooms with baths, 3 suites. Air-conditioning, cable TV, phone, and refrigerator in rooms, turndown service, concierge. $235–$355; Continental breakfast, afternoon tea. AE, MC, V. Restricted smoking.*

KINGS COURTYARD INN 🐚
198 King St., Charleston 29401, tel. 843/723–7000 or 800/845–6119, fax 843/720–2608, www.charminginns.com

It is easy to overlook the small doorway that leads into the shady courtyard of this European-style inn, a soothing oasis wedged between the city's best antiques shops and fashionable boutiques on King Street, one of Charleston's oldest shopping thoroughfares. Guests will quickly recognize the ambience, service, and respect for privacy that are characteristic here.

Built in 1853, the two structures that compose this Greek Revival inn have the appearance of being only one because of their exterior stucco, which was added after the great earthquake of 1886. Prior to the Civil War, plantation owners and shipping magnates stayed here when they did business in Charleston. The rooms are furnished with 18th-century reproductions, including French armoires and beds hung with hand-tied fishnet canopies, and decorated in elegant, traditional fabrics, with Oriental rugs accenting the original heart-pine floors. Two have pressed-tin ceilings, 14 have gas-burning fireplaces, and one has a private balcony. Most of the rooms open onto one of the two inner courtyards with fountains; the rest overlook King Street. A large whirlpool bath is the center of a rear garden area.

In a small formal room off the main courtyard, a fire burns in winter—complimentary wine and sherry are always available, as is brandy after dinner. Guests may have breakfast here, in one of the courtyards, the breakfast room, or their bedroom; a full meal is available and costs extra. Breakfast comes with a morning newspaper, and the nightly turndown service includes chocolates. ♨ *37 double rooms with baths, 4 suites. Air-conditioning, cable TV and phone in rooms, VCR available, small meeting room, turndown service with chocolates; outdoor whirlpool bath. $175–$260; Continental breakfast. AE, D, DC, MC, V. Restricted smoking.*

LAUREL HILL PLANTATION 🐚
8913 N. Hwy. 17 (Box 190), McClellanville 29458, tel. 843/887–3708 or 888/887–3708

Down an unpaved, winding road off Highway 17, this inn almost effortlessly replaces the original 1850s plantation home that stood here until Hurricane Hugo demolished it in 1989. Built using the original floor plan of two large rooms on both sides of a wide hall, the home has wide plank pine floors. The outstanding feature, though, is the huge wraparound piazza and heated sunporch with magnificently unending views of the wildlife-studded creeks, salt marshes, and ocean of Cape Romain Wildlife Refuge. Guests idle the afternoon away here, on the dock, or in the nearby sleepy, shrimping village of McClellanville, which is about 45 minutes from Charleston and 30 minutes from Georgetown.

Jackie and Lee Morrison, who live on the first floor, have a longtime passion for this area; Lee's family has owned this property for generations. A relaxed mix of American primitive and Amish-style antiques, with lots of blue and red plaids and ginghams, decorate the rooms. Folk art and collections of Depression glass and pitchers create a feeling of bygone days. Everywhere are sweet touches like vintage hand mirrors on dressing tables, extra pillows on the beds, piles of handmade quilts, and fresh mint for iced tea. Guest rooms make imaginative use of antique linens as shower curtains, window curtains, and canopies; three have antique queen-size beds and one has two beds of three-quarter size.

Guests help themselves to sodas, tea, beer, and wine. Afternoon refreshments might be homemade cheese dip with tomatoes from Lee's garden; the country breakfast, served on the porch or in the dining room around a big round table, is likely to be whole wheat pancakes with hot fruit compote and sausage, or artichoke strata with homemade breads and jam. ♠ *4 double rooms with baths. Ceiling fan, TV available on request; fishing, horseshoes. $95–$115; full breakfast, evening refreshments. AE, D, DC, MC, V. No smoking indoors.*

MIDDLETON INN ☜
Ashley River Rd., Charleston 29414, tel. 843/556–0500 or 800/543–4774

A stay at Middleton Inn is a juxtaposition of the grand sort. The modern, boxy, many-windowed inn, off scenic Highway 61 and 30 minutes from downtown Charleston, nearly rubs shoulders with the 18th-century Middleton Place Gardens. Inn guests enjoy unlimited access to Middleton Place until dark; walking from your streamlined, Scandinavian-style guest room to roam the landscape at dusk after the gardens have closed is an eerily beautiful experience. During the day, you can explore the stable yards (bustling with sheep, geese, and peacocks) and see blacksmiths and candle dippers at work.

Both the inn and the gardens sit high above the banks of the wide Ashley River. The river and its surroundings teem with wildlife such as alligators, herons, egrets, eagles, and snakes. All rooms have floor-to-ceiling windows with views, birch cabinets, oak floors, and light pine paneling. The inn offers bike tours of the original rice fields, kayak tours of the river, tennis, and a pool. For breakfast, you can take bagels and omelets made-to-order out to the picnic tables overlooking the river. The Restaurant at Middleton Place serves a good southern lunch every day and dinner on Saturday and Sunday. ♠ *52 double rooms with baths. Air-conditioning, TV, phone, and refrigerator in rooms, conference center; pool, bicycles, tennis, croquet, free admission to Middleton Place. $129–$149; full breakfast. AE, D, DC, MC, V. Restricted smoking.*

RHETT HOUSE INN ☜
1009 Craven St., Beaufort 29902, tel. 843/524–9030, fax 843/524–1310, www.innbook.com/rhett.html

This 1820 Greek Revival mansion in Beaufort's historic district was the home of Thomas Rhett, a rich planter, who summered here with his wife, Caroline Barnwell, and their children. The house exemplifies the rich and lavish lifestyle of prosperous southern planters prior to the Civil War—nowhere in the South was wealth flaunted more than in Beaufort. The three-story, square white building has black shutters and double-decker verandas on the second and third floors, supported by 14 fluted Doric columns. It stands on the edge of Craven Street, with a huge live oak dripping with Spanish moss directly in front and gardens to the side and the rear.

The mansion was looking somewhat sad when Steve and Marianne Harrison, executives in New York's garment industry, first spied it on a vacation in 1986. The Harrisons completely renovated the mansion and filled it with their own English and American antiques and art. Though elegant, the inn is warm and friendly with a French country-cottage look; guests feel comfortable in sweaters and tennis shoes, and boaters on the Intracoastal Waterway (only a block away) often drop in. Some rooms have private entrances. Famous guests have included

Barbra Streisand and Nick Nolte (when they were filming *Prince of Tides*), Dennis Quaid, and Demi Moore.

Two rooms have working fireplaces, and the honeymoon suite has a private porch and a whirlpool bath. Amenities in the rooms include fresh flowers and miniature African violets, a CD player (there's a CD library in the sitting room), a full-length mirror, and four pillows.

The inn expanded in 1997, renovating another building across the street (which has been totally regutted and therefore hasn't the historic ambience of the main inn). The seven guest rooms offer the amenities and privacy of a small hotel, each with gas fireplace, whirlpool tub, honor bar, private entrance, and outdoor sitting area.

Guests can eat breakfast in the breakfast room, in the garden, on the porch, or in their room. Picnics can be arranged on request. ♧ *8 double rooms with baths, 1 suite in main house; 7 double rooms with baths in Carriage House. Air-conditioning, ceiling fan, cable TV, phone, and CD player in rooms, turndown service with robes; bicycles. $160–$250; full breakfast, afternoon tea and cookies, evening hors d'oeuvres. AE, MC, V. No smoking.*

TWENTY-SEVEN STATE STREET BED & BREAKFAST ♥
27 State St., Charleston 29401, tel. 843/722–4243

This circa 1800 inn has the advantage of being in the heart of the historic district, in walking distance of the waterfront and most sights, yet on a quiet side street. Guest rooms are in the former main house as well as the original carriage house and slave quarters; a gated brick courtyard garden with wrought iron unites the different buildings and is a relaxing spot where you can listen to the chimes of nearby churches. A room on the third floor has high ceilings, three big windows, a Queen Anne bed, and dainty floral linens. The Carriage House Suite on the courtyard level has brick walls, a four poster rice bed, and a sitting area. All the rooms are furnished with antiques and reproductions, but each is different, so discuss options before you reserve.

Paul Craven, a native, and his wife, Joye, have run the B&B since early 1994 with loving attention to detail: There are fresh flowers, ironed sheets, and fruit, cold drinks, coffee, and tea in all rooms. A first-rate breakfast of fresh muffins and fruits comes with a newspaper. The Cravens are available to guests but also respect privacy. While other local B&Bs may be more prissied up—more grand, more deliberately historic—this place leaves you with a greater sense of everyday life in 19th-century Charleston. ♧ *2 double rooms with baths, 3 suites for long-term visitors. Air-conditioning, ceiling fan, kitchenette, cable TV, and phone in rooms; bicycles. $85–$145; breakfast extra. No credit cards. No smoking.*

TWO MEETING STREET ♥
2 Meeting St., Charleston 29401, tel. 843/723–7322

This Queen Anne Victorian, built in 1892, is one of the most beautiful houses in the city's historic district and is usually included in spring and fall house tours. You know this is a special place the minute you step through the iron gates onto a walk lined with flowers and shrubs. The landscaped gardens are manicured to perfection; the curved verandas, with their arched columns and balustrades, are freshly painted. The sparkle of the beveled glass and the polished brass on the heavy wooden door add to the welcome of the innkeeper's official greeting.

Its location, overlooking the Battery and the harbor, makes it convenient to all of Charleston's pleasures. In 1931, it was turned into an inn, and it eventually passed to Jean and Pete Spell. Together with their daughter, Karen Spell Shaw, the Spells have made the house a showplace, one of the city's most popular lodgings, and raised innkeeping to an art. All three are locals with insider's advice— Pete is a Citadel grad, and Jean is a licensed city guide who will enthusiastically help guests tailor a day of sightseeing around their interests. The Spells' fascination with Charleston and the Lowcountry is evident in the many books around the house.

You enter the foyer, a large open room with richly carved English oak paneling, stained-glass windows, and a heavy stairway over which hangs a huge crystal chandelier. The reception rooms are also paneled, and the house has nine stained-glass windows in all, two of them Tiffanys. The formal parlors, off the foyer, are furnished with Victorian reproduction love seats, 18th-century chairs, family heirlooms, and photos; the formal dining room has a dazzling crystal chandelier and highly polished silver. Guests can enjoy a firelit breakfast here in winter.

Each guest room has its own personality, and all are furnished with antique four-poster or canopy beds and Oriental rugs. The two honeymoon suites have working fireplaces and French doors that open to the outside, creating a feeling of privacy. The rooms on the first and second floors are the most sought after, but those on the third floor are just as appealing except that you must climb the stairs.

The staff members at Two Meeting Street go out of their way to make each stay memorable. Guests can enjoy afternoon tea with homemade cakes, Lowcountry sweets, cheese, and crackers. Breakfast is a treat, too, with fresh fruit salad and oversize "Texas" muffins. △ *9 double rooms with baths. Air-conditioning and TV in rooms. $175–$295; Continental breakfast, afternoon tea. No credit cards. No smoking, 2-night minimum weekends, closed Dec. 24–26.*

WENTWORTH MANSION 🐚
149 Wentworth St., Charleston 29403, tel. 843/853–1886 or 888/466–1886, fax 843/723–8634, www.wentworthmansion.com

It's hard to believe this spectacular four-story brick mansion was once the private home of one family. Built around 1886 by cotton merchant and phosphate manufacturer Francis Silas Rodgers, the house eventually served as headquarters for an insurance company until the early 1990s. Opened as an inn in summer 1998, it's near the College of Charleston, and about five blocks from shops and historic sites.

Amid hand-carved marble fireplaces, dark mahogany woodwork, Tiffany stained-glass windows, and Second Empire antiques (a few original to the house), guests enjoy complimentary afternoon tea, wine tastings, and evening cordials. The parlor has a carved plaster ceiling, marble mantel, and chandelier. Velvet drapes and fabrics in neutral shades of olive and gold accent the spacious guest rooms, each of which has at least one antique, a dramatic king bed, oversize bathroom with whirlpool, and sitting areas; most have gas fireplaces. The Grand Mansion Suite, originally the other half of the home's double parlors, has dramatic pocket doors between its huge sitting room and bedroom, both with a fireplace.

You can take your after-dinner cordial up a spiral staircase that leads to the mansion's cupola for a fantastic view of the city and the harbor. Breakfast is a buffet of fresh fruit, cereal, smoked salmon, bagels, muffins, and yogurt served on the sunporch. There is also a window-lined library, perfect for a quiet afternoon tea, which includes cheese, fruit, canapés, and sweets. Guests have only to stroll behind the inn to the carriage house for an elegant dinner at Circa 1886 Restaurant. ☖ *14 double rooms with baths, 7 suites. Air-conditioning, cable TV and phone in rooms; turndown service with robes; restaurant, lounge, meeting facilities, concierge. $275–$675; Continental breakfast, afternoon tea, evening cordials. AE, D, DC, MC, V. No smoking.*

THOROUGHBRED COUNTRY
AND THE OLD NINETY SIX

The Sandhills region, with its moderate climate, first lured the wealthy to western South Carolina in the 1890s. They settled in and around Aiken, wintering in stately mansions, throwing lavish parties, and spending their time hunting and racing. Many of their palatial vacation "cottages"—often surrounded by walls or hedges—are preserved in Aiken's three Winter Colony historic districts.

Among the top race horses that have been stabled and trained here are Kentucky Derby champion Sea Hero and Summer Squall, a Preakness winner. In late March and early April, people come to Aiken for the Triple Crown: three successive weekends of steeplechasing, Thoroughbred trials, and harness racing. Polo matches are held at Whitney Field on Sunday afternoons from September through November and March through July. On Saturday mornings, guided tours will take you to some of the local stables; at several you can ride and take lessons.

Golf is also popular; most of the year you can play any of two dozen nearby courses. In April, the tour of homes welcomes spring, and in May, the Strawberry Festival celebrates a luscious local product. Aiken's Makin' heralds autumn with arts-and-crafts demonstrations and displays, and then comes the Christmas Crafts Show.

History buffs interested in the Colonial and antebellum eras, the American Revolution, or the Civil War should explore some nearby towns in the Old Ninety Six District, 30 mi or so northwest of Aiken. At Abbeville, the Southern Cause was born and died. In 1860, the first organized secession meeting was held here, and scarcely less than five years later, Confederate president Jefferson Davis convened his last Council of War. The friendly town's historic Abbeville Opera House is a thriving venue for community theater.

In Greenwood, founded by Irish settlers in 1802, Andrew Johnson, the 17th president, ran a tailor shop at Courthouse Square before migrating to eastern Tennessee. In mid-June, the city hosts the South Carolina Festival of Flowers at the Park Seed Company, with home-and-garden tours, live entertainment, and a beauty pageant. Anglers, swimmers, and boaters head for nearby Lake Greenwood's 200-mi shoreline.

Along a Native American trade route near Greenwood is the little community of Ninety Six, located that number of miles from the Cherokee village of Keowee in the Blue Ridge Mountains. Two miles south, at the Ninety Six National Historic Site, South Carolina's first Revolutionary War battle was fought, in 1775. Also commemorated is a more significant engagement in 1781, which pitted General Nathaniel Greene against a force of British Loyalists.

PLACES TO GO, SIGHTS TO SEE

Abbeville County Museum (215 Poplar St., tel. 864/459–4600). Historic memorabilia and a log cabin are housed in an old 1850s jail designed by Robert Mills, architect of the Washington Monument.

Abbeville Opera House (Town Sq., tel. 864/459–2157). Built in 1908, the structure has been restored to its original grandeur, and current productions range from contemporary comedies to Broadway musicals.

The **Aiken County Historical Museum** (433 Newberry St. SW, Aiken, tel. 864/642–2015), in a wing of *Banksia*, an 1860 estate, depicts the area's early history, with rooms furnished to reflect late-18th- and early 19th-century lifestyles, a firearms collection, and Native American artifacts. On the grounds stand an 1890 one-room schoolhouse and an 1808 log cabin thought to be Aiken County's oldest building.

The **Burt-Stark House** (306 N. Main St., Abbeville, tel. 864/459–4297), site of Jefferson Davis's last Council of War, is open for tours Friday and Saturday or by appointment.

George W. Park Seed Co. (Rte. 254, 7 mi north of Greenwood, tel. 864/941–4213 or 800/845–3369). Colorful experimental gardens and greenhouses put on vivid displays in summer. There are guided tours, and you may buy seeds and bulbs in the company's store.

The **Greenwood Museum** (106 Main St., tel. 864/229–7093) has more than 7,000 items in eclectic displays: Native American artifacts, natural history and geology exhibits, and a replica of a turn-of-the-century community.

Hickory Knob State Resort Park (7 mi southwest of McCormick via U.S. 378, tel. 864/391–2450 or 800/491–1764) has a lodge, pool, nature trails, tennis courts, an equestrian center, and an 18-hole championship golf course. There's a lake where you can fish, rent sailboats and motorboats, and go waterskiing.

Hitchcock Woods (Enter from junction of Clark Rd. and Whitney Dr., Berrie Rd., and Dibble Rd.) is a serene and wild 2,000 acres of southern forest with hiking trails and bridal paths in the heart of Aiken.

Hopelands Gardens/Aiken Racing Hall of Fame (Dupree Pl. and Whiskey Rd., tel. 803/642–7630). The gardens have seasonal plantings, summer concerts and plays, and a Touch and Scent Trail lined with plaques in Braille. The hall of fame honors champion Thoroughbreds from Aiken.

Montmorenci Vineyards (U.S. 78, east of Aiken, tel. 803/649–4870) produces more than 10 varieties of wine, including several award winners. Tours of the family-operated winery are available by appointment with two weeks' notice.

The **Ninety Six National Historic Site** (Rte. 248, 2 mi south of Ninety Six, tel. 803/543–4068) has a reconstructed fort, a frontier settlement, and a trading post. National Park Service archaeological digs and historic restorations continue. A visitor center displays relics and has exhibits.

Parsons Mountain Park (Off SC 28, 7 mi south of Abbeville) offers a 24-mi motorcycle trail, 26-mi horse trail, swimming, fishing, and camping on Strom Thurmond Lake.

Sumter National Forest (200 Caroline Sims Rd., Hopkins, tel. 843/776–4396) is a 118,529-acre woodland with wildlife, recreation areas, and hiking and biking trails.

RESTAURANTS

Malia's (120 Laurens St., Aiken, tel. 803/643–3086) serves international "fusion cuisine," including a sandwich with veal, shiitake, baked ham, Brie and Portobello mushrooms, and lamb soup with curry. For the real flavor of Aiken, head to the **Track Kitchen** (420 Mead Ave., tel. 803/641–9628) to overhear the latest horse gossip over a no-frills breakfast or lunch. On mild days, ask for a table on the sunny terrace of the **West Side Bowery** (151 Bee La., Aiken, tel. 803/648–2900), a popular casual spot. Across the street, **Up Your Alley** (222 In the Alley, Aiken, tel. 803/649–2603) offers steaks, seafood, and healthful alternatives. **No. 10 Downing St.** (241 Laurens St., Aiken, tel. 803/642–9062) offers upscale dining in an early 19th-century cottage. Ten minutes from Aiken, in Warrenville, barbecue lovers head to **Bobby's** (1897 Jefferson Davis Hwy., tel. 803/593–5900) for hearty lunch and dinner buffets, plus barbecue and ribs to go. The casual but classy **Village Grille** (114 Trinity St., Abbeville, tel. 864/459–2500) specializes in herb rotisserie chicken, ribs, homemade pastas, and cordial-laced desserts. **Yoder's Dutch Kitchen** (U.S. 72, Abbeville, tel. 864/459–5556) has a daily lunch buffet and an evening smorgasbord and sells homemade pies and Dutch bread. In Camden, **Avanti's** at the Greenleaf Inn (1308 N. Broad St., tel. 803/713–0089) serves wonderful pastas and pork with Italian family-style side dishes, plus a great cannoli.

SHOPPING

Abbeville's town square is lined with attractive gift, antiques, and specialty shops in restored historic buildings dating from the late 1800s. Near McCormick, the **Barn at John De La Howe** (12 mi east of Abbeville, off SC 28 on U.S. 378, tel. 864/391–2131) sells plants and crafts made by the schoolchildren each Saturday. **Aiken,** too, has a historic main street with small boutiques and antique shops.

VISITOR INFORMATION

Greater Abbeville Chamber of Commerce (104 Pickens St., Abbeville 29620, tel. 864/459–4600). **Greater Aiken Chamber of Commerce** (400 Laurens St. NW, Box 892, Aiken 29802, tel. 803/641–1111 or 800/542–4536). **Greenwood County Chamber of Commerce** (Box 980, Greenwood 29648, tel. 864/223–8431). **Ninety Six Chamber of Commerce** (Box 8, Ninety Six 29666, tel. 803/543–2900).

RESERVATION SERVICE

Southern Hospitality B&B Reservations (110 Amelia Dr., Lexington 29464, tel. 803/356–6238 or 800/374–7422).

ANNIE'S INN ✍

U.S. 78 E (Box 300), Montmorenci 29839, tel. 803/649–6836, fax 803/642–6709

You won't be a stranger at this inn long. Before you know it, you'll be sipping coffee by the wood cook stove in the friendly atmosphere of the kitchen, getting acquainted with the other guests (usually businesspeople during the week and couples on weekends).

The oldest B&B in town, this nearly 200-year-old farmhouse in the rural community of Montmorenci, just outside Aiken, stood at one time on a 2,000-acre cotton plantation. The crop is still grown nearby, but only 2 acres of the original tract remain with the house.

There were originally three floors, but the top floor was hit by a cannonball during the Civil War and was thus subsequently removed. The house's most distinguishing features are its big front porch and second-floor balcony. Scottie Rwark, who runs the inn with her husband, Dallas, has combined antiques, handmade quilts, area rugs, and lace. Guests who are staying for a long time usually choose one of the six housekeeping cottages behind the house.

Scottie serves a breakfast of waffles with fresh steamed apples, popovers with locally produced honey, or eggs Benedict in the kitchen or in the dining room (when she has a full house).

On nice days, guests gather at the swimming pool, play croquet, or pitch horseshoes, and Scottie always has plenty of books, magazines, and games on hand for rainy days. ♣ *5 double rooms with baths, 6 cottages. Ceiling fan, TV, phone in rooms. $65–$95; full breakfast. AE, D, DC, MC, V. Restricted smoking.*

BELMONT INN ✍

Court Sq., 104 E. Pickens St., Abbeville 29620, tel. 864/459–9625 or 888/251–2000

This three-story hotel, with its long, arched double veranda, planted on one corner of Court Square, has played a prominent role in the history of the town. Built in 1903 and called the Eureka, in its heyday it was the resort of famous statesmen, lawyers, and judges during court sessions, and of drummers and vaudeville actors. The hotel went through hard times, closed in 1974, reopened in 1984, then closed again in a tattered state. Audrey and Alan Peterson reopened it in 1996 after giving the inn a major sprucing-up.

Since its rebirth, the Belmont has developed quite a following. Its guests like to combine a visit with an evening at the Opera House (theater packages include dinner and tours of the Burt-Stark house), following the example of stars like Jimmy Durante, Fanny Brice, Sarah Bernhardt, and Groucho Marx, who made overnight stops in Abbeville. The town calls itself the "birthplace and deathbed of the Confederacy," and there is a Confederate memorial in the town square.

Guest rooms have high ceilings and are furnished with Victorian reproductions, including four-poster beds and armoires; only rooms facing the town square have a noteworthy view. Though the heart-pine floors are original, the fireplaces are now only decorative. The John C. Calhoun Room opens onto the second-floor balcony that it shares with an adjacent room. The fancy Lafayette Room is accessorized completely in red and gold. The inn's original registration desk is now on the first floor; it and the two parlors upstairs have rich hunting colors and are furnished with Victorian reproductions, some period antiques, and wicker.

Timothy's restaurant, serving regional cuisine, offers dinner and Sunday brunch. Guests help themselves to a Continental buffet breakfast served here and may take it out to the veranda overlooking the square. Light fare is served in the Curtain Call Lounge on the basement level. The meeting rooms, also on this level, were originally used by traveling salesmen to display their merchandise. ♿ *25 double rooms with baths. Air-conditioning, cable TV and phone in rooms; restaurant, lounge, parking. $69–$129; Continental breakfast, afternoon wine and cheese. AE, D, DC, MC, V. Restricted smoking.*

BRODIE RESIDENCE 🐚
422 York St. SE, Aiken 29801, tel. 803/648–1445

Aiken's first B&B, the Brodie Residence is the home of native Aikenites Sissy and Wade Brodie. The minute you see the hand-painted cushions on the veranda of their 1929 New England–style home on a wide, tree-lined avenue, you know you will bask under their careful attention.

The foyer's whitewashed oak floors are painted with gold-leaf diamonds; the dining room (with two large, round tables, suited to the Brodies' favorite pastime, entertaining) and living room are also decorated in posh creams and golds. There is an indoor hot tub, hibiscus-lined pool in the backyard, warmly decorated pastel guest rooms, and family photos and portraits.

The Brodies—Wade is a retired banker, Sissy a corporate events planner—regularly host community and charity functions (their B&B was home to the U.S. women's rowing team during 1996 Olympic training). Antiques are absent but not missed, since Sissy's refined touch is everywhere: Her iced tea comes garnished with fresh mint, and she offers guests a complimentary walking, auto, or bike tour of Aiken. ♿ *2 double rooms share 1 bath. Ceiling fan in rooms, turndown service with chocolates; pool, indoor hot tub, bicycles. $55; Continental breakfast, afternoon refreshments. No credit cards. No smoking.*

GREENLEAF INN 🐚

1308 N. Broad St., Camden 29020, tel. 803/425–1806 or 800/437–5874

Charming Camden, with its horsey history and grand southern Colonial homes, is a bit reminiscent of Aiken. As in Aiken, Camden's fanciest roads are left unpaved for horses. Because General Sherman spared the town, most of its antebellum homes still stand, and the inn, which opened in 1983, is its prize accommodation.

Alice Boykin, whose name is to Camden what Carnegie's name is to Pittsburgh, owns the inn, but you're more likely to be greeted by innkeeper Jack Branham. The B&B includes three buildings on several parklike acres: The Reynolds House (circa 1805) has four rooms; the McLean House (circa 1890) has a small restaurant on the first floor and four rooms on the second; and a guest cottage sleeps four. Rooms are done in classic Victoriana. Many have four-poster beds, wide-plank uneven floors, Oriental rugs, and period wallpapers. They're clean and spacious, and all have modern baths and ceiling fans. You won't find a better value in the region—or a more serene place to rock your cares away. A breakfast of pancakes or French toast, fresh-squeezed orange juice, and fruit salad is brought to your room. ♨ *8 double rooms with baths, 3 suites, 1 cottage. Phone in rooms; free use of nearby health club. $65–$80; full breakfast. AE, D, MC, V. Pets with prior approval.*

ROSEMARY HALL ☙

804 Carolina Ave., North Augusta 29841, tel. 803/278–6222 or 800/531–5578

This gem in North Augusta spares no possible elegance. Parlors have down-stuffed love seats, period antiques, and luxurious drapes; guest rooms have canopy beds, European pillows, antique linens, and rugs custom-made in India, Pakistan, and Romania. About 10 mi from Aiken and 3 mi from downtown Augusta, Georgia, Rosemary Hall is an opulent feast for the senses, with service to match. Completed in 1902, the antebellum-style inn has an L-shape veranda with 50-ft columns, intricate curly-pine paneling and ceilings, and a fireplace in all but one room.

Guests can enjoy smoked salmon, cheese, and crackers in the jewel-toned gentlemen's parlor or the elegant ladies' parlor. The Georgian Suite has a gorgeous rug woven with tassle images, a tassle-draped fireplace, and an enormous bathroom with a claw-foot tub. Other guest rooms have private verandas or whirlpool tubs. Across the street is Lookaway Hall, another magnificent, three-story mansion; both homes were built by the Jackson brothers, who flipped a coin to see who got which property. ♨ *8 double rooms with baths. Air-conditioning, cable TV and phone in rooms, turndown service with robes, concierge. $75–$200; full breakfast, afternoon tea and cookies, evening hors d'oeuvres. AE, D, DC, MC, V. No smoking.*

TOWN & COUNTRY INN ☙

2340 Sizemore Circle, Aiken 29803, tel. 803/642–0270, fax 803/642–1299, www.bbonline.com/sc/towncountry

Marlene and David Jones turned their modest brick home into a B&B in 1996, adding a second floor with five guest rooms. On 5 acres about 4 mi from historic Aiken, the inn is in a restful, green spot where horses graze and pine trees dot the lawn.

There's a pleasant pool area with a kitchen, a five-stall barn, pasture, and round pen. A landscaped back garden has several inviting sitting areas, blueberry bushes, and pear, apple, fig, and pecan trees. Guest rooms have handmade quilts, candles, and an assortment of antiques and auction goodies. Room No. 4 is furnished completely with family antiques. The upstairs common room has a simple sofa and stuffed chairs and plenty of magazines; there's a porch with rockers off the common room.

Downstairs are David's collections from the Philippines, where he lived and worked for a few years, including a carved wooden bar, eelskin coffee table, and stone table. The clientele is a mix of relocating retirees, businesspeople, and riding enthusiasts. Before heading to bed, guests choose several items from a menu including blueberry pancakes, French toast, eggs, grits, and oatmeal. Each evening, Marlene serves coffee and dessert, usually made from something grown in her garden (blackberry cobbler, pear or apple pie). ♨ *5 double rooms with baths. Air-conditioning in rooms; pool. $65–$95; full breakfast, evening coffee and dessert. AE, D, MC, V. No smoking, pets with prior approval.*

VINTAGE INN ☜

1205 N. Main St., Abbeville 29620, tel. 800/890–7312 or 864/459–4784

This two-story Princess Anne home with wraparound veranda is a 15-minute walk from Abbeville's town square. Built in the 1870s, the building was falling apart when Gail and Jim Uldrick began renovating it in 1991. Originally the two Abbeville natives planned to sell the house, but it worked its charms and they now call it home. (Gail later discovered that her great-grandparents had once lived in the house.) Jim and the Uldricks' four sons meticulously refurbished the home, including the scarred pine floors, fireplaces, wide foyer, and double doors. The inn sparkles now: Gail has decorated the three guest rooms upstairs with homey quilts, lace curtains, antique books, and sweet knickknacks. The upstairs sitting area has plenty of magazines and a collection of antique hats for guests to try on. Or they can pop in the kitchen for a chat with Gail at the long, antique pine table in front of the carved fireplace mantle. That Abbeville is a family-centered community is evident here: Gail's mom lives in the carriage house out back, all four sons live nearby, and a portrait of one daughter-in-law holds the place of honor in the pink parlor. ♨ *1 double room with bath, 2 double rooms share 1 bath. Ceiling fans in rooms, refrigerator stocked with drinks in sitting area. $65–$125; full breakfast. AE. No smoking.*

WILLCOX INN ☜

100 Colleton Ave., Aiken 29801, tel./fax 803/649–1377 or tel. 800/368–1047, fax 803/643–0971

Were it not for the white paint on this three-story classic inn, you would hardly notice the building amid the trees and shrubbery in Aiken's historic district. But it's right there with the elaborate estates and horse farms belonging to the winter people, who come from everywhere each year for the riding, racing, and hunting.

Frederick Sugden Willcox, an Englishman, came to Aiken around 1891 with his Swedish wife, Elise, and soon started the inn. The Willcox family managed the inn until 1957; Jim Bargren, who owns several other inns, took over in 1994.

Second Empire and Colonial revival in architectural style, the weatherboard inn has a front porch supported by six Doric columns, over which there is a balcony. The rosewood-paneled lobby has heart-pine floors, a stone fireplace at either end, and a smaller fireplace on the second landing; decorated in leather and hunting-color plaids, it's a grand and handsome room. The Polo Lounge, with dark paneling and leather chairs, is a perfect setting for the horsey set during racing season. The Pheasant Room Restaurant serves lunch, dinner, and Sunday brunch; the duck with raspberry sauce is wonderful. Guest rooms are large, with reproduction antiques, four-poster beds, and floral wallpapers. The Winston Churchill Suite has a separate sitting room, a private entrance, two fireplaces, and a porch. Room 106, on the back side, is cool and quiet; its large bathroom has a claw-foot tub. ♨ *24 double rooms with baths, 6 suites. Air-conditioning, cable TV and phone in rooms, restaurant, lounge, meeting room; free use of nearby health club. $90–$135; Continental breakfast. AE, D, DC, MC, V.*

Georgia

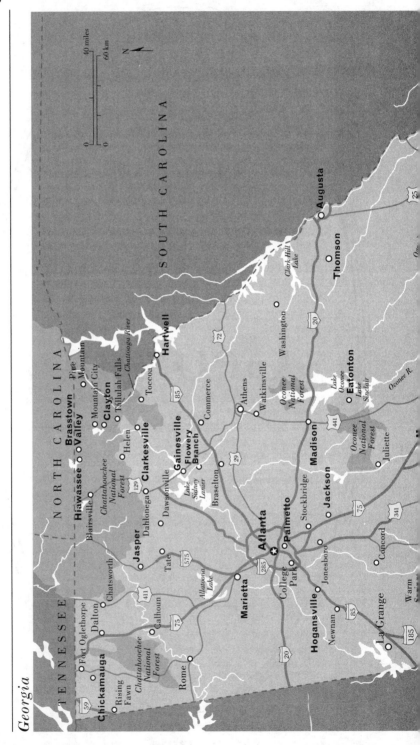

Georgia

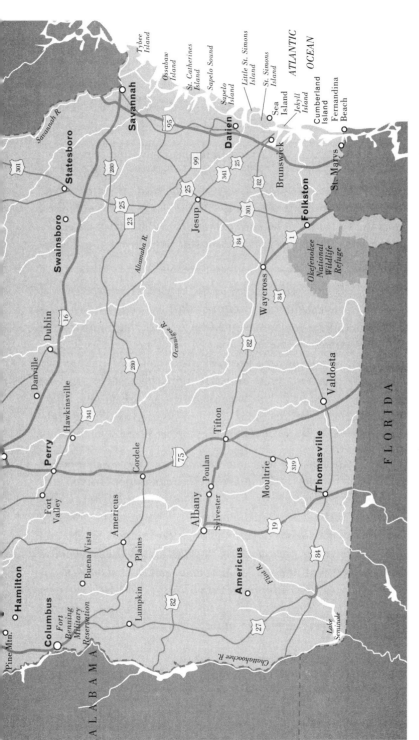

NORTH GEORGIA AND ATLANTA

No other part of Georgia is as diverse in temperament and appearance as the area that encompasses Atlanta and stretches northward. Cosmopolitan Atlanta seems a world away from the rural mountain areas steeped in the lore of the Cherokees and dotted with Civil War battle sites. The region's rich heritage dates back to the early 1800s, when adventurous pioneers moved from the crowded coastal settlements into the untamed upland territories.

Though Atlanta is deservedly known as the City of Trees, development has drastically altered the state capital and its environs. Today steel-and-glass skyscrapers—many designed by John Portman, a Georgia Tech graduate—punctuate the city's downtown and northern perimeters. A lingering presence of the area's earlier history is found only outside these populated centers, where the high-rise silhouettes fade into the distance and are replaced by quaint town squares and lush valleys. Then, almost as suddenly as they appeared, the open green spaces lining highways and side roads give way to the smoky blue peaks of the mountains.

Atlanta, which catapulted into the international spotlight when it hosted the 1996 Olympic Games, is the undisputed boomtown of the Southeast. It has such big-city pleasures as the tony shops and restaurants lining the streets of upscale Buckhead and the quirky art scene found in Little Five Points. It also has a six-block underground mall and a pavilion with an unparalleled collection of Coke memorabilia. Just outside the city at Stone Mountain is the nation's largest Civil War monument, carved into a granite cliff. Driving east from Atlanta brings visitors to the charming town of Athens, site of the state's botanical garden and its largest university as well as the birthplace of alternative music groups like REM. Picture Mayberry meets MTV.

The rural appeal of the country north of Athens is epitomized by the year-round presence of roadside apple-cider, vegetable, and crafts stands along the winding backroads and highways. In Dahlonega, in the uplands northeast of Atlanta, panning for gold is a favorite pastime, as are kayaking and river rafting along the Chattooga River's white-water rapids. Popular resorts rim the shores of pristine Lake Rabun and Lake Burton. Both lakes are reputed among weekend visitors and vacation-home residents to be the "in" spots for the pursuit of fishing, waterskiing, or sipping dockside cocktails. Only 45 minutes from Atlanta's northern suburbs lies Lake Lanier, a 38,000-acre reservoir with 540 mi of shoreline. It attracts boaters, sailors, and anglers and offers camping, day-use parks, and other facilities for fans of water sports.

Annual crafts and cultural festivals, county agricultural fairs, and weekly markets are year-round attractions. The ideal time for a visit to Atlanta is spring, when azaleas and dogwood trees are in full bloom and temperatures are mild. The mountains draw visitors all year long, but especially in summer for their coolness and in autumn for their spectacular red and gold foliage.

PLACES TO GO, SIGHTS TO SEE

Amicalola Falls State Park (Hwy. 52, 16 mi northwest of Dawsonville via Rte. 183, tel. 706/265–8888) is where the state's highest waterfall (729 ft) is found and where the Georgia portion of the Appalachian Trail begins.

Ashley Oaks (144 College St., Jonesboro, tel. 770/478–8986). Built between 1879 and 1880, this Jonesboro mansion remains the town's most elegant residence. It is furnished with period pieces and is open for tours by appointment.

Athens. This small town is the northern gateway to the state's Antebellum Trail. It is also home of the nation's oldest state university, whose buildings date to the early 1800s, and the *Georgia Museum of Art* (PVAC Complex, 90 Carlton St., South Campus, tel. 706/542–4662). The *State Botanical Garden* (2450 S. Milledge Ave., tel. 706/542–1244) is about 1 mi off the Loop 10 bypass that goes around Athens (S. Milledge Ave./Whitehall Rd.–Madison/Watkinsville exit).

Atlanta Botanical Garden (1345 Piedmont Ave., tel. 404/876–5859). Composing 30 acres of Atlanta's Piedmont Park are 15 acres of formal gardens, a 15-acre hardwood forest, a Japanese garden, and a conservatory for unusual and flamboyant tropical and desert plants.

Atlanta Cyclorama (800 Cherokee Ave., tel. 404/658–7625). A panoramic battle painting, more than a century old and 350 ft in circumference, is the focal point of this Civil War museum complex. A guided tour and short film are provided.

Brasstown Bald (In north Georgia southeast of Hiawasee off GA 180). Often referred to as the "top of Georgia," this 4,784-ft peak is the state's highest point. Georgia, Tennessee, and the two Carolinas can be seen from here on a clear day.

Château Élan Winery (100 Tour de France, Braselton, tel. 770/932–0900 or 800/233–9463). Vineyards surround this elegant château, inn, spa, and conference center, offering casual and formal restaurants, an art gallery, and wine tastings. The manicured grounds also include four golf courses, an equestrian center, and tennis courts.

Chattooga River. A first-class white-water river that forms the border between Georgia and South Carolina, the Chattooga annually draws more than 100,000 visitors eager to ride its rapids. For information about river outfitters, contact the U.S. Forest Service's Tallulah Ranger District (tel. 706/782–3320).

Chickamauga National Military Park (U.S. 27, Fort Oglethorpe, tel. 706/866–9241). The historic clash of Union and Confederate troops here in 1863 resulted in 34,000 casualties. Today, visitors can take a 7-mi self-guided tour following the battle's stages and, at the visitor center, see the largest collection of Civil War shoulder arms in the nation. The gift shop has an excellent inventory of appropriate books.

Chief Vann House (Rte. 52A, Chatsworth, tel. 706/695–2598). This handsomely furnished Federal-style house was built by Cherokee chief James Vann in 1805; it's now a showplace of Cherokee culture.

Cloudland Canyon (122 Cloudland Canyon Park Rd., Exit 133 [Resaca–Hwy. 136] off I–75, Rising Fawn, tel. 706/657–4050). This 2,300-acre scenic park, which straddles a deep gorge on the western side of Lookout Mountain, has waterfalls and dramatic land formations.

Dahlonega Courthouse Gold Museum (1 Public Sq., tel. 706/864–2257). The first major American gold rush (1828–29) happened in Georgia, not California. Ore samples, early photographs, and mining tools are displayed in the former Lumpkin County Courthouse. Visitors can pan for gold in nearby old mining properties.

Ft. Mountain Park (181 Ft. Mountain Park Rd., east of Chatsworth, tel. 706/695–2621). Ft. Mountain's origins are unknown, but this 875-ft-long rock wall, built by prehistoric people, is believed to have been a Native American religious site.

Helen (I–85 to I–95 to GA 365, then take Exit 7 [Jesse Jewell Pkwy./GA 129] to Cleveland. GA 75 out of Cleveland, 9 mi to Helen). This mountain town reinvented itself as a Bavarian alpine village and steeps itself in Germanic traditions with an annual Oktoberfest. Souvenir shops filled with European imports, Christmas ornaments, and local crafts line its main streets.

Kennesaw Mountain National Battlefield Park (Old U.S. 41 and Stilesboro Rd., 900 Kennesaw Mountain Dr., tel. 770/427–4686). This 2,900-acre park with 16 mi of hiking trails outside Atlanta commemorates the entire 1864 Atlanta campaign, which included the Battle of Kennesaw Mountain, one of the Civil War's most decisive battles. Casualties at Kennesaw Mountain alone totaled 3,000 Union soldiers and 1,000 Confederates, chiefly at nearby Cheatham Hill.

Lake Burton (12 mi west of Clayton off U.S. 76). The lake is a reservoir that offers 2,775 surface acres and breathtaking scenery along its 62 mi of shoreline.

Lake Hartwell. Covering nearly 60,000 surface acres, and with an average depth of 50–60 ft and 960 mi of shoreline, this artificial lake's thriving populations of largemouth bass, catfish, and crappie make it a fisher's paradise. Exit 59, I–85, at the South Carolina–Georgia state line; the lake lies on both sides of the states' borders.

Lake Lanier (GA 400, Exits 14–17, or I–85 to I–985, Exits 2–3) one of Atlanta's and north Georgia's major attractions, offers sailing, fishing, boating, and other water activities.

Lookout Mountain (On Rte. 2, near Chattanooga, TN). Hang gliders take off from the *Lookout Mountain Flight Park* (7201 Scenic Hwy., Rising Fawn 30738, tel. 706/398–3541), but you can simply stop at the overlooks to get the view of the surrounding mountains and patchwork of farmlands and forest.

Marietta (I–75 to Exit 113 [N. Marietta Pkwy.]; Marietta Welcome Center, 4 Depot St., Marietta 30060, tel. 770/429–1115). Well-preserved homes, churches, a renovated business district, and a national and a Confederate cemetery are some points of interest along this town's extensive walking and driving tour.

Monastery of the Holy Spirit (2625 Hwy. 212, 8 mi southwest of Conyers, tel. 770/483–8705). The grounds of this Trappist monastery are a pastoral spot for picnics and contain a greenhouse where bonsai trees are sold and a retail area with religious articles that also sells baked goods, cheeses, jams, books, videos, and tapes.

New Echota (Rte. 225 NE, 1211 Chatsworth Hwy., Calhoun, tel. 706/624–1321). Restored and reconstructed period buildings represent the history of the Independent Cherokee Nation, which resided here from 1825 until the Cherokees were removed to Oklahoma in 1838.

Panola Mountain State Conservation Park (2600 Rte. 155 SW, Stockbridge, I–20 east to exit 36 [Wesley Chapel Rd.], tel. 770/389–7801), in Rockdale County, has hiking trails, picnic areas, covered shelters, a nature center, and playgrounds.

Stone Mountain Park (16 mi east of Atlanta, U.S. 78, Stone Mountain Fwy., tel. 770/498–5600) is a 3,200-acre recreation and amusement park centered on a massive Civil War relief sculpture. Also here are an antebellum plantation, a paddle-wheel riverboat, restaurants, and recreational sports, including bicycling, hiking, and golfing.

Tallulah Gorge State Park (GA 441, Tallulah Falls, tel. 706/754–7970), the deepest gorge (1,100 ft) east of the Mississippi River, provides some of the best hiking in the Southeast, as well as magnificent fall foliage. The visitor center (338 Jane Hurt Yarn Dr.) has exhibits on the area's natural resources and pioneer past.

Traveler's Rest (Jarrett Manor, U.S. 123, on the Tugaloo River, 6 mi east of Toccoa, tel. 706/886–2256). This two-story plantation-plain frame house, built in two phases in 1815 and 1835, was a stagecoach inn and plantation home; it is furnished with locally crafted antiques, many by Caleb Shaw, originally from Massachusetts.

Underground Atlanta (50 Alabama St., tel. 404/523–2311) comprises six redeveloped city blocks on the site of the old Atlanta railroad terminus. It is filled with shops, restaurants, and entertainment.

World of Coca-Cola Pavilion (55 Martin Luther King Jr. Dr., Atlanta, tel. 404/676–5151). This building's dazzling architecture is nearly as compelling as its collection of memorabilia related to the Atlanta-based soft drink's history.

Zoo Atlanta (800 Cherokee Ave., Grant Park, tel. 404/624–5600) delights both children and grown-ups with its natural environments and exhibits. The Reptile House is a sure winner, with its exhibits of reptiles of all sizes and types. A self-guided path begins with Flamingo Lagoon and continues through Willie B. (a mountain gorilla) and his entourage of ladies. A petting zoo entices the youngest children.

NIGHTLIFE

In Atlanta, blues dominates at **Blind Willie's** (828 N. Highland Ave., tel. 404/873–2583) and **Fat Matt's Rib Shack** (1811 Piedmont Rd., tel. 404/607–1622). The best local groups perform blues and rock at **Fuzzy's Place** (2015 N. Druid Hills Rd., tel. 404/321–6166). Salsa seekers will enjoy **Sanctuary** (28 E. Andrews Dr., tel. 404/262–1377). For jazz with dinner, it's **Dante's Down the Hatch** (80 Peachtree Rd., tel. 404/266–1600 in Buckhead; or Underground Atlanta, Lower Pryor St., tel. 404/577–1800 downtown) or **Cafe 290** (Balconies Shopping Center, 290 Hilderbrand Dr., tel. 404/256–3942). **Carbo's Cafe** (3717 Roswell Rd., Buckhead, tel. 404/231–4433) has Continental cuisine in the dining room and music in the piano bar. For comedy, hit the **Punchline** (tel. 404/252–5233), which showcases major national acts.

Near the square in Marietta, you'll find **Java Blues** (10 Whitlock Ave., tel. 770/419–0095), with its outrageously painted (purple and blue) walls. There's live nightly entertainment—everything including jazz, blues, alternative, and rock. Monday is chess night. Country-and-western music and line dancing are the entertainment at the **Buckboard Country Music Showcase** (2080 Cobb Pkwy., Windy Hill Plaza, Marietta, tel. 770/955–7340) and **Cowboys Concert Hall** (1750 N. Roberts Rd., Kennesaw, tel. 770/426–5006).

RESTAURANTS

To capture the feeling of the Old South while dining on contemporary southern cuisine, find **Anthony's** (3109 Piedmont Rd., tel. 404/262–7379), which is in an antebellum house. The **Colonnade Restaurant** (1879 Cheshire Bridge Rd., tel. 404/874–5642) serves the classics of homestyle southern cooking: fried chicken, catfish, salmon patties, and ham steak. The **Horseradish Grill** (4320 Powers Ferry Rd., tel. 404/255–7277), near Chastain Park in Atlanta, has a witty menu of nouvelle southern cooking, but its fried chicken is perfect and traditional. **South City Kitchen** (1144 Crescent Ave., tel. 404/873–7358) has a definite Lowcountry spirit (she-crab soup and many shrimp dishes) and gives new twists to the standards, with dishes such as fried green tomatoes with goat cheese. For barbecue, try **Fat Matt's Rib Shack** (1811 Piedmont Rd., tel. 404/607–1622) in Atlanta or **Old South** in Marietta (601 Burbank Cir., tel. 770/435–4215). The dining room at the **Glen-Ella Springs Country Inn** (*see below*) focuses on mountain treats, such as fresh trout. In northwest Georgia, the **Woodbridge Inn** (*see below*) in Jasper has a dining room whose food is as good as its view. In Dahlonega, **Renée's Cafe & Wine Bar** (136 N. Chestatee St., tel. 706/864–6829) serves southern cuisine with a Mediterranean accent. In Gainesville, dine on contemporary Continental fare at **Luna's** (Hunt Tower, 200 Main St., tel. 770/531–0848). In Athens, head to **East-West Bistro** (351 E. Broad St., tel. 706/546–9378). Hartwell innkeeper Parke Skelton (*see Skelton House, below*) is chef-owner at **Vickery Parke** (21 Vickery St., tel. 706/376–2006).

VISITOR INFORMATION

Calhoun Welcome Center (300 S. Wall St., Calhoun 30701, tel. 706/625–3200 or 800/887–3811). **Clayton County Convention & Visitors Bureau** (104 N. Main St., Jonesboro 30236, tel. 770/478–4800 or 800/662–7829). **Dahlonega-Lumpkin County Chamber of Commerce** (13 S. Park St., Dahlonega 30533, tel. 706/864–3711 or 800/231–5543). **Fannin County Chamber of Commerce Welcome Center** (399 Appalachian Hwy. [Rte. 515], Blue Ridge 30513, tel. 706/632–5680 or 800/899–6867). **Gainesville–Hall County Convention & Visitors Bureau** (424 Green St., Gainesville 30501, tel. 770/536–5209). **Greater Rome Convention & Visitors Center** (Box 5823, Rome 30162, tel. 706/295–5576 or 800/444–1834). **Habersham County Chamber of Commerce** (668 Clarkesville Hwy., Cornelia 30531, tel. 706/778–4654 or 800/835–2559). **Marietta Welcome Center** (4 Depot St., Marietta 30060, tel. 770/429–1115). **Rabun County Welcome Center** (U.S. 441 N, Clayton 30525, tel. 706/782–5113).

RESERVATION SERVICES

Atlanta Hospitality Bed & Breakfast Reservations (2472 Lauderdale Dr., Atlanta 30345-2231, tel. 770/493–1930 or 800/484–2058 [code 1930]). **Bed & Breakfast Atlanta** (1608 Briarcliff Rd., Suite 5, Atlanta 30306, tel. 404/875–0525 or 800/967–3224, fax 404/875–8198). **R.S.V.P. Grits** (541 Londonberry Rd., Atlanta 30327, tel. 404/843–3933 or 800/823–7787). For a list of 65 inns, contact **Great Inns of Georgia** (tel. 404/843–0471, fax 404/252–8886), a marketing group.

SHOPPING
The discount shopper will want to explore the outstanding **North Georgia Premium Outlets** (GA 400 at Dawson Forest Rd.), about 45 minutes north of I–285. Here, more than 70 stores cover the waterfront from Barney's clothing to designer outlets, music, and even vitamins. Shop for carpeting and other floor finishes in Dalton, where you'll find carpet outlets along I–75. Here, too, is **Dalton Factory Stores** (80 mi north of Atlanta; Exit 136 off I–75), with specialty stores including Jones New York, West Point Pepperell, Mikasa, and more. Two **Tanger Factory Outlet Centers** (Exit 53, Commerce, about 60 mi north of Atlanta, off I–85, tel. 706/335–4537; Exit 68, Hampton/Locust Grove, about 30 mi south of the city, off I–75, tel. 770/957–0238), one off I–85 north of Atlanta and the other off I–75 south of the city, cover everything from kitchen gear to designer fashions. For posh shopping within the city, head to **Phipps Plaza** (3500 Peachtree Rd., tel. 404/262–0992 or 800/810–7700). Across the road is **Lenox Square** (3393 Peachtree Rd., tel. 404/233–6767). Dunwoody's **Perimeter Mall** (4400 Ashford Dunwoody Rd.) added a Nordstrom in 1998.

BEECHWOOD INN ☙
220 Beechwood Dr., Clayton 30525, tel. and fax 706/782–5485

Rustic with a natural-look finished siding, the inn has a fine view of the north Georgia mountains, making it ideal for either a spring or autumn stay. Impatiens fill the flower boxes that ring the wraparound porch, which has inviting rockers and wicker furniture. It is also the location of choice when contemplating a white-water trip on the Chattooga River, as put-in is only a few minutes away toward South Carolina.

Terraced gardens slope down from the front elevation, enhancing the view toward the mountains. The inn sits on Beechwood Hill, and the flower and herb gardens sweep up the hill from the rear of the structure.

In 1987, Marty Lott, an experienced restorationist, and her then husband, Tom, began a painstaking rehabilitation of a historic inn that was completed in 1993. A resident innkeeper, Marty greets her guests in a warmly lit reception room filled with fine antiques and good reproductions of Colonial-period American furniture. Primitive prints in the folk tradition line the walls of the public spaces. Filled with fine antiques and period reproduction paintings, the interior exudes an authentic Colonial-period feeling. Rich, rustic colors trim the woodwork, wainscoting, and shutters, while off-white walls suggest Colonial "buttermilk" walls.

Marty's breakfasts might include French toast, crustless quiches, or egg casseroles, served in the sun parlor. With its expansive wraparound windows, the porch faces east and provides a classic mountain view of pines and Buford hollies.

The five guest rooms, furnished with reproduction period-style furnishings, are all inviting. Toasty quilts warm the beds. All rooms have private porches or balconies; five have woodburning fireplaces; and some have adjacent sitting areas or dressing rooms. ♨ *5 double rooms with baths. Air-conditioning, cable TV in den, fireplaces in rooms. $95–$125; full breakfast. No credit cards. No smoking, closed Nov.–May 1.*

BRASSTOWN VALLEY RESORT ☞

6321 U.S. Hwy. 76, Young Harris 30582, tel. 706/379–9900 or 800/201–3205, fax 706/279–9999, www.brasstownvalley.com

The Blue Ridge Mountains shelter one of Georgia's and the South's most encompassing resorts, Brasstown Valley, a cooperative venture between state and private entities. Opened in 1995, Brasstown Valley is an ecologically sensitive design, with a lodge whose sweeping 72-ft fieldstone fireplace and floor-to-ceiling windows seem perfectly suited to the surrounding lush canopy of hardwoods and pines. Massive chandeliers made from shed deer antlers make the soaring ceilings glow with warm light.

The lodge itself contains 120 generously configured rooms, 33 with working fireplaces. Eight adjacent log cottages each hold four guest rooms and a grand parlor with a woodburning fireplace, kitchenette, and veranda. Color schemes are forest green, burgundy, and navy, and furnishings suggest Early American twig furniture. Decorative elements showcase the work of local artisans, supporting the culture of this mountain environment.

With its Dennis Griffiths–designed par-72 Scottish links golf course and a well-equipped conference center, Brasstown Valley is ideal for business meetings. Mountain South Outfitters, which is on site, is a good place to acquire last-minute fishing and hiking items. They lead white-water rafting, trout fishing, hiking, biking, and lake and river kayaking trips. Nearby Brasstown Bald, the highest point in Georgia, offers a challenging hike to its peak. Reserve a 25-gear mountain bike for the day to explore the terrain, or get serious at the Unicoi World Championship Course, a 6-mi Olympic test for mountain bikers.

Off-site, guests will find plenty of antiques shops, art galleries featuring local crafts, cultural activities (mountain music at Georgia Mountain Fair in nearby Hiawasee and theater at Young Harris College), and natural attractions.

The resort does both bed-and-breakfast packages throughout the week and golf packages (Sunday through Thursday only), with prices varying according to the season. Off-season prices are excellent values. ⚑ *129 rooms with baths, 5 suites. Air-conditioning, cable TV, desk, and phone in rooms, fireplace and kitchenette in cabins, 2 restaurants; conference center. $149–$174; not including breakfast (packages including breakfast are available). AE, D, DC, MC, V. Restricted smoking.*

DUNLAP HOUSE ☞

635 Green St., Gainesville 30501, tel. 770/536–0200 or 800/276–2935, fax 770/503–7857, www.bestinns.net/USA/gadunlap.html

In Gainesville's Green Street Historic District, which is on the National Register, the white frame Dunlap House was built in 1910. Its style is a bit difficult to categorize. A centered dormer recalls Palladian forms; a wide street-front veranda references Victorian architecture; sturdy, somewhat squat columns suggest a Craftsman influence. The white wicker furniture on the veranda, with its twirling ceiling fans, is especially inviting on lazy summer days.

The inn's owners, Toledo natives David and Karen Peters, decided to ditch the corporate world and purchased the Dunlap House in 1997. Accustomed to providing hospitality, they ran a summer charter fishing service on Lake Erie for about a decade. David is a former corporation comptroller, while Karen still works as a systems analyst for a software company.

In their two-room unit, the Peters are joined by seven chirping cockatiels and a black Labrador named Mavrick, who is not allowed to visit guests' rooms.

The Dunlap House is popular with business guests, and with visitors attending events at Road Atlanta and the nearby ½-mi NASCAR Lanier International Speedway. Famous guests have included actors Paul Newman, Dennis Weaver, and Tom Cruise, and the much-loved late TV journalist Charles Kuralt. In addition to the racing facilities nearby, Gainesville enjoys proximity to Lake Lanier; the town is busy with special festivals throughout the year.

Breakfast is fresh fruit, cereals, juices, and breads, and Karen may make muffins or "monkey bread"—which is redolent of cinnamon—and egg casseroles. Scrambled eggs may contain the Peterses' favorite onion-and-pepper cheese. ⚠ *10 rooms with baths. Air-conditioning, cable TV, phone with data-port in rooms. AE, MC, V. $110–$160; full breakfast. No smoking.*

GLEN-ELLA SPRINGS COUNTRY INN & CONFERENCE CENTER 🐚
Bear Gap Rd. (Rte. 3, Box 3304), 8½ mi north of Clarkesville, 30523, tel. 706/754–7295 or 888/455–8891, fax 706/754–7295, www.glenella.com

Just outside of Clarkesville, the Glen-Ella Springs Country Inn, a hideaway more than a century old, was lovingly renovated in 1987 by Barrie and Bobby Aycock. The small hotel, listed on the National Register of Historic Places, sits by a gravel road on 17 acres of meadows and gardens.

At first glance the Glen-Ella, with its heart-pine floors, walls, and ceilings, appears down-home, but its uptown flair soon becomes evident. The front lobby, filled with chintz and antiques, serves as a parlor, and fires are lit here against the cool night air. From welcoming porches furnished with country-style rocking chairs, you enter the guest rooms, where quilts, chintzes, original artwork, painted reproduction antiques, and Oriental and area rugs convey an English country feeling within naturally finished and painted pine-paneled interiors.

The hotel's dining room, which has a fireplace, is the realization of Barrie's original dream: to own her own restaurant. Her kitchen is the source of the sweet baked goods—blueberry-granola pancakes and oat scones—served at breakfast and regional southern cuisine served at dinner. The food here has so enhanced the inn's reputation that it has become a culinary hot spot for Atlantans, who will drive the two hours for the sumptuous meals.

Those not involved in special occurrences such as mystery weekends and herb-gardening conferences may relax by the pool on the large sundeck surrounded by flower gardens. Sports lovers will find excellent hiking at nearby Tallulah Falls. Golf (as well as tennis) is found at the Orchard, a championship course within a few miles of the inn. Kayaking and white-water rafting on the Chattooga River also are popular, and the inn arranges horseback riding.

During the week, the conference center is frequently booked by Fortune 100 companies. ⚠ *14 double rooms with baths, 2 suites with fireplaces and whirlpool tubs. Air-conditioning, phone with voice mail in rooms, satellite TV in lobby; pool, conference center. $100–$180; full breakfast. AE, MC, V. No smoking.*

GORDON-LEE MANSION 🐚
217 Cove Rd., Chickamauga 30707, tel. 706/375–4728 or 800/487–4728, fax 706/375–9499, www.fhc.org/gordon-lee

Built between 1840 and 1947 by James Gordon, an early Scottish settler from Virginia, the Gordon-Lee Mansion has been rightly made a National Historic Site. The Greek Revival–style house survived the ravages of the Battle of Chicamauga that raged on the plantation's land more than a century ago. Renovated in the early 20th century, when it acquired its now-famous classical-style columns, the mansion sits in the middle of 7 acres, containing formal English and vegetable gardens.

During the Battle of Chicamauga, the house was used by the Union Army as a headquarters and hospital. Its last resident was Member of Congress Gordon Lee, a descendent of James Gordon, and his wife, Olive Emily Berry. Lee served this district for 22 years in the early part of this century. His log-house office on the grounds has been refurbished and now offers two guest rooms, two baths, a living room, and a full kitchen. This space, which is reserved for families or groups, has its own kitchen, so rates for guests here do not include breakfast.

One suite attached to the main house contains a kitchen area but lacks the charm of the other spaces. From 1976 until 1989, the house was opened to the public as a museum. A wide driveway lined with elms and maples frames the grand Doric columns on the front veranda as you approach. The remaining brick slave cabin now is used as a dressing room for the many weddings that take place at the inn. The mansion's expansive rooms have 10- and 12-ft ceilings and are furnished with English, American, and French period antiques. The living room, library, and dining room downstairs are furnished in museum-quality antiques as well.

Frank Green, a retired dentist, and his wife, Maria, began the bed-and-breakfast operation in 1989. They live on the grounds nearby, as does the manager, Richard Barclift. ⌂ *6 double rooms with baths. Air-conditioning, cable TV in rooms. $75–$125; Continental breakfast. MC, V. No smoking.*

MOUNTAIN MEMORIES ☙
285 Chancey Dr., Hiawasee 30546, tel. 706/896–8439 or 800/335–8439, www.whc.edu/users/mtnmem

From the expansive windows in the spacious dining room of this mountaintop country inn, there's a spectacular view of the surrounding Appalachian Mountains as the morning mist clears the tops of nearby peaks. Built in 1963, the inn, completely renovated in 1994, clings to a slope near Lake Chatuge. Sandy gray siding and white trim give the exterior a homey look. After breakfast, guests may relax on the wraparound deck or in the gazebo, take a brisk stroll around the lake, or go sailing on its placid waters in the inn's pontoon boat, which cruises in nice weather in the evening.

Or, with accommodations this inviting, guests may wish to return to their rooms to spend time in the generously sized, two-person bedside whirlpool tubs. Mountain Memories Inn is definitely for romance. Three downstairs rooms and three upstairs rooms each have private outside entrances, individually controlled thermostats, and fluffy, feminine decor in soft colors (lavender, pink, and blue).

Should a guest prefer activities off site, there's plenty to do: Climbing to the top of Brasstown Bald pays off at dusk with a spectacular sunset. In summer, visitors attend theater at Young Harris College, where *Reach of Song*, based on the poetry of mountain man of letters Byron Herbert Reece is performed June through August. Antiques and crafts shopping is excellent.

Resident innkeepers Yolanda and David Keating specialize in pampering and offer a complimentary evening dessert buffet in the dining room aglow with candlelight. Breakfast is a huge affair, especially famous for Yolanda's breakfast lasagna (lasagna noodles baked with sausage gravy, sliced hard-boiled eggs, and assorted cheeses), baked eggs with mushrooms and tomato, puffed pancakes, or homemade quiche. ♨ *6 rooms with baths. Air-conditioning, cable TV/VCR, and whirlpool tubs in rooms, 400-film tape library, lounge. $100–$145; full breakfast, complimentary dessert buffet. D, MC, V. No smoking.*

NICHOLSON HOUSE 🐚

6295 Jefferson Rd., Athens 30607, tel. 706/353–2200, fax 706/353–7799, www.bbonline.com/ga/nicholson/

Only about 15 minutes outside Athens, the Nicholson House is perfect for anyone attending functions at the nearby University of Georgia. The early 19th-century, 4,000-square-ft house rests majestically on 6 acres of a land grant originally awarded in 1779 to William Few, one of Georgia's two signers of the Constitution. Deer routinely parade across the front of the property. With its landscaped natural setting, the property is perfect for small weddings.

Originally built by Ransom and Nancy Nichols as a two-over-two log house, the building was given a Colonial revival–style face-lift after 1947, totally concealing the log exterior. The Nicholsons, for whom the inn is named, purchased the property in that year, added a few rooms, and redesigned the appearance of the house. Within, random-width planking and uneven floors and ceilings reveal the original 19th-century structure. A wide front veranda offers restful rocking chairs from which to view the surrounding countryside and take in the sunset.

The bright, warm dining and living rooms are decorated in deep green and burgundy, with a paisley wall covering in adjoining spaces and gleaming white trim that ties the decorative elements together. They are furnished with period reproductions and antiques, and along with the kitchen, they are both available to guests. The six bedrooms in the main house are furnished with period-style reproduction pieces. In addition to those in the main house, there's a nearby hillside cottage and a carriage house. The carriage house has two guest rooms, and romance-seekers enjoy the cottage with its bedroom, living room, and kitchenette. The cottage also has a fine view of the surrounding woods and fields.

The breakfast, which focuses on healthy foods and often includes a fresh fruit entrée, yogurt, juice, fresh muffins, rolls, and croissant, is served in the dining room. Innkeeper-owner Stuart Kelley, a former Eastern Airlines operations executive, lives on the property. ♨ *9 double rooms with baths. Air-conditioning, cable TV, phone in rooms, $75–$95; Continental breakfast. AE, D, MC, V. No smoking.*

SERENBE 🐚

10950 Hutcherson Ferry Rd., Palmetto 30268, tel. 770/463–2610, fax 770/463–4472, www.serenbe.com

Marie and Steve Nygren are not the kind of folks one expects to find in rural Fulton County, a short distance from Atlanta. This urbane, enterprising young couple with a professional history in the hospitality industry and a young family had been searching for a weekend retreat when they found this now almost 300-acre farm. Marie named it Serenbe, combining the words *serenity* and *being*.

Now the family dog, Miz Scarlett, counts as her companions horses, cattle, chickens, rabbits, and pigs. The complex includes a carefully restored farmhouse, a barn and bungalow converted to bed-and-breakfast accommodations, and a painstakingly designed garden. No detail is spared: Classical music wafts over this pastoral setting through a cleverly hidden system of 30 speakers. The Nygrens have added 5,000 square ft to the main house, much of which is a state-of-the-art conference center.

The weathered 1930s-vintage restored barn is a study in adaptive reuse. Beneath its rooms, a sheltered cabana looks out onto the carefully designed swimming pool. A common area, filled with fine art by local and national artists, opens onto a patio. Its fireplace burns on both sides, warming the large common living space and the outside patio. A less dramatic cottage holds two bedrooms and also has its own kitchen; it must be taken as a unit.

The guest rooms are "country comfortable," decorated with quilts on beds, and folk art, family antiques and pieces gathered on travels. Painted white with green-and-red accents, one room, with a painted white headboard and a whirlpool tub, has French doors that lead to a vegetable garden. Another room has a reading nook, primitive American chest, skirted table with lamps, and overstuffed chairs upholstered with big purple-and-white checked fabric. The room's plank wood walls are painted a high gloss white and its three-sided exposure affords plenty of light. Throughout, handwoven rugs in purples and beige brighten honey-color pine floors. The cottage has a brick fireplace in the center of the living room and glassed-in eat-in porch overlooking the lake, and is simply furnished with items such as a primitive American bench and an old cabinet from a Tennessee cabin.

Guests may stroll the expansive pastures; read in the cabana, where a full southern-style breakfast—grits and all—may be served; cool off in the pool; or meander through the geometric garden. Breakfast may also be enjoyed in the family's home, where it is served in a large glassed-in porch. At a nearby facility, guests seeking a more active experience may rent horses on which to explore the farm's trails. ♙ *4 double rooms with baths, 1 cottage; common area with satellite TV/VCR and video library, fireplace, patio; whirlpool bath in 1 room; pool and hot tub, canoeing, hiking, fishing, lake. $115–$150; full breakfast. No credit cards. No smoking.*

SHELLMONT BED & BREAKFAST 🐚
821 Piedmont Ave., Atlanta 30306, tel. 404/872–9290, fax 404/872–5379, www.innbook.com/shell

Atlanta's Midtown, lying between Piedmont Park and Downtown, developed in the late 19th and early 20th centuries. The neighborhood's spacious, ornate Victorian homes exhibit a wealth of period detail. This fine example of Victorian-era classical eclecticism, listed on the National Register of Historic Places and a City of Atlanta Landmark, reflects that taste for detail. It was designed in 1891 by the Massachusetts-born, Atlanta-reared architect Walter T. Downing for Dr. William Perrin Nicholson. The exterior proudly displays classical architectural elements, including heavily carved woodwork, columns with shell-adorned capitals, and finely detailed stained-glass windows. One is particularly dramatic: The magnificent, huge window behind the staircase in the reception space casts a warm light throughout.

The urban pocket garden is filled with Carolina jasmine, azaleas, and hostas. An herb garden supplies fragrant additions to breakfast, especially herbed mint tea. A wrought-iron bench, a reproduction 19th-century Charleston bench, invites contemplative moments.

Owners and resident innkeepers Debbie and Ed McCord established the Shellmont in Nicholson House in 1983. Coming to hospitality from pharmaceutical marketing (Debbie) and real estate development (Ed), the McCords have established a following among business visitors to the city. Desks and phones with dataports have been added to the rooms.

BONUS MILES MAKE
GREAT SOUVENIRS.

Earn Miles With Your MCI Card.

Take the MCI Card along on this trip and start earning miles for the next one. You'll earn frequent flyer miles on all your calls and save with the low rates you've come to expect from MCI. Before you know it, you'll be on your way to some other international destination.

Sign up for MCI by calling
1-800-FLY-FREE

Is this a great time, or what? :-)

Earn Frequent Flyer Miles.

AmericanAirlines'
A'Advantage

▲ Delta Air Lines
SkyMiles

MIDWEST EXPRESS AIRLINES

US AIRWAYS
DIVIDEND MILES

Besides restoring the stained-glass window with painstaking care, the couple has reproduced another Victorian detail: most of the house's original stenciling, above sponge-painted walls. Upstairs bedrooms have reproduction period wallcoverings and lace panels at the windows. The Eastlake Room has an antique bed with an 8-ft-high headboard and matching marble-topped dresser. Curved windows fitted with curved glass in that room are an original architectural feature.

In a green, yellow, and burgundy color scheme, the carriage house has white plantation shutters and an antique reproduction four-poster bed. Recessed lighting warms the spaces and hardwood floors gleam under Oriental rugs. There's a kitchen, a bath with a ceramic tile and marble steam shower/bath, a sleigh bed, two TV/VCRs, and two phones.

Breakfast varies; some favorites are Belgian waffles and frittatas. Always on hand are gourmet coffee, fresh juice, and homemade breads (pumpkin, blueberry, pear and nutmeg, banana), scones, or cinnamon rolls. ♠ *2 double rooms, 2 suites, 1 carriage house. Air-conditioning, TV and phone in rooms, kitchen and 2 TV/VCRs in carriage house. $90–$169; full breakfast, turndown service with gourmet chocolates. AE, DC, MC, V. No smoking.*

SKELTON HOUSE ☞
97 Benson St., Hartwell 30643, tel. 706/376–7969, fax 706/856–3139

Ruth Skelton, resident innkeeper, says she was surprised when a relative bequeathed the old family home to her son, Parke, a chef and restaurateur in Hartwell. One day she asked the man's secretary why he had done that. "Because," the woman answered simply, "he knew Parke wouldn't tear it down."

Parke not only didn't tear it down, he spruced it up. Restoring the house completely, Parke turned it into a bed-and-breakfast inn and asked his mother to operate it. In the commercial kitchen, mother and son turn out the breads and pastries for his restaurant, Vickery Parke.

The gleaming white-frame Victorian structure, ablaze with lights at night, is impossible to miss. Whirling fans push cooling breezes across the wide front porch during hot days. The house was built in 1896 by Jim Skelton and his wife Jessie, for their family, which ultimately included 10 children. Parke is his great-grandson. Family memorabilia and heirlooms, antiques–such as the Weaver upright grand piano in the front parlor–and photographs of the house in its early years fill the public spaces and appoint some of the guest rooms.

Rooms are individually decorated and full of references to family members. Parke's namesake room, which has a whirlpool tub, a deck with a rooftop garden, and a private entrance, is for romance-seekers. Annie Grace has its own second-story porch.

Ruth's cooking is much in demand for catered luncheons, arranged by prior reservation. For weekend breakfast, get her to make the upside down apple pancake. Stuffed French toast with apple cider syrup also wins favorites, and the bacon is locally produced. Weekday breakfast is Continental. ♠ *7 rooms with baths. Air-conditioning, cable TV, phone in rooms. $85–$100; full breakfast. AE, D, DC, MC, V. No smoking.*

WHITLOCK INN ☞

57 Whitlock Ave., Marietta 30060, tel. 770/428–1495, fax 770/919–9620,
www.mindspring.com/~whitlockinn/

The 1900 Dobbs house (which became the Whitlock Inn) had seen better days, after having been used as an adult day care facility by the city of Marietta. Suffering badly from deferred maintenance, the elegant, white (now) Victorian frame home in Marietta's historic district was to be razed for a parking lot.

Native Mississippians Nancy (a former publisher), and Sandy (who owned a computer business) Edwards and their daughter (now innkeeper) Alexis lived down the street in another historic home, and couldn't bear the impending doom facing the Dobbs house. On land that once held a 150-room resort that was destroyed in a fire more than a century ago, the house had sheltered Herbert C. Dobbs, his wife, Annie, and their family of eight.

After a painstaking—and painful—restoration that the Edwardses have chronicled in a scrapbook sitting on the coffee table, the Whitlock Inn emerged as the phoenix from the ashes of the Dobbs house, now a jewel in this urban historic district. From this location, guests may stroll the streets and alleyways of this Civil War–era town and walk to theater, fine dining, open-air concerts in Glover Park, and antiques stores around the square in Marietta.

Ablaze with lights at night, the inn has generous spindled verandas, an upstairs rooftop porch, pocket doors, hardwood floors, and leaded-glass windows in the reception parlor. Reproduction Chinese Chippendale furnishings and authentic antiques fill the individually styled guest rooms and public spaces. Terry cloth robes are supplied. One room has a queen-size sleigh bed; and another, the bridal suite, a queen-size poster bed. A ballroom added onto the rear of the house is popular for weddings and special events.

Continental breakfast with quiche is served in the dining room, and freshly baked cookies are always available in the front parlor. ⌂ *5 double rooms with baths. Air-conditioning, cable TV and phone in rooms. $100–$125; Continental breakfast. AE, D, MC, V. No smoking.*

WHITWORTH INN

6593 McEver Rd., Flowery Branch 30542, tel. 770/967–2386, fax 770/967–2649,
www.whitworthinn.com

Ken and Christina Jonick built an inn from scratch so they could live and work in the same space. Christina, who holds a doctorate in education, still teaches at a nearby college. Ken, who used to be with Pan Am, devotes his entire work effort to the inn.

The simple dormered structure is comfortably but not luxuriously furnished, and all rooms are bright and well lit. Baths are strictly functional. On 5 acres of beautifully wooded land just north of Atlanta, the inn is popular with business guests and with families, because it's so handy to Lake Lanier. Children under 12 stay free. The inn is not so appealing for romance.

Breakfasts are substantial, with pancakes, French toast, and bacon and eggs among the hefty dishes offered, providing plenty of sustenance for a day of busy activities. ⌂ *10 rooms with baths. Air-conditioning, cable TV and phone in rooms. $65–$75. MC, V. No smoking.*

WOODBRIDGE INN 🐦

411 Chambers St., Jasper 30143, tel. 706/692–6293, fax 706/692–9061

In 1977 a young German, Joe Rueffert, and his Georgia-born wife, Brenda, bought a slightly worn, slightly post–Civil War hotel on a lark and moved into its second level with their two young children, Hans and Sonya. On the ground floor of the former Lenning Hotel, the couple established one of the area's most popular restaurants. Diners, who have included former President and First Lady Jimmy and Rosalynn Carter, enjoy a splendid view of Sharptop Mountain from the large picture window in the dining room.

Renaming it the Woodbridge for the wooden bridge that leads from the street to the inn's parking lot, the Ruefferts built a 12-unit shed-roofed lodge, which Brenda decorated, achieving an airy, modern look with light colors, comfortable contemporary furnishings, and a minimum of fuss. These rooms may not be the antiques-filled spaces of many other historic bed-and-breakfast inns, but they charm with their simplicity. The units are on three levels, and the top-floor units, called Eagle's Nest, each contain a loft with a table and chairs and a sleeper sofa. All units have some kind of outdoor private space—patios on the low level, balconies on the upper two levels. The middle level emerges at the street.

In 1997 the couple moved into a log house nearby and converted the upper floors into six guest rooms. Carefully retaining old fixtures wherever possible, the Ruefferts designed these rooms to have more historic appeal than those in the lodge.

Rooms have tables and chairs, coffeemakers, and a supply of doughnut sticks; the Ruefferts do not serve breakfast.

The restaurant in the lower level of the original structure is regionally famous for its fresh trout, steaks, and desserts, and it has a good wine list. Joe's son-in-law, Tobin Walcott, cooks with him in the kitchen, and his son, Hans, sometimes helps out as well. △ *18 double rooms with baths. Restaurant (limited lunch; dinner), air-conditioning, cable TV, phone in rooms; pool, gazebo, ponds. $75–$90; no breakfast. AE, D, MC, V. No smoking, pets and children over 10 extra, children under 10 free.*

MIDDLE GEORGIA

The landscape of middle Georgia has remained relatively undisturbed since the days when cotton was king. You can drive for hours past flat fields planted in razor-straight rows of soybeans, tobacco, tomatoes, corn, peanuts, cotton, the famous Vidalia onions, and, of course, groves of peach trees. The daily rhythm of rural life has been colorfully captured in works by native writers: Flannery O'Connor's irony-laden short stories, the Uncle Remus *tales by Joel Chandler Harris, and* The Color Purple *and other books by Alice Walker. You may have glimpsed the charm of the area on the critically acclaimed TV series* I'll Fly Away, *which was set and filmed in Madison.*

The sheer beauty of Madison, a cultural and aristocratic town, is preserved in its fine antebellum homes. Nearby Eatonton, also a showcase of period domestic architecture, was home to Joel Chandler Harris and Alice Walker. In Macon, crowds gather annually in March for the cherry-blossom festival; it has almost 200,000 of the Japanese trees, surpassing even Washington, D.C. Washington, Georgia, with its distinctive antebellum and Victorian homes, was incorporated in 1780, when it briefly served as the state's capital. It was the first city in the country to be named for George Washington. Many antebellum plantation and town houses, as well as Victorian mansions and bungalows, have been handsomely restored and stand as reminders of bygone years. Well-marked driving trails bearing names like Peach Blossom and Antebellum take you through small towns dotted with homes of architectural distinction and past lushly landscaped gardens.

PLACES TO GO, SIGHTS TO SEE

Callaway Plantation (U.S. 78, 5 mi west of Washington, tel. 706/678–7060). This 50-acre portion of a once-thriving 3,000-acre plantation was under the control of the same family from the late 18th century until 1962, when the buildings and this plot were given to the city of Washington as a historic site. Today, it shows how the area's early settlers lived. Tour a circa 1869 Greek Revival house, a log cabin (1785), and a two-story Federal plain-style house (1790).

Hard Labor Creek State Park (I–20 east to Exit 49, tel. 706/557–3001) convenient to Madison, Rutledge, and Eatonton, has more than 20 mi of trails, a golf course, a lake with a beach, and cottages. A telescope-equipped observatory—one of the finest in the southeast—is open March through October on Saturday evenings to study the night sky.

Hawkinsville Historic Opera House (100 N. Lumpkin St., tel. 912/783–1717). The original turn-of-the-century glamour of this elaborately decorated performance hall has been restored, and cultural events, concerts, and plays are presented here once more.

Jarrell Plantation (Off GA 18, Jarrell Plantation Rd., Juliette, tel. 912/986–5172), outside Macon, consists of 20 historic buildings dating between 1847 and 1940, including a gristmill, a cotton gin, a cane mill, and smokehouses, as well as beehives and an extensive collection of domestic artifacts of the period.

Macon, incorporated in 1823, has three national historic districts, which have large garden squares and wide streets lined with Greek Revival mansions and Victorian bungalows. *Pleasant Hills Historic District,* one of the first African-American neighborhoods on the National Register of Historic Places, and the *Harriet Tubman Museum* (340 Walnut St., tel. 912/743–8544) are dedicated to the preservation of African-American history. The *Ocmulgee National Monument* (1207 Emery Hwy., tel. 912/752–8257) commemorates 12,000 years of Southeast Indian culture with a museum, a film, and exhibits from the excavated Indian mounds. *Hay House* (934 Georgia Ave., tel. 912/742–8155), a spectacular 24-room Italian Renaissance Revival mansion (circa 1855–59), was built with an elevator, a hidden storage room, stained-glass panels, murals, and an early ventilating system. Today it is filled with art and antiques, some of which come from the original Johnston collection and others from the Hay family, which donated the house to the Georgia Trust for Historic Preservation. *Woodruff House* (988 Bond St., tel. 912/752–2715), by noted local master builder Elam Alexander, is a Greek Revival mansion built in 1836 and owned and operated by Mercer University. It was the scene of a ball for Winnie Davis, daughter of Confederate president Jefferson Davis. Macon's most recent addition in the attractions arena is the *Georgia Music Hall of Fame* (200 Martin Luther King Jr. Blvd., tel. 912/750–8555), devoted to Georgia-born musicians from all genres who have left their marks on the musical world.

In **Madison,** stringent restoration codes have preserved the city's architectural heritage. Federal and Victorian mansions, churches, and public buildings make it the state's antebellum showcase. Good walking-tour maps and audiotapes are available at the Madison-Morgan County Chamber of Commerce (*see* Visitor Information, *below*).

Male Academy Museum (30 Temple Ave., Newnan, tel. 770/251–0207). In a restored 1883 schoolhouse, Coweta County's history is interpreted through education, industry, architecture, and costume, from pre-settler days through the late 19th century. Civil War and *Gone With the Wind* collections are displayed with rotating exhibits.

Massee Lane Gardens (Rte. 49, between Fort Valley and Marshallville, tel. 912/967–2358) is the home of the American Camellia Society. The 9 acres of gardens are in full bloom from November to March; azaleas, banksia roses, daylilies, and other bulbs take their turn in season.

Museum of Aviation at Robins Air Force Base (7 mi from I–75 at Exit 45 [Warner Robins/Centerville], outside Warner Robins, tel. 912/923–6600). This collection on 43 acres contains about 90 historic airplanes, including a U–2, a Flying Tigers P–40, a MIG 17 from the Romanian Air Force, and an SR–71 Blackbird spy plane.

Terrell Plantation (Exit 51, I–20, Harmony Rd., U.S. 441 10 mi south of I–20 toward Eatonton, tel. 706/485–2655). Owner Dottie Billingsley has restored an antebellum Greek Revival house (call to reserve a tour) and specializes in heirloom plants and seeds, chemical-free plants, and cut flowers. Her Garden Store is open Monday–Saturday 11–5 or by appointment.

Robert Toombs House (216 E. Robert Toombs Ave., Washington, tel. 706/678–2226). Once the home of Confederate general Robert Toombs, a successful lawyer and, briefly, Secretary of State for the Confederacy, this house, built before 1800, is now a state historic site whose exhibits tell the story of the fiery planter and lawyer.

Washington Historical Museum (308 E. Robert Toombs Ave., tel. 706/678–2105). Elegant antebellum furnishings, Civil War mementos, and a Native American collection are on display in this house.

RESTAURANTS

Another Thyme Cafe (5 E. Public Sq., tel. 706/678–1672), on the square in Washington, serves grilled chicken, fried catfish, and specials such as Irish stew. **Fincher's Barbecue,** with two Macon locations (891 Gray Hwy., tel. 912/743–5866; 3947 Houston Ave., tel. 912/788–1900) and one in Warner Robins (519 N. Davis Dr., tel. 912/922–3034), has been serving pit-cooked pork, ribs, chicken, and Brunswick stew for more than 50 years. In Macon, **Natalia's** (2720 Riverside Dr., tel. 912/741–1380) specializes in northern Italian food. A native of Aix-en-Provence, France, Daniel Adam has found a home in Macon and cooks French fare at his **Café Provence** (3267 Vineville Ave., tel. 912/474–2100). The **New Perry Hotel** (800 Main St., Perry, tel. 912/987–1000) specializes in down-home southern fare. Near Madison, the **Yesterday Café** (120 Fairplay St., Rutledge, tel. 706/557–9337), a revamped turn-of-the-century drugstore, is famous for blueberry pancakes and buttermilk biscuits as well as southern specialties such as country-fried steak with mashed potatoes for lunch and Continental cuisine for dinner. Taking its cue from the popular film, the **Whistle Stop Cafe** (Rte. 1, tel. 912/994–3670) in Juliette, north of Macon, is wildly popular for its fried green tomatoes and other staples of southern fare. Near Eatonton, **Magnolia House** (1130 Greensboro Rd., tel. 706/484–1833) gives southern fare a whole new dimension, with glorious smoked and fresh trout cakes and fresh fruit fried pies (shaped like a turnover). **Oak Tree Victorian Dinner Restaurant** (U.S. 27, Hamilton, tel. 706/628–4218) is popular for casual but refined Continental dining.

SHOPPING

Discount shoppers will quickly spot the "Big Peach" on the east side of I–75 near Byron, just south of Macon, at **Peach Outlet Mall** (Exit 46), which has the usual run of discount shops. Don't miss the produce, preserved items, relishes and pickles, and excellent barbecue at **Peach Parkway Produce and B.B.Q.** (tel. 912/956–4774) across the road from the outlet mall. Hint: Get the hot sauce; it's worth the hiccuping.

VISITOR INFORMATION

Forsyth-Monroe County Chamber of Commerce (Box 811, Forsyth 31029, tel. 912/994–9239 or 888/642–4628). **Macon-Bibb County Convention and Visitors Bureau** (Terminal Station, 300 Cherry St., Box 6354, Macon 31208, tel. 912/743–3401 or 800/768–3401). **Madison-Morgan County Chamber of Commerce** (115 E. Jefferson St., Box 826, Madison 30650, tel. 706/342–4454 or 800/709–7406). **Newnan-Coweta Chamber of Commerce** (23 Bullsboro Dr., Box 1103, Newnan 30264, tel. 770/253–2270). **Peach County Chamber of Commerce** (Box 1238, Fort Valley 31030, tel. 912/825–3733). **Perry Area Con-**

vention & Visitors Bureau (Box 1619, Perry 31069, tel. 912/988–8000). **Washington-Wilkes Chamber of Commerce** (104 E. Liberty St., Box 661, Washington 30673, tel. 706/678–2013).

CARMICHAEL HOUSE 🦜
149 McDonough Rd., Jackson 30235, tel. 770/775–0578, www.carmichael.com

Painted in shades of teal and sand, the 1897 Queen Anne Victorian house, built by the noted Atlanta architectural firm of Bruce and Morgan, for the then-princely price of $16,000, the Charmichael House is named for its builder, Mr. J. R. Carmichael Sr. It was a family home for him, the town buggy maker and banker, his wife, and his 11 children. Unique architectural features include a distinctive two-story rotunda. A large wraparound porch, turrets, and plenty of gingerbread signal its Victorian lineage.

John Herdina, a commercial roofing contractor, and his wife, Linda Sullivan, purchased the house from J. R. Carmichael Jr. in 1992 to make it both their home and an inn. Many of the antiques in the inn are Carmichael family originals, such as the wicker baby carriage carefully positioned in the upstairs hall. Herdina and Sullivan renovated the rear structure, which predates the house, as another pair of bed-and-breakfast accommodations.

Much of the house is devoted to public space, much of it with details such as superior woodwork and stained glass windows. The kitchen has a unique stove and an old-fashioned feeling.

Jackson is about 7 mi east of I–75, and just 40 minutes south of Hartsfield Atlanta International Airport. Walking around Jackson is a pleasing experience, and much of the city's streetscape has recently been upgraded, with new sidewalks and lighting. Although there's a lot to do in and around Jackson (there are lakes and state parks nearby), most guests visit the area on business.

Breakfast is substantial if not gourmet, and the service from John and Linda is friendly and devoted to detail. ⌂ *5 rooms with baths, 1 suite. Air-conditioning, cable TV, and phone in rooms. $75–$150; full breakfast. AE, D, DC, MC, V. No smoking.*

CROCKETT HOUSE 🦜
671 Madison Rd., Eatonton 31024, tel. 706/485–2248, www.bbonline.com/ga/crocketthouse/

When the spinster Jones sisters died in the 1970s, the 1895 Victorian house on Madison Road still lacked indoor plumbing and electricity. The pair, reared in luxury and educated in Europe, had dutifully returned home from their studies in Munich when their mother summoned them. Musicians, they made a living publishing magazine articles that one wrote and the other illustrated. After their deaths, the house was, some said, haunted.

But innkeepers Christa and Peter Crockett, who live on the ground floor of the inn, never have found it so. The pair bought the place in 1992 and today operate what Christa calls a "traditional" bed-and-breakfast inn. Guests arrive to find a classic Victorian veranda set with rockers and hanging baskets full of pink petunias. Ceiling fans whirl and wind chimes tinkle.

The Crockett House's rooms are decorated with great taste and, for a Victorian ambience, restraint. The individually styled bedrooms have woodburning fireplaces; two have claw-foot tubs in front of the hearths. One room, with two full-size white iron beds, is perfect for friends traveling together. The Crocketts serve hefty breakfasts with fresh juices and a hot dish. Specialties include a splendid apple bread and ham-and-cheese soufflé.

Eatonton, Georgia, has much to recommend it for anyone eager to view historic homes and to touch base with Georgia's literary roots. It was home both to Joel Chandler Harris (*Uncle Remus*) and to Alice Walker (*The Color Purple*). Nearby are ample recreational facilities, from the boating and fishing at Lake Sinclair to golf. Just a few miles up U.S. 441 on the north side of I–20 lies Madison, with its own historic homes. **♙** *4 double rooms with baths, 2 double rooms share 1 bath. Air-conditioning, fireplaces in rooms, cable TV in common area and in one guest room. $65–$95; full breakfast. AE, MC, V. No smoking.*

1842 INN ☙
353 College St., Macon 31201, tel./fax 912/741–1842 or tel. 800/336–1842, the1842inn@worldnet.att.net

Established in 1823, Macon has 11 historic districts with more than 5,500 buildings on the National Register of Historic Places. One of the events that make a stay at the 1842 Inn special is "Lights on Macon," a self-guided walking tour that guides visitors past more than 30 of its neighborhood's splendid homes. An imposing Greek Revival mansion a few blocks from Mercer University and a five-minute drive from downtown, the inn has luxurious rooms both in the main house and the charming Victorian cottage in back.

Named for the year its oldest portion was built, the inn was enlarged around the turn of the century. Professionally restored in 1986, it has earned many preservation and hospitality awards. It was bought in 1991 by Phillip Jenkins, a Georgia native and management consultant, and his silent partner, Richard Meils, a Michigan physician.

The grand, white-pillared front porch—dramatically lit at night—opens to a traditional center hall. The parlors are furnished with fine period antiques, including European tapestries, paintings, and a collection of period export porcelain. In the front parlor Phillip sometimes enjoys playing the Baldwin baby grand for guests, who often add their own musical acumen to the evening's complimentary cocktail hour.

The elegant bedrooms, some furnished with period antiques, have ceiling fans whirling overhead and brass or four-poster beds. Breakfast is served along with the morning paper in your bedroom's sitting area, the parlor, or, in fine weather, in the courtyard. Fresh flowers perfume the rooms. **♙** *12 double rooms with baths in house, 9 doubles with baths in cottage. Air-conditioning, cable TV and phone in rooms, fireplaces in 6 rooms, whirlpool baths in 4 rooms, turndown service with chocolates. $115–$185; Continental breakfast (full breakfast is extra), afternoon refreshments. AE, MC, V.*

FARMHOUSE INN ☙
1051 Meadow La., Madison 30650, tel. 706/342–7933, members.aol.com/fhinn

Pat and Melinda Hartney moved their family, including toddlers Jordan and Hannah, to a farm that has been in Melinda Hartney's family for generations. The land, gently rolling and fertile, lies near the Apalachee River, which flows into nearby Lake Oconee. There is a walking trail on the property.

The farmhouse that rests on top of a hill looks as though it's been on this site for generations, but in fact, the structure, complete with a traditional red tin roof, is mostly Melinda's design. This innkeeper knows her ridge poles from her soffits, as she is a graduate in architectural interior design from Auburn University. Krista Schauer, Melinda's roommate at Auburn, did the final drawings.

The rambling effect conveyed in the structure is carefully planned: The family abides in a private residence connected by porches and breezeways to other major segments, including the inn's three rooms. Luck won out, and the Hartneys finished their project in time to host Olympic Games–bound guests.

Three country-style rooms have private baths and entrances, twin or queen-size beds, and sitting areas with queen-size sofa beds. Quilts lend a homey feel, and beadboard wainscoting is just one of the Early American architectural details. Fabrics and colors reference Early American style but with sophistication.

The common room invites guests to read, watch TV, and chat and is the setting for breakfasts. Eggs strata, rosemary biscuits, cheese grits, and carrot-cake muffins are a typical breakfast. Buttermilk pancakes with blackberry syrup and local country ham are another specialty. The family chickens supply the eggs.

In addition to being ideally located for exploring nearby Madison, the inn has a 1 mi-long River Trail that crisscrosses the farms pastures, as well as a stocked pond for fishing. To reach the inn, take U.S. 278 out of Madison. ⚓ *3 rooms with baths. $95; full breakfast. Air-conditioning, cable TV and phone in one room and common room. MC, V. No smoking.*

GRAND HOTEL ☞

303 E. Main St., Hogansville 30230, tel. 706/637–8828 or 800/324–7625, fax 706/637–4522, www.gomm.com

Visitors zooming through Georgia along I–85 (Exit 6 for the hotel) may enjoy a stop at this authentic old-fashioned hotel in a small Georgia town that's fit for a movie set. Hogansville, first settled in the 1820s, is a typical railroad crossroads town that took its name from its first settler, William Hogan. Once bustling with churches, industry, and several hotels, the town now has settled into charming obscurity.

One of its old lodgings, built in the 1890s, is the Grand Hotel, a veranda-encircled Victorian building with a spacious, wood-paneled and brass-trimmed lobby. Its 10 rooms are distinctively and individually styled with a mix of antiques and colors ranging from pale yellow to intense pink. There are original prints and oils and fireplaces with gas logs; five rooms have whirlpool tubs.

The upstairs lobby is the scene of the hotel's complimentary cocktail-and-hors-d'oeuvres hour. Other areas to explore include an outdoor patio, gardens, conference room, and banquet hall. An adjacent sweet shop tempts with all kinds of rich treats, and the back of the hotel now is a Victorian tearoom, with high tea available by reservation.

From the hotel, managed by Glenda M. Gordon, visitors may stroll through the small town's charming Victorian neighborhoods, past the cemetery where founder Hogan and many of his family are buried, or across the railroad tracks to any of the town's restaurants. Most popular is Hogan's Heroes, especially worthy for Italian cuisine. Across the street from the hotel are a number of charming retail shops.

Hogansville, 30 minutes south of Hartsfield Atlanta International Airport, is handy for visitors to Warm Springs, Callaway Gardens, and Newnan, which are all within 20 mi. ⚓ *5 double rooms, 5 suites. Air-conditioning, cable TV and phone in rooms; conference and banquet facilities. $75–$150; Continental breakfast, afternoon cocktails and hors d'oeuvres. AE, MC, V. No smoking.*

HENDERSON VILLAGE ✺

125 S. Langston Cir., Perry (1 mi west of Exit 41, I–75), tel. 912/988–9009
or 888/615–9722, fax 912/988–9009, www.hendersonvillage.com

About 20 years ago, German electronics entrepreneur Bernhard Schneider bought an 8,000-acre ostrich and cattle operation in middle Georgia. He had wanted a farm in the southeastern United States—anywhere he could reach on a nonstop flight from Munich. Schneider's offices, at the intersection of GA 26 and U.S. 41, were in a neighborhood whose aesthetic character he found less than appealing. While he was looking for a way to enhance it, one of the owners of a nearby early 20th-century residence asked him to buy the property, and he was on his way to developing one of the state's most exquisite lodging-and-dining resorts.

On pristine, rolling farmland, Henderson Village is a cluster of buildings, three original to the site; the others Schneider acquired and moved to the complex. He plans to find, acquire, move and restore more, creating ultimately a study in area vernacular architecture. Within the transformed residences, some of them formerly simple farm homes, are sumptuously decorated interiors. One of the orig- inal-to-the-site structures, an 1838 Greek Revival house, is the Langston House 1838, the village's restaurant. Here, French-American chef François de Mel- ogue has developed a superior menu, with such entrées as squab with foie gras, grilled diver scallops on minced asparagus, extraordinary desserts, and a fine col- lection of wines, including some German ones in deference to the owner. Break- fast includes fresh juices, house-baked breads, stone-ground grits, and egg dishes that take advantage of local ingredients like country ham and Vidalia onions.
♤ 24 rooms, 4 suites with whirlpool tubs. Air-conditioning, gas-log fireplace, robes in rooms, restaurant, pool. $145–$205; full breakfast. AE, MC, V.

COASTAL GEORGIA

Sandy white beaches and saltwater marshes rim the state's 100 mi of coast, from the mouth of the Savannah River at the South Carolina border south to the St. Marys River. The islands (called the Golden Isles) and mainland towns that dot this coastline attracted Colonial settlers and later became the winter retreats of Carnegies, Rockefellers, and Vanderbilts. All were lured, as visitors are today, by the balmy winters, the promise of escape on sun-drenched beaches, and calm afternoons spent drifting along winding tidal creeks. Along with these timeless pleasures come exciting Independence Day celebrations, rowdy beach music, wonderful seafood, and jazz, blues, and art festivals. The area's diverse pursuits and sunny climate combine to make it a year-round vacation spot.

Historic Savannah has a Colonial setting, with cobblestone squares and parks draped with Spanish moss. The city's River Street waterfront gift shops and jazz bars bustle with visiting crowds, and the annual St. Patrick's Day parade is one of the country's largest. Augusta, founded in 1736 and named for the then Princess of Wales, is called the Garden City of the South. Its six historic districts can be viewed from a trolley or on foot. Of particular interest are Broad Street, Riverwalk, Olde Town (one of the largest neighborhoods of Victorian homes in the state), and Summerville. Known as the Hill, this once-separate town, originally established as a summer resort, later attracted notable winter visitors such as John D. Rockefeller, who often resided at the Bonair Hotel. Today Summerville is a thriving restored neighborhood. President Woodrow Wilson spent his childhood in Augusta, living here during the Civil War. His childhood home still stands and is being restored by Historic Augusta (tel. 706/724–0438). His father served as pastor at the First Presbyterian Church, which also still stands. Bike trails along the Savannah River provide a pleasant way to enjoy the wildlife—blue herons, river otters, and wild turkeys—that abounds. Travelers seeking a more informal setting can continue south toward St. Simons Island for swimming, fishing, golf, and tennis.

Little of urban America is evident in these rural, coastal areas, but glimpses of the lavish lifestyle of the 19th-century rich and famous remain on

Jekyll Island in Millionaire's Village, where stately Victorian and shingled manses line the waterway compound. Cumberland Island National Seashore's protected forests and 16 mi of pristine white-sand beaches and dunes offer isolated serenity. Inland near the Georgia-Florida state line lies the 730-square-mi Okefenokee National Wildlife Refuge, whose tea-color waters are dotted with water lilies and inhabited by alligators.

During the off-season, before Memorial Day and after Labor Day, the crowds leave these seashore communities, and the already remote beaches become virtually private playgrounds. If you visit at this time of year, you discover what locals already know: that the humid temperatures and the insects leave with the crowds.

PLACES TO GO, SIGHTS TO SEE

Augusta. This beautiful port city, the third oldest in Georgia (laid out June 1736), was named for the then Princess of Wales. International attention focuses here when it hosts golf's Masters Tournament each spring. A five-block area with stores, restaurants, entertainment, and the *Ft. Discovery's National Science Center* (One 7th St., Augusta, tel. 706/821–0200 or 800/325–5445) and the excellent *Morris Museum of Southern Art* (One 10th St., Augusta, tel. 706/724–7501) line the riverwalk. In the walkable historic district, Broad Street is known for its antiques stores. Augusta has the state's second-oldest opera, a symphony, and a ballet company, all of which perform in the Romanesque revival–style *Sacred Heart Cultural Center* (1301 Greene St., tel. 706/826–4700).

Cumberland Island. A national seashore, this island is distinguished by an undisturbed landscape. Accessible only by boat, it is a sanctuary for wild horses, deer, and bobcats. It is popular for day trips and overnight camping, and the park service (Box 806, St. Marys 31558, tel. 912/882–4335) operates a ferry service ($10.17 plus $4 day-use fee) on a limited, reservations-only schedule.

Darien. The British *Ft. King George* (Box 711, Darien 31305, tel. 912/437–4770), built in 1721, today contains a reconstructed block house and a renovated museum focusing on the site's history, which included a large Indian village and a Spanish mission. Founded on January 19, 1736, when Scottish Highlanders landed and began building, Darien itself has 19th-century houses and historic churches (including the smallest one in the United States).

The **Green-Meldrim House** (1 W. Macon St., Savannah, tel. 912/232–1251), a Gothic Revival mansion with wraparound wrought-iron balconies, was built in 1850 for cotton merchant Charles Green. General Sherman stayed here during his occupation of Savannah; it was later occupied by a Judge Peter Meldrim and is now the parish house of St. John's Episcopal Church. The house, in its original condition, is furnished with period antiques and is open for tours.

Hofwyl-Broadfield Plantation (Hwy. 17, Brunswick, tel. 912/264–7333), established in the early 1800s, was one of the few that functioned around the turn of the 20th century. In this century, the plantation became a thriving dairy farm until it was bequeathed to the State of Georgia as a historic site. Visitors can tour the 1858 plantation house and walk along the canals that were used to flood the rice fields lining the riverbanks.

Jekyll Island. Named for Sir Joseph Jekyll, the largest contributor to Georgia's colonization, the island is reached from Brunswick by causeway. There are 63 holes of golf, 10 mi of Atlantic Ocean beachfront, and a historic district that was a turn-of-the-century private winter playground for the Rockefellers, Cranes, Pulitzers, and Vanderbilts. Many of their brick, shingle, and tabby manses stand today as architectural landmarks of a bygone era.

Melon Bluff Nature Center (near Midway, off I–95 at Exit 13, tel. 912/884–5779 or 888/246–8188), is the ideal spot for bird-watching, canoeing, kayaking, bicycling, and myriad outdoor activities on a 3,000-acre plantation that has been in the same family since the early 18th century. Lodging is available, and more is being developed.

Okefenokee Swamp Park (5700 Swamp Park Rd., off U.S. 1, 8 mi south of Waycross, tel. 912/283–0583). This wildlife sanctuary is at the north end of the Okefenokee National Wildlife Refuge, one of the country's most acclaimed wilderness areas. Guided boat tours highlight the swamp's flora and fauna, and a network of bridged walkways allows visitors to penetrate the park on foot.

St. Simons Island. This seashore haven, connected to the mainland by a causeway, is the most developed of the Golden Isles. Its southern tip is rimmed by white-sand beaches and dotted with souvenir shops, gift boutiques, and restaurants; a network of bike paths extends across the marshlands into the center of the island. Historic sites established by early settlers include *Ft. Frederica* (Off Frederica Rd., just past Christ Episcopal Church, tel. 912/638–3639) and *St. Simons Lighthouse* (101 12th St., tel. 912/638–4666).

Sapelo. After the Creek Indians, Spanish missionaries, British soldiers, and rice planters came tobacco magnate R. J. Reynolds, who bought this barrier island in the 1930s for his own agricultural projects. Today the island is a state-owned protected area, which operates as an institute for the study of marine life and marshland. It's accessible only by boat by prior arrangement. The Department of Natural Resources (tel. 912/437–3224), at the visitor center in Meridian, Georgia, 7 mi north of Darien, conducts tours Wednesdays and Saturdays year-round and adds Fridays June 1 to Labor Day. Admission is $10.

Savannah. Colonial Savannah, with the nation's largest historic district, lures visitors with its 21 cobblestone squares, giant parterre gardens, waterfront gift shops, jazz bars and parks draped in Spanish moss. *Midnight in the Garden of Good and Evil*, the wonderful best-seller and movie, has provoked a boom in tourism. Savannah's main attractions include *Factor's Walk* and *River Street* (Riverfront Plaza), the restored harbor area; the *Ralph Mark Gilbert Civil Rights Museum* (460 Martin Luther King Jr. Blvd., tel. 912/231–8900), which tells the story of Savannahians who took part in the city's civil rights history; the *Isaiah Davenport House* (324 E. State St., tel. 912/236–8097), whose threatened demolition spurred the preservation of the city's landmarks; *Chippewa Square* (Bull St. between Whitaker and Drayton Sts.), site of the imposing Daniel Chester French statue of General James Edward Oglethorpe, the city's founder.

Tybee Island, east of Savannah on Victory Drive (U.S. 80), is a popular seashore escape for families. Seafood restaurants, typically touristy souvenir shops, and summer cottages crowd the island. Accessible only by boat, adjacent "Little" Tybee Island, actually larger than Tybee, is remote and completely undeveloped. Campers' tents dot its hard sand-packed beaches.

RESTAURANTS

In Savannah, **Elizabeth on 37th** (105 E. 37th St., tel. 912/236–5547) is famed for regional specialties. In the historic district, the **Olde Pink House** (23 Abercorn St., tel. 912/232–4286) prepares classic Lowcountry fare and serves it in an elegantly restored 19th-century residence. **Mrs. Wilkes Dining Room** (107 W. Jones St., tel. 912/232–5997) serves southern breakfasts and lunches in an appealing elbow-to-elbow family-style setting, as does **Nita's Place** (140 Abercorn St., tel. 912/238–8233), which even does freshly squeezed homemade lemonade. **The Lady & Sons** (311 W. Congress St., tel. 912/233–2600) has made a hit with both locals and tourists for its fine Savannah country fare, especially the crab stew. **Sapphire Grill** (110 W. Congress St. tel. 912/443-9962) explores the richness of and updates traditional plantation fare. **45 South** (20 E. Broad St., tel. 912/233–1881) serves gourmet regional cuisine in cozy, contemporary settings. **Blanche's Courtyard** (440 Kings Way, tel. 912/638–3030) on St. Simons Island prepares fine fresh seafood in traditional southern and American presentations, and on Tybee Island the **North Beach Grill** (41-A Meddin Dr., tel. 912/786–9003) demonstrates that you can dine well in your sandals and swimsuit. In Statesboro the dining room in the **Statesboro Inn** (*see below*; tel. 912/489–8628) serves Continental cuisine Tuesday through Saturday night. Darien's best choice for dining is **Archies** (Hwy. 17, tel. 912/437–4363), especially for southern-style fish and other specialties. In a renovated Victorian storefront in downtown Augusta is the **White Elephant Café** (1135 Broad St., tel. 706/722–8614), serving Caribbean fare. For elegant Continental dining in Augusta, **La Maison on Telfair** (404 Telfair St., tel. 706/722–4805) is a standout.

SHOPPING

Downtown Savannah offers myriad antiques shops, art galleries, touristy gift shops, and book shops (both old and new). Just south of the city on I–95, **Savannah Festival Factory Stores** (11 Gateway Blvd. S, I–95, exit 16, tel. 912/925–3089) specializes in merchandise sold at 25%–75% off retail. Upscale discount shopping is found at **Magnolia Bluff Factory Stores** (I–95, exit 10, Darien).

VISITOR INFORMATION

Cotton Exchange Welcome Center (32 Eighth St., Augusta 30901, tel. 706/724–4067 or 800/726–0243). **Jekyll Island Convention and Visitors Bureau** (381 Riverview Dr., Jekyll Island 31527, tel. 912/635–3636 or 800/841–6586). **St. Simons Visitors Center** (530 Beachview Dr., St. Simons Island 31522, tel. 912/638–9014 or 800/933–2627). **Savannah Visitors Center** (3303 Martin Luther King Jr. Blvd., tel. 912/238–1779). **Tybee Visitors Center** (U.S. 80 and Campbell Ave., Box 491, Tybee Island 31328, tel. 912/786–5444 or 800/868–2322).

RESERVATION SERVICES

For a list of 65 inns, contact **Great Inns of Georgia** (tel. 404/843–0471, fax 404/252–8886), a marketing group. **RSVP Savannah** (9489 Whitfield Ave., Box 49, Savannah 31406, tel. 912/232–7787 or 800/729–7787). **Savannah Historic Inns** (147 Bull St., Savannah 31401, tel. 912/233–7660 or 800/262–4667).

BALLASTONE INN ☙

14 E. Oglethorpe Ave., Savannah 31401, tel. 912/236–1484 or 800/822–4553, fax 912/236–4626

This handsome, eclectic inn takes its stylistic notes from a variety of periods, beginning with the Federal era, when it was first built, to the Victorian, when it was last substantially altered. The mansion was home to a well-to-do Savannah shipping magnate and later a bank president; today it is run by Jean Hagens, a former executive with Sunoco. Its central location along Savannah's Oglethorpe Avenue in the historic district puts you on the bus line, a quick walk from the Civic Center.

The Ballastone fairly exudes classic Savannah elegance. Period Victorian European and American antiques with some reproductions fill the double parlor. Many of the rooms have rice poster and canopy beds and are decorated with antiques from the Regency period and Victorian era. Resident designer Scott Simms has added deft faux finishes even to the elevator, whose door sports a wainscot look, imitating the Victorian paneling in the hallway. Mixed kudzu and wisteria vines trail around the banister and mirrors and through light fixtures; Simms changes the embellishments with the seasons. His hand also graced the entrance hall's ceiling, which now has a blue-sky fresco with clouds and angels.

Full breakfast with a hot dish, such as light-as-a-sigh blueberry pancakes, is served in the back parlor or the courtyard. The courtyard, with ligustrums in jardinières and potted palms, is an ideal spot for a leisurely breakfast. Coffee, tea, and complimentary sherry are available around the clock. Additional cocktails may be purchased (automatically charged to the room) from the back-parlor bar and enjoyed anywhere in the inn. ♨ *14 double rooms with baths, 9 suites. Air-conditioning, cable TV/VCR and phone in rooms, fireplaces and whirlpools in some rooms, video library, 24-hr concierge, elevator, turndown service with chocolates and brandy; off-street parking. $255–$375; full breakfast, afternoon tea and nightcaps. AE, MC, V.*

BED AND BREAKFAST INN 🐚

117 W. Gordon St., Savannah 31401, tel. 912/238–0518, fax 912/233-2537,
www.travelbase.com/destinations/savannah/bed-breakfast/

A restored 1853 Federal row house on historic Gordon Row (now Gordon St.) lies at the edge of Forsyth Park, with its expansive green space for jogging and its tennis courts. The inn's lush courtyard brims with seasonal flowers and leafy trees, making it a breezy cool spot for enjoying the city's warm summer evenings.

Just down the street is Chatham Square, and at the Bull Street end lies Monterey Square, where visitors busily snap photos of Jim William's Mercer House from *Midnight in the Garden of Good and Evil.*

Innkeeper Robert McAllister, whose son Jim and daughter-in-law Janet handle day-to-day operations, is among the few remaining original innkeepers in Savannah: This establishment has been a fixture in Savannah hospitality and lodging for nearly two decades.

The inn remains one of the city's better lodging values, and perhaps its best bed-and-breakfast value. For this reason, it's popular for family reunions. Best rooms are the garden suites (which have full kitchens), living rooms, and dining areas. At these prices, don't look for robes or turndown service, and the dining space is not charmingly decorated. But the staff is warm and wonderful; the breakfast ample if not gourmet; and the value substantial.

Full breakfast features a hot dish, and afternoon tea could include freshly made brownies. ♨ *12 rooms, 1 suite, 2 cottages with kitchens (one without oven). Air-conditioning, cable TV, phone in rooms. $85–$110; full breakfast, afternoon tea. AE, MC, V. No smoking.*

COLEMAN HOUSE INN 🐚

323 N. Main St., Swainsboro 30401, tel. 912/237–9100, fax 912/237–8656

This rambling Queen Anne Victorian house, with a classic wraparound veranda, corner turrets, and whimsical asymmetry, is ideal as a bed-and-breakfast inn. Within, the beadboard walls and ceilings are finished in a rich, dark tone. The house sits on a large city lot, just outside of downtown, making it a good site for gatherings.

The eight large guest rooms, individually decorated, are furnished in period-style pieces. One room has a white wooden swing, white wicker furniture, and blue bed coverings and drapes. Another has a huge oak poster bed and enjoys private access to an upstairs porch.

Resident innkeepers David and Connie Thurman do much of the catering in the Swainsboro area, and the inn's commercial kitchen is their base of operation. The Thurmans' fried chicken is superior. Breakfast is substantial and very southern, with grits, eggs, and biscuits.

Popular for its dinner service (chiefly steak) on Friday night only, as well as for Sunday dinner, as Southerners call the noon meal, the Coleman House specializes in home-style dishes. Served buffet style, the dishes are set on a long table in the central hallway. The inn's main common rooms are set with strictly utilitarian, church basement–style tables and chairs, but this doesn't prevent the place from being a frequent site for weddings, showers, and other events.

The inn is very popular for business guests, too, who conduct small meetings in the downstairs parlors. The inn is close to George L. Smith State Park, and other small municipal parks are even closer. Swainsboro lies just north of I–20 west of Savannah. △ *8 rooms with baths. Air-conditioning, cable TV and phone in rooms. $55–$85; full breakfast. AE, MC, V.*

ELIZA THOMPSON HOUSE ☞

5 W. Jones St., Savannah 31401, tel. 912/236–3620 or 800/348–9378, fax 912/238–1920, www.bbonline.com/ga/savannah/elizathompson/index.html

In those years before the Civil War, Savannah was bustling and busy and beginning to push out beyond its boundaries. That's when (around 1847) a socially prominent widow, Eliza Thompson, built her fine town house on a brick-paved street in what was known as the trading district. A side gate opens to one of the city's most enchanting courtyards, centered by a flowing Ivan Bailey fountain, the work of one of the state's best contemporary iron sculptors. One can almost imagine the entertaining, elegant parties the auburn-haired widow hosted in the 1840s and '50s.

In recent times, the house had become an inn but had fallen into neglect. In 1995 Carol and Steve Day left the corporate world, purchased the house and repainted, refinished, and refurnished it in period style. English antiques fill the public spaces and appoint some of the guest rooms; the baths are now marble. The former carriage house has been converted to lodging space, offering 13 accommodations.

The public spaces, where guests gather for afternoon wine and cheese, with Carol often hosting, have especially benefited from their uplift. Dessert and coffee are offered nightly. Breakfasts feature pancakes, waffles, egg dishes, fresh fruit, and homemade pastry. △ *25 rooms with baths. Air-conditioning, cable TV and phone in rooms. $89–$199; full breakfast. MC, V. No smoking.*

FOLEY HOUSE ☞

14 W. Hull St., Savannah 31401, tel. 912/232–6622 or 800/647–3708, fax 912/231–1218, www.bbonline.com/ga/savannah/foley/index.html

Danish native Inge Moore and her husband, Mark, an investor born in Tennessee, have done a masterful job renovating an inn that had fallen victim to almost malevolent neglect. Purchasing the inn in 1994, they stripped the peeling paint from its walls and ripped up worn carpeting to reveal rich wood floors. Today, the inn is elegant with fine antiques. Many rooms have working fireplaces and some have generously sized whirlpool tubs. The staff, available 24 hours a day, is cheerful and welcoming at all hours.

The Moores' commitment to the inn is ongoing: In 1988 they built a carriage house to the rear of the property. These four fine rooms are less expensive simply by virtue of not being in the historic house.

Built more than 50 years apart on Chippewa Square, this pair of handsome Jacobean town houses is named for Kirby Foley, an Irish immigrant who, as a retailer and real estate investor, made a fortune in Savannah. His widow, Honoria, built the second one after the Civil War and there reared her five grandchildren, whose parents had died. Henry Urban, who also designed the sanctuary in the adjacent Independent Church, was the architect.

Continental breakfast, with fresh seasonal fruits and yogurt, may be served in your room, the lounge, or outdoors in the courtyard. Afternoon tea is complimentary, and wine is available for an extra charge.

Across the street in front of the inn is the First Baptist Church, the only church that would allow Yankees to attend services after the Civil War. Behind it is the Independent Church. Don't miss the Daniel Chester French statue of General Oglethorpe in Chippewa Square. ⌂ *19 rooms with baths. Air-conditioning, robes, cable TV/VCRs and phone in rooms, fireplaces in 15 rooms, film library, oversized whirlpool in 5 rooms. $135–$250; Continental breakfast. AE, DC, MC, V. No smoking.*

FOUR CHIMNEYS ⌃
2316 Wire Rd., Thomson 30824, tel. 706/597–0220

Maggie and Ralph Zeiger are justifiably proud of the personal attention they lavish on guests in this early 19th-century classic southern home in the middle of Georgia's hunt country. (The hunt season runs November through March.) Jasmine sends up its summer scents from a corner of the front porch, set with rocking chairs and a swing. The name comes from the four chimneys that anchor each side of the house. Maggie loves to show off her garden, while Ralph, a former law enforcement officer in Cleveland, Ohio, chimes in with praise for her sausage ring.

The house sits in the countryside just outside of town. Entering the front hall, the guest notices the hand-planed wide boards, a hallmark of early 19th-century construction. Stenciled ceilings, hand-planed wood floors, and working fireplaces add charm to the carefully restored house. Ralph thinks the house might have been built by Quakers, who spent some time in this region before leaving in opposition to slavery.

Only 50 mi east of Augusta just off I–20, Thomson is home to the fall Blind Willie Blues Festival, a tribute to bluesman "Blind" Willie McTell, a native son. Nearby Mistletoe State Park tempts with myriad outdoor activities, including hiking. The inn is handy for guests attending the Masters Golf Tournament in the spring.

For breakfast, Maggie always provides fruit, juice, and muffins, and on weekends she adds a hot dish (such as a sausage ring) to the menu. This is one of the state's best bed-and-breakfast values. ⌂ *3 rooms with baths. Air-conditioning, cable TV and phone in common area. $45–$50; Continental breakfast during the week, full breakfast weekends. No credit cards. No smoking.*

THE GASTONIAN

220 E. Gaston St., Savannah 31401, tel. 912/232–2869 or 800/322–6603, fax 912/232–0710, www.gastonian.com

Two blocks from Savannah's Forsyth Park and 12 from River Street stands the Gastonian. Hinting of the comforts within, a pineapple, symbolic of hospitality, is engraved on the brass sign at the entry. The two Regency Italianate mansions that compose the inn had been constructed for two prosperous merchants after the Civil War. In October 1996 Ann Landers (not the advice columnist) bought and redecorated much of the inn.

Authentic Georgian and Regency-period antiques set the 19th-century ambience. In the front parlor and formal dining room, the antiques have the patina that comes from being well loved and much-polished. Guests are encouraged to lounge in the coral upholstered wing chairs on either side of the drawing-room fireplace or pick out tunes on the antique baby grand piano in the front parlor. Scalamandré's Savannah-collection wallpapers adorn the hallways. One guest room has rustic country decor, ladder-back cane chairs, and antique trunks; another recalls Colonial America, with crewel draperies and bedspreads. Most have rice poster or Charleston canopy beds. Romance seekers should ask about the Caracalla Suite, with its huge bedside hot tub.

A sumptuous southern breakfast is served in the large country kitchen or the dining room. Dishes feature such specialties as ginger pancakes. Late risers may opt for a Continental breakfast delivered bedside on a silver tray along with the local paper. An elevated sundeck with chaise longues, a wisteria- and jasmine-draped pergola, and a large hot tub are pleasant spots to laze away the afternoon. The concierge has plenty of suggestions for terrific restaurants and will arrange for transport by horse-drawn carriage. March, April, May, September, and October are the inn's busiest times, so call well in advance. △ *14 double rooms with baths, 3 suites. Air-conditioning, cable TV, phone, and gas fireplace in rooms; off-street parking. $150–$350; full breakfast, afternoon tea, turndown service, evening cordials. AE, D, MC, V. No smoking.*

GREYFIELD INN ☜

Cumberland Island (Box 900, Fernandina Beach, FL 32035), tel. 904/261–6408 (reservations and information), fax 904/321–0666, www.greyfieldinn.com

Greyfield Inn is accessible only by boat (passage on the inn's *Lucy R. Ferguson* is free to guests) or by private plane, landing only by prior arrangement on a grass strip.

The imposing house with wide colonnade porches was the setting for John F. Kennedy Jr.'s 1996 wedding to Carolyn Bessette. It was built in 1901 by tycoon Thomas Carnegie for his daughter, Margaret. Operated by Mitty Ferguson, Carnegie's great-great-grandson, and his wife, Mary Jo, the inn contains family photographs, tabletop collections of seashore memorabilia, and antique rugs. A resident innkeeper, Brycea Merrill, takes care of day-to-day details.

Dark, heavy, late-19th-century furniture, some of it original to the house, appoints the inn's rooms. Bathrooms have antique tubs, and an enclosed backyard shower house is another full bath. Downstairs, the library bedroom has its own bath. The top floor holds two suites with king-size beds and private baths. Two cottages each contain two bedrooms with private baths and a common living area. All guest rooms were air-conditioned in 1998. By 1999, half-baths will be added to those guest rooms that share baths.

Rates include all meals. Breakfast is informal but substantial. Hors d'oeuvres start the cocktail hour; then a bell rings to announce the formal gourmet evening meal. Dressing for dinner (jackets for gentlemen and dressy casual attire for women) transforms the nightly ritual into a festive occasion, but the atmosphere still is relaxed.

The best times to visit are in spring and early autumn, when the insect population and humidity level remain low. *⚘ 7 double rooms with baths, 7 doubles and 1 suite share 3 baths, outdoor shower house. Air-conditioning; shuttle to ferry, bikes, guided nature tours. $275–$395; AP, afternoon refreshments. MC, V. No smoking.*

INN AT FOLKSTON ☞

509 W. Main St., Folkston 31537, tel./fax 912/496–6256 or tel. 888/509–6246, www.folksinn@planttel.net

Genna and Roger Wangsness, natives of the American Midwest, stumbled, literally, onto Folkston, where a rundown Craftsman bungalow just happened to be for sale. A local tourism booster told the couple how badly Folkston wanted a bed-and-breakfast inn; the house would make an excellent inn; and wouldn't they love to buy it and run it?

All that was true, so the Wangsnesses moved in and began to restore. Months went into removing paint from fine gray brick surrounding the living-room fireplace, stripping away layers of paint from fine old woodwork, and uncovering handsome wainscoting obscured by plasterboard. The effort paid off, revealing a classic 1920s-era Craftsman jewel.

A slow southern afternoon will beckon you to dawdle in the swing on the wide porch that's sheltered under a deep front gable. Inside, the front parlor is furnished with period pieces, and original doors have polished brass fixtures. Four guest rooms are individually styled, with soft colors, down comforters, and quilts. One is a suite, with a two-person whirlpool tub, a sitting area, and king-size bed; another has its own screened-in porch.

The inn is the best spot for exploring the Okefenokee, but other nearby activities attract as well. Sporting Clays, 10 mi outside Folkston, is designed for clay target shooting (you must bring your own equipment, including ammunition).

Breakfast begins early for guests who may have canoeing on their agendas, with coffee served on the hallway hutch. One unusual dish is the baked lemon yogurt, which is light, zingy, and packed with needed protein. *⚘ 4 double rooms with baths, 2 suites. Air-conditioning; off-street parking. $90–$125; full breakfast. AE, D, DC, MC, V. No smoking.*

JEKYLL ISLAND CLUB HOTEL ☞

371 Riverview Dr., Jekyll Island 31527, tel. 912/635–2600 or 800/535–9547, fax 912/635–2818, www.jekyllclub.com

Originally settled by Guale Indians, Jekyll Island was colonized first by Spanish missionaries, then by William Horton, one of General James Edward Oglethorpe's most trusted officers. Oglethorpe had named the island for a friend, Sir Joseph Jekyll. Horton developed a thriving plantation, and the remains of his second home still stand, begging for restoration.

The island was developed in the late 19th century as a private hunting club for New York's most wealthy. For its 100 members, the island became a vacation home. Its elite members included William Rockefeller, J. P. Morgan, Joseph Pulitzer, and William Vanderbilt. The centerpiece of this development was the dramatic Victorian clubhouse designed by architect Charles A. Alexander and built in 1887. With its Queen Anne–style turret, wraparound porch, and sweeping landscape, the club became famous for its fine dining and exquisite service. In 1896 a syndicate of selected wealthy members constructed the Sans Souci apartments, where J. P. Morgan resided. Finally, in 1901, an annex containing eight privately owned apartments was built at the end of the clubhouse.

These buildings, abandoned when the club ceased to function after World War II, form the nucleus of this unique resort. Custom-decorated guest accommodations in both the restored clubhouse and the Sans Souci apartments have warm color schemes, mahogany beds, luxurious baths, and some fireplaces. A croquet lawn, 22 mi of bicycle trails, tennis, golf, beaches, and swimming are among the amenities that recall the opulence of the club era. Bed-and-breakfast packages are available Sundays through Thursdays for $59 to $69 per person, depending on the season. The main dining room remains a culinary destination. ♨ *117 rooms, 17 suites. Air-conditioning, concierge, meeting and banquet rooms; off-street parking, 2 restaurants, pool, 9 tennis courts, croquet, bicycles. $119–$169; full breakfast with bed-and-breakfast package only. AE, D, DC, MC, V.*

KEHOE HOUSE ☜

123 Habersham St., Savannah 31401, tel. 912/232–1020 or 800/820–1020, fax 912/231–0208

Irish immigrant William Kehoe, who became wealthy in the ironworks business, built this imposing house to shelter his 10 children. Rich in classical and Italianate details, with typical Victorian elements, the 1892 Renaissance revival–style house sits imposingly on Columbia Square. Terra-cotta moldings, iron railings, and Corinthian columns are its most notable architectural details. The cost of construction was $25,000—a princely sum in that day.

Opened in 1993 as an inn, Kehoe House counts as its neighbor the famous Isaiah Davenport House, whose threatened demolition spawned the Historic Savannah Foundation.

Furnished with important period antiques, the inn has brass-and-marble chandeliers and a music room. Handwoven carpeting adorns the gleaming wood floors, made of pine, oak, and maple. The honeymoon suite, which has a sitting room, has access to a veranda. The beamed, high-ceiling attic space, decorated in period antiques and reproductions, has a large boardroom, making it ideal for meetings and banquets. Several small windows admit natural light, enhanced by track lighting and lamps.

The double parlor, with 14-ft ceilings and two fireplaces, is the ideal spot to enjoy the substantial breakfast. Chef Arthur Geiger's famous dishes include his superior pecan waffles. Costing $15 per person, full English tea is served in the afternoon; available by 48-hour reservation only, it features assorted tea sandwiches, scones, tartlets, or other baked goods made on the premises. Daily complimentary tea with cakes is served from 4 to 5 PM in the music room. The cocktail hour begins at 5 PM, with hors d'oeuvres set up at 6 PM. Chocolates, a Kehoe House robe, wine, and bottled water are the main ingredients in the Kehoe's turndown service. ♨ *13 double rooms with baths, 2 suites. Air-conditioning, concierge, meeting and banquet rooms; off-street parking, turndown service. $195–$250; full breakfast, afternoon tea, cocktail hour with hors d'oeuvres. AE, D, DC, MC, V. No smoking.*

LODGING AT LITTLE ST. SIMONS ISLAND ☛

Box 21078, St. Simons Island 31522, tel. 912/638–7472 or 888/733–5774,
fax 912/634–1811, www.pactel.com.au/lssi

To describe this island retreat as unique does it little justice. Nowhere in Georgia is a sunset more glorious than over the marshes that ring this still privately owned island. Most likely, you will be exhausted after a day exploring its 7 mi of pristine beaches. Trails crisscross the island and are excellent for hiking or bicycling. More than 200 different species of birds have been observed here. Canoe the island's waterways, or maybe go fly fishing under the direction of an Orvis-endorsed guide. Ride horses along the trails. You'll hear armadillos thrash through the underbrush and cranes call and spot alligators snoozing in the sun.

Family programs educate and entertain the smaller guests, who learn about the environment in a natural classroom. Parents and children may go on safari with an island naturalist or conduct a scavenger hunt.

Romance seekers will enjoy the privacy of a freestanding cottage, Michael's Cottage, which has a living room and kitchenette (no oven). The River Lodge and Cedar House are simply but comfortably furnished, with four bedrooms, each with its bath and deck. The bedrooms are arranged around a common living room with fireplace and screened-in porch across the back. The very rustic original lodge, now air-conditioned, has two bedrooms. The 1929 Helen House, made of traditional tabby (a shell-and-mortar material), has two baths, a living room, fireplace, and screened porch.

Rates include all three meals, prepared by a staff headed by chef Charles Bostick. His emphasis is on regional cuisine, so dishes include peach pecan pancakes for breakfast, fried chicken, blue crab cakes, crispy flounder with ginger peach sauce, and prickly pear sorbet. Lunch may be served in the dining room or packed in picnic baskets. ♨ *15 rooms with baths. Air-conditioning; hiking, bicycling, horseback riding, birding, canoeing, fly-fishing. $350–$550; AP. MC, V. No smoking.*

MANOR HOUSE ☛

201 W. Liberty St., Savannah 31401, tel. 912/233–9597 or 800/462–3696,
fax 912/236–9419, www.bbonline.com/ga/savannah/manorhouse/index.html

This 1830s Federal-style home is the city's oldest building south of Liberty Street. It hosted a group of Federal officers after Savannah was taken in 1865 and presented by its conqueror, General William T. Sherman, to Lincoln as a Christmas gift. The building once housed a tavern called Harry's and had fallen into serious neglect.

Now completely renovated, the Manor House is an all-suites bed-and-breakfast inn, with rooms furnished with period reproductions and antiques. Each suite has a master bedroom, living rooms, and bath; three have two-person whirlpool tubs; two have kitchens. The only inconvenience is that, in most of the suites, the baths are across the living room from the bedrooms.

Double parlors with fireplaces are furnished with fine English and American antiques, and Oriental rugs adorn the burnished heart-pine floors. Floor-to-ceiling windows open to a view of old oak trees lined with Spanish moss.

Across the back of the inn is a veranda set with rocking chairs for afternoon relaxation. Breakfast is a simple Continental affair with fresh juices, fresh-baked muffins or croissants, seasonal fruit, yogurt, coffee, and tea.

Small gatherings are easily held in the back part of the main parlor, but owner Tim Hargus, an experienced innkeeper, has renovated a large space at Savannah Station for a special events–conference facility. Off Martin Luther King Jr. Drive, the facility is about eight blocks from the inn. △ *5 suites with baths. Air-conditioning, cable TV/VCRs and phone in rooms, whirlpool tubs in 3 suites, turndown service; off-street parking. $185–$225; Continental breakfast, tea, wine and cheese. AE, MC, V.*

OPEN GATES 🐦
Vernon Square (Box 1526), Darien 31305, tel. 912/437–6985

A brick and white-picket fence outlines the perimeter of Open Gates bed-and-breakfast, the home of Carolyn Hodges. The white-frame Victorian house with Italianate details, gray shutters, and a red front door was built in 1876. It is tucked beneath a canopy of Spanish moss cascading from live oaks on Vernon Square, a national historic district, near the Altamaha River. Founded in 1736, the town was a shipping center for cotton and a busy lumber port.

An avid preservationist and nature lover, Hodges eagerly shares her knowledge with interested visitors. She conducts bird-watching expeditions on her excursion boat, which she gets to the water by pulling it behind her vintage Mercedes-Benz.

In a sunny den, a game table is set for Chinese checkers and shelves are filled with books on coastal history, including the diary of the English actress Fanny Kemble, who recorded her stand against slavery while living on one of the rice plantations owned by her husband, Pierce Butler of Philadelphia. Carolyn prepares a breakfast of plantation pancakes, served with an assortment of jams in her collection of fruit-shape jam pots.

One guest bedroom, in Savannah blue, has a sleigh bed and a display of antique clothes and books; another, done in peach and blue, has twin beds and antiquarian children's books; an upstairs room, painted light green, has wooden floors (cypress and heart-pine), pine furnishings, and botanical materials. A room above the garage with a private entrance has natural wood walls adorned with antique quilts.

The canoe standing on the back porch, the aquarium gurgling away in the den, and the baby grand, family portraits, and photographs in the Pompeiian-red front parlor remind you that this is a well-loved, lived-in family's home. △ *2 double rooms with baths, 2 doubles share 1 bath. Air-conditioning, cable TV in common area; large pool. $61–$66; full breakfast. No credit cards. No smoking.*

PERRIN GUEST HOUSE INN 🐦
208 Lafayette Dr., Augusta 30909, tel. 706/731–0920 or 800/668–8930,
www.innsandouts.com

Edward Perrin built a fine plantation home on his 5,000-acres in 1863, right in the middle of the raging Civil War. Today, much of that land constitutes the Augusta National Golf Course, home of the Masters tournament. The grounds surrounding the original plantation house lie off busy Washington Road, just off I–20, and provide a welcoming buffer from the nearby urban noise. In 1984, a similarly styled structure was built on this parcel as a bed-and-breakfast inn, but the enterprise was not successful.

Enter fifth-generation Augustan Ed Peel and his wife, Audrey, who also claims many generations in Augusta. The couple rescued the inn at bankruptcy auction in 1993. Audrey did all the redecorating. This is a busy pair: She owns a project engineering management company and employs her husband. "I work for her," he gleefully says. They also own a hunting club in Emmanuel County, on a 3,500-acre preserve.

With their offices in the original plantation house on the property, the couple keeps a steady eye on the inn, which is popular for special events, particularly weddings.

Styled in the manner of a 19th-century plantation house, with a wide veranda, the 1984 building has a large parlor and dining room furnished with period antiques. Rooms have a mix of antiques and period-style reproductions. Breakfast is meager Continental, with store-bought pastries, commercial cereal, fruit, and weak coffee, the sole unfortunate note at this otherwise nicely done bed-and-breakfast. The communal kitchen makes it easy to stash upgraded provisions in the refrigerator, and if you bring your own wine, decent glasses are available. ♣ *10 double rooms with baths. Fireplaces in rooms; 6 rooms with whirlpool tubs; gazebo, scuppernong arbor, patio. $100–$150; Continental breakfast. AE, MC, V. No smoking.*

PRESIDENT'S QUARTERS 🕊

225 E. President St., Savannah 31401, tel. 912/233–1600 or 800/233–1776, fax 912/238–0849, www.presidentsquarters.com

It's difficult to take a pair of 19th-century town houses and adapt them for contemporary hospitality purposes, especially when the project lies in the nation's largest historic district. But this gem—one of the best bed-and-breakfast values in Savannah—achieves that and more.

The inn is on Oglethorpe Square. Its two town houses, which have antiques and period-style reproductions, were built in 1863. The 16 gracious rooms, furnished with period-style reproduction pieces, are each named for an American president. Some have whirlpool tubs, the perfect cure for fatigue following walking tours of the district.

White wine awaits guests in their rooms, while fruit baskets are available on each floor. Sumptuous afternoon tea features delicious homemade cakes. The Continental breakfast, which includes home-baked breads, is served in each room. Pampering continues with the turndown service, which comes with surprises such as a glass of sherry or port and a nibble.

The inn is not smoking free, but smokers are limited to the first-floor rooms. An elevator is cleverly hidden to satisfy restoration requirements.

Formerly in the insurance industry, partners Stacy Stephens and Hank Smalling purchased the inn in 1997. Their expansion plans include acquiring the town house across the street for an additional three rooms. The original hand-painted ceiling murals are still intact there. ♣ *8 double rooms with baths, 11 suites. Air-conditioning, cable TV and phone in rooms, whirlpool tubs in 7 suites; gazebo, off-street parking. $137–$215; Continental breakfast. AE, D, DC, MC, V. Restricted smoking.*

STATESBORO INN 🕊

106 S. Main St., Statesboro 30458, tel. 912/489–8628 or 800/846–9466, fax 912/489–4785, www.statesboroinn.com

This large cream-colored Victorian frame house with shaded verandas was built in 1905 by W. G. Raines. Renovated and opened as a B&B in 1985, it offers such simple old-fashioned pleasures as rocking chairs on the front porch and such modern luxuries as whirlpool tubs.

In a quiet downtown area, the inn is 1 mi from Georgia Southern University and its botanical gardens. Visiting lecturers and professors are routinely housed at the inn during their stay in Statesboro. Savannah is an hour away via I–16.

The Garges family—Michele, Tony, and their daughter, Melissa—purchased the inn in 1993 and moved to Statesboro from Long Island, New York. Michele was in health care and Tony was a real estate agent. Bedrooms have brass beds, love seats, and country charm; some have private porches. Four bedrooms and three common rooms have working fireplaces. In a restored cabin behind the house, so the story goes, Willie McTell wrote "Statesboro Blues," a hit song for the Allman Brothers Band. McTell, a renowned blind blues musician, hailed from Thomson, Georgia, near Augusta.

Added to the rear of the main house and discreetly attached to it is a wing of rooms—distant from the street—that are especially quiet. A banquet facility that accommodates 100 is part of this addition; wedding receptions and other special events frequently take place in this space and in the garden outside. An adjacent Craftsman-style bungalow contains four rooms, each with a porch but sharing a common living room. The Garges live on the property.

The inn's public dining room is known for casual but elegant dining. The 50-seat, award-winning restaurant cooks up such regional specialties as crab cakes in tarragon cream sauce. The daily specials, such as a grilled duck breast with red-pepper glaze, are often particularly irresistible. The wine list is not lengthy, but it contains good selections. Breakfast is served in the same dining room and typically includes fresh fruit and an egg dish. Chef Tom Williams has good command of this kitchen. ⬧ *13 double rooms with baths, 1 suite, 4 rooms with baths in adjacent bungalow, bungalow with common living room. Restaurant, air-conditioning, cable TV and phone in rooms; off-street parking. $80–$150; full breakfast. AE, D, MC, V. No smoking, no large pets.*

SOUTHWEST GEORGIA

Though it's steeped in Civil War history, landscaped with lush gardens, and rich in plantation lore, this corner of Georgia is frequently overlooked. A hundred years ago, however, southwest Georgia's low-key charm developed a following among the celebrated and wealthy, and the area is associated with two American presidents. Franklin D. Roosevelt's Little White House in Warm Springs, the only home he ever owned, is now a museum, preserved as it was on the day he died there. When Jimmy Carter was elected president, the small town of Plains, west of Americus, became instantly famous.

Columbus, on the Chattahoochee River, is the region's largest city. Surrounded by the huge Fort Benning Military Reservation, it was the home of John Pemberton, the inventor of Coca-Cola, and is the site of the PGA Southern Open Golf Tournament. North of Columbus, in the Appalachian foothills, are Franklin D. Roosevelt State Park and Callaway Gardens, a resort development on 14,000 acres comprising woodlands, lakes, gardens, and wildlife that's the center of the spring Azalea Festival and an annual November steeplechase.

Near the Florida border lies Thomasville, a town of architectural grandeur, where the turn-of-the-century elite built hunting lodges and plantations and spent the winters entertaining. Many of the sporting retreats are still occupied, and a few are open to the public.

The southwest corner of Georgia also has good outlet shopping, camping, hunting, and white-water rafting. At the Andersonville National Historic Site, Civil War buffs can delve into the past. Those intrigued by Native American culture should explore Kolomoki Mounds State Historic Park, which contains seven mounds built during the 12th and 13th centuries by some of the most advanced tribes in the United States.

PLACES TO GO, SIGHTS TO SEE

Andersonville National Historic Site (Rte. 49, 10 mi north of Americus, tel. 912/924–0343). In 14 months between 1864 and 1865, 13,000 Union prisoners died in the Confederate prison on this site. The reconstructed portion of the stockade is open for tours, and the museum chronicles prisoners of war in all the American conflicts from the Revolution to Vietnam. In 1998, a new Prisoner of War memorial opened, detailing in prisoners' own words and with startling imagery the sacrifices of soldiers held in captivity. A nearby village has a log church, prison officials' quarters, a pioneer farm, and crafts and antiques stores.

Bellevue (204 Ben Hill St., LaGrange, tel. 706/884–1832). This Greek Revival house, famous for its Ionic columns, portico, and upstairs balcony, was built in the early 1850s. Tours are available Tuesday–Saturday.

Callaway Gardens (U.S. 27, Pine Mountain, tel. 706/663–2281 or 800/225–5292). Spread across 14,000 acres of woodlands, lakes, and gardens near LaGrange, this excellent family resort has four golf courses, soft and hard tennis courts, swimming, waterskiing, sailing, quail hunting, and the *Cecil B. Day Butterfly Center,* North America's largest free-flight, glass-enclosed conservatory in which you can walk among the butterflies (tel. 706/663–2281 or 800/225–5292).

The **Chattahoochee Valley Art Association** (112 Hines St., LaGrange, tel. 706/882–3267), in a restored Victorian building, displays a permanent collection of regional and local artists' works Tuesday through Saturday and puts on special monthly exhibits.

Columbus has a downtown historic district with well-preserved residential and commercial buildings that you can see on a walking tour. The *Columbus Museum* (1251 Wynnton Rd., tel. 706/649–0713) has an excellent folk-art collection, an outstanding regional history section, a fine-arts area, and a hands-on exhibit for children. The *Confederate Naval Museum* (202 4th St., tel. 706/327–9798), on the riverfront, contains the remains of two Confederate warships, the *Muscogee* and the *Chattahoochee.* The *Coca-Cola Space Science Center* (701 Front Ave., tel. 706/649–1470) has an observatory, a planetarium, and a *Challenger* Learning Center, where people high-school age and older go through one of three simulated space missions.

Cordele. This small town, established in 1888 by the Americus Investment Company, grew from the junction of two railroads and was the state capital during the final stage of the Civil War. The chamber of commerce (*see* Visitor Information, *below*) has brochures detailing walking tours of the turn-of-the-century downtown, which is on the National Register.

The **Fort Benning National Infantry Museum** (Building 396, Baltzell Ave., Fort Benning 31905, tel. 706/545–2958) traces the evolution of the infantry from the French and Indian War to the present. Original objects from American infantry history are on exhibit.

Jimmy Carter National Historic Site (300 N. Bond St., Plains 31780, tel. 912/824–3413). The 39th president's first campaign headquarters, in his hometown, was in the old depot, which today houses a collection of materials (photos, campaign buttons, posters, videos) relative to the 1976 campaign. The former Plains High School, where both Carters attended school, has a visitor center and informative collections of pictures and memorabilia from Carter's boyhood. The National Park Service has restored the Carter family farm (about 2½ mi from the visitor center) home and commissary, which is open to the public on an irregular basis. Plans call for developing 17 acres of the farm as a typical family farm of the 1920s and '30s, a project to be completed in a few years.

Little White House (Hwy. 85W and U.S. 27A, Warm Springs, tel. 706/655–5870). Franklin D. Roosevelt, afflicted with infantile paralysis, built this small house in Warm Springs as a vacation retreat during the early 1900s, so he could be near the beneficial waters. It's open daily for tours.

Pebble Hill Plantation (U.S. 319, Box 830, Thomasville 31799, tel. 912/228–2344), designed by Abram Garfield, son of President James A. Garfield, is a gracious, antiques-filled, country estate that belonged to one of the Hanna (*see*

Melhana Plantation, *below*, for background) family members, Mrs. Elisabeth Ireland Poe. Filled with objets d'art, fine old books, and hunt memorabilia, it hosted the Duke and Duchess of Windsor as well as numerous other important guests. The grounds contain a stable with museum and the old dairy.

Providence Canyon (43 mi south of Columbus, Rte. 1, Box 158, Lumpkin 31815, tel. 912/838–6202), a natural wonder of spectacular color and shape, was formed entirely by rainwater erosion. There's an interpretive center, picnic areas, and hiking trails.

Thomasville. This storybook town in a scenic setting was a booming winter resort during the late-19th and early 20th centuries. The rich and famous invested in its development by buying acreage and building mansions. Today, 71 plantations still operate in the area on 300,000 acres. The *Lapham-Patterson House* (626 N. Dawson St., tel. 912/225–4004), a landmarked Queen Anne 20-room cottage, is an architectural tour de force without a single right angle. It is open for tours. Memorabilia from the 1800s is displayed in the *Thomas County Museum* (725 N. Dawson St., tel. 912/226–7664).

Westville (S. Mulberry St., Lumpkin, tel. 912/838–6310). This living-history museum south of the town square depicts 19th-century Georgia life with its authentically restored buildings and daily crafts demonstrations.

RESTAURANTS

The cafeteria-style **Yoder's Deitsch Haus** (Hwy. 26, tel. 912/472–2024), 3 mi east of Montezuma on GA 26, is famous for its southern food, an adjacent gift shop selling local crafts from the Mennonite community, and bakery. In Americus, the **Windsor Hotel Dining Room** (125 W. Lamar St., tel. 912/924–1555) serves Continental cuisine. In historic Newnan, **Ten East Washington Street** (10 E. Washington St., tel. 770/502–9100) is a good spot for stylish Continental dishes. In Columbus, dine divinely on contemporary Continental fare at the **Olive Branch** (1032 Broadway, tel. 706/322–7410), and after dinner, slip upstairs to listen to music at the **Loft.** Other good spots are the **Garlic Clove** (6060 Veterans Pkwy., tel. 706/321–0882) and **Horizons Bistro** (5935 Veterans Pkwy., tel. 706/324–2566). In Thomasville, search out excellent fine dining (reservations essential), with lots of regional specialties, at **Melhana Plantation** (*see below*).

SHOPPING

Discount shopping draws visitors to a spot along I–75 near Valdosta (Exit 2, Lake Park), where both sides of the highway are virtual meccas for bargain hunters. The **Lake Park Mill Store Plaza** (tel. 912/559–6822) and the **Factory Stores of America Outlet Stores** (tel. 912/559–0366) are worth at least a half day's attention. In "Uptown" Columbus check out **10th Street** for the Galleria Riverside and the clusters of antiques shops and unique stores that dot this renovated historic district.

VISITOR INFORMATION

Albany Area Welcome Center and Chamber of Commerce (225 W. Broad Ave., Albany 31701, tel. 912/434–8700 or 800/475–8700). **Americus–Sumter County Chamber of Commerce** (Box 724, Americus 31709, tel. 912/924–2646). **Americus–Sumter County Tourism Council** (Box 724, Americus 31709, tel. 888/278–6837). **Andersonville Welcome Center** (Old Railroad Depot, Andersonville 31711, tel. 912/924–2558). **Columbus Convention & Visitors Bureau** (Box 2768, Columbus 31902, tel. 706/322–1613 or 800/999–1613). **Cordele Chamber of Commerce** (Box 158, Cordele 31010, tel. 912/273–1668).

Plains Visitors Information Center (U.S. 280, Plains 31780, tel. 912/824–7477). **Thomasville Welcome Center** (135 N. Broad St., Ground Floor, Thomasville 31792, tel. 912/227–7099 or 800/704–2350).

 RESERVATION SERVICE
R.S.V.P. Grits (541 Londonberry Rd., Atlanta 30327, tel. 404/843–3933 or 800/823–7787).

1884 PAXTON HOUSE ✎
445 Remington Ave., Thomasville 31792, tel. 912/226–5197, fax 912/226–9903,
www.1884paxtonhouseinn

Built, as the name suggests, in 1884, this elegant Victorian Gothic house has been well restored by Susie Sherrod, a retired army nurse (rank of colonel), who lives on the premises. The inn is in the Tockwotton Historic District—one of Thomasville's two historic districts, where the houses date from the 1850s to the 1920s. The center of town is just a short stroll away.

One of only two Victorian Gothic homes left in Thomasville, the house has a splendid wraparound veranda with rockers. The downstairs parlor, the former "women's parlor," has a molded plaster ceiling, original brass Victorian light fixtures, and a heart-pine fireplace. The dining room, centered by a solid mahogany table, is illuminated by a shimmering Austrian crystal chandelier. The main house has four fine bedrooms; an adjacent cottage has four more rooms. One bedroom (called the getaway room) is adjacent to the lap pool and hot tub. Antiques fill the nooks and crannies in both public spaces and guest rooms. Splendid collections of Meissen porcelain, dolls, Lladró figurines and clocks, as well as hand-painted Russian lacquer boxes fill the house.

The 18th Century Suite is ideal for the business traveler: It has an 18th-century-style secretary good for working moments, as well as a separate sitting room. The deep antique tub in the bath is a perfect spot to unwind.

Susie is justifiably proud of her sumptuous breakfast, which often includes juice, an egg dish, stuffed French toast, and good coffee. She also usually adds an aromatic batter bread or jam-filled pastry to the breakfast table. An on-site gift shop specializes in handmade Victorian-style Christmas ornaments and gifts.

Running the width of the house in the back and halfway down the side, the garden room contains a sitting room and a breakfast space. The garden beyond includes rose arbors, beds of blooming flowers, and a swing under the tree. ♠ *9 double rooms with baths. Air-conditioning; cable TV, phone, robes, iron and ironing board, and hair dryer in rooms; VCRs in 4 rooms, whirlpool tub in 1 room; garden, lap pool, hot tub. $90–$185; full breakfast, fruit, and sodas. AE, MC, V. No smoking.*

1870 ROTHSCHILD-POUND HOUSE ✎
201 7th St., Columbus 31901, tel. 706/322–4075 or 800/585–4075,
www.awts.com/poundhouse

Built in 1870, the Rothschild-Pound House, defined by a classic mansard roof, is one of two remaining Second Empire houses in Columbus. The inn is convenient to Columbus' restored historic district, downtown, and the Chattahoochee Riverwalk. Innkeepers Garry and Mamie Pound moved the house to its present location in 1993, restored its hardwood floors and fireplaces, and filled it with dramatic antiques. A working artist from a well-known family of artists, Garry shows his work in the house. Mamie looks after the inn and her young son, Murphy.

Fourteen-foot ceilings, a carved mahogany staircase, and marble and carved mahogany mantels in the rooms are among the house's architectural features. Two parlors frame either side of a generous entrance hall. A large veranda welcomes guests with its comfortable rocking chairs.

The three rooms in the main house all have antique beds (among them, mahogany and heart-pine four-posters) and private baths—one with a whirlpool—and working fireplaces. Next door, on the other side of a cheerful landscaped garden, a cottage has four more rooms, also with antique beds and private baths—one with a whirlpool tub. The cottage is excellent for business conferences; it has a large communal space, screened-in back porch, and kitchen. Plans include converting an adjacent vernacular Victorian house to suites, a project that should be finished in 1999.

Breakfast is substantial, with fresh or curried fruit and a main course, such as quiche, French toast, or pancakes. Mint juleps and peach daiquiris are specialties of the house. △ *7 double rooms with baths. Air-conditioning, cable TV/VCR and phone in rooms, whirlpool tub in 2 rooms, kitchenettes in 3 rooms; living room, garden, in-room coffee and tea. $85–$140; full breakfast, evening hors d'oeuvres and wine. AE, D, MC, V. No smoking.*

MAGNOLIA HALL 🐚
127 Barnes Mill Rd. (Box 326), Hamilton 31811, tel. 706/628–4566, www.bbonline.com/ga/magnoliahall

Resident innkeepers Dale and Kendrick Smith have varied backgrounds: Dale directed a city library in West Point, Georgia, and Ken still is a certified financial planner, a field he has been in for more than 25 years, with clients in several states. Ken also serves as mayor of Hamilton, seat of Harris County. Seeking something "different to do," the Smiths completely renovated the old Walton house that had sat empty for years. Special insulation for soundproofing and ramping for guests who use wheelchairs, originally planned for Ken's 102-year-old still-living father, make this intimate inn special.

This handsome Victorian cottage displays its original gingerbread trim and has a striking red roof, magnolia-leaf green siding, taupe shutters, and classic wraparound porch with rockers and hanging porch swing. Trudy, the resident cat, stays on the veranda, where she keeps an eye on comings and going from her own chair and cushion. On the main floors, which has three guest rooms, a wide central hallway separates the parlor and library; the two suites are upstairs. Each room has its own thermostat. The Victorian theme continues into the guest rooms, which have Eastlake walnut beds. One bedroom has cream striped wallcoverings and lace curtains while another has rose-and-cream bird-themed wallpaper and floral tapestry window treatments. Modern bathrooms, most with double sinks and seated showers, have color schemes that match the bedrooms.

The well-landscaped grounds are fragrant with the aroma of tea olives and other aromatic blooms. Climbing roses on an arbor near the stone terrace create the look and feel of an English garden. The giant magnolia tree lends its shade as well as its name to the inn.

Breakfast is served in the formal dining room. French toast baked and stuffed with fresh fruit served with baked eggs, Callaway Gardens stone-ground grits (cooked in cream!), and bacon, and fresh fruit pancakes topped with real whipped cream are among the most requested dishes. Room rates include passes to nearby Callaway Gardens. ♿ *3 rooms with baths, 2 suites. VCRs in 3 rooms. $90–$105; full breakfast, hors d'oeuvres. No credit cards. No smoking.*

MELHANA PLANTATION ✖

301 Showboat La., Thomasville 31792, tel. 912/226–2290 or 888/920–3030; fax 912/226–4585, www.melhana.com

Wealthy from oil money and industrial enterprises, Howard Melville Hanna of Cleveland, Ohio, represents just one of many monied northern families who bought plantations in southwest Georgia in the late-19th and early 20th centuries. He purchased this plantation, originally built in the 1820s and known as Melrose, in the late-19th century. Nearby Pebble Hill (*see* Places to Go, Sights to See, *above*) was a Hanna-owned plantation, and another daughter owned yet a third plantation.

Charlie and Fran Lewis purchased a piece of the plantation land and shared their home, Owl's Nest, on that parcel with their two sons Zachary and Nick. In 1997, the couple purchased the adjacent Pink House, the heart of the original 3,000-acre plantation, and some 40 acres to develop a luxury resort property. Listed on the National Register of Historic Places, the Pink House, the former Hanna family residence, now contains 11 sumptuously furnished guest rooms, many with whirlpool tubs and fireplaces. Lewis family businesses include insurance brokerage and marketing for Charlie, who also manages investments, and jewelry design for Fran. But most of their energies these days are devoted to developing the resort.

To enjoy Melhana, explore the exquisite gardens, which are being carefully restored and reinvigorated. Relax on the porch with a book, or ride a horse from nearby stables down an easy trail. The theater on the site is thought to have been used for a first screening of *Gone With the Wind*, as neighbor Jock Whitney was one of the film's investors.

Breakfast might include fresh fruit and juices, baked egg dishes or omelets, and homemade breads. The menu in the restaurant changes weekly, but look out for fried green tomatoes with Vidalia onion relish, rosemary-skewered shrimp, and game when the region's hunting season is in full swing. ♿ *33 rooms with baths. Air-conditioning, robes in rooms, whirlpool tubs in 16 rooms; restaurant, conference center, theater. $250–$550; full breakfast. AE, D, DC, MC, V.*

1906 PATHWAY INN ✖

501 S. Lee St., Americus 31709, tel. 912/928–2078 or 800/889–1466, www.bestinns.net/usa/ga/pathway.html

Americus is, in many ways, a classic country Victorian town. At its center lies the restored Windsor Hotel (*see below*), linchpin for the well-done downtown redevelopment. In the heart of Americus's historic district, the Pathway Inn, a classic Victorian residence built in 1906 with a wide veranda, columned portico, and glorious stained-glass windows, has been pristinely restored.

Angela and Chuck Nolan, from England and Michigan respectively, moved up from the Florida Keys when they purchased the inn in 1998. The upstairs spaces are the hub of the inn, with its large rooms, some with whirlpool tubs, and some with king-size beds. An upstairs hallway serves as a sitting area; its entrance privatizes these guest rooms from the rest of the house.

One of three upstairs suites is the Carter Room, named for the nearby former citizen who became president. It has a king-size bed, a desk for working, comfortable chairs, a TV/VCR, and a small video library. Carter portraits and memorabilia decorate the room. The Roosevelt Room, one of the two downstairs suites, has a queen-size bed and a bath with a marble shower.

Breakfast often features regional specialties, such as locally made sausage and syrup made from blueberries grown in neighboring Marion County. Hot dishes often include French toast à l'orange, blintz casserole topped with apricot preserves, and a western breakfast casserole. Wine and cheese are available upon arrival; daily afternoon tea is served. ♙ *5 double rooms with baths. Air-conditioning, cable TV and phone in rooms, whirlpool tubs and ceiling fans in some rooms, VCR in 1 room. $75–$125; full breakfast. AE, D, MC, V. No smoking, pets by prior arrangement.*

WINDSOR HOTEL ℘
125 W. Lamar St., Americus 31709, tel. 912/924–1555 or 888/297–9565, fax 912/928–0533

Among Georgia's and America's most intriguing historic hotels is the Windsor Hotel, a seeming maze of redbrick turrets and Romanesque arcades by Swedish-born (1846) Atlanta architect Gottfried L. Norrman. Norrman's work was all over this small (population 18,000) southwest Georgia town, as well as across the entire southeast. Built in 1892, and named for John Windsor, one of its developers, the Richardsonian Romanesque eclectic hotel is on the National Register of Historic Places and is one of the National Trust's Historic Hotels of America.

Time was not kind to the hotel, which had disintegrated by the 1960s and was threatened with demolition. But Americus's citizens rose up to reclaim their grande old dame before she could be leveled for, yes, a parking lot. The original 100 rooms were reduced to 53 rooms and suites, and all were given private baths. Today, there is a small meeting room and a fine dining room.

Entering the hotel, one is amazed by its lobby, a study in neo-Moorish design. Norrman was influenced to some extent by the Hotel Alcázar in St. Augustine, Florida. Moorish-style arches sweep to the second story, and the entrance floor tiles, made of Georgia marble and oak and installed in 1912, were laid in a complex geometric pattern reminiscent of floors in southern Spain.

Reproduction gold oak furnishings, deeply carved, appoint the rooms. One of the suites served as home to Hume Cronin and Jessica Tandy while she was filming *Fried Green Tomatoes*. Amenities include a Ladies Tea Parlor, a pub, and a fine gifts gallery. Street level retail shops include an antiques shop.

Special events at the hotel include holiday madrigal dinners with singing by faculty and students from nearby Georgia Southwestern University. ♙ *51 double rooms with baths, 2 suites. Air-conditioning, cable TV and phone in rooms, hair dryers; in-room coffee and tea. $80–$195; no breakfast. AE, D, MC, V.*

In case you want to see the world.

At American Express, we're here to make your journey a smooth one. So we have over 1,700 travel service locations in over 120 countries ready to help. What else would you expect from the world's largest travel agency?

do more ®

http://www.americanexpress.com/travel

Travel

In case you want to be welcomed there.

We're here to see that you're always welcomed at establishments everywhere. That's why millions of people carry the American Express® Card – for peace of mind, confidence, and security, around the world or just around the corner.

do more®

Cards

In case you're running low.

We're here to help with more than 118,000 Express Cash locations around the world. In order to enroll, just call American Express before you start your vacation.

do more

Express Cash

And just in case,

We're here with American Express® Travelers Cheques and Cheques *for Two*.® They're the safest way to carry money on your vacation and the surest way to get a refund, practically anywhere, anytime.
Another way we help you...

AMERICAN EXPRESS

do more ®

Travelers Cheques

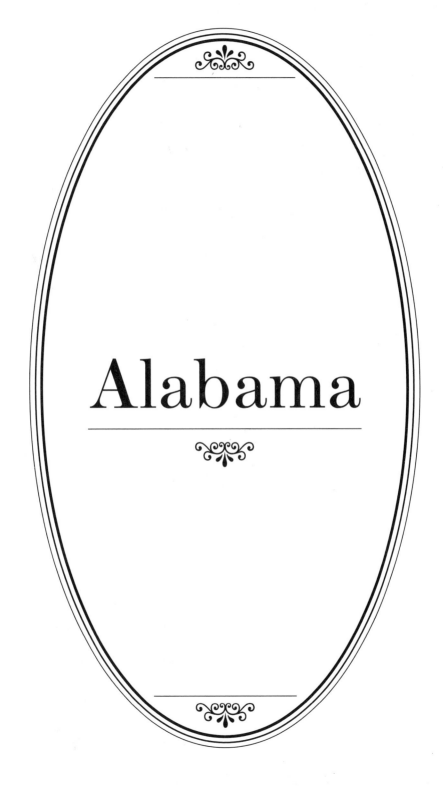

Alabama

Alabama

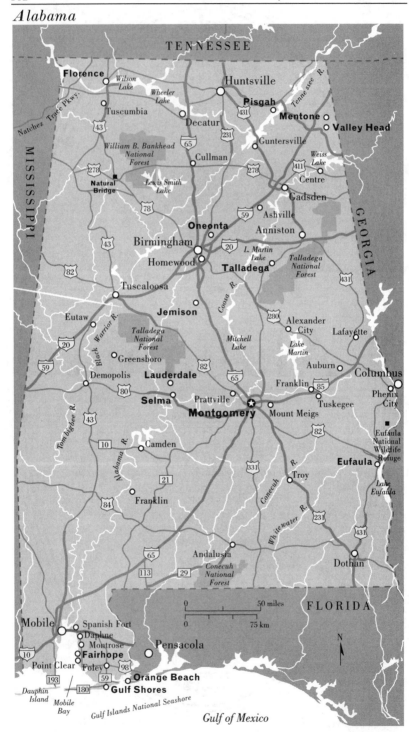

TENNESSEE

Florence
Wilson Lake
Wheeler Lake
Huntsville
Pisgah
431
Mentone
○ **Valley Head**
Tuscumbia
43
Decatur
231
Guntersville
411 Weiss Lake
William B. Bankhead National Forest
65
Cullman
278
Centre
278
Natural Bridge
Lewis Smith Lake
Gadsden
78
59
Ashville
GEORGIA
Oneonta
Birmingham
20
L. Martin Lake
Talladega National Forest
Anniston
Homewood
Talladega
431
Coosa R.
Tuscaloosa
43
82
Jemison
280
Alexander City
Lafayette
Eutaw
Talladega National Forest
Mitchell Lake
Lake Martin
20
Black Warrior R.
Greensboro
82
Auburn
Columbus
59
Demopolis
Lauderdale
65
Franklin
85
Phenix City
80
Selma
Prattville
★
Tuskegee
43
Montgomery
Mount Meigs
Eufaula National Wildlife Refuge
10
Camden
82
Eufaula
Alabama R.
21
331
Conecuh R.
Troy
Lake Eufaula
84
Franklin
Tombigbee R.
Whitewater R.
231
431
65
Andalusia
Dothan
113
29
Conecuh National Forest
FLORIDA
0   50 miles
0   75 km
Mobile
Spanish Fort
Daphne
Montrose
Pensacola
N
10
Fairhope
Point Clear
Foley
193
59
98
Orange Beach
180
Gulf Shores
Dauphin Island
Mobile Bay
Gulf Islands National Seashore
Gulf of Mexico

Natchez Trace Pkwy.
MISSISSIPPI
278
82
59
10

NORTH ALABAMA

Alabama can easily be divided into three parts: the upland country from Birmingham north; the central section, known for its fertile black soil; and the Gulf Coast, with picture-postcard perfect beaches. The rocky and mountainous land in the northern section is filled with lakes and hideaways, small towns that time seems to have forgotten, and cities like Huntsville, where the Redstone Arsenal is credited with putting the first man on the moon. Huntsville also is home to the Twickenham Historic District, with more pre–Civil War houses than anywhere else in the state. Many date to 1814.

There are several covered bridges left in this part of the state, as well as a number of state and national parks that offer recreation and noteworthy sights. The longest natural bridge east of the Rockies is near Haleyville; in DeSoto State Park there's the 110-ft DeSoto Falls in the beautiful Little River Canyon. Russell Cave National Park has the remains of Native American tribes dating back 8,000 years.

Farther south, set in a valley amid rolling hills, is Birmingham, the state's largest city and in the '20s and '30s the South's major industrial area. Atop Red Mountain on the city's south side is the towering statue of Vulcan, symbol of the iron and steel industry on which the city's wealth was founded. Steel is no longer the major employer, but roots of the industry are remembered at Sloss Furnaces, which is today a tourist attraction and an outdoor theater for concerts. The city, now dedicated to medicine instead of steel, is one of the country's leading centers of medical care and study. An impressive fine-arts museum specializes in Asian and French art, hosts traveling exhibitions from national galleries, and contains a scholarly library.

 PLACES TO GO, SIGHTS TO SEE

The **Birmingham Botanical Gardens** (2612 Lane Park Rd., tel. 205/879–1227) comprise 67 acres in which a Japanese garden, a rose garden, and fern and rock gardens are intermingled with fountains and plantings of azaleas, camellias, and dogwoods.

Birmingham Museum of Art (2000 8th Ave. N, tel. 205/254–2565) has the S. H. Kress collection of Asian porcelains and bronzes, paintings, and silver and the Hitt collection of 18th-century art and decorations.

Historic Huntsville Depot (320 Church St., Huntsville, tel. 800/678–1819) is in one of the country's oldest surviving railway stations, built in 1860. The museum covers the history of the region's transportation.

Ivy Green (300 W. North Commons, Tuscumbia, tel. 256/383–4066) is the birthplace of Helen Keller and the house where her teacher, Annie Sullivan, taught her to communicate despite her deafness and blindness. It is complete with Keller's furniture, schoolroom, and clothes.

Museum of Art in Huntsville (In the Von Braun Civic Center, 700 Monroe St., tel. 256/535–4350) has changing exhibits and permanent collections of American paintings, sculpture, and Japanese netsuke (small, intricately carved toggles). It is closed Monday.

Sloss Furnaces National Historic Landmark (20 32nd St. N, Birmingham, tel. 205/324–1911), a former mill, hosts concerts and festivals and is open for self-guided tours. It is closed Monday.

U.S. Space and Rocket Center (1 Tranquility Base, Huntsville, tel. 256/837–3400 or 800/637–7223), the largest space museum in the world, depicts the development of space exploration. You can see the 354-ft *Saturn V* moon rocket, experience effects of weightlessness, and try a thrill ride that takes you on a 4G, 45-mph trip straight up a 180-ft tower and then drops you back down to earth.

VisionLand (5051 Prince St., Bessemer, tel. 205/481–4758), 16 mi southwest of Birmingham, opened in the spring of 1998, with a themed water park, rides for adults and children, and an amphitheater. Rampage, a wooden roller coaster, has 18 crossovers, a dozen turns, and dramatic 120-ft drop.

Vulcan Park (U.S. 31 S at Valley Ave., Birmingham, tel. 205/328–6198) surrounds a huge statue of Vulcan, the god of metalworking, which stands atop Red Mountain overlooking the city. You can climb to Vulcan's top or take the elevator for a bird's-eye view of downtown.

RESTAURANTS

In Birmingham, **Highlands Bar & Grill** (2011 11th Ave. S, tel. 205/939–1400) is known for its innovative southern cooking prepared by a Cordon Bleu–trained chef. **Hosie Barbecue** (321 17th St. N, tel. 205/326–3495) features an outstanding barbecue created by Hosie King. If you've never tried soul food, this is your chance for pig ears. At **Nabeel's Cafe** (1706 Oxmoor Rd., Homewood, tel. 205/879–9292) expect foods prepared with some artistry, whether it's an eggplant casserole, spinach-and-feta croissant, or spinach pie. Cozy, high-backed booths add a welcome touch. The **Irondale Cafe** (1906 1st Ave. N, Irondale, tel. 205/956–5258), the inspiration for novelist Fannie Flagg's Whistlestop Cafe, serves those famous fried green tomatoes. **Furnace Master's** (At Tannehill Ironworks Historical State Park, tel. 205/477–6102) has an extravagant Friday- and Saturday-night seafood buffet. Post-dining rocking on the front porch of this log structure is recommended. At **Classical Fruits/Bar-B-Que** (8831 Ala. Hwy. 157, Moulton, tel. 256/974–8813), Hoyt and Franny Adair make great barbecue, chicken stew, chicken finger plate, catfish, fudge, and chocolate-covered apples. Memorable barbecue has been the norm for years at **Big Bob Gibson Bar-B-Q** (1715 6th Ave. SE, Decatur, tel. 256/350–6969), where grandson Don McLemore carries on the family tradition. Don't miss the cream pies, smoked turkey, and white barbecue sauce.

SHOPPING

South of Birmingham, the **Riverchase Galleria** (Intersection of I–459 and U.S. 31S, tel. 205/985–3039) is one of the largest shopping malls in the Southeast. The bi-level mall, which adjoins the Wynfrey Hotel, has a huge food court and more than 200 stores, including anchors **Macy's, Rich's, JCPenney, McRae's, Sears,** and **Parisian.** Clothiers include Laura Ashley and Banana Republic. **Brookwood Village** (623 Brookwood Village, between U.S. 280 and U.S. 31S, tel. 205/871–0406) is an upscale mall with 75 specialty stores, **Rich's, McRae's,** and a food court. About 60 mi north of Birmingham, **Boaz** (tel. 800/746–7262) has more than 200 outlet and specialty stores. **Mountain Top Flea Market** (6 mi west of Attalla on Hwy. 278, tel. 800/535–2286) opens every Sunday at 5 AM and consists of 1,000 dealers selling antiques, collectibles, new merchandise, handicrafts, and fresh produce.

VISITOR INFORMATION

Birmingham Convention and Visitors Bureau (2200 9th Ave. N, Birmingham 35203–1100, tel. 205/458–8000 or 800/458–8085). **Huntsville/Madison County Convention and Visitors Bureau** (700 Monroe St., Huntsville 35801–5570, tel. 256/533–5723 or 800/772–2348).

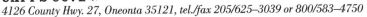

CAPPS COVE

4126 County Hwy. 27, Oneonta 35121, tel./fax 205/625–3039 or 800/583–4750

Thirty miles north of Birmingham, Capps Cove is the handiwork of retirees Sybil and Cason Capps, Alabama natives who searched far and wide before falling in love with the rushing stream that dissects their 20 Blount County acres. Their compound, begun in 1995, includes their two-story brick home, a 10-pew wedding chapel, two guest cabins, an antiques store, and a barn suitable for parties.

A wide, oak stair landing between guest bedrooms holds a collection of antique mirrors in oak frames; one dates to the 1700s. Nearby are a Victorian wicker baby buggy and a black mourning dress from the early 1900s. The balcony also has antique wicker furnishings and a view of the nearby stream and woods.

In the main house, the Ladies Room has an antique brass-and-iron bed covered with crisp, white vintage linen. Feminine, white vintage clothing decorates this room that has an antique dresser and dressing table. Across the hall, the Gentlemen's Room has a mahogany bedroom suite with an antique red-and-white, double Irish chain quilt covering the bed. Accents are an assortment of men's hats and accessories from the late 1800s and early 1900s.

The Rustic cabin is made of board and batten with a sleeping loft upstairs and another bedroom and sitting area downstairs. The cabin has a porcelain wood cookstove, stacked-stone fireplace, rocking chairs, game table, small refrigerator, and microwave.

The Honeymoon cabin, with white walls and cathedral ceiling, has an antique brass-and-iron bed, reclining love seat, stacked-stone fireplace, refrigerator, and microwave. A front-porch swing overlooks the Blackburn River.

In spring and summer, guests may have breakfast on the screened porch. Other times, breakfast, always elaborate, is served in the formal dining room, where china cabinets display Sybil's collection of flow blue china and Cason's pearl-handle flatware collection. **⚘** *2 double rooms with baths, 2 cabins with baths. Air-con-*

ditioning, fireplace, refrigerator, and microwave in cabins; hiking trails, free home tour. $80–$150; full breakfast, soft drinks and snacks. MC, V. No smoking.

LODGE ON GORHAM'S BLUFF ☙
101 Gorham Dr. (Box 160), Pisgah 35765, tel. 256/451–3435, fax 256/451–7403

In the early 1990s, the McGriff family began to develop their land, 3 mi north of Pisgah, into a new town that will eventually have scores of homes, shops, an artists' workshop district, meetinghouse, town green, and post office. This new town, or neighborhood, is being built with a nod to tradition: Sidewalks and front porches, for instance, are common. The Lodge on Gorham's Bluff is the crown jewel of the endeavor.

The three-story, clapboard lodge has upstairs and downstairs porches across the front. It is strategically built with a view of the Tennessee River and passing barges. The McGriffs, with deep roots in nearby Sand Mountain, where Bill is a CPA and Clara is a former schoolteacher, have outfitted their lodge with thick robes, smooth cotton sheets, down-filled pillows and comforters, bath salts, and whirlpool tubs. Soft music plays throughout common areas and in bedrooms; guests have volume controls at bedside.

Third-floor rooms, ideal for honeymooners, have whirlpool tubs for two and fireplaces that open both into the bedroom and bath. Second-floor rooms have one-person jetted tubs, and balconies with rocking chairs and abundant planters. The glass-enclosed tower with a widow's walk is a good place to savor the view.

In the first-floor living area, guests have access to a VCR, a collection of videotapes, abundant books, and a small kitchen stocked with snacks and cold drinks. A 20-seat restaurant at the lodge serves Sunday lunch and candlelight dinner nightly. Reservations are required; lodge guests have priority.

The Overlook Pavilion is a good place to watch the river and spot soaring eagles. This new Appalachian town is a welcome respite from the bustle of big-city living. ⏃ *6 double rooms with baths. Restaurant, air-conditioning, phone, whirlpool tub, robes, and fireplace in rooms, VCR in common area; fishing, kite flying, hiking. $110–$165; full breakfast, snack-filled kitchen. AE, MC, V. Some age restrictions for children.*

MENTONE INN ☙
Rte. 117 (Box 290), Mentone 35984, tel. 256/634–4836 or 800/455–7470

Lookout Mountain, in extreme northeastern Alabama, forms the backdrop for the Mentone Inn, a building perfectly suited to its setting. Stone steps, dark wood, flagstone paths, flowers, and evergreens invite visitors to the inn's entrance. A stone foundation supports the screened-in porch, set with rocking chairs, a swing, and small tables. Rolling hills and valleys on all sides are ablaze in the fall with foliage too dramatic to seem real.

The inn is owned and operated by Frances Waller, a retired social worker who perceives her innkeeper's role as a continuing way to serve people. (She even offers reduced rates to fellow social workers and therapists.) Mrs. Waller, who bought this hideaway in 1995, has a way with people, pausing often to listen and to talk. Her grandmother's sheet music and handwritten recipes fill walls in the inn and create the feel of a favorite relative's home you visited as a child. A glance around shows family photos from the 1920s—the same era as the house— plus china hand-painted by Mrs. Waller's mother.

Near a stone fireplace, guests play dominoes or bridge in the cozy parlor, then for a change sit on the porch. In the glassed-in dining area, paneled walls oversee a long table and several smaller ones, all with views of the mountains. There's complimentary coffee—and sometimes homemade cookies—in the kitchen. Everything feels the way a relaxed country inn should.

A handsome staircase made of pale wood leads upstairs. Walls in the house are wood-paneled in natural beaded pine; some are painted, some left their natural color. Five of the bedrooms, all with period furnishings, have two beds so that more than two guests may stay comfortably. ♣ *12 double rooms with baths. Air-conditioning, cable TV in living room. $70; full breakfast, afternoon refreshments. AE, MC, V. No smoking.*

RAVEN HAVEN ☞
651 County Rd. 644, Mentone 35984, tel./fax 256/634–4310

Tucked away off the beaten path in quiet Mentone, Raven Haven is a welcome retreat owned and operated by Tony and Eleanor Teverino, who are gracious, easygoing hosts. Lookout Mountain is the backdrop for this rock home with a wide front porch filled with rocking chairs.

Guest rooms do not have the distraction of telephones and televisions, but in the common areas there is a good supply of books and a TV/VCR with a video library. Spacious, manicured grounds, including 10 acres outside the back door, are the place to sit in a swing chair or take a 2-mi walk around the property.

The Nautical Room, with private entrance and deck, has pine paneling, a cannonball bed, port holes, and rope hammock. The Queen Anne Room, fashioned after an 18th-century boudoir, has a skylight in the shower and a stained-glass window above the bed.

The Casablanca Room, with archways replacing what once were closets, is set up as a tropical getaway that Bogie would have liked. The bath includes a large walk-in shower that is handicap accessible. The Little Room on the Prairie, the only guest room with air-conditioning, has a stone fireplace with gas logs, ceiling beams covered with rough-cut pine, and walls that are rough boards and batten. The bath has a walk-in shower.

Tea, hot chocolate, a selection of coffees, and home-baked snacks are left out for guests. ♣ *4 double rooms with baths. TV in common area, VCR in library, fax. $70–$90; full breakfast, snacks. No credit cards. No smoking, children over 14 only, 2-night minimum Apr.–Oct.*

WINSTON PLACE: AN ANTEBELLUM MANSION ☞
353 Railroad St. (Box 165), Valley Head 35989, tel. 256/635–6381 or 888/494–6786, www.virtualcities.com

In the 150-year-old town of Valley Head, centrally located between Chattanooga, Birmingham, and Atlanta, Winston Place is nestled on 25 acres dotted with hardwood trees, set against picturesque Lookout Mountain Parkway. The innkeeper is science teacher Leslie Bunch, who is married to Alabama all-American Jim Bunch. Leslie's effervescent personality makes a stay here memorable. The couple and their school-age children live in a small home just behind the main house.

On the National Register of Historic Places, the stately home, dating to 1831, was originally the residence of the Winston family of Winston Hall, Yorkshire, England. Sweeping verandas and majestic columns are a simple statement of Winston's financial success and a tribute to the master craftsmen he assembled to perfect his home. During the Civil War, the home became headquarters for 30,000 Union soldiers. Winston Place has four massive columns and 2,000 square ft of verandas, both upstairs and down. For those resting on the verandas, the mountain view from porch swings and rockers is framed by large columns.

Spacious suites offer modern conveniences, including cable TV, luxury bedding by Crown Crafts, central heat and air, and private baths. Winston Place has original antique furniture, family mementos throughout, a huge kitchen open to guests, and front-porch rockers. An upstairs suite has two queen poster beds, curtains with soft valances, and designer fabric; a seating area with a fireplace is the perfect place to curl up with a book.

Each morning, a full, formal breakfast is served with china and crystal. A bonus for traveling families is that the entire house, which sleeps from 12 to 18, is available for rent for $650 per night, $3,000 per week, or $6,000 per month. ⚠ *1 room with 2 queens, 1 room with king and queen, 1 with 2 doubles, 1 suite with 2 kings and 1 queen, all with baths. Air-conditioning, cable TV, kitchen, free home tour. $125–$150; full breakfast. MC, V. No smoking.*

WOOD AVENUE INN 🐚
658 Northwood Ave., Florence 35630, tel. 256/766–8441

Square and octagonal towers rise high above the garden of this three-story Queen Anne house. On a tree-lined street in a college town, this inn, built in 1889, is pure Victorian, with 14-ft ceilings, nooks, crannies, and bay windows.

Owners Alvern and Gene Greeley have both worked in various fields, he as a clergyman turned auto-parts salesman, she as the dean of a Bible college and then as a real estate agent. With her radiant smile and enveloping warmth, Alvern makes innkeeping an art form. Since she likes to pamper people, she is doing what comes naturally in running a bed-and-breakfast and delights in making home-cooked delicacies. Her zucchini bread is unsurpassed.

The house has an inviting porch with green wicker furniture and begonias in flower boxes. The formal parlor opens off the wide central hall, which bisects the two lower floors. One drawing room has dark-green walls with gleaming white woodwork, a 150-year-old red velvet sofa, and a cabinet in a corner. Its rosewood shelves have held china for more than a century. But it's the bric-a-brac that sets the tone. Arranged among and around the furniture are enough figurines, artificial flowers, bows, wreaths, footstools, and ruffled cushions to stock a theatrical warehouse. Five minutes in that room and you know exactly how the well-to-do characters in a Dickens novel live.

Fireplaces are in every room, even the bathrooms, two of which have narrow tubs resting on claw feet. Beside the tub a table holds a bottle of sparkling cider and two silver-wrapped chocolates. After a good soak, you climb into a huge bed, its pale rose-colored spread topped by matching pillows against the 19th-century-look wallpaper.

Outside the back door, wisteria climbs over an arbor, and a black carriage handmade by the Amish stands under a protective roof. ⚠ *6 double rooms and 2 singles with baths, 2 suites. Air-conditioning in rooms, cable TV in lounge; badminton, horseshoes. $62–$95; full breakfast. MC, V. No smoking.*

CENTRAL ALABAMA

Central Alabama, sometimes called the Black Belt because of its rich black soil, runs through the midsection of the state from the Mississippi line to the area around Montgomery. This is the land that produced King Cotton and that until the Civil War supported immensely rich plantations. It is flat, gentle land, wooded with oak, hickory, sweet gum, beech, magnolia, sycamore, and semitropical bay trees and palmettos. Most of the large holdings have become cattle farms.

On the eastern edge of the central region lies Tuskegee, where in 1881 Booker T. Washington founded a university for African-Americans. Here, in what remains a predominantly African-American town, the university provides an intellectual and educational haven and carries on the research begun by George Washington Carver, whose work with peanuts and sweet potatoes helped to change the lives of southern farmers.

The Black Belt now provides a background for towns like Selma, Franklin, Demopolis, and Greensboro, full of antebellum houses and cemeteries—the one in Selma holds the grave of Abraham Lincoln's sister-in-law. Many of these homes are in a fine state of preservation and look as though Scarlett O'Hara should come strolling through the white columns to rest on encircling porches. Some of the homes are open to the public during spring festivals and pilgrimages, for a few weeks allowing visitors to relive the days when Great-great-grandmother's silver teapot was used regularly and had no need to be hidden from the Yankee soldiers.

Montgomery, the state capital, was the site of major events in both the Civil War and the civil rights movement. Martin Luther King Jr. preached here regularly from the pulpit of the Baptist church on Dexter Avenue. The church is within the shadow of the renovated state capitol; the bronze star where Jefferson Davis stood to be sworn in as president of the Confederacy is still kept brightly polished. The Montgomery bus boycott began here and the Selma March ended here, not far from the First White House of the Confederacy.

PLACES TO GO, SIGHTS TO SEE

Alabama Shakespeare Festival (1 Festival Dr., Montgomery, tel. 334/271–5353 or 800/841–4273) is the world's fifth largest Shakespeare company. It has two theaters and a professional repertory company. The season runs October through August.

Alabama State Capitol (Bainbridge St. at Dexter Ave., Montgomery, tel. 334/242–3935), a neoclassical building, has been restored to antebellum magnificence.

Civil Rights Memorial (400 Washington Ave., Montgomery, tel. 334/264–0286) was designed by Maya Lin, who also designed the Vietnam Memorial in Washington. This one of black granite and flowing water honors those people killed in the struggle for black equality.

Dexter Avenue King Memorial Baptist Church (454 Dexter Ave., Montgomery, tel. 334/263–3970), where Martin Luther King Jr. was pastor during his early civil rights struggles, has a large civil rights mural in the basement. It is open to the public weekdays.

F. Scott Fitzgerald Museum (919 Felder Ave., Montgomery, tel. 334/264–4222) is the world's only museum devoted to the noted author. The Fitzgeralds lived here briefly.

Montgomery Zoo (North Blvd. between Coliseum Blvd. and Lower Wetumpka Rd., Montgomery, tel. 334/240–4900) is a sprawling complex with a miniature train and many rare and endangered species.

Montgomery Museum of Fine Arts (1 Museum Dr., tel. 334/244–5700) is in the same park as the Alabama Shakespeare Festival and includes a café and children's hands-on gallery.

Old Alabama Town (301 Columbus St., Montgomery, tel. 334/240–4500) is a recreation of structures and landscapes detailing how people lived in central Alabama from 1818 to 1900.

Jasmine Hill Gardens and Outdoor Museum (Jasmine Hill Rd., Wetumpka, tel. 334/567–6463) is a "Little Corner of Greece." Gardens are filled with art objects and colorful plantings.

Tuskegee Institute, a national historic site on the campus of Tuskegee University, is managed by the National Park Service. The *Carver Museum* (Tuskegee campus; 1212 Old Montgomery Rd., tel. 334/727–3200) has artifacts, photo displays, and films on the institute and on George Washington Carver's research with peanuts and sweet potatoes. Park rangers conduct guided tours of *The Oaks* (1212 Old Montgomery Rd., tel. 334/727–3200), home of Booker T. Washington and a fine example of Queen Anne Victorian architecture designed and built in 1899 by blacks. Nearby **Tuskegee National Forest** (tel. 334/727–2652) is ideal for hiking and fishing.

RESTAURANTS

In Montgomery, **Sassafras Tearoom** (532 Clay St., tel. 334/265–7277) is a Victorian-style restaurant in the Cottage Hill district. Sassafras tea is served with accompaniments such as chicken salad, buttermilk pie, and other home-cooked goodies. **Vintage Year** (405 Cloverdale Rd., tel. 334/264–8463), which serves dinner only, has built a reputation for new American cuisine–style dishes such as snapper, salmon, and shrimp. **Jubilee Seafood** (1057 Woodley Rd., Cloverdale, tel. 334/262–6224) is small in size but big on fresh seafood. West Indies salad and barbecue shrimp are especially tasty. In a former filling station, **Sinclair's** (1051 Fairview Ave. E, tel. 334/834–7462) has salads, sandwiches, pasta, fresh seafood, and steak. **Heart of the Melon Cafe** (1031 Fairview Ave. E, tel. 334/269–5000) serves upscale southern foods and homemade desserts. Just across the river from Tuscaloosa, in the small town of Northport, the **Globe**

(430 Main Ave., tel. 205/391–0949) is a trendy eatery decorated with theatrical paraphernalia. It serves eclectic and ethnic gourmet cuisine from around the world.

SHOPPING

In Montgomery, **Eastdale Mall** (East Blvd. and Atlanta Hwy., tel. 334/277–7359) has some 100 specialty stores plus **McRae's, Parisian, Gayfer's, Sears**, restaurants, a movie theater, and the Southeast's only mall-enclosed ice rink. **Montgomery Mall** (East Blvd. and Hwy. 231S, tel. 334/284–1533) has more than 100 specialty stores, a food court, **Gayfer's, JCPenney**, and **Parisian. Mulberry Street District** (Mulberry St. exit off I–85, tel. 334/262–0013) is a collection of unique shops nestled among the trees of a friendly, old Montgomery neighborhood. **Herron House Antiques** (422 Herron St., tel. 334/265–2063) has a large stock of porcelain, glass, and silver, plus 18th- and 19th-century furniture displayed in one of the city's stately homes.

VISITOR INFORMATION

Montgomery Visitor Center (401 Madison Ave., Montgomery 36104, tel. 334/262–0013). **Alabama Bureau of Tourism & Travel** (401 Adams Ave., Montgomery 36103–4927, tel. 334/242–4169 or 800/252–2262).

GRACE HALL 🐚
506 Lauderdale St., Selma 36701, tel. 334/875–5744, fax 334/875–9967,
www.olcg.com/selma/gracehall.htm

Grace Hall, built in 1857, also is known as the Ware-Baker-Jones House, after the three families who lived here for more than 110 years. The mansion became run-down apartments and then a grungy boardinghouse but today is resplendent again, with many original antiques. The owners are Coy and Joey Dillon, he a former steel executive, she a semi-retired interior designer. Since the age of 16, when Joey bought her first antique (an oval mirror for $10), she has been interested in old buildings. She jumped at the chance to buy and restore Grace Hall. The Dillons drifted into B&B management when the mayor of Selma asked them to house a visiting dignitary.

The house, a certified restoration of an antebellum home, is stunning, with double parlors, a pressed-tin ceiling in the study, red stained glass, Romantic portraits in the hallway, heart-pine floors, and windows 10 ft tall. The dining room has its original mahogany pedestal table, seating 12, and a smaller room behind used for guests' three-course breakfast. Solid brass chandeliers light the house; on the south porch overlooking the manicured garden and its huge live oak is original wicker furniture.

The large bedrooms in the main house have marble fireplaces. Other features include oak desks, Oriental rugs, hand-painted enamel clocks, and antique, step-up carved rosewood beds. Wallpapers are copies of 19th-century designs; in one bedroom, the Brighton pattern fits perfectly with a four-poster bed flanked by brother-and-sister walnut chests. TV sets are concealed in cabinets. Leading off the back is a latticed, galleried wing, whose porches, facing the garden, provide open-air sitting space for three more smaller, but just as charming, bedrooms. Fitting the southern surroundings, an overhead fan turns lazily above a large bowl holding branches full of cotton bolls. The Dillons occasionally give tours to bus groups on weekdays during the day. ⚓ *6 double rooms with baths.*

Air-conditioning, cable TV and phone in rooms, free home tour. $69–$99; full break-fast, evening refreshments. AE, D, MC, V. No smoking, pets by prior arrangement, children over 6 only.

JEMISON INN

212 Hwy. 191, Jemison 35085, tel./fax 205/688–2055, www.bbonline.com/al/jemison

The 1930s redbrick, red-roof Jemison Inn—with arches and a wraparound porch filled with ferns and antique wicker—was built by the small town's first physician. Rumor has it that the house was built close to the road so the doctor's spinster sister could swing on a porch swing while gossiping with passersby. Gracious and hospitable innkeepers Joe and Nancy Ruzicka, both retired, spent their careers dealing with people—she as a university librarian, he in the family publishing business.

B&B guests arrive to find a front-porch easel with a welcome message including their names. It is the first of many thoughtful touches. The home has a Victorian air, although it was completed in 1929. The parlor, with a mix of furniture from 1890 to 1930, sets the rose theme that follows in public areas. Set against rose, cream, and green, the look continues with moire draperies, Oriental rugs, crushed velvet and tapestry upholstery, collections of Nippon, Roseville pottery, Victorian silver, and walnut Eastlake furnishings. There are 1930s facings on doors and windows, lots of glass, hardwood floors, crown molding, and period wallpaper.

The McNeil Room has a king-size bed created from 1880s walnut twin beds, hand-stitched quilts, an Eastlake marble-top walnut dresser, a walnut chest, needlepoint rugs, and tapestry draperies. The Johnson Room, down the hall, has 1900 mahogany classic furnishings with appointments in gold, blue, and white. The attached bathroom has a whirlpool tub for two. Across the hall, the Duffee Room has a 1900 golden-oak high-back bed, North Wind chairs, a large oak armoire, ball-and-claw oak tables, a crocheted bedspread, floral wallpaper, a hooked rug, oil paintings, and beaded purses. The private bath has a claw-foot tub, pedestal sink, and oak baker's rack.

Across from the house, only a few miles from I–65, is the Ruzickas' antiques shop, which they open for guests' private viewings. There's a different dinner theme package monthly. ♨ *3 double rooms with baths. Air-conditioning, ceiling fans, cable TV/VCR in 2 common areas and guest rooms, video library, fax, copier, free home tour, fruit and flowers in room, turndown service with mints, champagne in room for honeymooners; gardens, swimming pool. $75–$135; full breakfast, afternoon refreshments, in-room snacks, poolside snacks. AE, D, DC, MC, V. No smoking, children by prior arrangement.*

KENDALL MANOR INN

534 W. Broad St., Eufaula 36027, tel. 334/687–8847, fax 334/616–0678, www.bbonline.com/al/kendall

Kendall Manor stands majestically on a hill in historic Eufaula, a town filled with the state's second most abundant collection of structures on the National Historic Register. Filled with moss-draped trees, Eufaula draws visitors to its spring Pilgrimages and fish-laden Lake Eufaula. Built in 1872, the inn offers weekend dining, by reservation, to the public.

Transplanted northerners, Timothy and Barbara Lubsen left the corporate world to live out their dream of owning a B&B. It was an ambition they harbored more than a decade while he worked as a consumer products researcher and she as a travel agent, tour director, and interior designer.

Ruby-etched glass panels accent 10-ft entrance doors that open to reveal spacious rooms with 16-ft ceilings and elaborate moldings. The parlor, with original furnishings, has detailed carvings in rosewood and walnut, windows topped with gold-leaf cornices, antiques, and Oriental rugs. A rosewood square grand piano and a sunroom are available for guests' use. There is an adult-size rocking horse in the upstairs sitting area.

Rooms upstairs have wood floors, Oriental-style rugs, 10-ft windows with Venetian blinds, and cloud shades. The Alabama Room, with yellow and black accents, includes a king rice bed (which has wood posts carved with a rice motif), antique armoire and chest, love seat, chair, and ottoman. Floral wallpaper is the backdrop in the Georgia Room. Flowers in rooms and goodies such as lemon bars or brownies are standard. Wine is by request.

Verandas extend around three sides of the home. A second-story sitting porch, with comfortable chairs, overlooks the front lawn's dogwood and magnolias. Chippendale railings surround the rear deck, which leads to a fountain, bench, and gardens where breakfast sometimes is served.

In the rooftop belvedere, earlier visitors have left their mark: Hundreds of signatures, some dating to the home's early years, have been scrawled on the walls. Overnight guests are invited to continue the tradition. ⚓ *6 double rooms with private baths. Air-conditioning, cable TV and phone in rooms, ceiling fans, fax, copier, free home tour; bikes, croquet. $89–$114; full breakfast, welcome beverage, afternoon refreshments, dinner by request. AE, D, MC, V. No smoking, children over 14 only, minimum stay during special events.*

LATTICE INN 🍃

1414 S. Hull St., Montgomery 36104, tel. 334/832–9931 or 800/525–0652, fax 334/264–0075, members.aol.com/latticeinn

Follow the aroma of freshly baked cookies through Montgomery's historic garden district to this turn-of-the-century Craftsman bungalow. Proprietor Michael Pierce bakes more than 2,000 cookies a month and even slips a bag of them into your suitcase as you depart. The renovated house, 1 mi from downtown Montgomery, is set among wild gardens with oak and pine trees, an ornamental fishpond, and lots of flowers. The shady front porch has just enough lattice to provide privacy, while an intricately designed multilevel deck overlooking the pool is great for sitting and dozing. The terra-cotta-colored walls and mahogany paneling in the living room add to the dark and serene mood.

Spacious bedrooms have brick or stone wood-burning fireplaces, high coffered ceilings, stained-glass windows, and antique furnishings. William J.'s Room has a high-posted bed and bath with 19th-century claw-foot tub, porcelain basin mounted on an antique chest, and original art. Aunt Myrtle's Room has a queen high-poster bed, family pieces, fireplace, picture windows, bath with shower, and unusual art pieces.

On the garden level, two rooms with private entry can be combined to create a suite. Lucille's Hide-A-Way has a kitchenette, bath with shower and tub, and a choice of twin or king bed. Lynn's Place has a king bed with an antique door as its headboard, an armoire, and a large, walk-in shower.

The private cottage, with a plain pink wooden exterior, has a bedroom, bath, dining and living rooms, cable television, fully equipped kitchen, and queen-size, single, and day beds. ♨ *4 double rooms with baths, 1 cottage. Air-condition-ing, phone in rooms, cable TV in library and some rooms; pool, outdoor hot tub, sun-deck, pond. $75–$90; full breakfast, cookies. AE, D, MC, V. No smoking, one child under 12 per adult.*

ORANGEVALE PLANTATION ☙
1400 Whiting Rd., Talladega 35160, tel. 256/761–1827, fax 256/761–8794

Orangevale Plantation, on 150 acres 4 mi south of Talladega, once was the center of a 3,000-acre cotton plantation. Built in 1854, the main house is Greek Revival with six 25-ft-tall pillars and white exterior.

Orangevale is run by Billy Bliss and her husband, Richard, a physician who served in three branches of the U.S. military. With two married sons living nearby, the Blisses maintain cattle, sheep, horses, ducks, geese, an orchard, cornfields, fishponds, and a vineyard. Guests may stroll a nature trail lined with azaleas, dog-woods, and ferns.

The Blisses live downstairs in their antiques-filled home and leave the upstairs, which has its own living-room area, to guests. In typical antebellum fashion, the bedrooms open off a central hall, and, though these rooms have their own bath-rooms, you have to tiptoe down the hall to reach them. Both bedrooms have four-poster beds with down comforters, Sheraton chests, brick fireplaces, and large windows.

There are three outbuildings. The farthest, which the innkeepers reach via golf cart, overlooks the orchard. Each of its two rooms, connected by a dogtrot, has a queen-size and single bed, a freestanding brick fireplace, a rocking chair, and walls and ceiling made of rough-hewn wood.

Behind the main house and within view of the tree-canopied brick patio are two units, both with exposed wood, kitchenettes, living areas, and baths. Cabin inte-riors, smelling of old pine logs, appear rustic but are exceptionally comfortable.

Guests find fresh fruit and produce and Billy's specialty—iced tea sweetened with mint sprigs from the grounds. Breakfast often is served at the kitchen's lazy Susan, where the Blisses' four children once gathered when growing up here. Orangevale gives a true taste of the Old South, and the Blisses, who welcome families, are well suited for their roles as caretakers of the past. ♨ *2 double rooms with baths, 1 cottage, 2 cabins. Air-conditioning, TV in common areas, kitchen, fax, copier, washer/dryer, free tour of house and grounds; nature trail, 2 fishing ponds. $95; full breakfast. No credit cards.*

RED BLUFF COTTAGE ☙
551 Clay St., Montgomery 36104 (Box 1026, Montgomery 36101), tel. 334/264–0056 or 888/551–2529, fax 334/263–3054, www.bbonline.com/al/redbluff

Built to accommodate guests, this raised cottage sits high above the Alabama River and has public rooms on the second floor and bedrooms below. It is run by Mark Waldo, tall, slim, and congenial, a retired Episcopal rector, and his wife, Anne, a master gardener, chef, and musician. The lower level's porch has an unusual swinging bed that invites a snooze. The upper-level porch has comfortable seat-ing and a magnificent view of the State Capitol, downtown, and the river plain.

The public rooms have Oriental rugs, a fireplace, and the kind of soft lamplight that makes you want to sit down and indulge in good conversation or a good book borrowed from the ample library. Guests may play the harpsichord in the music room, where Bach sheet music and wooden recorders are scattered about.

Breakfast is served on family china and silver at a mahogany table that sits beneath a crystal chandelier, and sometimes on the porch amid the hanging baskets. The gazebo in the garden is a pleasant gathering place. The bedrooms are full of light, thanks to large windows hung with light net curtains. Antiques, along with many family mementos, decorate all the rooms. One room is a suite, with a small attached room suitable for children.

Red Bluff Cottage is convenient to historical sites, state buildings, the Alabama Shakespeare Festival Theater, the Museum of Fine Arts, the Montgomery Zoo, Garrett Coliseum, and the Civic Center. ⌂ *4 double rooms with baths, including 1 family suite. Air-conditioning, TV in living room, games, washer/dryer. $65–$75; full breakfast, prebreakfast coffee, soft drinks. AE, D, MC, V.*

ST. JAMES HOTEL 🐾

1200 Water Ave., Selma 36701, tel. 334/872–3234 or 888/264–6788, fax 334/872–0332, www.stjamesselma.com

Outlaw Jesse James once was a guest in the St. James Hotel, which dates to the 1830s, when parlors bustled with wealthy cotton planters, merchants, and politicians. The completely restored St. James reopened in late 1997, almost 100 years after closing as a hotel. In intervening years, the riverfront structure housed various businesses. The hotel today is a private and public partnership owned by the City of Selma, which united government, community, and private investors in the $6 million restoration. A management company oversees the property with southern hospitality.

Outside, lacy ironwork trims balconies, just as it did when the hotel was in its glory days. The lobby has antiques, heart-pine floors, an original hotel mantel, and draperies made from antique French fabric.

Guests are served afternoon tea and lemonade on the hotel's front balcony, which has views of Lafayette Park, the Alabama River, Water Avenue, and the Edmund Pettus Bridge, best remembered as the setting for Bloody Sunday, when marchers, in 1965, headed to Montgomery, some 50 mi away, to seek voting rights for blacks.

Guest rooms are furnished with 19th-century plantation reproductions from the Vestiges collection of Lexington Furniture. Carpets, draperies, and bedspreads were designed and woven especially for the hotel. Bathroom tiles, clustered in mosaic designs, were created for the St. James. All guest rooms have private baths. The hotel's four suites, each with jetted tub and bidet, have fireplaces with gas logs, original oil paintings, four-poster beds, and walk-in closets. Suites, with some 800 square ft, open onto balconies with views of the river and nearby bridge.

Antique reproductions fill the Drinking Room, where French silk draperies of muted bronze-color reproduction fabric made in France puddle on floors. The quietly elegant, white tablecloth Troup House Restaurant, furnished with a mixture of antiques and reproductions, oversees a fountain-centered courtyard. ⌂ *38 rooms, 4 suites, all with baths. Restaurant; lounge; air-conditioning, valet parking, turndown service, cable TV in rooms; use of nearby fitness center. $64–$128; Continental breakfast. AE, D, DC, MC, V. Restricted smoking.*

GULF COAST DELTA

The southwestern part of Alabama, the Gulf Coast Delta, is dominated by water: by the rivers and streams of the delta draining into Mobile Bay and by the Gulf of Mexico, whose beaches have sand so gleaming white it looks as though it has been scooped up from the streets of paradise. Throughout much of the region large trees support gray-green curtains of Spanish moss that festoon their branches, hanging down 10 or 15 ft in irregular clusters and adding an air of mystery to the silent landscape.

Mobile, with its active shipping industry, is Alabama's only important port. The French settled it in 1711, and many of the older parts of the city hold fast to bits and pieces of their French ancestry. Live oaks, 100 years old and riotous, and exploding stretches of azaleas turn the town into a fairyland in early spring.

Strung along the eastern shore of Mobile Bay is a scattering of small towns with evocative names: Point Clear, Fairhope, Daphne, Montrose, and Spanish Fort. Point Clear has one of the South's most famous hostelries, the 140-year-old Grand Hotel, whose half-moon dining rooms overlook the bay and whose sweeping lawn is so manicured guests are almost afraid to walk on it.

 PLACES TO GO, SIGHTS TO SEE

Bellingrath Gardens and Home (12401 Bellingrath Gardens Rd., Theodore, tel. 334/973–2217 or 800/247–8420), 65 acres of gardens set amid a 905-acre semitropical landscape 20 mi south of Mobile, are famous for their imaginative landscaping with traditional southern flowers, shrubs, and trees. The house contains a collection of Boehm porcelain. Southern Belle Riverboat offers 45-minute narrated tours on nearby Fowl River.

Bon Secour National Wildlife Refuge (Hwy. 180 at Mile Marker 13, tel. 334/540–7720) has more than 2 mi of beachfront accessible by nature trails. Six miles west of Gulf Shores, the oasis of wildlife is where you can fresh- and salt-water fish and hike trails. (In mid-April you may witness the arrival of migratory songbirds.) Year-round at the park, you can see pelicans, bobcats, and alligators.

The **Dauphin Island Sea Lab** (101 Bienville Blvd., tel. 334/861–2141) spotlights the unique local ecosystems of the Mobile Bay estuary. Exhibits follow a drop of water through the Mobile–Tensaw River Delta, Mobile Bay, and the barrier islands to the Gulf of Mexico. A 9,000-gallon aquarium simulates the brackish underwater environment of Mobile Bay; a 16,000-gallon tank is filled with sea life from the Gulf of Mexico.

Fairhope was settled about 1900 by a group of midwesterners, who established the country's oldest and largest single-tax colony. The system remains in operation and is studied by economists worldwide. The village is a growing art colony with antiques shops and several potteries and is also a center for fishing, boating, and marine services.

Gulf Shores and **Orange Beach** are coastal towns with miles of sugary white beaches and plenty of places to play, including amusement parks, golf courses, miniature-golf courses, and sailboat charters going into back bays and bayous. On the coast is the 6,000-acre **Gulf State Park** (tel. 800/544–4853), with a 825-ft pier.

The **Marriott Grand Hotel** (Hwy. 98 Point Clear, tel. 334/928–9201 or 800/544–9933), originally built in 1847, housed Confederate soldiers during the Civil War.

Mobile. In an old fire station, *Phoenix Fire Museum* (203 S. Claiborne St., tel. 334/434–7554) remembers early firefighters with exhibits and two engines. *Exploreum Museum of Science* (65 Government St., tel. 334/471–5923) is a hands-on place for kids to learn about science and technology. Several historic homes (tel. 334/471–6365) are now museums: *Richards-DAR, Condé-Charlotte, Oakleigh,* and *Bragg-Mitchell.* Moored offshore in Mobile Bay is the USS *Alabama* (Battleship Pkwy., tel. 334/433–2703 or 800/426–4929), which was called "The Hero of the Pacific." Adjacent to the battleship is a submarine and a hangar filled with aircraft. At Mobile Bay, *Fort Gaines* (tel. 334/861–6992) and *Fort Morgan* (tel. 334/540–7125) remain, as though still obligated to protect the bay from invaders.

Wildland Expedition Swamp Tour (Chickasaw Marina, Hwy. 43, Chickasaw, tel. 334/460–8206) takes visitors on two-hour trips into swamps north of Mobile. There are no trips Sunday–Monday.

Zooland Animal Park (Hwy. 59, Gulf Shores, tel. 334/968–5731) has exotic animals, a petting zoo, and elevated decks.

RESTAURANTS

Along Mobile Bay, dining options are plentiful. **Guido's** (29154 Hwy. 98, Daphne, tel. 334/626–6082), in a corner of a former grocery store, has a chalkboard menu and all-fresh foods. Expect choices such as a rolled steak stuffed with feta cheese and mushrooms or a sandwich made with slices of eggplant. On the bay, **Gambino's** (18 Laurel Ave., Fairhope, tel. 334/928–5444) is known for Italian dishes, seafood, and prime rib.

In Mobile, **Drayton Place** (101 Dauphin St., tel. 334/432–7438) serves American fare prepared on-site from scratch. At **Port City Brewery** (225 Dauphin St., tel. 334/438–2739) wash down beer sausage and oak-fried pizza with a microbrew. **Justine's Courtyard & Carriageway** (80 Saint Michael St., tel. 334/438–4535), in an antebellum setting in downtown Mobile, offers traditional Gulf Coast cuisine, including seafood, pasta, steaks, and specialty dishes prepared table-side.

Near downtown Dothan, 203 mi from Mobile, **Garland House** (200 N. Bell St., Dothan, tel. 334/793–2043) is known for its chicken divan and quiche. Service is limited to weekday lunches. **Poplar Head Mule Company Brewpub and Grill** (155 S. Saint Andrews St., Dothan, tel. 334/794–7991) serves food and home-brewed beer in an old livery in the downtown district. You can find authentic Italian food at **Papparazzi's** (U.S. 231 S, Dothan, tel. 334/671–5823).

Along the coast, **Bayside Grill** (27842 Canal Rd., Orange Beach, tel. 334/981–4899) overlooks Sportsman Marina and serves pastas, steaks, salads, and chicken. Coconut shrimp, black-bean soup, Creole-style gumbo, and banana Foster strudel are especially popular. Sunday brunch is lavish. **Fish Camp Restaurant** (County Rd. 6 off Hwy. 59 on Bon Secour River in Gulf Shores, tel. 334/968–2267) has front doors flanked by palm trees, whimsical and nautical things hanging on walls, and some of the best seafood in town.

SHOPPING

In Mobile, **Bel Air Mall** (1 block east of I–65 Beltline off Airport Blvd., tel. 334/478–1893) has 175 stores under one roof, including **JCPenney, Parisian, Target, Dillards**, and **Sears**. **Springdale Mall-Plaza** (Airport Blvd. and I–65, tel. 334/479–9871) is anchored by **Gayfer's, McRae's**, and **Montgomery Ward** and has more than 100 stores. Eight miles north of Gulf Shores, **Riviera Centre** (AL 59S, Foley, tel. 334/943–8888) is a complex of some 200 outlet stores with savings up to 75% off regular retail prices. Included are **Danskin, Calvin Klein, Liz Claiborne, Polo/Ralph Lauren, Bass Shoes**, and **Pfaltzgraff**.

VISITOR INFORMATION

Alabama Gulf Coast Convention and Visitors Bureau (Drawer 457, Gulf Shores 36547, tel. 334/968–7511 or 800/745–7263). **Fort Condé Welcome Center** (150 S. Royal St., Mobile 36602, tel. 334/434–7304). **Mobile Convention and Visitors Corporation** (Box 204, Mobile 36601-0204, tel. 334/208–2000 or 800/566–2453).

BAY BREEZE

742 S. Mobile St. (Box 526), Fairhope 36533, tel. 334/928–8976,
fax 334/928–0360, www.bbonline.com/al/baybreeze

Not far from downtown Fairhope, a winding white-shell driveway leads through a landscaped camellia and azalea garden to a stucco-and-wood guest house built in the early 1930s. Owners Bill and Becky Jones, who have restored and enlarged her childhood home, live in their own wing, while guests enjoy the main house and nearby cottages, which offer privacy. The house fronts Mobile Bay, where, not far away, is the Yankee ironclad *Tecumseh*, which sank with 116 sailors. Stretching into the bay is a private 462-ft pier with a kitchen, where Bill often cooks Saturday breakfast or a seafood supper. Fortunate guests may find themselves here for Jubilee—a natural phenomenon that takes place only two places in the world when a lack of oxygen forces bottom dwellers—crab, shrimp, flounder—to shore.

A large front lawn has a stone fountain and pine benches. In the sunny living room are china and rare books in a cabinet next to a musket from the War of 1812. The Bay Room has white wicker chairs facing large French windows and the bay. A cozy sitting room hides an upright piano and brick fireplace. Breakfast is served in the dining room; a view of ducks and the bay enhances the meal.

The three bedrooms in the main house have wooden floors, brass queen beds, old family portraits, large windows, and antique furnishings. Cottage suites are light and spacious, decorated with antiques, Oriental and hooked rugs, brick floors, and white pine paneling. In one suite, the bedroom has a large queen brass bed, mini-kitchen, and comfortable sofa sleeper that increases accommodations to four.

Becky, a retired biology instructor, loves sitting at the end of the pier and weaving tales while guests revel in this casual escape on historic Mobile Bay. ♨ *3 double rooms with baths, 2 cottages. Air-conditioning, cable TV in rooms, games, VCR in game room, ceiling fans, fax, free home tour; bikes, pond, pier. $95–$105; full breakfast, refreshments on arrival. AE, MC, V. No smoking, pets and children by arrangement only, minimum stay during special events.*

THE BEACH HOUSE, A BED & BREAKFAST BY THE SEA ☜
*9218 Dacus La., Gulf Shores 36542, tel. 334/540–7039
or 800/659–6004, bbchannel.com*

Wrapped in porches and nestled among dunes, the Beach House is a tribute to owners Russ and Carol Shackelford, former therapists who know well how to promote relaxation. The couple designed their haven to showcase views of the beach and ocean. A favorite spot is the screened porch, a grand vantage point for spotting dolphins at play from "swing" chairs, which are suspended from the ceiling.

French doors open into a large living room where rough-hewn columns look like masts of an old sailing ship. (The look was not happenstance but by design.) Exposed beams and book-lined walls are bathed in the filtered light from tall windows draped in billowing gauze. An overstuffed sofa and deep club chairs are accented by an occasional wicker piece, while nautical knickknacks, a library table, and an antique armoire from Indonesia (laden with board games) add inviting touches.

The five guest rooms are uncluttered, breezy, and let the ocean seem almost to come indoors. Pine floors are scattered with Oriental rugs, and walls are painted with soft colors. Each guest room has a waveless water bed covered with a plush featherbed. Cape May and Key West rooms share a second-floor porch with a hammock, swing chairs, and a skywalk that leads to an open deck with a hot tub. Third-floor suites have king-size beds, whirlpool tubs, private decks, and floor-to-ceiling windows offering gulf views.

Guests may choose to eat breakfast on the front porch or in the kitchen, where a refrigerator is stocked with snacks. Breakfasts include choices such as apple-puff pancakes drizzled with maple syrup and homemade biscuits topped with melted cheese and smothered in tomato-basil gravy.

A favorite pastime for many visitors is traipsing through nearby Bon Secour National Wildlife Refuge (see above) or running along the beach to catch salty breezes. ♨ *5 rooms with baths. Air-conditioning, TV in rooms by request, ceiling fans in rooms, snacks in guest refrigerator; kites. $130–$231, 3-night minimum; full breakfast, snacks. No credit cards. No smoking.*

CHURCH STREET INN ☜
*51 S. Church St. (Box 526), Fairhope 36533, tel. 334/928–8976, fax 334/928–0360,
www.bbonline.com/al/churchstreet*

This early 20th-century white stucco house, on the National Register, was formerly the home of Becky Jones's mother. The Joneses, who made few changes to convert the home into a B&B, stay at Bay Breeze (*see above*) and leave daily duties to a capable manager.

Filled with five generations of family antiques and heirlooms, the house is within walking distance of downtown Fairhope and its boutiques, galleries, antiques shops, and unique restaurants. In the living room's bay window is Becky's mother's "memory book," with love letters and her first teaching contract, dated 1926, for $40. There are mahogany tables and Tiffany lamp shades downstairs. Downstairs bedrooms, always with fresh flowers, have four-poster beds, oak rocking chairs, and lace curtains. Upstairs is a large bedroom with dark pine floors, walk-in closet, and secret passage surrounding the room. There's also an adjoining original bathroom with claw-foot tub and turtle-back, bead-board ceiling. All have queen-size beds. ♨ *3 double rooms with baths. Air-conditioning, TV, ceiling fans in rooms, free home tour; bikes. $85; full breakfast, snacks in kitchen. AE, MC, V. No smoking, pets and children by special arrangement, minimum stay during special events.*

THE ORIGINAL ROMAR HOUSE ☞

23500 Perdido Beach Blvd., Orange Beach 36561, tel. 334/974–1625 or 800/487–6627, fax 334/974–1163, www.bbonline.com/al/romarhouse/

When Jerry Gilbreath bought the Original Romar House in 1980, he began renovations with an eye to creating a place reminiscent of family vacation homes. Gilbreath has entrusted the care of the home and its guests to innkeeper Darrell Finley, a retired electrical engineer who is gifted at making visitors feel welcome.

One of the oldest homes along the Alabama coast, Romar House was built in 1924 on the sand and later was raised, with the space below the house enclosed to add five guest rooms in addition to the one in the main portion of the house. An adjacent cottage sleeps four and has a living-dining room combination, kitchen, cable TV/VCR, and stereo.

The cypress-sided home is the place to hear palm trees rustling in the wind, and smell the salty air while sipping a tropical drink on the deck of the Purple Parrot Bar. The front entrance has Caribbean mahogany doors and arched stained-glass windows. A wraparound screened porch is the place to feel Gulf breezes that muffle the sounds of the nearby highway. Antique lanterns and a brick walkway lead visitors to the beach.

Filled with art deco furniture, guest rooms are named for area festivals. The Shrimp Festival room, for instance, has rich shrimp and coral tones; the Sea Oats Festival room features pale shades of pink and teal. Cypress doors in the bedrooms are from an old New Orleans hotel.

Breakfast is served on the deck overlooking the Gulf or inside on the 60-year-old dining table. Plates often hold fresh strawberries, melon, scrambled eggs, biscuits, and honey. After breakfast, there's time to venture to a private stretch of white sandy beach to collect seashells—or to curl up in a cypress swing or hammock. ♨ *5 double rooms with baths, 1¾-bed with bath, 1 cottage. Air-conditioning, cable TV in living room and bar; hot tub, hammock, bicycles. $79–$200; full breakfast, wine and cheese. AE, MC, V. No smoking, children over 12 only.*

Mississippi

Mississippi

ARKANSAS

TENNESSEE

Memphis
Hernando
Holly Springs
Corinth
78
55
Senatobia
Holly Springs National Forest
45
Tishomingo State Park
Clarksdale
Oxford
6
Tupelo
Tallahatchie R.
Holly Springs National Forest
Tombigbee National Forest
Tombigbee R.
61
Cleveland
49E
Greenwood
82
Columbus
Greenville
French Camp
West
Starkville
Chatham
Yazoo R.
3
Glen Allen
Yazoo City
Kosciusko
45
Delta National Forest
Big Black R.
Tombigbee National Forest
Satartia
55
Pearl R.
Natchez Trace Pky.
49
Ross Barnett Reservoir
Vicksburg
Ridgeland
20
Meridian
Mississippi R. R.
Jackson
Bienville National Forest
Natchez Trace Pky.
Bayou Pierre
59
Port Gibson
Lorman
45
Church Hill
Brookhaven
84
Laurel
Natchez
61
84
De Soto National Forest
Homochitto National Forest
Chickasaw
55
Pearl R.
Hattiesburg
De Soto National Forest
98
LOUISIANA
59
Mobile
Pascagoula R.
Ocean Springs
10
Long Beach
Biloxi
Bay St. Louis
Gulfport
Pascagoula
Waveland
Pass Christian
Lake Pontchartrain
Gulf Islands National Seashore
N
New Orleans
Gulf of Mexico
0   50 miles
0   75 km

NORTH MISSISSIPPI
HILL COUNTRY

The clean and green Hill Country of the Magnolia State is a place where shared memories and respect for tradition surely influenced some of the great writers who hail from there, among them William Faulkner of Oxford. The Nobel Prize–winning Faulkner and another Oxford writer, John Grisham, have helped to cast the region as a literary mecca. This is, after all, the birthplace of Faulkner's mythical Yoknapatawpha County, and the setting for a few of Grisham's popular thrillers. The University of Mississippi (Ole Miss) at Oxford has excellent museums, one with an extensive collection of Greco-Roman antiquities, and maintains Faulkner's Greek Revival home, Rowan Oak.

Even before Faulkner made the region famous, the Union soldiers who were bivouacked at Holly Springs during the Civil War were quite enamored of it. Rumor has it that because of certain blandishments of local women determined to save their columned and colonnaded homes, the Yankees chose not to burn the town. Today those private houses are open for the Pilgrimage tour in late April; some may be visited by appointment year-round. The entire Courthouse Square, with its neat box of shops and offices, is on the National Register of Historic Places.

Two other pretty towns, Corinth and Columbus, are steeped in yet more Civil War history—and herstory. In 1866, the women of Columbus helped to heal the nation by placing flowers on the graves of both Confederate and Union soldiers at Friendship Cemetery. "Decoration Day," initiated by those genteel ladies, evolved into the nation's Memorial Day. In 1884, the first state-supported college for women was founded here. Corinth, a town of tree-canopied streets and quiet, historic neighborhoods, was of strategic importance during the Civil War because the railroads met and crossed here. It changed hands more than once, and the Battle of Corinth cost thousands of lives. The major Battle of Shiloh occurred just across the state line in Tennessee.

Between the two towns, along the northern stretches of the Natchez Trace, is Tupelo, which has museums, mall shopping, and Elvis Presley's birthplace-museum. Nearby are several state parks and lakes.

Starkville, west of Columbus, is the home of many museums and Mississippi State University, where SEC (Southeastern Conference) sports offer year-round activities.

PLACES TO GO, SIGHTS TO SEE

Antebellum Home Tours (Columbus, tel. 601/329–3533 or 800/327–2686). The town opens at least three of its antebellum mansions—with period antiques—for tours every day, year-round.

Antique Doll Collection (Blue Mountain College, Blue Mountain 38610, tel. 601/685–4771) displays unique dolls that date to 1875, the first graduating class of the college.

Blues Archives (Farley Hall, University of Mississippi, Oxford, tel. 601/232–7753). See how singin' the blues evolved from Mississippi Delta roots. B. B. King's collection of memorabilia and recordings is exhibited, as are the works of other blues musicians, to make this the world's largest collection of blues music.

The **Center for the Study of Southern Culture** (Barnard Observatory, University of Mississippi, Oxford, tel. 601/232–5993) examines the region's music, folklore, and literature.

Corinth National Cemetery (tel. 601/286–286-3759 or 800/748–9048), once a major battlefield, is now the gravesite of 6,000 Civil War soldiers.

Elvis Presley Birthplace and Museum (306 Elvis Presley Dr., Tupelo, tel. 601/841–1245). The museum is called "Times and Things Remembered" and has a collection of unique and never-published candid photographs and other Elvis memorabilia.

The **Jerry Lee Lewis Ranch** (1595 Malone Rd., Nesbit 38651, tel. 601/429–1290) will prove to be an interesting house tour for those who appreciate the music of this rock legend.

The **Kate Freeman Clark Art Gallery** (292 E. College Ave., Holly Springs, tel. 601/252–4211 or 601/252–2511) exhibits more than 1,000 paintings by the Holly Springs native who left her home in the 1890s to study with William Merritt Chase at the Art Students League in New York. By choice, she never sold a painting.

Marshall County Historical Museum (220 E. College Ave., Holly Springs, tel. 601/252–3669) is full of interesting local artifacts and war relics from 1812 to the Korean conflict; there is also a Civil War room.

Natchez Trace Parkway Visitor Center (Mile Marker 266, Natchez Trace Pkwy., tel. 601/680–4025), open every day but Christmas, has exhibits, a hands-on area for children, a bookstore, and the "Official Map and Guide," which opens to 4 ft and lays out the Trace mile by mile.

The **Northeast Mississippi Museum** (204 4th St., Corinth, tel. 601/287–3120) has Native American relics and artifacts and Civil War maps and battle plans.

Rowan Oak (Old Taylor Rd., Oxford, tel. 601/234–3284) is writer William Faulkner's antebellum home. His outline of the prize-winning story *A Fable* is still written on the wall of his study.

At **Tishomingo State Park** (Mile Marker 302.8, tel. 601/438–6914), in northeast Mississippi, the Appalachian Mountains begin. The park has nature trails, canoe trips, and beautiful rustic settings.

The **Tupelo City Museum** (Ballard Park, tel. 601/841–6438) has permanent and traveling exhibits that range from the arts to astronauts to remembrances of Elvis Presley.

Waverley Plantation (Between Columbus and West Point, tel. 601/494–1399) is a spectacular mid-1800s showplace built around an octagonal rotunda. Tours are offered daily, year-round.

RESTAURANTS

Oxford favorites include the sophisticated **City Grocery** (1118 Van Buren Ave., tel. 601/232–8080), with gourmet New Orleans-style fare, and the **Downtown Grill** (110 Courthouse Sq., tel. 601/234–2659), serving dishes like gumbo and catfish. **Harvey's**, in Tupelo, Columbus, and Starkville, specializes in mesquite-grilled fish, steak, and chicken, and dressed-up hamburgers and salads. All locations are relaxed and casual, and the service is unusually good. In Tupelo, **Jefferson Place** (823 West Jefferson St., tel. 601/844–8696) serves the finest cuts of beef and lighter fare—sandwiches, salads, and burgers. **Woody's** (619 N. Gloster St., tel. 601/840–0460) is the place to find steak, prime rib, and seafood; it's open for dinner only. Folks from all over the country say that the upscale **Portobella's** (309 Main St., tel. 601/245–1007) in Columbus serves the best Italian food this side of Italy.

VISITOR INFORMATION

Columbus Convention & Visitors Bureau (Box 789, Columbus 39703, tel. 601/329–1191 or 800/327–2686). **Corinth Area Tourism Promotion Council** (Box 1089, Corinth 38834, tel. 601/287–5269 or 800/748–9048). **Holly Springs Chamber of Commerce** (154 S. Memphis St., Holly Springs 38635, tel. 601/252–2943). **Oxford Tourism Council** (Box 965, Oxford 38655, tel. 601/234–4680). **Starkville Visitors & Convention Council** (322 University Dr., Starkville 39759, tel. 601/323–3322). **Tupelo Convention & Visitors Bureau** (P.O. Drawer 47, Tupelo 38802, tel. 601/841–6521 or 800/533–0611).

RESERVATION SERVICES

Greater Golden Triangle Welcome Center (300 Main St., Columbus 39701, tel. 601/328–0222 or 800/689–3983). **Lincoln, Ltd. Bed & Breakfast Mississippi Reservation Service** (Box 3479, Meridian 39303, tel. 601/482–5483 or 800/633–6477).

ALEXANDER HOUSE 🐚

Anderson and Green Sts. (Box 187), West 39192, tel. 601/967–2266 or 800/350–8034

When Ruth Ray and Woody Dinstel retired and came back to her native West, Mississippi, after living overseas while working for an oil company, they did not expect to be B&B proprietors of a house that was built around 1880. They are, and they love it. The Dinstels bought the then run-down house in 1993 after it had been empty for 25 years and began the restoration process. They had help from other locals—West's population is under 100—and the West Historical Society, which salvages and restores old buildings. Also on the property is a one-bedroom circa 1900 cottage-cum-B&B, offering complete privacy in an old, but not rustic, setting.

Guests have said that the Alexander House is like a "big, happy dollhouse." The house is so authentically decorated in Victorian colors, fabrics, and furnishings that a visit is like a step back in time. Some of these furnishings include antiques that the Dinstels brought from England, where they lived while working at the oil company; among them are vintage quilts, chintz, original beaded-wood walls, and iron beds.

Ruth Ray cooks up hearty breakfasts, offering a choice of ham, bacon or sausage, eggs, grits, fruit, great fluffy biscuits, and wonderful homemade jellies and jams. Dinner is available with advance reservations. ♣ *3 double rooms with baths, 2 doubles share 1 bath. TV in 2 rooms and upstairs common area. $85; full breakfast. D, MC, V. No smoking, children and pets by prior arrangement.*

AMZI LOVE HOUSE 🕊

305 7th St. S, Columbus 39701, tel. 601/328–5413

In the town of Columbus, where women have made significant historical contributions, one of the many antebellum homes was built for a woman. Her descendant Sid Caradine and his wife, Brenda, now run it as a bed-and-breakfast. Built in 1848 for the bride of Amzi Love, the Italian-style villa in the historic district is much the way it was originally because seven generations have intentionally preserved its unique character. In fact, Sid tells his guests that it's like a journey back in time, complete with original Empire and Victorian furnishings and such accessories as the crocheted bedspreads and needlepoint done by Amzi Love's five daughters.

Sid returned to his birthplace in 1989, after deciding that writing poetry and gardening were preferable to working in the stock market. He and Brenda have also restored the Love-Lincoln Carriage House, which provides a favorite overnight stay for many of their guests. Refreshments are served upon arrival, and weather permitting, a short cruise on a 1962 Chris Craft yacht is possible. ♣ *3 double rooms with baths, 1 suite. Air-conditioning, robes, and phones in rooms. $100–$150; full breakfast, welcome refreshments. AE, MC, V. Restricted smoking.*

ARBOR HOUSE 🕊

518 College St., Columbus 39701, tel. 601/241–5596, historic/columbus.org

This colorful downtown residence is a prime example of the Italianate architecture that was a design favorite in certain parts of the South just before the Civil War. Local historians say that Arbor House was built in two stages—the first part in 1841, and the villa-style town house emerged around 1875. Inside are exceptional antiques that came directly from Aunt Mimi's house on St. Charles Avenue in New Orleans.

Owners Michael and Shelia Jessyl are avid collectors of antique furniture, Victorian silver, and Old Paris porcelain, all of which are displayed in their home. Shelia is also an artist whose work graces a few walls. The Jessyls were passing through the area in the mid-1990s en route to their home in Memphis when they saw the house, fell in love with it, and quickly made plans to purchase it.

All the bedrooms have Oriental carpets and family antiques. One bedroom, informally known as the Oak Room because of its four-poster oak bed and other oak furnishings, is decorated in reds with deep green drapes. The French Room, done primarily in pale greens, has twin beds and peach chintz fabrics. A deep green bedroom is known as the Rosewood Room because of its 8-ft carved rosewood headboard and a rosewood armoire. The fourth bedroom, recently redecorated in ocher yellow tones, contains a Georgian dresser, secretary, and wing chairs.

Breakfast, which can include bagels, croissants, homemade jams, sausages, and eggs, is served each morning on the Jessyls's antique silver and china service.

Arbor House is a Columbus Pilgrimage tour home. It is one block from the heart of town, within easy walking distance of restaurants, shops, churches, and the first home of playwright Tennessee Williams, which now serves as the Columbus Welcome Center. ♨ *4 double rooms with baths. Air-conditioning, cable TV, phones in rooms. $95–$135; full breakfast. MC, V.*

BACKSTROM B&B ☞
4567 Hwy. 182 E (Box 2311), Columbus 39704, tel. 601/328–0222 or 800/698–3983

Bill and Betty Jo Backstrom's B&B could be a house in the middle of a lush, green forest. Tall pines and hardwood trees surround it, though it's less than 5 mi from Columbus. With its natural wood construction and porches across the front and back, it has the appearance of an authentic rustic country place, even though it is barely a decade old. The Backstroms had wanted to buy an old house but were unable to find one, so they used old timbers and material from Betty Jo's daddy's old store in Tennessee and built their old-new country house.

The house is filled with rustic decorative pieces with family connections, among them quilts and old spool tables now in service as desks. Interspersed with family treasures is exquisite stained glass from the Backstroms' stained-glass business. Guest rooms are furnished with antiques and old things, not too frilly and not too sparse—just comfortable. After the sumptuous southern breakfast, guests can wander with their coffee to the front or back porch, where rocking chairs and swings await. ♨ *3 double rooms with baths. Air-conditioning, TV/VCR, and phones in rooms. $75; full breakfast. MC, V. No smoking.*

BARKSDALE-ISOM HOUSE ☞
1003 Jefferson Ave., Oxford 38655, tel. 601/236–5600

From its humble beginnings in 1838 as a three-room office for local physician Dr. T. D. Isom, the Barksdale-Isom House has become an upmarket southern planter-style B&B filled with fine French antiques and its own chef, who serves a sumptuous gourmet buffet each morning.

The original builder would be amazed at the Continental rebirth of the structure he built of hand-planed native timber. According to local legend, as Dr. Isom's practice grew, so did his office-home, and it took on the planter style of the era. Owner Susan Barksdale renovated the house a few years back and gave it its new lease on life, and new names for each room. The Rose Room is so named because of a rumored connection with Oxford native William Faulkner's "A Rose for Emily." The owners have used a rose motif, and the room has a working fireplace and mid-18th-century French furniture. The Barksdale Room, done entirely in red, from the wallpaper to the canopy and bedspread, is notable for three sets of French doors. The Worthy Room has two double beds and a wisteria motif. The dark gray and green Saunders Room contains a king-size canopy bed. The Weems Room is yellow and white, and the golden beige Miss Sallie Room has a private kitchen and entrance. All bedrooms have a number of antiques.

Guests are pampered here: Massages are available with advance reservations, and for the gourmand, the chef may share a recipe or two. The breakfast buffet includes two choices of cereals, various breakfast breads, fruit, cheese grits, juice, and coffee. The hosts serve hors d'oeuvres in the afternoon and tea on weekends. ♨ *5 double rooms with baths. Air-conditioning, TV, phones in rooms. $120–$150; full breakfast. AE, MC, V. No smoking.*

CARAGEN HOUSE 🐚
1108 Hwy. 82 W, Starkville 39759, tel. 601/323–0340

Though this most unusual steamboat Gothic-style Victorian house was built in 1890 in downtown Starkville, in 1981 it was cut in half and moved in two parts to its present site on 22 acres, still in the city limits. The Caragen House is as grand today as it must have been in the 1890s; it resembles a steamboat, with its oval-shape wraparound porches on the first and second story and spindle railings helping to create the illusion. Either porch offers an excellent view of the adjoining fields and woods.

Owner Kay Shurden—a caterer who stays busy with weddings and other special events—says that "Caragen" means "beloved spirit" in Italian. The Caragen House is a popular place for parents of nearby Mississippi State University students; since Southeastern Conference sports draw thousands of fans, call early for reservations during peak football season.

For furnishings, Kay chose to stay within the period of the home's construction. She found very good reproductions and selected nice fabric and paint that enhanced the original floors, windows, and ornate Italian mantels.

Each room has an entertainment center cleverly tucked away in a massive piece of furniture, and a wet bar is also hidden from view. Rooms are named according to color: The Yellow Room, for instance, is light and airy, with wickerlike furniture and a daybed for children. Each room has special elements of the period, such as leaded beveled glass. Bathrooms are new and modern, though Kay had to do some creative planning to add two bathrooms upstairs without altering the basic design of the house.

Guests tend to gather in the sunroom, which was originally a screened porch. Adjoining it is a deck with a swing, fans, ferns, and a view of a field. Hearty breakfasts feature homemade breads and sweets. △ *5 double rooms with baths. Air-conditioning, cable TV, wet bar in rooms. $100; full breakfast. AE, MC, V. No smoking.*

CARPENTER PLACE 🐚
120 Oak Ridge St., Starkville 39759, tel. 601/323–4669

Down a long, narrow road through a pecan orchard, amid rolling hills and fields, sits this rambling old house. The county's oldest home (circa 1835), Carpenter Place has won awards for its astute restoration—-the update of the structure has maintained its architectural integrity. The two-story plantation-style house now has its original interior colors—sunny light yellow in most areas—and is filled with fine old linens and lace, antiques, and family treasures. Old sits nicely with the new: The house has modern amenities, including plush bathrooms.

It was the birthplace and boyhood home of Roy Carpenter, the great-great-grandson of the builder. With his wife, Lucy, Roy now owns and manages it as a B&B, keeping it in mint condition. There are two bedrooms in the main house and a suite in the carriage house. Roy teaches at a local university, and Lucy, a former educator, contributed much of the interior-design expertise. It was she who planned the English gardens, where something is always in bloom. Exploring the approximately 120 acres will keep you busy; fishing in the pond is possible. The hosts are happy to show the house's treasures or explain its Civil War history. △ *2 double rooms with baths, 1 suite. Air-conditioning, TV in suite and kitchen, phone in suite. $65–$150; full breakfast. MC, V. No smoking, no children under 12.*

CARTNEY-HUNT HOUSE ☜
408 7th St. S, Columbus 39703, tel. 601/329–3856

This 1828 house is thought to be the oldest brick structure in north Mississippi, but it is still light and airy. This has as much to do with the young owners as with the decor. Vicky Hicks Hardy, a former teacher, and her CPA husband, Kirk, treat guests hospitably. They are pleased to share the history of the residence and the surrounding community, Columbus's Southside Historic District, a neighborhood of lovely old places.

The house, restored in 1982–83, has won coveted restoration awards. It is not ornate; rather, it exhibits the no-nonsense Federal style of the period. The blue, formal parlor is small and furnished with Victorian and period pieces, while the bedrooms are spacious and have a pleasing mix of antiques. Pastel colors highlight the warm woods. A shaded brick patio with wrought-iron furniture is a good place from which to enjoy the often pleasant climate. ♨ *2 double rooms with baths. Air-conditioning, TV and phone in rooms. $85; full breakfast. MC, V. No smoking.*

HIGHLAND HOUSE ☜
810 Highland Circle, Columbus 39701, tel./fax 601/327–5577

Once known by locals as the Lindamood House, this imposing Greek Revival mansion has dominated Highland Circle in Columbus since the early 1900s, when it was rebuilt after a disgruntled housekeeper purportedly set fire to the original 1862 wood structure. Now Jim Holzhauer, a physician, and his wife, Celeta, are the proud owners-innkeepers of this 9,000-square-ft showplace B&B. The house boasts a widow's walk, 78 windows, 13 working fireplaces, 14-ft ceilings, two parlors, and three dens.

Downstairs to the left, two parlors are separated by faux marble columns. To the right are two festively decorated dining rooms, with a huge brick fireplace directly ahead. The fireplace is a replica of a brick kiln once used by brick-maker Mr. Lindamood. Above it all is a hand-painted ceiling that took two years to complete. Jim's chess-set collection is displayed throughout the house.

One guest room is downstairs, near the wide staircase behind the fireplace that winds up to the second story, where three more guest rooms await. Antiques and Asian pieces are used in the colorful guest rooms, giving them an eclectic, interesting feel. Even amid the architectural excellence and expensive furnishings, the Highland House is quite comfortable, and guests are made to feel as though they've "come home." Upon arrival, Celeta offers a wonderful minted lemonade and a tour of the house. She's from a small town in Alabama and is a soft-spoken southern belle who gives guests her undivided attention.

Other nice touches include various exotic birds, a pool, a hot tub, and a video library of 3,000 movies, plus mint juleps on the veranda, Bailey's and coffee in the evening, and a breakfast extravaganza with menu items that might include orange-poached pears with white chocolate and raspberries, baked apples, homemade breads, jams, and casseroles. ♨ *4 double rooms with baths. Fireplace, phone, TV/VCR in rooms; pool, exercise room, tanning bed. $100–$160; full breakfast, champagne brunch on Sun. AE, MC, V. No smoking.*

LIBERTY HALL ☜
Armstrong Rd., Columbus 39701, tel. 601/328–4110

This 1832 planter's home is inhabited by the W. S. Fowler family, descendants of the builder. Some of their ancestors now grace the halls and walls in fine old oil paintings, while others, including a South Carolina senator of the early 1800s, lie in the wrought-iron-enclosed family burial plot in the front yard. Though Liberty Hall is only 6 mi from Columbus, its split-rail fence and tall timbers recall a distant time. The white, two-story Greek Revival house has tall columns, a gallery, and plenty of room to roam. A lovely wooded path leads to a clear, bubbling creek. Inside, the house is an antiques lover's delight. Many furnishings are original to the home, among them Empire pieces in the formal parlor. In the dining room, French country scenes were painted on upper panels before the Civil War and left unfinished when the war began.

All bedrooms have antiques, pine floors, 10-ft ceilings, ceiling fans, and working fireplaces. The Preacher Room, named after the Methodist minister who would stay in the room when ministering in the area, has floral wallpaper and a high wooden headboard. Another room, also decorated with floral patterns, has wicker furniture; a third room has two double beds, an Oriental rug, and a marble-top table.

The Fowlers are close-knit and traditional: There's still a big family dinner each Sunday. Guests can arrange dinner with advance notice and an additional fee.
△ *3 double rooms with baths. Air-conditioning; pool, walking trails. $85; full breakfast. No smoking.*

MOCKINGBIRD INN ☜
305 N. Gloster St., Tupelo 38801, tel. 601/841–0286, fax 601/840–4158

Jim and Sandy Gilmer decided to leave the corporate world and strike out on their own. So in addition to starting a recycling business, they transformed a spacious old two-story home on a shady street corner into a B&B. In researching the home's history, the Gilmers found that the original builders from 1925 loved to entertain and had theme parties relating to various countries. The globe-trekking Gilmers named their B&B the Mockingbird Inn, after the state bird—a symbol of hospitality. It's only fitting that a mockingbird appears at the porch windows periodically.

It's also only fitting that people who have seven favorite places in the world and seven rooms to decorate should re-create those places in the decor of the rooms and the bathrooms. You can almost hear gondolas gliding across a canal in the Venice Room, where rich Venetian tapestry and old lace make it more authentic. The Mackinac Island Room resembles a wonderful whitewashed lakeside cottage, light and airy, with pickled wood. A pewter wedding canopy bed and chaise longue are two of many elements that leave no doubt as to the inspiration for the Paris Room. The large Athens Room has Greek columns and an L-shape whirlpool for two. Even Isak Dinesen would feel at home in the Africa Room, where faux jungle-animal skins and mosquito netting around the bed set the scene. Pastels and seashells make the Sanibel Island Room as authentic as possible; add the verdigris iron bed and wicker furniture, and it's Florida revisited. Finally, in the Bavaria Room, lots of knotty pine, a sleigh bed, antique skis, and typical lace-trimmed windows bring southern Germany to northern Mississippi.

Guests linger on the indoor porch, with its wicker furniture and coffee and tea makings. The inn is popular with businesspeople who attend one of the two Tupelo furniture markets and with tourists of the rock-and-roll persuasion, who like to look across at the school where Elvis Presley attended sixth and seventh grades. △ *7 double rooms with baths. Air-conditioning, cable TV and phones in rooms; fireplace in 1 room, whirlpool bath in 1 room. $75–$125; full breakfast, afternoon refreshments. D, MC, V. No smoking, no children under 13.*

PUDDIN PLACE 🐚
1008 University Ave., Oxford 38655, tel. 601/234–1250

Since 1992, when Ann and Guy Turnbow decided to turn an 1892 house near the Ole Miss campus into a Victorian B&B, its name has piqued the interest of guests. Puddin Place was named for a former resident, Miss Mary "Puddin" Sims, a dear friend of the current owners. The general consensus, though, is that it is "a puddin' of a place," to use an old southern phrase.

Because the same family owned the house until 1980, it didn't go through the major changes often imposed by multiple owners. The current owners have made it very comfortable while maintaining the home's early character through colors and decor. The suites are furnished with antiques and collectibles, and they all have open fireplaces and ceiling fans. In addition to the tangible reminders of yesteryear, there's an unhurried pace here. Guests can let the porch swing lull them into a nap on a summer day. Those who relish more activity can find, within a short walk, the university museums, the downtown square, and Rowan Oak, William Faulkner's home. ⚘ *2 suites. Air-conditioning, cable TV, fireplaces, ceiling fans in rooms. $90; full breakfast. No credit cards. No smoking.*

RAMBLING ROSE 🐚
621 10th St. N, Columbus 39701, tel. 601/327–2952

There's something inexplicably inviting about a gray Victorian-style house with a big front porches, swings, and rockers—especially if it's on a quiet corner of a tree-lined street. This describes Rambling Rose, where guests are likely to find new friends in owners Phyllis and William Wallace. The Wallaces are young retirees from financial planning and higher education, and they enjoy their unhurried new lifestyle. They can be found tending to the flower garden, basking in the hot tub, or playing the grand piano in the parlor.

Rambling Rose, which has a thoroughly relaxed atmosphere, is a house of good conversation, good books, and good music. Furnishings are an eclectic collection of antiques and old things. The Blue Room has pale blue walls and an antique walnut bed and dresser, while the Pink Room contains a four-poster double bed and mahogany furnishings. Guests in the Salmon or Melon Room can view the old-fashioned porch from a large picture window.

A full breakfast with homemade breads and jellies might also include eggs, pancakes, waffles, cheese grits, bacon, sausage, and fruit. ⚘ *2 double rooms with baths, 1 double shares a bath. Air-conditioning, cable TV/VCR in common room; hot tub. $70; full breakfast. MC, V.*

SASSAFRAS INN 🐚
785 Hwy. 51, (Box 612), Hernando 38632, tel. 601/429–5864 or 800/882–1897, fax 601/429–4591

Just south of Memphis, in a town depicted in one of John Grisham's novels, this English Tudor home is almost hidden by trees and landscaping. As guests arrive, owners Dennis and Frances McClanahan extend a hospitable southern welcome. Dennis, a builder, and Frances, a floral designer, have a home with plenty of flowers and architectural extras such as skylights in one of the bedrooms and eight stained-glass windows in the indoor pool area. Amenities include a climate-controlled indoor pool, hot tub, and a recreation room with Ping-Pong and pool tables. There's a cottage on the grounds where honeymooners—or anyone else who appreciates romantic settings—can enjoy absolute privacy.

The guest-room decor is lacy Victorian. All bedrooms have queen-size beds, CD players, sound machines (you can listen to the ocean, for example), and bathrobes. The Victorian Room contains cherrywood furniture from that period, including a four-poster bed, and delicate lace and satin drapes. The Magnolia Room combines oak furniture with a bedspread and wallpaper in a magnolia motif. Ivy-patterned decor complements the bright cheeriness of the Skylight Room.

Business travelers will enjoy the inn's technological amenities: A computer, copier, and fax are all available. Guests can choose from a choice of breakfast locations: poolside table, formal dining room, or room service. △ *3 double rooms with baths, 1 cottage-suite with microwave and mini-refrigerator, TV and phone in rooms; indoor pool, hot tub, business facilities. $85–$225; full breakfast. AE, D, MC, V. No smoking.*

SPAHN HOUSE 🐦

401 College St., Senatobia 38668, tel. 601/562–9853 or 800/400–9853, spahnhouse.com

Senatobia, just 30 minutes south of Memphis, is a pretty-as-a-picturebook small town, where you'll find what's quickly becoming one of the state's most popular B&Bs: the Spahn House. The owners are Joe and Daughn Spahn. He's a building contractor, and she's a former partner in a brokerage firm who came "back home" to the Magnolia State via Chicago, New York City, and Miami after she married Joe. Their 15-room southern mansion, built in 1904, is on a tree-canopied street in a quiet, historic neighborhood.

The grand old house was a true Victorian until its renovation in 1948, which left it bearing a slight resemblance to the Greek Revival style. When the Spahns bought the house in 1994, they transformed it into a B&B. The parlor's recessed arches give the first inkling that this is no ordinary house. High ceilings, original pine floors, and rich woods add to the turn-of-the-century ambience. Throughout the house, window treatment may be lace left over from a wedding or vines carefully crafted as valances. A wide staircase leads to the second-story common area, which connects to all the guest rooms. Antiques were purchased in Memphis and New Orleans and "all in between," according to Daughn. Each room has a different theme, including the Gentlemen's Room, where antique clothing and hats are casually displayed. Quaint old chests have been converted to vanities; this utilitarian use of odd pieces of furniture adds to this B&B's appeal.

Daughn is now a caterer with a full staff, and guests can arrange a private gourmet dinner. Breakfasts are elegant: Expect a soufflé that may be filled with ham and cheese or strawberries and whipped cream, fresh fruits, and an assortment of other gourmet offerings, all served with panache. Also on-site is a business office for the use of guests. △ *4 double rooms with baths. Whirlpool baths in 2 rooms, TV in common area. Private candlelight dinner available with advance reservation. $75–$110; full breakfast. AE, MC, V. No smoking.*

NEAR THE NATCHEZ TRACE
AND THE MISSISSIPPI DELTA

The two-lane paved road crossing Mississippi from southwest to northeast, connecting Natchez to Nashville, Tennessee, has had a long and colorful past. It began about 8,000 years ago, when a path was "traced out" by buffalo and Native Americans. By 1800, the well-worn Old Trace was the route used by post riders, settlers, outlaws, peddlers, and "Kaintucks," or boatmen, from all points north. They came down the Mississippi River to New Orleans, sold their goods and boats, then headed home via the Trace, hoping not to encounter hostile tribes, bandits, or wild animals on the way. Those who could spare a few pennies slept inside—often on the floor— at inns (called stands) scattered along the Trace, sharing "mush and milk" with other wayfarers pleased to have the simple luxury of hot food and a roof over their head.

After the late 1820s, when steamboats began to offer better accommodations and shorter trips, the wilderness path to the new frontier fell into disuse. The Old Trace had been taken over by weeds when, in about 1909, the Mississippi chapter of the Daughters of the American Revolution waged a campaign to mark it. Their exemplary efforts resulted in the 450-mi, limited-access Natchez Trace Parkway, a long, thin park running from Natchez to Nashville.

Travelers today who seek historic places and a slower pace choose this road. The Trace is safe, scenic, and impeccably maintained by the National Park Service and has been landscaped to open up peaceful vistas in the dense woodland. Uniformed rangers patrol it, enforcing the 50 mph speed limit, and commercial vehicles and outdoor advertising are prohibited. You can drive the Trace from Natchez to Tupelo in seven hours, but to fully appreciate its beauty and history requires a more leisurely approach—perhaps a weeklong odyssey.

Expect to see abundant tall timber, historic markers, wild game, and nature trails, but plan to leave the Trace for restaurants, shops, and city sights. They're available in Natchez, Jackson, and Tupelo (see North Missis-

sippi Hill Country, above), right on your way, and in Vicksburg, on the Mississippi River, 15 mi west.

In Natchez, one of the South's favorite destinations, many antebellum houses are open for daily tours throughout the year, and travelers today catch a glimpse of the way things were in the Old South.

Near Jackson, swaying pines and moss-draped oaks are replaced by sailboats and the glistening waters of the Ross Barnett Reservoir. Jackson is the best choice for restaurants, museums, and entertainment.

Head northwest of Jackson and you're en route to the Mississippi Delta, known only as the Delta in these parts. The land is vast and flat and attracts visitors from around the world, searching the juke joints of Highway 61 for Delta blues and those who wail them.

PLACES TO GO, SIGHTS TO SEE

The **Delta Blues Museum** (114 Delta Ave., in the Carnegie Public Library, tel. 601/624–4461 or 601/627–6820) is the local source for blues and blues artists, complete with memorabilia and videos.

The **Florewood River Plantation State Park** (Hwy. 82 W, 2 mi west of Greenwood, tel. 601/455–3821) is the state's best example of an actual Delta cotton plantation. This living-history presentation documents life on the plantation circa the 1850s.

French Camp Log Cabin (Natchez Trace, Mile Marker 180.8, tel. 601/547–6657) is a "dogtrot" cabin: A center hall, open on both ends, separates the two sides. Built in the early 1800s, it contains Native American and French artifacts and has an operating sorghum mill.

Jackson, Mississippi's capital, is the place to stop for cultural events and tours of historic sites and old government buildings. The town has become something of a regional arts mecca thanks to blockbuster events such as the USA International Ballet Competition (tel. 601/355–9853), held in June every four years (the next is 2002), and huge art exhibitions such as "Splendors of Versailles" (1998). You can see the *Governor's Mansion* (300 E. Capitol St., tel. 601/359–3175) on 30-minute tours Tuesday–Friday. The *Old Capitol* and *State Historical Museum* (100 S. State St., tel. 601/359–6920) are open daily for self-guided tours. The *Jackson Zoological Park* (2918 W. Capitol St., tel. 601/352–2585) is open year-round, and the *Russell C. Davis Planetarium* (201 E. Pascagoula St., tel. 601/960–1550) gives multiscreen space and nature shows Tuesday through Sunday. The *Mississippi Museum of Art* (201 E. Pascagoula St., tel. 601/960–1515) contains continuing and changing exhibits, often international in scope, and a gallery with interactive high-tech exhibits for children. At the *Jim Buck Ross Mississippi Agriculture and Forestry/National Agricultural Aviation Museum* (1150 Lakeland Dr., tel. 601/354–6113), which has farm buildings and exhibits on the state's agrarian roots, you can see an orientation film and a re-created small town, circa 1920, with farm animals and living-history enactments. Juried works and native crafts are sold here at the *Chimneyville Crafts Gallery* (1150 Lakeland Dr., tel. 601/981–2499).

Mississippi Crafts Center (Ridgeland, just north of Jackson on the Natchez Trace, tel. 601/856–7546), a quaint log cabin with front-porch rockers, sells local crafts, including quilts, baskets, and jewelry.

The **Mississippi Delta** is a little over an hour's drive west of the Trace on U.S. 82, but it's worth a visit. It's a land of mood and mystique where vast, flat fields seem to go on forever. This is the heart of the state's cotton country. The rich Delta soil spawned numerous writers and artists and the unique music of hot days and hard times—the inimitable Delta blues. You can hear the blues throughout the Delta, on front porches and in juke joints, at festivals and church socials.

Mount Locust Inn (Mount Locust ranger office–bookstore, Mile Marker 15.5 of the Natchez Trace Parkway, tel. 601/445–4211), is the only remaining example of a frontier stand, or inn. Built around 1780, it is furnished accordingly and is closed during December and January.

Natchez's grand mansions attest to the former wealth of this old and colorful river town, recalling a time when lavish entertaining was de rigueur for the landed gentry. About 30 of the more than 500 historic structures are on parade during the spring and fall "Pilgrimages." A carriage ride through the historic district is a memorable way to see the houses and hear their stories. The riverboats *Delta Queen, American Queen,* and *Mississippi Queen*—calliopes playing, flags flying, passengers cheering—make regular stops at Natchez Under-the-Hill, the riverbank area that was the former hangout of rowdy boatmen and gamblers. And due to the recent influx of casino boats such as *Isle of Capri* and *Lady Luck,* today you can gamble there again. To help plan your visit to Natchez, stop in the Natchez Visitors Reception Center, a state-of-the-art, interactive resource with films and multimedia exhibitions that opened in summer 1998.

Port Gibson has quaint churches, historic houses of varying architectural styles, and the towering columns at the *Windsor Ruins,* remnants of another time. In contrast, you can visit the *Grand Gulf Nuclear Station* (Bald Hill Rd., tel. 601/437–6317), a futuristic facility.

Vicksburg, on the Mississippi, approximately 25 mi west of the Trace, is a lively and appealing river town known for its Civil War significance. Its historic antebellum houses are open for tours year-round. The *Vicksburg National Military Park* (3201 Clay St., tel. 601/636–0583) encompasses more than 1,800 acres of hills, fortifications, monuments, and the USS *Cairo,* a Union gunboat. The gaming industry has come to Vicksburg: The river is now lined with gambling boats, though one only hopes they never have to prove their water-worthiness. The *Old Court House Museum* (1008 Cherry St., Vicksburg, tel. 601/636–0741) is an 1858 building with area artifacts from Indian cultures through the steamboat era. *McRaven Tour Home* (1445 Harrison St., tel. 601/636–1663), built over three periods from 1797 through 1849, has 3 acres of gardens.

RESTAURANTS

In Jackson, **Nick's** (1501 Lakeland Dr., tel. 601/981–8017) is the choice of both Jacksonians and visitors for fine dining. For retro regional flavor and fresh seafood, you can't beat the **Mayflower Cafe** downtown (123 W. Capitol St., tel. 601/355–4122), one of the few remaining Jackson restaurants still serving the region's trademark "comeback sauce" with its seafood salads. **Bravo!** (4500 I–55 N, Highland Village, tel. 601/982–8111) earns the exclamation point, say lovers of Italian fare. Seafood, veal, steak, and wood-fired pizzas are popular items. The prime rib and gulf seafood at **Primo's** (4330 N. State St., tel. 601/982–2064) are another Jackson favorite. **Hal & Mal's** (200 S. Commerce St., tel. 601/948–0888) features regional food and music, including blues, rock, bluegrass, and Celtic, and draws the local arts and media crowd. Proprietor Monday Agho of **Monte's Seafood & Pasta** (896 Avery Blvd., tel. 601/957–0450) serves with both Caribbean and Cajun flair. Families flock to **Cock of the Walk** (141 Madison Landing Circle, Ridgeland, tel. 601/856–5500) for catfish, cornbread, and greens with a peaceful view overlooking the Reservoir.

The most talked-about new restaurant in Natchez Under-the-Hill, **John Martin's** (53 Silver St., tel. 601/445–0605), brings a touch of class and gourmet cuisine to the area, while the casual **Wharf Master's House** (57 Silver St., tel. 601/445–6025) is known for seafood, charbroiled steaks, and local fare. Hickory smoked prime rib, legends, and ghosts are on the menu at **King's Tavern** (619 Jefferson St., tel. 601/446–8845). For lunch in Natchez, the best place to get a taste of the real old South is at the **Carriage House Restaurant** (401 High St., tel. 601/445–5151) on the grounds of the beautiful Stanton Hall. It serves lunch only except during Pilgrimage time, and the fare is all the foods Southerners love. Locals and visitors rave about both the quality and presentation of the contemporary regional cuisine at **Liza's** (657 S. Canal St., tel. 601/446–6368), where the menu changes seasonally.

Among Vicksburg's popular restaurants are the rather formal **Delta Point** (4144 Washington St., tel. 601/636–5317), overlooking the Mississippi River and serving a variety of good food, from Cajun to Continental, and **Walnut Hill** (1214 Adams Street, tel. 601/638–4910), where everyone passes the down-home food—including fresh vegetables galore and, some say, the best fried chicken in the South—around the table. For delicious variations on a theme, the French chef prepares catfish seven delectable ways at **Jacques' Cafe** (4137 I–20 Frontage Rd., in Park Inn International, tel. 601/638–5811), or dine by candlelight at **Andre's** (2200 Oak St., tel. 601/636–1000 or 800/862–1300), which is part of Cedar Grove bed-and-breakfast (*see below*). The casinos that line the river in Vicksburg are known to serve good food, as well. Among the most popular are **Americastar** (tel. 800/700–7770), **Harrah's** (tel. 800/427–7247), and **Isle of Capri** (tel. 800/843–4753).

While in the Delta that begins north of Vicksburg, see how Deltans live and dine: For lunch, there's no better place for either than the **Crystal Grill** (423 Carrollton, Greenwood, tel. 601/453–6530), which has been in the same spot, owned by the same family, since 1913. Here you'll find down-home vegetables, the best beef and seafood, and homemade pies with meringue 3 inches high. **Lusco's** (722 Carrollton Ave., Greenwood, tel. 601/453–5365), famous for steaks and seafood, is one of the best-known restaurants in the Delta and has remained almost unchanged since it opened in 1933. You walk through the old kitchen and tamale machine at **Doe's Eat Place** (502 Nelson St., Greenville, tel. 601/334–3315) into a small, no-nonsense little dining room for steaks and shrimp that have drawn national celebrities (including Liza Minnelli and Tom Cruise) for years. The elegant, expensive **KC's** (Hwy. 61, Cleveland, tel. 601/843–5301) has garnered rave reviews from food critics from Memphis to New Orleans.

SHOPPING

C. W. Fewel III & Co., Antiquarians (840 N. State St., Jackson, tel. 601/355–5375) specializes in fine 18th- and 19th-century furnishings and accessories. If you're in the mood for a treasure hunt, the **Fairground Antique & Flea Market** (900 High St., Jackson, tel. 601/353–5327), with 220 dealers, often harbors some fine pieces among the simply fun stuff. It's open on Saturdays and Sundays. The **Chimneyville Crafts Gallery** (1150 Lakeland Dr., Jackson, tel. 601/981–2499) sells the work of members of the Craftsmen's Guild of Mississippi. Pottery, jewelry, woodwork, glasswork, quilts, and paper are among the offerings. **Mississippi Cultural Crossroads** (507 Market St., Port Gibson, tel. 601/ 437–8905) has an enviable collection of quilts on display and for sale.

VISITOR INFORMATION

Greenville Convention & Visitors Bureau (410 Washington Ave., Greenville 38939, tel. 601/334–2711 or 800/467–3582). **Greenwood Convention & Visitors Bureau** (Box 739, Greenwood 38930, tel. 601/453–9197 or 800/748–9064). **Metro Jackson Convention & Visitors Bureau** (Box 1450, Jackson 39215, tel. 601/960–1891 or 800/354–7695). **Mississippi Department of Economic Development, Division of Tourism Development** (Box 1705, Ocean Springs 39566, tel. 800/927–6378). **Natchez Convention & Visitors Bureau** (Box 1485, Natchez 39120, tel. 601/446–6345 or 800/647–6724). **Natchez Pilgrimage Tours** (Box 347, Natchez 39121, tel. 601/446–6631 or 800/647–6742). **Port Gibson Chamber of Commerce** (Box 491, Port Gibson 39150, tel. 601/437–4351). **Vicksburg Convention & Visitors Bureau** (Box 110, Vicksburg 39181, tel. 601/ 636–9421 or 800/221–3536). **Yazoo County Convention & Visitors Bureau** (Box 186, Yazoo City 39194, tel. 601/746–1815).

RESERVATION SERVICES

Lincoln, Ltd. Bed & Breakfast Mississippi Reservation Service (Box 3479, Meridian 39303, tel. 601/482–5483 or 800/633–6477). **Natchez Pilgrimage Tours Bed & Breakfast Reservations** (Box 347, Natchez 39121, tel. 601/ 446–6631 or 800/647–6742).

ANCHUCA 🕊

1010 First East St., Vicksburg 39180, tel. 601/661–0111

Time seems to have stood still at Anchuca. It may be the most authentic—in style, decor, and attitude—of Vicksburg's antebellum bed-and-breakfasts. The owner, Loveta Byrne, who formerly ran the Burn B&B in Natchez, refurbished and re-opened Anchuca in 1997 and has kept its antebellum flavor intact. Anchuca (circa 1830) was the first Vicksburg B&B, and for years guests there have experienced the South the way it must have been in the pre-1860 days.

Loveta has invested a lifetime of antiques collecting in Anchuca, and you'll find few post–19th-century pieces in any of the rooms or parlors. When talking about the house, Loveta is well informed and exhibits a delightfully dry wit. (You'll want to ask her about the balcony where Confederate president Jefferson Davis addressed Vicksburg.)

Former servants' quarters, now used as suites, serve as cozy, romantic hideaways, whose brick walls and floors keep them cool in the heat of summer. Also lovely are the gardens and pool, which has fountains. Anchuca has two master bedrooms in the mansion and four bedrooms in the 1890 guest cottage. ♙ *6 double rooms with baths, 2 suites. Air-conditioning and TV in rooms; kitchen, microwave, and mini-refrigerator in suites; pool. $95–$190; full breakfast. MC, V. Restricted smoking.*

ANNABELLE 🕊

501 Speed St., Vicksburg 39180, tel. 601/638–2000 or 800/791–2000, fax 601/636–5054, www.missbab.com/annabelle

Luckily for the old Victorian Italianate house and the guests who voted it among the 10 best B&Bs in the state, George and Carolyn Mayer came up from New

Orleans and purchased Annabelle in 1992. The Mayers have traveled extensively and understand the expectations and needs of travelers. George is European and bilingual; languages spoken at Annabelle include German, Portuguese, some Spanish, and American South, y'all.

In the historic River View Garden District, Annabelle, circa 1868, sits just east of the Mississippi River bed and is reminiscent of a home in New Orleans's French Quarter. A brick patio adjoins the house and is a great place to relax prior to or after exploring Vicksburg. Inside, Victorian antiques are set off by bright colors, but best of all, the house lacks the fussiness often found in early Victorian houses. Two bedrooms in the cottage can be converted to a suite, and the Natchez Suite in the 1880 Federal guest house consists of a living room, bedroom, and kitchen. The suite is separated from the main house by a sparkling pool. ♦ *6 double rooms with baths, 1 suite. Air-conditioning, phone and cable TV in rooms, 1 room with whirlpool; pool, off-street parking. $93–$125; full breakfast. AE, D, DC, MC, V. No smoking, no large pets.*

BAILEY HOUSE ❦

400 S. Commerce, Natchez 39120, tel. 601/442–9974, fax 601/442–9939, www.bestinns.net/usa/ms/bailey.htm/

The personality of owner Lisa Brunetti is literally etched onto the walls of the Bailey House (circa 1897), with its murals and fanciful paintings of kudzu or wisteria sometimes cleverly disguising a crack in the plaster. A watercolor artist and art teacher, Lisa has applied her fine sense of line and aesthetics to this centrally located Natchez Garden District property, where her paintings are displayed throughout.

Rooms are uncomplicated and bright. Don't look for a lot of fussy antiques, just tasteful things old and new that keep the clean, allergen-free atmosphere informal and breezy. One of the most striking elements of the Victorian Colonial-revival style house is a large, expressive stained-glass window over the landing (the 1870 painting it was derived from is hanging in the front parlor). "I saw it and felt sorry for the house," says Lisa, who was originally looking for an art studio when she bought Bailey House with her husband, Mike, a Louisiana farmer.

Bedrooms overlook picturesque Natchez street scenes that include an Episcopal church and a synagogue, as well as the home's courtyard, with its camellias, wisteria, old sweet-olive tree, and bubbling fountain with goldfish pond. Two second-story bedrooms share a veranda reachable through the large windows. (One small drawback to the house, where sound carries, is the somewhat-too-intimate proximity of one guest bathroom to an upstairs common area.)

Guests have commented on the warmth of the atmosphere and their quick rapport with both Lisa and her cook, Margaret, who lays out a breakfast that, like the rest of the house, is a work of art (butter served with cut violets was a particularly sweet touch). ♦ *5 double rooms with baths. Air-conditioning, cable TV in rooms. $125–$145; full breakfast. MC, V. No smoking, no children under 12.*

BALFOUR HOUSE ❦

1002 Crawford St. (Box 781), Vicksburg 39181, tel. 601/638–7113 or 800/294–7113, fax 601/638–8484

Civil War historians will surely be familiar with the Balfour House (circa 1835), for it was the home of diarist Emma Balfour, who kept a daily account of the

Siege of Vicksburg in 1863. The diary is now part of the Emma Balfour Collection of the Mississippi Department of Archives and History. After the fall of Vicksburg, the Union army used the house, an outstanding example of the Greek Revival, as its local headquarters.

The Balfour House was the scene of a Christmas ball in 1862, where Confederate officers and their ladies had come for holiday festivities. The dance, however, was interrupted when a Confederate courier rushed into the ballroom to announce that Yankee gunboats had been sighted on the nearby Mississippi River. The festivities quickly ended as the men dashed out the door to defend the Confederacy. Each year, the Reenactment of the 1862 Christmas Ball at the Balfour House is a much-anticipated event in Vicksburg.

The house was meticulously restored in the early 1980s, won the 1984 Award of Merit from the Mississippi State Historical Society, is listed on the National Register of Historic Places, is featured at the Smithsonian, and is a designated Mississippi Landmark.

Period purists will be pleased to know that owner Sharon Humble has remained as authentic to the era of the house as possible. The graceful, elegant redbrick structure, with bold white trim, has a rare, three-story elliptical spiral staircase. In the three guest suites, the antique—predominantly Empire—furnishings reflect the age and style of the house. Guest-room colors range from dark green to mauve and pale green to pale pink, each with matching color schemes in the adjoining bath.

Breakfast menus vary, but guests can expect fare such as quiche Lorraine and fruit or an egg-and-cheese casserole with fruit and bread. ♣ *3 suites. Air-conditioning, TV and phone in rooms. $85–$150; full breakfast. AE, D, MC, V. No smoking.*

BELLE OF THE BENDS 🐚
508 Klein St., Vicksburg 39180, tel. 601/634–0737 or 800/844–2308, fax 601/638–0544, www.belleofthebends.com

Built by a state senator in 1876, Belle of the Bends is named for a steamboat that once plied the Mississippi, and it indeed evokes Mark Twain–era river life. On a bluff just a block from the Yazoo Diversion Canal off the Mississippi, the house itself is reminiscent of a steamboat, with two-story verandas wrapping around three sides, as well as wonderful river views from two of its bedrooms.

Owners Wally and Jo Pratt, who bought the house in October 1990, have stayed true to the Victorian Italianate character of the structure, with plenty of period antiques, Oriental rugs, and, of course, steamboat memorabilia such as photos of *Belle of the Bends,* which was owned by Jo's grandfather, Captain Tom Morrissey.

The only possible drawback to being so close to the river is that a train runs nearby (including a couple of times a night), but the Pratts supply each guest with earplugs. And some guests say the train lends authenticity to the sense of nostalgia. "You hear the whistle blow in the distance," says guest Leslye Gibbens of Houston. "It is actually very soothing and adds to the ambience of the place."

And the next morning you are rewarded with a breakfast spread that may include pancakes made with homegrown blueberries or omelets, cheese grits, and homemade breads. ♣ *4 suites with baths. Air-conditioning, TV/VCR, and phone in rooms; video library. $95–$135; full breakfast. AE, MC, V. No smoking.*

THE BURN 🐦
712 N. Union St., Natchez 39120, tel. 601/442–1344 or 800/654–8859,
fax 601/445–0606

This impressive Greek Revival house has been home to more than one Natchez mayor and has been the site of lavish entertaining since it was built in 1832. Once called a Greek Revival cottage, the Burn is actually a full-fledged three-story mansion, one of the oldest pure Greek Revival homes in America. From the transomed and sidelighted Grecian doorway, the first thing guests notice is the unique spiral staircase with its delicate spindle banisters. Dramatic and original furnishings characterize the rooms, with original crystal gasoliers flickering in the ladies parlor. Outstanding woodwork and plaster moldings enhance the quality so obvious at the Burn.

Guest rooms in the main house are on the first floor in the original house's servants' quarters, where quiet and comfort prevail. Guests may enjoy the pool, patio, and fountained garden off the ground floor. All bedrooms and suites have fine antiques, pastel walls, and exquisite Belgian fabrics on windows and beds. Three additional guest rooms and one suite are across the courtyard in the Garçonnière, a building formerly used by male family members and out-of-town guests.

Though it's in the city, the Burn has a country feel about it, for tall trees and flowering shrubbery are plentiful on its 5 acres of terraced gardens. Great southern breakfasts include the most delicious little biscuits you'll ever taste, a specialty of one of the favorite cooks in Natchez. △ *4 double rooms with baths, 3 suites. Air-conditioning, fireplaces, and cable TV in rooms; pool. $125–$200; full breakfast. AE, MC, V. No smoking.*

CANEMOUNT PLANTATION 🐦
Hwy. 552 W (Rte. 2, Box 45), Lorman 39096, tel. 601/877–3784 or 800/423–0684

This 6,000-acre working plantation near Port Gibson, just off the Natchez Trace, is nestled quietly among vast forests and fields, flowing streams, and hills, welcoming guests to an idyllic escape. Canemount was built in 1855 in the Italianate revival style. The house is almost unchanged, except that the butler's pantry has been converted to a small kitchen for the owners, Ray John and Rachel Forrest, and their son John. When it was built, the kitchen was out of doors, as is today's cozy, wood-paneled kitchen with a brick fireplace, where guests gather for breakfast.

Canemount, in all its Spanish moss–draped glory, is a haven for wildlife. The Forrests, formerly of Morganza, Louisiana, purchased it in 1981 as a hunting retreat, but according to Rachel, they "fell in love with the place and decided to stay permanently." White-tailed deer are so plentiful that Canemount was selected for a Mississippi State University study of their life span. Meandering paths and trails offer opportunities to see deer, Russian boar, and wild turkey. Certain areas are designated for wildlife photography, and a guided Jeep wildlife safari is offered every afternoon.

Guests are invited to have dinner with the Forrests at no extra charge and to tour the antiques-filled main house. Accommodations are in nearby, private, restored antebellum structures: Rick's Cottage, with brick walls, original wood floors, and a tester bed; Grey Cottage, which has a whirlpool bath; and Pond House, with a whirlpool tub. In addition, a restored 1829 carriage house has six guest rooms. Each cottage is furnished with antiques and contemporary pieces and is wonderfully quiet and undisturbed except for the sounds of birds and an occasional deer.

The plantation acreage includes the historic Windsor Plantation, where the haunting ruins—23 towering Greek columns—still stand, though the massive house was destroyed by fire in 1890. The Persnickety Pig dining area, also on the plantation, is in a converted dairy. It's where festive Cajun pig roasts are held, as well as catered parties and group dinners, by reservation. ♨ *6 double rooms with baths, 3 cottage suites. Air-conditioning, TV in some rooms and common area; pool, ponds. $165–$195; full breakfast, cocktails, hors d'oeuvres, dinner. AE, MC, V. No smoking, no children under 12.*

CEDAR GROVE ☙

2200 Oak St. (Box B), Vicksburg 39180, tel. 601/636–1000 or 800/862–1300, fax 601/634–6126, www.cedargroveinn.com

The imposing Cedar Grove gets lots of attention among B&B aficionados, perhaps because of its history, certainly because of its bold color schemes and lush furnishings. Built in 1840, the massive mansion has an eclectic architectural pedigree, though it is predominantly Greek Revival. There's still a Union cannonball lodged in a parlor wall from when Vicksburg was under siege during the Civil War. Federal troops later used the home, a National Historic Landmark and on the National Register of Historic Places, as a hospital. Amazingly, after all this time, the original heavy furniture made for the house remains in the master bedroom and the children's rooms, along with a few pieces attributed to Prudent Mallard, a prominent New Orleans furniture maker of the day.

The house sits on 4 acres, with contoured lawns, fountains, pool, croquet, gazebos, and a playable, smaller-than-average "Victorian-style" tennis court on the back grounds. Tennis rackets and balls and croquet mallets are available at the front desk. The Mississippi River is just across the street, and sometimes the sound of riverboat calliopes can be heard in the distance.

The main house has an array of wall colors, including gold, red, violet, deep yellow, and, in some rooms, festive combinations of two colors. The woodwork and molding in the ballroom and parlor are ornate and elaborate, with heavy window treatments. The guest rooms in the main house are colorful and spacious, with gaslit chandeliers, pier mirrors, Italian marble mantels, and other elements of the house's earlier eras. There are also two rooms in a poolside building, eight carriage-house suites, and five cottages.

Breakfast is served inside the mansion, at the restaurant, Andre's, which overlooks the garden. The plantation breakfast consists of eggs, sausage, grits, fruit, and breads. The restaurant at Cedar Grove opens at 6 PM for dinner; walk-ins are welcome. ♨ *9 double rooms with baths, 15 suites, 5 cottages. Restaurant, air-conditioning, TV and phone in rooms; pool, croquet, Victorian-style tennis court, gift shop. $85–$165; full breakfast. AE, D, MC, V. Restricted smoking.*

CEDAR GROVE PLANTATION ☙

617 Kingston Rd., Natchez 39120, tel./fax 601/445–0585, www.travelbase.com/destinations/natchez/cedar-grove

A delightful discovery in the countryside off Highway 61 south of Natchez is secluded, pastoral Cedar Grove Plantation, which combines southern antebellum charm with a lodgelike atmosphere that tends to appeal especially to men. Although furnished in antiques, the warm dens and library of Cedar Grove and its sprawling grounds offer a refreshing respite from the cool quaintness of many other B&Bs.

The former 900-acre cotton plantation, built in the 1830s by New Jersey native Absalom Sharp, is brick Greek Revival, with porches overlooking a rose garden, a pond, a swimming pool, and the grounds.

The surrounding 150 acres teems with wild game, and there are bass and bream in the five ponds. When it comes to fishing, friendly and knowledgeable John Holyoak, who manages and lives on the property, can provide assistance. Guests may fish, bike, and hike here, and dog owners are encouraged to bring their canine companions, who can stay in a large kennel on the grounds.

For those who would like extra privacy, away from the main house, the converted stables–carriage house has two cozy rooms overlooking the pool. Unlike rooms in the main house, which share a TV/VCR in a common area, carriage-house guests have in-room TVs. ♠ *5 double rooms with baths. Air-conditioning and phone in rooms; pool, ponds, trails, kennel. $65–$145; full breakfast. AE, MC, V. No smoking, no children under 12, pets with prior approval.*

CEDARS PLANTATION ☞
Rte. 2 (Box 298), Church Hill 39120, tel. 601/445–2203, fax 601/445–2372, www.thecedarsb&b.com

The Cedars Plantation was built as a one-story planter's cottage around 1830, with four big rooms surrounded by porches. In the 1850s, the elegant Greek Revival portion was added, blending amazingly well with the original structure. Now the stately, columned, 2½-story house sits atop a slight incline, surrounded by a seemingly endless white picket fence, mirrorlike ponds, old oak trees laden with lazy Spanish moss, and colorful flowers of the season.

Once a working plantation, the Cedars adorns the lush green rolling hills about 20 mi north of Natchez, just off the scenic Natchez Trace Parkway on Route 553 and within walking distance of the historic Christ Episcopal Church, thought to be the oldest Episcopal parish in the region.

Prominent Natchezians have owned the Cedars, as has Hollywood actor George Hamilton (at which time it was featured in *Architectural Digest*). It is now owned by Glenda and Dick Robinson of Chicago; a resident staff manages this National Register property.

A parlor is to the right of the foyer, a formal dining room to the left. Look upward from the center of the foyer, and see the staircase spiraling up to the third floor. Fine period antiques, some European and some southern, decorate each room. The airy house is painted in light pastels; it has numerous tall jib windows that also serve as doors. Some of the original decorative painting is intact, as are plaster cornices, center medallions, and ornate moldings. Guest rooms are spacious and "of-the-period" perfect.

The pale yellow suite on the third floor was once an attic and is now a treetop perch from which to view the grounds through Palladian arched windows. The suite also has a working fireplace, a wet bar, and a whirlpool bath by the windows.

Special big, fluffy biscuits complement the ham, eggs, grits, fruit, or casserole. Breakfast can be served in the breakfast room, the formal dining room, or weather permitting, on a porch for an outstanding view of the gently rolling hills and lovely trees. ♠ *3 double rooms with baths, 1 3-room suite. Mini-refrigerator, ice maker, robes, and phone in rooms. $150–$200; full breakfast, complimentary beverage. AE, MC, V. No smoking, no children under 12.*

THE CORNERS

601 Klein St., Vicksburg 39180, tel. 601/636–7421 or 800/444–7421,
fax 601/636–7232, www.thecorners.com

The Corners has had a happier history than many other Vicksburg dwellings. No cannonballs are lodged in the walls, and there are no stories of the siege, just interesting anecdotes about the house. The Corners sits almost in the shadow of Cedar Grove (*see above*), because John Klein, Cedar Grove's builder, presented the smaller and more intimate two-story brick house to his daughter as a wedding gift.

The late Greek Revival–early Victorian house was built in 1873 and bought by Texans Bettye and Cliff Whitney in 1986. You can enjoy the river sights and sounds from the 68-ft front gallery. The guest rooms, many of which have working fireplaces, are furnished with antiques, each with a different color combination. The master bedroom is "on the mauve side," with a canopy bed (circa 1842) and a river view.

On the National Register of Historic Places, the house sits on 2 acres of grounds with a rose garden and parterre garden in front, as well as a more old-world backyard landscaping.

A full southern breakfast is served every day, with grits and eggs and all the trimmings sometimes giving way to casseroles, a Cajun corn dish called *macque choix,* and caramelized French toast. ♦ *14 double rooms with baths, 1 suite, 1 2-bedroom cottage. Air-conditioning, TV and phone in rooms, whirlpool baths in 8 rooms. $85–$125; full breakfast. AE, D, DC, MC, V. No smoking.*

DUNLEITH

84 Homochitto St., Natchez 39120, tel. 601/446–8500 or 800/433–2445

Dunleith is one of the South's most beautiful houses, from the colonnaded galleries that encircle it to the superior antiques within and the 40 acres of landscaped grounds, wooded bayous, and green pastures without. It is constantly photographed, often written about, and occasionally appears in films. Dunleith is also a National Historic Landmark on the National Register of Historic Places.

The palatial mansion (circa 1856) is owned by William Heins III of Natchez. A resident manager and staff run the business of daily tours and lodging, and it is, quite noticeably, a business. Fortunately, the magnificence of Dunleith's architecture and interiors neutralizes the regimented recitations of the staff, and the grandeur of the place prevails.

Among the elegant furnishings are the dining room's French Zuber wallpaper, printed from woodblocks circa 1855 that were hidden in a cave in France during World War I. The V'Soske carpet in the front parlor determined the color scheme for the room's walls, draperies, and upholstery; the greenish-gold walls and draperies perfectly complement the peachy pinks and gold tones in the carpet. A Louis XV ormolu-mounted mahogany Linke table is in a prominent place in the front parlor.

Three of the guest rooms at Dunleith are in the main house, and eight are in the former servants' wing, built in 1856. The rooms are quiet and private and are well decorated in mid-19th-century style, with a mixture of reproductions and antiques. A Victorian color scheme with peaches, blues, and pastels is used throughout. Each guest room has a working fireplace, original from the era of construction.

Another nice feature: The grounds are subtly lighted at night so that guests can stroll in the "moonlight" or enjoy the romantic views from wicker rockers on the galleries.

Old brick and warm woods set the stage for the big plantation breakfast served in the former poultry house. Exposed beams, lots of windows, and wooden floors add a homey touch that guests may have pined for in the elaborate, museumlike main house. ♙ *11 double rooms with baths. Air-conditioning, TV, phone, fireplaces in rooms. $95–$140; full breakfast. D, MC, V. No smoking, no children under 18.*

FAIRVIEW 🐚

734 Fairview St., Jackson 39202, tel. 601/948–3429, fax 601/948–1203, www.fairviewinn.com

The Colonial-revival Fairview, built in 1908, was designed by the architectural firm Spencer & Powers of Chicago for local lumber baron Cyrus G. Warren. It occupies an enviable tract of land in Jackson's Belhaven historic district, not too far from downtown, yet far removed from the hustle and bustle. Innkeeper-owners Carol and William Simmons have been B&B proprietors since 1993, though the house has been in William's family since 1930.

The three-story facade sets the scene for what's inside, like the oak-paneled library, with its ornate molding, leather sofa and chairs, and extensive Civil War book collection. When they decided to transform their private residence into a public house, the Simmonses adapted and redecorated family bedrooms into guest rooms, converted a parking area to a versatile ballroom, and found a use for every nook and cranny. The result is a well-planned, elegantly decorated, beautifully furnished showplace. The French furniture looks particularly grand paired with polished marble floors and mantels, as in the foyer.

The suites and guest rooms have deep, rich reds or soft, gentle golds and cream pastels, as well as outstanding fabric choices for beds and window treatment. Antiques and reproductions are used in conjunction with contemporary pieces. All the beds are either king or queen, some rooms have whirlpool tubs, and the third-floor suite has two queen beds and a whirlpool tub.

The Simmonses keep the sprawling house filled with leisure travelers, wedding parties, and business meetings, which all also keep their full-time chef and catering staff busy. Guests rave about the French toast served with dressed-up grits, bacon, fresh fruit, and the special blend of Louisiana's own Community coffee. Dinner, available for groups with advance reservations, is generally a pasta with beef, seafood or veal, salad, seasonal vegetable, and luscious dessert. ♙ *3 double rooms with baths, 5 suites. Air-conditioning, TV and phone in rooms, whirlpool tub in 2 rooms. $100–$150; full breakfast. AE, D, MC, V. No smoking.*

FRENCH CAMP BED AND BREAKFAST INN 🐚
1 Bluebird La., French Camp 39745, tel. 601/547–6835 (recorder)

The settlement on the Natchez Trace called French Camp got its name when Louis le Fleur built an inn here in 1812. Le Fleur, a French Canadian, married a Choctaw woman; their son changed his name to Greenwood Leflore and became a Choctaw chief, a state senator, and a colorful figure in Mississippi history. Today, Leflore's ornate carriage is on display at French Camp Academy, a small secondary school begun in 1885.

Sallie and Ed Williford, both associated with the school (she tutors math; he is director of development), manage the academy's nearby bed-and-breakfast. The inn (circa 1850), on the Natchez Trace, is intentionally rustic; it is made from two log cabins now joined together, each more than 100 years old. Rich warm wood, chinked log walls, antiques, iron beds, and handmade quilts give the

B&B the right touch of old-world charm mixed with its 20th-century conveniences. Big windows with forest views plus Sallie's homemade bread and jams are a bonus. **△** *5 double rooms with baths. Air-conditioning. $60; full breakfast. MC, V. No smoking.*

GOVERNOR HOLMES HOUSE 🐚
207 S. Wall St., Natchez 39120, tel. 601/442–2366 or 888/442–0166, fax 601/442–0166

Built in 1794, this Federal brick town house was the residence of David Holmes, the last governor of the Mississippi Territory and the first governor of the state of Mississippi. The house is also rumored to have been owned by Jefferson Davis, president of the Confederacy.

Perhaps these high-powered former occupants inspired the present owners when they set about making the remarkably well-preserved house reflect its history and happenstance; it is now on the National Register of Historic Places.

In the Governor's Suite, beamed ceilings and ecru walls provide a perfect background for the colorful Oriental carpet and canopies that cover the three twin beds. The fabric is by Scalamandré. Leather wing chairs positioned beside the fireplace are inviting. Owner and manager Bob Pully, former manager of the Algonquin Hotel in New York, gives tours every day from 10 to 4. **△** *4 suites. Air-conditioning, TV in rooms. $105–$140; full breakfast. AE, D, MC, V. No children under 12.*

GUEST HOUSE HISTORIC INN 🐚
201 N. Pearl St., Natchez 39120, tel. 601/442–1054, fax 601/442–1374, gsthouse@bkbank.com

This small, elegant hotel in the heart of Natchez's downtown historic district was built around 1840. It has tall Greek columns across the front and a wide porch on two sides, an inviting spot to enjoy morning coffee or a late-afternoon beverage. The Guest House is within walking distance of many historic tour homes, fine antiques shops, and restaurants—a prime location, whatever your plans.

Guest rooms, which were totally renovated following a tornado in spring 1998, are individually decorated with antiques—including tester beds in some rooms—and excellent reproductions of early to mid-1800s furnishings. Good quality is notable in the rich, bold color of the fabric used on beds and windows, in the many dark woods, and in the soft-print wallpaper. A room in this friendly property feels more like it's in a private home than an inn in a tourist-busy town.

Listed on the National Register of Historic Places, the Guest House is locally owned. It's a favorite place for corporate retreats, family reunions, and weddings. **△** *17 double rooms with baths. Restaurant, air-conditioning, cable TV, phone, small refrigerator, and coffeemaker in rooms; meeting rooms. $94; Continental breakfast. AE, D, DC, MC, V. No smoking.*

LINDEN 🐚
1 Linden Pl., Natchez 39120, tel. 601/445–5472 or 800/254–6336, fax 601/442–7548

Linden's ornately carved Federal-style doorway may be familiar to movie fans, because it was copied for the doorway to Scarlett O'Hara's Tara in *Gone With the Wind.* The house was built around 1800 and sold in 1818 to the first U.S. senator from Mississippi. Linden—a sprawling, two-story house with wings on each side—is known for its 98-ft front gallery and for the Federal furniture found inside. Hepplewhite, Sheraton, and Chippendale are well represented at Linden; other treasures include three original paintings by Audubon.

The guest rooms are furnished with antiques and some heirlooms, for one family's descendants have been in residence here since 1849. The east-wing bedrooms open onto a back gallery that overlooks the garden and courtyard.

The owner, Jeanette Feltus, a former teacher, conducts tours of the house and joins guests for a full plantation breakfast of hot biscuits, eggs, grits, fruit, sometimes meat and gravy, and plenty of juice and coffee. The house is listed on the National Register of Historic Places. ⌂ *7 double rooms with baths. Air-conditioning. $90–$120; full breakfast. No children under 10.*

LINDEN-ON-THE-LAKE ☜
1262 East Lake Washington Rd. (Box 117), Glen Allan 38744, tel. 601/839–2181, fax 601/839–2182

Don't look for the spit-polished preciousness of Natchez at Linden-on-the-Lake, just pure down-home Delta hospitality on a property that is a work in progress. Linden, which even has two Delta-style shotgun shanties (housing two guest accommodations) on the estate, would be a perfect spot for blues lovers during the annual Delta Blues Festival in September.

The turn-of-the-century home, which overlooks 8,900-acre Lake Washington, is said to be the third structure on that land and is built in a neo-Greek Revival style. Rooms feel lived in and, despite many antiques, are as comfortable as an old shoe. Especially charming are the original bathroom fixtures, including a remarkable-looking "umbrella" shower.

There may be a few piles of wood or concrete in the yard, and the surrounding property is hardly clutter-free, but don't go for perfection of presentation. Go for the genuine warmth of hard-working owners John and Nancy Bridges, who make a stay at Linden an authentic Delta experience. John will take you to see the operating saw mill he runs (interested guests have even been allowed to saw wood), show you a small, overgrown cemetery behind the house; or scout a place where you can catch a mess of catfish or brim as the sun sets through the moss-draped cypresses of Lake Washington. Bicycles are also available.

Nancy will go out of her way to make you comfortable. She has been known to improvise extra accommodations out of thin air for tired and desperate travelers when not a room was to be found in the Delta. ⌂ *1 double room with bath, 3 doubles share 1 bath, 2 cabins. Air-conditioning, TV in rooms. $75–$85 for doubles, $65–$80 for cabins; full breakfast. No smoking, pets by arrangement.*

MILLSAPS BUIE HOUSE ☜
628 N. State St., Jackson 39202, tel. 601/352–0221 or 800/784–0221, fax 601/352–0221

The Millsaps Buie House's location on the busiest street in Jackson, Mississippi, sets it apart from the Magnolia State's many plantation-like bed-and-breakfast inns. An elegant Victorian mansion, built in 1888 in the heart of downtown, it is grand, historic, and filled with antiques. Everything about the house says "quality," from exterior construction to interior details like the hand-molded plaster frieze work, bay windows, and other elements representative of the Queen Anne style.

Once the home of Major Reuben Webster Millsaps of the Confederate army—as well as a banker, financier, and founder in 1892 of the distinguished Millsaps College—the house has been in the same family for five generations. It has been a B&B since 1987 and is described as "a 19th-century urban retreat for the 20th-century traveler." One might add "business traveler," for although the house contains priceless heirlooms, each room has a telephone with computer data-port and a small, unobtrusive bedside radio, and TVs are concealed in old armoires. For health-conscious guests, a fitness center is nearby.

Guests are encouraged to relax in the drawing room, parlor, or library before retiring to their room for the evening. Pier mirrors in the parlor reflect the grand piano, and the house as a whole reflects the style and taste of the distinguished interior designer, Berle Smith, who also refurbished the Governor's Mansion, the New State Capitol, and Florewood Plantation in Greenwood.

Bedrooms are furnished in a pleasing mixture of period antiques and reproductions, including canopy beds, rosewood chairs, and marble-top tables. Original mantelpieces add detail, while old family portraits add authenticity. The rich, pleated draperies in one of the rooms are a soft-green fabric and match the carpet and the dominant color in the flowered wallpaper.

A hearty southern breakfast is served, with specialties such as homemade banana bread, cheese grits, bran muffins, and hot biscuits. Whether serving or giving directions to Jackson attractions, the staff members are at all times hospitable. ♠ *11 double rooms with baths. Air-conditioning, cable TV and phone with data-port in rooms. $100–$170; full breakfast. AE, D, DC, MC, V. No smoking, no children under 12.*

MISTLETOE PLANTATION ☞
176 Airport Rd., Natchez 39120, tel. 601/445–8511

Mistletoe Plantation is striking in its conservative, yet elegant adherence to the home's Federal style origins in 1807. While some Natchez mansions and B&Bs get carried away with frilly overstatement, Mistletoe has real character, and testifies to a loving restoration in the 1940s by the descendants of its original owners, the Bisland family.

Additions have been made over the years to what was originally a four-room floor plan, separated by a center hall. The surrounding 1,300 acres are what remain of a Spanish land grant to John Bisland in 1788.

The home, which is now owned by Alan and Rachelle Henseler of Fairhope, Alabama, is furnished with antiques and reproductions, and the three spacious bedrooms have antique beds. One room has a four-poster, wood paneling, floral-pattern fabrics, and a large bathroom with a whirlpool tub. A yellow room has a four-poster as well as a door that leads directly outside. The blue room upstairs has a sitting area and a modern bathroom.

The grounds are perfect for bird watching—hundreds of hummingbirds return every spring—and wild turkeys and deer roam the nature trails. A pond beckons cane-pole fishers, and a swimming pool was in the planning stages at press time. There is an enclosed courtyard with a fountain for relaxing with a book or with the complimentary wine and cheese served afternoons by on-site caretaker John Clarks. ♠ *3 double rooms with baths. Air-conditioning, phone in rooms, whirlpool bath in 2 rooms, TV in common area. $100–$170; full breakfast. MC, V. No smoking, no children under 12.*

MOLLY'S ☞
214 S. Bolivar Ave., Cleveland 38732, tel. 601/843–9913

Postmodern art and sculpture lovers will enjoy the *Pee-Wee's Playhouse* atmosphere of Molly's, which is not only a bed-and-breakfast but also a working sculpture studio and gallery.

Everywhere you turn is the playful, colorful, and surreal sensibility of nationally known artist Floyd Shaman. He and wife Molly have blended Victorian, Art Deco, and Art Nouveau furnishings with his figurative, laminated wood sculpture and other artwork, most of which is for sale, to fun and frolicky effect. Floyd, who has mounted one-man shows in New York and around the country, will take guests on a studio tour upon request.

Once a genteel boardinghouse, the house now has rooms painted with western motif murals, reflecting Floyd's Wyoming roots; a hall lined with hundreds of soda and beer bottles and cans; and a living room arranged around a giant wooden roller skate.

Molly's draws the Delta Blues Festival crowd in September, as it does those coming to Cleveland year-round to eat at renowned KC's restaurant, nearby. Breakfast, including Molly's famous muffins, is served on a porch in the shade of Chinese umbrella trees and overlooking a pleasant courtyard out back. Guests have access to a common TV and phone. **△** *3 double rooms with baths. Air-conditioning, TV in common room. $55–$65; full breakfast. MC, V. No smoking, pets boarded nearby with advance arrangements.*

MONMOUTH 🖋

36 Melrose Ave., Natchez 39120, tel. 601/442–5852 or 800/828–4531, fax 601/446–7762, www.monmouthplantation.com

The massive Monmouth (circa 1818) is not only one of Mississippi's best-known B&Bs, it's also the state's unofficial Hollywood connection. Monmouth appears to be the choice of the movie industry, according to reports from members of the Hollywood press corps who often accompany filmmakers to this most photogenic part of the sunny South. Actors and crew stayed here while in Natchez filming John Grisham's *A Time to Kill*.

Owners Ron and Lani Riches live in Los Angeles but stay at Monmouth as much as possible. The Richeses (he's a land developer) bought Monmouth about 20 years ago and have worked hard at restoring the grand old house. Monmouth's Greek Revival portico was added in 1853, at which time the original brick was covered with eggshell stucco and scored. The grounds, all 26 acres, are immaculate, and there's always something in bloom.

The interior mood is formal, with the blue-silk-covered rococo-revival furniture in the double parlor made even prettier by the glow of a Waterford crystal chandelier. The windows are done with fanciful swags, valances, fringes, and lace.

The bedrooms in the main house are a decorator's dream. The peach bedroom, a favorite, has peach walls and fabrics made into magnificent draperies on the windows and the canopy bed. Other grand accommodations include the four garden cottages, the carriage house, the former servants' quarters, and the six Plantation Suites. The suites have fireplaces, whirlpool baths, and period furnishings. The Quitman Retreat is richly decorated in blues and creams and is the most exquisite of all. There's also a conference center to accommodate up to 120 for meetings. Those suites farthest away from the main house are the most elaborate in style.

Monmouth is the only property in Mississippi that's a National Trust–designated Historic Hotels of America, and it is a National Historic Landmark.

During the cocktail hour, complimentary hors d'oeuvres are served. In the morning, the full southern breakfast takes on a special elegance: It's served on fine china in a formal setting. **△** *6 double rooms with baths and 1 suite in main* *house, 11 doubles with baths and 7 suites in outbuildings. Restaurant (dinner only, 1 seating nightly), air-conditioning, TV and phone in rooms, robes and luxury bath products in rooms; croquet course, fishing pond, walking trails. $135–$275; full breakfast, hors d'oeuvres during cocktail hour. AE, D, MC, V. No smoking, no children under 14.*

OAK SQUARE ☙

1207 Church St., Port Gibson 39150, tel. 601/437–4350 or 800/729–0240, fax 601/437–5768

Port Gibson's massive, white-frame Greek Revival–style Oak Square (circa 1850), whose white columns support a second-story porch, was built as the town home of a cotton planter who apparently wanted his family to enjoy culture as well as comfort. The house has a foyer-ballroom with a wide stairway leading to a "minstrel gallery." The gentility of the old house has been retained by the William Lum family, the owners. The Lums were formerly retail merchants in Port Gibson. Oak Square and the dependencies are filled with outstanding antiques inherited from family plantations.

Elaborate crown moldings and ornate plasterwork adorn the ceilings, and Empire and rococo-revival furniture fills all 30 rooms in the mansion. Guest rooms are in the Guest House and the French House, both adjoining the property and both comfortably furnished with a mixture of antiques and other great old pieces.

Southern breakfast of eggs, grits, breads, and meat is served in the shady, cool, glass-enclosed garden room, with unobstructed views of the courtyard, tall trees and flowers, and the architecturally superb main house. ☙ *9 double rooms with baths. Air-conditioning, TV and phone in rooms. $95–$125; full breakfast. AE, D, MC, V. No smoking, no children under 12.*

RAVENNA ☙

8 Ravenna La., Natchez 39120, tel. 601/445–8516 or 800/647–6742, fax 601/445–0052

Built in 1835 for a cotton broker who spared no expense, Ravenna has a memorable, dramatic feature: its elliptical stairway, which gracefully spirals from the first to the third floor. A magnificent hallway arch sets the stage for the stairway and the other architectural elements of the interior.

The home of Catherine Morgan, the Greek Revival building is furnished mostly with period antiques and family heirlooms and has a nice lived-in appeal. The guest rooms, with old armoires and tester beds, are gracious, and their decor matches the age and style of the house, with no unnecessary adornment. Catherine is known for her culinary talent, and each morning she serves southern delicacies with all the trimmings.

Ravenna is surrounded by 3 acres of lush informal gardens, with foliage so thick the house appears to peek from behind the leaves and Spanish moss. In springtime, azaleas and dogwoods provide a haven of color. ☙ *2 double rooms with baths, 1 cottage. Air-conditioning, TV and fireplace in cottage; pool. $95–$110; full breakfast. AE, MC, V. Restricted smoking.*

REDBUD INN ☙

121 N. Wells St., Kosciusko 39090, tel. 601/289–5086 or 800/379–5086, fax 601/289–5086, www.theredbudinn.com

The 1884 Victorian Redbud Inn is as pretty as the name sounds. Right in the heart of Kosciusko, it is a fine example of Queen Anne architecture and is listed on the National Register of Historic Places. It is within walking distance of the town square and other charming Victorian houses.

Owner Maggie Garrett, a teacher, has decorated each room with period antiques and individual colors and appointments. The Peach Room, for example, has a big Victorian bed so tall it has a set of antique steps leading up to it. Flowers and accessories complement the decor. The Dogwood Room has a balcony.

A popular restaurant on the first floor serves lunch to the public and can also prepare private candlelit dinners for B&B guests, if requested in advance. The inn also has an antiques shop, specializing in English and Victorian items; there you can pick up the delightful cookbook *A Taste of the Redbud*. ♨ *4 double rooms with baths, 1 double with ½-bath (shower downstairs). Restaurant, air-conditioning, TV, and phone in rooms. $75–$100; full breakfast. AE, D, MC, V. Restricted smoking.*

STAINED GLASS MANOR 🦜

2430 Drummond St., Vicksburg 39180, tel. 601/638–8893 or 888/842–5262, fax 601/636–3055, www.vickbnb.com

Running a bed-and-breakfast may not be rocket science, but don't tell Werner von Braun protegé and NASA veteran Bill Smollen, the colorful, talkative proprietor of Stained Glass Manor.

For fans of the *Titanic* era and vestiges of turn-of-the-century wealth, Stained Glass Manor represents a respite from the area's trademark antebellum and Victorian homes. Once lived in by Fannie Vick Willis Johnson, a philanthropist and owner of the famous Panther Burn Plantation, the B&B is believed to have been designed by George Washington Maher, one of the creators of indigenous American architectural styles.

You enter the mansion through the huge, lofty Great Oak Hall; most rooms here are oversize. One huge "family-style" guest room has four beds and can sleep as many as nine. Some rooms have antebellum heirlooms, belonging to the owner and his wife, while others have a more Victorian theme. The mix of real antiques from various periods, and reproductions, adds an extra layer of intricacy to the home's oaky, woody atmosphere, with all its nooks and crannies. Stained-glass fans will enjoy the many Louis J. Millet designs that compose "one of the most lavish residential displays of leaded and stained glass," according to the National Register of Historic Places.

NASA buffs headed for the John C. Stennis Space Center in Bay St. Louis will find owner Smollen ready with plenty of insider dope on the early days of America's space program. He also has NASA memorabilia. The full New Orleans breakfast, with chicory coffee, is distinguished by Smollen's rich, sweet wine jelly. ♨ *2 double room with baths, 1 double shares a bath, 1 suite sleeps 9, 1 suite in carriage house. Air-conditioning, TV and phone jack in rooms. $85–$185; full breakfast. AE, D, MC, V. Restricted smoking, small pets by previous arrangement.*

WENSEL HOUSE 🦜

206 Washington St., Natchez 39120, tel. 601/445–8577 or 888/775–8577, fax 601/442–2525

A pretty Victorian town house in a town dominated by pre–Civil War mansions, Wensel House has one of the best addresses in town. It is directly across from Natchez's Canal Street Depot, which houses shops, Natchez Pilgrimage Tour headquarters, and a stage where it's not uncommon to hear great jazz on a weekend. It's also one short block east of the mighty Mississippi River.

Owner-innkeepers Ron and Mimi Miller, both affiliated with the Historic Natchez Foundation, are recognized for their knowledge and expertise of historic preservation of houses, furnishings, and fabric.

Guests have full use of the circa 1888 house, which is painted in pastels and has wonderful ornamental plaster ceilings. Rooms have 12-ft ceilings and are decorated with family heirlooms. The Millers, who eschew frilliness, have created a pleasant, friendly, and old-fashioned atmosphere. Reading material includes three daily newspapers. Rooms and baths are spacious and light, either white or pastel, and sparsely furnished, except for the one—Mardi Gras room—that is more fanciful and festive. All rooms have a double and a single bed. Continental breakfast is available at your leisure, and complimentary fresh fruit and beverages are available throughout the day. ⚠ *3 double rooms with baths. Phone and TV in rooms. $75; full breakfast. No smoking, no children under 10.*

WEYMOUTH HALL ☜
1 Cemetery Rd., Natchez 39120, tel. 601/445–2304, fax 601/445–0602

For a stunning and uninterrupted view of the Mississippi River, this is the place. High on a bluff, this H-shape, cupola-topped Greek Revival mansion (circa 1855) probably would be in the river by now if former owner Gene Weber had not shored up the bluff with 500,000 yards of hauled-in dirt, terraced it, and planted it with grass to stop the erosion.

The house, which was bought in 1997 by Troyce and Linda Guice, provides solitude, for no other house is close by; the river is in front and the National Cemetery is behind. For greater peace and quiet, recessed porches beckon.

Weymouth Hall still has the look and feel of the mid-1800s. It's not as commercialized as some other historic homes, and it is furnished with period antiques. Each guest room has private entrances, and two have river views. A plantation breakfast, including homemade breads, eggs, grits, fruit, and beverage, is served in the breakfast room. The owners ask that guests arrive by 5 PM. ⚠ *5 double rooms with baths. Air-conditioning, cable TV in bedrooms. $95–$105; full breakfast. AE, MC, V. No smoking.*

MISSISSIPPI GULF COAST REGION

The Gulf Coast is perhaps the state's most dynamic region, with tourism exploding in the last decade thanks to a gaming industry that, since the first casino was constructed in 1992, increasingly defines the area. What was a quiet, family destination characterized by antebellum homes lining the waterfront, local seafood, and quaint, artsy towns has become a sort of southern Atlantic City. Yet, the region has also managed to preserve much of its sense of history and charm, as underscored by 1999's yearlong Tricentennial Celebration celebrating the French landing near Biloxi—the region's first permanent European settlement.

Today, the international influence in this seaside resort area comes from workers in the seafood business, which, along with tourism, ranks as the leading industry. A drive along scenic U.S. 90 reveals palatial beach "cottages" and a 26-mi strip of artificial beach, said to be the world's longest. Coastal towns range from antiquing meccas to artists' settlements, and whether you're in Biloxi, Gulfport, Long Beach, Pass Christian, or Bay St. Louis, a stop at any one of many restaurants will turn up the coast's specialty: fresh seafood. Daily excursions can be made to the barrier islands, where water is blue and beaches are white; there are scheduled departures on daily cruise ships, and West Ship Island can be reached by passenger ferry. Charter boats go out deep-sea fishing (more than 200 species of fish populate nearby waters), and upwards of 20 golf courses attract players year-round.

Inland from the gulf is Hattiesburg, the site of the University of Southern Mississippi, where there's a plethora of university-related diversions—theater, art galleries, and SEC sports. Hattiesburg also hosts the popular Deposit Guaranty Golf Classic, on the PGA tour, each April. Outdoor recreational areas and water parks abound along the nearby Pat Harrison Waterway. Northeast of Hattiesburg, Laurel has one of the country's best small museums, the Lauren Rogers Museum of Art. The privately endowed museum, in a neo-Georgian building, is known for the quality of its exhibits and permanent collections.

Still farther inland lies Meridian, whose Highland Park has a museum for country-music legend Jimmy Rodgers and a one-of-a-kind antique carousel. Meridian's downtown is much as it was in the 1940s and appears to be thriving.

PLACES TO GO, SIGHTS TO SEE

Beauvoir: The Jefferson Davis Home & Presidential Library (2244 Beach Blvd., Biloxi, tel. 228/388–1313). With its comprehensive library devoted to Jefferson Davis, opened amid much fanfare in 1998, this beachfront dwelling was the last home of the president of the Confederate States of America. Along with the new archives, the 1854 house-museum contains Civil War artifacts and Confederate memorabilia.

Biloxi Lighthouse (U.S. 90, tel. 228/435–6308). This 65-ft cast-iron structure, built in 1848, is the area's major landmark. The base holds a permanent exhibit of the lighthouse's history.

De Grummond Children's Literature Research Collection (University of Southern Mississippi, Hattiesburg, tel. 601/266–4345). More than 1,100 authors and illustrators are included in this extensive collection of original children's works.

Dentzel Carousel (Highland Park, Meridian, tel. 601/485–1801). Painted ponies and other hand-carved animals on this antique carousel, one of three in the United States, have thrilled children and adults since 1892.

Fort Massachusetts (West Ship Island, tel. 228/875–9057) was built in 1858, captured by Union forces, and used as a prison for Confederate soldiers and civilians. The ferry trip takes 1 hour and 15 minutes and costs $16 for adults.

Grand Opera House (2206 5th St., Meridian, tel. 601/693–5239). The state's grand lady of opera has been restored. See the stage where Lillian Gish, the Barrymores, Sarah Bernhardt, and others performed after 1890.

George E. Ohr Arts and Cultural Center (136 G. E. Ohr St., Biloxi, tel. 228/374–5547) displays 175 works by influential American potter George Ohr, known as "the mad potter of Biloxi." There are also traveling exhibitions and shows by local artists.

Gulf Islands National Seashore (3500 Park Rd., Ocean Springs, tel. 228/875–9057). The National Park Service runs this 400-acre park on the mainland (with a visitor center, campground, and nature trail). It offers fishing and, in summer, free bayou excursions and ferry trips to West Ship Island, 12 mi out in the gulf, where there are unspoiled beaches and blue water, bathhouses, umbrellas, and food stands.

Jimmy Rodgers Museum (Highland Park, Meridian, tel. 601/485–1808). Rodgers, called the "father of country music," was the first inductee into the Country Music Hall of Fame.

J. L. Scott Marine Education Center & Aquarium (115 Beach Blvd., Biloxi, tel. 228/374–5550). The 26 aquariums and other exhibits serve as an introduction to the sea life of the region.

John C. Stennis Space Center (Rte. 70, Bay St. Louis, tel. 228/688–2370 or 800/237–1821) offers a free tour, a look at space-shuttle testing, the *Apollo 13* spacecraft, and films on space.

Lauren Rogers Museum of Art (5th Ave. at 7th St., Laurel, tel. 601/649–6374) shows works by John Singer Sargent, Jean-François Millet, Winslow Homer, and Grandma Moses. It houses 19th- and 20th-century American landscapes, European salon paintings, a Georgian silver collection, and more than 600 baskets woven by Native Americans and others.

The **Lynn Meadows Discovery Center** (246 Dolan Ave., Gulfport, tel. 228/897–6039) is a children's museum with hands-on science exhibits, an art studio, a historic "attic" to explore, a tree-house village, a two-story "climbing sculpture," video equipment for budding broadcast journalists, and a market for local produce.

Magnolia Hotel/Mardi Gras Museum (119 Rue Magnolia, Biloxi, tel. 228/435–6245). Mardi Gras is a big celebration on the Gulf Coast, complete with parades and festive costumes. It warrants its own museum, which is in the only remaining pre–Civil War hotel on the gulf.

Marine Life Oceanarium (Hwy. 49 at Hwy. 90, Gulfport, tel. 228/863–0651). Sealife exhibits include bottlenose dolphins, California sea lions, and loggerhead sea turtles, sharks and stingrays, as well as tropical birds, and a touch pool.

Maritime & Seafood Industry Museum (Point Cadet Plaza, Biloxi, tel. 228/435–6320). A tribute to the industry that helps to keep the coast afloat, the museum displays tools of the trade and has an architectural exhibit called "The Houses That Seafood Built."

Old Spanish Fort & Museum (4602 Fort Dr., Pascagoula, tel. 228/769–1505). Built by the French in 1718, the oldest building in the Mississippi Valley has thick walls made of oyster shells, mud, and moss. The museum has a varied collection of 18th-century items and a children's hands-on exhibit.

Shearwater Pottery (102 Shearwater Dr., Ocean Springs, tel. 228/875–7320). See the unique works of celebrated artist Walter Anderson and his brothers. Family members have continued the brothers' traditions in pottery and prints; the showroom and sales gallery are open to the public.

Walter Anderson Museum of Art (510 Washington Ave., Ocean Springs 39564, tel. 228/872–3164). Impressive murals and rotating exhibitions of paintings, pottery, and sculpture by Mississippi's best-known artist are found here.

RESTAURANTS

For an authentic and very casual coast atmosphere and great gumbo, try **McElroy's Harbor House Seafood Restaurant** (Biloxi Small Craft Harbor, tel. 228/435–5001), overlooking the gulf. More elegant and upscale, with a cream-of-crabmeat soup that is worth the trip to Ocean Springs, **Germaine's** (1203 Bienville Blvd., Ocean Springs, tel. 228/875–4426) serves some of the best seafood on the coast. For pure coastal atmosphere and a local crowd, try the quirky **Blow Fly Inn** (1201 Washington Ave., Gulfport, tel. 228/896–9812), distinguished by its fly motif and pastoral bayou view. **Vrazel's** (3206 W. Beach Blvd., Gulfport, tel. 228/863–2229) is known all over these parts for its excellent French and Italian cuisine. For barbecue, locals flock to kitschy **An-jac's Acres** (1700 22nd St., Gulfport, tel. 228/865–9941). The famous **Mary Mahoney's Old French House** (138 Rue Magnolia, Biloxi, tel. 228/374–0163), a Mississippi tradition, is in one of the oldest houses in America, built in 1737, and has served two U.S. presidents with seafood and steaks. **Weidmann's** (210 22nd Ave., Meridian, tel. 601/693–1751) fresh vegetables and gulf seafood have delighted Mississippians since 1870.

SHOPPING

Gulfport Factory Shops (Exit 34A off I–10, 10,000 Factory Shops Blvd., tel. 228/867–6100) has more than 70 famous-brand shops offering factory-outlet prices. The shops are connected by a covered walkway. A food court, tourist information booth, and playground are also on the premises. **Hillyer House** (207

E. Scenic Dr., tel. 601/452–4810) sells jewelry, pottery, glass, and brass made by local and regional artists, plus packaged southern delicacies.

VISITOR INFORMATION

Lauderdale County Tourism Bureau (Box 5313, Meridian 39302, tel. 601/482–8001 or 888/868–7720). **Mississippi Gulf Coast Convention & Visitors Bureau** (Box 6128, Gulfport 39506, tel. 601/896–6699 or 800/237–9493).

RESERVATION SERVICE

Lincoln, Ltd. Bed & Breakfast Service (Box 3479, Meridian 39303, tel. 601/482–5483 or 800/633–6477).

BAY TOWN INN 🐚

208 N. Beach Blvd., Bay St. Louis 39520, tel. 228/466–5870 or 800/533–0407, fax 228/466–5668

The Bay Town Inn is in a prime location: one hour from New Orleans, a short drive to the coast's casinos, and practically next door to an up-and-coming Old Town arts and antiques district. If you seek solace and scenery, they are here, overlooking the pretty Bay of St. Louis. Owner Ann Tidwell, who hails from near Nashville, Tennessee, practically bought it on the spot.

Bay Town Inn is a nearly perfect Victorian house dating to 1899. It has antiques as well as many elements original to the sturdy house, including solid cypress doors, beaded board, and heart-pine flooring. The decor is Victorian but not cutesy. Ann says that some "early attic" furniture is in evidence, though each room has a few antique pieces and some old family favorites, such as her mother's pedal sewing machine. Colors in the rooms are burgundy, peach and green, or "sand and garden" colors of light golds and greens. Guests have full use of the house and property and can always find fruit and something freshly baked on the kitchen counter. Watching the sun come up over the bay from the inn's porch is a lovely way to start a day. ♣ *7 double rooms with baths. Air-conditioning. $85–$95; full breakfast. AE, D, MC, V. No smoking, no children under 14.*

FATHER RYAN HOUSE 🐚

1196 Beach Blvd., Biloxi 39530, tel. 228/435–1189 or 800/295–1189, fax 228/436–3063, www.frryan.com

Named for the poet laureate of the Confederacy, the Father (Abraham) Ryan home, built in 1841, overlooks the Gulf of Mexico and is now a National Historic Landmark. A palm tree grows tall and proud in the center of the front steps.

It has been owned and run by Rosanne McKenney and her physician husband since 1989, and they have spent years restoring it. Rosanne grew up in Naples, Italy, and she has brought Italian touches to the place, among them art and pottery from the Amalfi Coast. Furnishings include fine European antiques from the early 1800s, stained glass, and rich woods. All rooms have gulf views, with a wonderful terrace upstairs that is easily accessible from guest rooms.

The pool is in the backyard, and though big live oak trees are all around it, there are ample places to sunbathe.

The staff are fluent in Italian and Spanish. Some proceeds from the inn are earmarked for a foundation creating a charity hospital in Honduras. ♣ *13 rooms with baths, 3 suites. TV and phone with data-port in rooms, robes in rooms, whirlpool* *baths in some rooms; pool, gift shop. $77–$165; full breakfast and Continental breakfast for early-risers. AE, MC, V. No smoking.*

GREEN OAKS 🐚

580 Beach Blvd., Biloxi 39530, tel. 228/436–6257 or 888/436–6257, fax 228/436–6225, www.gcw.com/greenoaks

Perhaps nowhere on the Gulf Coast is the continuum of history more evident than at Green Oaks, a gracious antebellum mansion surrounded by 28 towering live oaks and caressed by the breezes of the Gulf of Mexico. The recorded family history of proprietor Oliver Diaz, a judge on the Mississippi Court of Appeals, dates to 1700, when his first American ancestor arrived on the Gulf Coast with the explorer d'Iberville.

Thanks to Diaz, who served in the Mississippi House of Representatives with novelist John Grisham, the atmosphere at Green Oaks exudes a genuine sense of regional and national politics (Diaz's two cats are named Bill and Hillary). In a nod to the state's rich literary tradition, the upstairs parlor has a library of first editions by Mississippi writers including Eudora Welty, William Faulkner, and Willie Morris.

Oliver's wife, Jennifer, has furnished the Greek Revival "raised cottage"—built high upon brick pillars to protect it from storm surge—with not only a rich assortment of Diaz heirlooms but also antiques from estates such as Myrtle's Plantation in St. Francisville, Louisiana. Green Oaks, with several rooms accessing a grand veranda overlooking the Gulf, is elegant but never seems fussy or stuffy.

A young, personable mother, Jennifer takes an active interest in her clientele, sometimes booking female guests on girls-only fishing trips. Green Oaks is also becoming famous for its afternoon teas, with mint juleps and traditional English fare served on the veranda with antique crystal, china, and silver. △ *5 double rooms with baths, 2 doubles and 1 suite in cottage. Air-conditioning, cable TV and phone with data-port in rooms, turndown service with chocolates. $125–$150; full breakfast. AE, D, MC, V. No smoking, 2-night minimum on holiday weekends.*

INN AT THE PASS 🐚

125 E. Scenic Dr., Pass Christian 39571, tel. 228/452–0333 or 800/217–2588, bbonline.com/ms/innatpass/

The Inn at the Pass has an enviable Pass Christian (pronounced *Christy*-Ann) address. The lovely little seacoast town is Mississippi's answer to Newport, Rhode Island, and is gaining a reputation as one of the South's best places.

The house was built in 1885 and was the home of the Emile Adam family for more than 75 years. The current proprietors, Brenda and Vernon Harrison, came to the Gulf Coast from Houston, where he practiced law and she was a psychologist. They have been instrumental in forming a Bed and Breakfast Association for Mississippi.

The Harrisons have turned the house they bought into Inn at the Pass, a pleasant, quiet B&B with Eastlake influences. The wide front porch with its wicker furniture offers a grand view of the Mississippi Sound, and inside, the furnishings complement each room's name. The Rose Room is Victorian; the Hunt Room is masculine in color and design elements, which include hunting trophies and plaid fabric. The Magnolia Room has bent-willow furniture and original art depicting beach scenes and landscapes. There is also a cottage that accommodates up to six.

A full breakfast, always delicious, is served. ♙ *4 double rooms with baths, 1 cottage. Air-conditioning, TV and phone in rooms, kitchenette in cottage. $75– $125; full breakfast. AE, D, MC, V. No smoking, kennel available for small pets.*

LINCOLN, LTD., BED & BREAKFAST
MISSISSIPPI RESERVATION SERVICE ☞
2303 23rd Ave. (Box 3479), Meridian 39303, tel. 601/482–5483 or 800/633–6477

For those who want complete privacy in a bed-and-breakfast suite with no owners around, Lincoln, Ltd., is just the place. The house—a 1905 cottage in Meridian's historic district—serves a dual purpose. The front portion is the office of Lincoln, Ltd. Bed & Breakfast Reservation Service, where B&B pro Barbara Hall and her staff work. They have all the answers to questions concerning B&Bs and inns in Mississippi (they also have a few listings in adjoining states). Their office closes at about 5 PM; from then until 9 AM or so, guests have the charming house to themselves.

The back suite has a private entrance, use of the kitchen, a carport, and other comforts of home. The suite's living room is cheerful, with pretty plaid sofas, nice woodwork and accessories, and, in the connecting bedroom, walls of a restful, light sea green with rich cream-color trim and curtains. A fireplace, a rocking chair, and flowered chintz cushions and spread enhance the antique walnut bed and chest. The adjoining bathroom has a claw-foot tub and plenty of storage space. ♙ *1 suite. Air-conditioning, TV, phone in rooms. $70; Continental breakfast. AE, MC, V. No smoking.*

SHADOWLAWN ☞
112A Shearwater Dr., Ocean Springs 39564, tel. 228/875–6945, fax 228/875–6595

A secluded retreat from the garish lights of casino row and noisy traffic along Highway 90, Shadowlawn is an idyllic escape to a time when life on the Mississippi Gulf Coast was about lazy summers spent fishing or crabbing off the pier. Built in 1907 on a hill overlooking the Mississippi Sound, Shadowlawn is a relaxing, turn-of-the-century experience that recalls the era when owner Nancy Wilson summered there with her grandparents as a child.

The home is next door to the Shearwater Pottery, which sells works by renowned Mississippi artist Walter Anderson; Nancy recalls playing with the Anderson family as a young girl. The 4½ acres of landscaped grounds, distinguished by a gnarled, sideways-growing Osage orange tree, are second to none on the coast and even have a small private beach.

Unlike the bright and airy antebellum houses that characterize most of the area's inns, Shadowlawn has a dimmer, almost northern ambience that is more Sagamore Hill than Tara. But the breezy, pine-floored, wide-screened porch that overlooks the gulf is a perfect spot to relax with a cold drink and a novel on a hot summer's day. ♙ *4 double rooms (one with twin beds). Air-conditioning, cable TV/VCR in rooms. $110–$135; full breakfast. MC, V. No smoking, no children under 14.*

TALLY HOUSE ☞
402 Rebecca Ave., Hattiesburg 39401, tel. 601/582–3467, fax 601/582–3467

The Tally House, a sprawling, all-wood 13,000-square ft Colonial revival–style house, is a showplace of South Mississippi's major product: timber. Painted bright white, the 2½-story house has dormers, identical top and bottom porches on three sides, railings, balusters, and a red roof. Surrounding the house are flower borders, a well-manicured lawn, and brick walkway.

Inside are 11 fireplaces, porcelain objects, clocks, and fine antiques collected by innkeeper-owners Sydney and C. E. Bailey. The guest rooms reflect the house's many moods. Each room is decorated in a style befitting the period for which it is named: Eastlake, French Provincial, Art Deco, and Country Victorian. The house was built in 1907 and has had as overnight guests three Mississippi governors, other national and international leaders, and just plain folk who enjoy an historic home and southern hospitality, plus a hearty breakfast with homemade jellies and jams. △ *4 double rooms with baths. Air-conditioning. $65–$75; full breakfast, welcoming beverage. MC, V. No smoking.*

WHO'S INN? ☞
623 Washington Ave., Ocean Springs 39564, tel. 228/875–3251
or after 5 PM and Sundays, 228/875–2900, fax 228/875–3251

In the heart of Ocean Springs, a quaint and artsy coastal town, Who's Inn? is for those who want cafés, boutiques, and antiques shops right outside their door. The tiny inn, run by botanical sculptor Trailer McQuilkin and his wife, Sharon, has a fairy-tale charm, as does the entire Ocean Springs historic district. The inn also serves as a gallery specializing in local and southern contemporary artists.

The two guest rooms open onto a pleasant porch with chairs and tables under ceiling fans. Each of the comfortable, modern rooms has a coffeemaker and a refrigerator stocked with sodas and bottled water, and bicycles are available for guests. One room has an ornate headboard made from an Indonesian wedding bed (which has, according to Sharon, fostered the fertility of at least one guest).

Breakfast is included, but you have to stroll across the street to a French bakery, where you are likely to meet locals eager to talk about their town and how it has maintained its character in the face of rapidly changing Gulf Coast life. On-site gallery director Bill Myers is friendly and knowledgeable about Ocean Springs and the local art scene. △ *2 double rooms with baths. Air-conditioning, cable TV, phone with data-port in rooms; bicycles. $85–$95; Continental breakfast served in French bakery across the street. AE, MC, V. No smoking.*

Louisiana

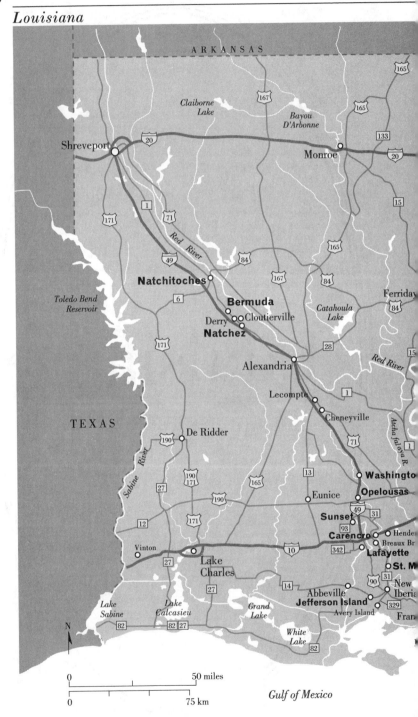

ARKANSAS

Claiborne Lake

Bayou D'Arbonne

Shreveport

Monroe

Red River

Natchitoches

Bermuda

Derry ○○ Cloutierville

Natchez

Catahoula Lake

Ferriday

Alexandria

Lecompte

Cheneyville

TEXAS

De Ridder

Toledo Bend Reservoir

Red River

Atchafalaya R.

Washington

Eunice

Opelousas

Sunset

Carencro

Hender

Breaux Br

Lafayette

St. M

Sabine River

Vinton

Lake Charles

Abbeville

Jefferson Island

Avery Island

New Iberia

Fran

Lake Sabine

Lake Calcasieu

Grand Lake

White Lake

N

0   50 miles

0   75 km

Gulf of Mexico

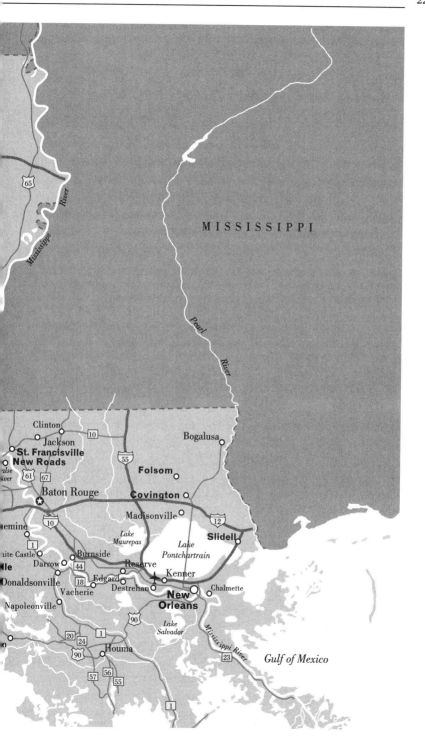

GREATER NEW ORLEANS

Internationally known for its wonderful Cajun and Creole cuisine and great jazz, New Orleans basks in the sun smack on the Mississippi River about 110 mi inland from where the river flows into the Gulf of Mexico. The city is something of a paradox: It's a major convention city and one of the world's largest ports; some 11 million visitors come to call annually; and Mardi Gras is but the best known of dozens of annual festivals (New Orleanians do love to party)—all of which means there is a great deal of activity here. And yet, this is a very laid-back, Caribbeanesque city that much prefers to operate on "island time." Not for naught is it called the Big Easy. The Crescent City (another sobriquet) is unlike any other American city; certainly it is different from other southern cities. It has been promoted as "America's European Masterpiece"—yet there is nothing quite like it in Europe, either. It is, in a word, unique.

Within the city proper, the French Quarter is the prime tourist target. Comprising about 1 square mi, the Quarter is an easily walkable, perfect grid. Its narrow streets are lined with picturesque, pastel-painted buildings garnished with fanciful ironwork or dollops of gingerbread. It is both a carefully restored living museum whose structures date from the 18th and 19th centuries and a residential district with about 3,500 somewhat smug inhabitants. Most of the famous restaurants are in the Quarter, and Bourbon Street is lined with music clubs of every description. This is a 24-hour town, which means there is no legal closing time. At almost any hour of the day or night, you can stroll down Bourbon and hear the syncopated rhythms of Cajun, rhythm and blues, gutbucket (that's low-down, mean blues), Dixieland, rinky-dink piano, ragtime, and even Irish music. The heartbeat of the Quarter is Jackson Square, a pedestrian mall where stately St. Louis Cathedral soars like a hymn over a riotous scene of Dixieland bands, red-nosed clowns, sidewalk artists, costumed kooks, tap dancers and break dancers, fire-eaters, bongo players, unicyclists, nonchalant New Orleanians, and curious tourists.

Almost as much activity, frivolous as well as serious, takes place in the Central Business District (CBD), adjacent to the Quarter. The Foot of Canal Street, as it's known to locals, boasts several splashy attractions. From the downtown area, the St. Charles Avenue streetcar, a National Historic Landmark, makes a jolly rumble upriver. It chugs through the Garden District, a residential area in which palatial mansions are surrounded by luxuriant gardens, and on past pretty Audubon Park, which has magnificent live oaks dressed in Spanish moss and a wonderful zoo. Lake Pontchartrain runs for 40 mi on the northern border of the city; the lakefront area is a favorite summertime playground for locals. There are several marinas, sailboats for rent, and a plethora of funky restaurants frequented by hard-core, no-nonsense seafood eaters. The metropolitan area extends to the piney woods on the north shore of the lake, where fishing and boating are popular and bed-and-breakfasts abound.

Six miles east of the city lies Chalmette National Historical Park, on whose rolling green fields Andy Jackson whipped the Brits in the 1815 Battle of New Orleans. And to the west of town, the Great River Road, which follows the meandering Mississippi from New Orleans to Baton Rouge, is decorated with handsome, restored antebellum plantation homes. Many are open to the public, and several companies offer tours to plantation country. If you fly into New Orleans, you'll note that dry land seems to sort of fizzle out the closer you get to the city. These flat marshlands are laced with waterways, and swamp tours, which sneak into erstwhile pirates' lairs and give you a tempting taste of Cajun country to the west, are extremely popular outings.

PLACES TO GO, SIGHTS TO SEE

Carriage Rides. Decatur Street at Jackson Square is lined with fringed carriages drawn by mules in silly hats. The lively raconteurs at the reins dispense a wealth of misinformation but give a pleasant half-hour overview of the Quarter.

Cemeteries. Reminiscent of Père Lachaise in Paris, New Orleans's aboveground cemeteries are usually high on visitors' must-see lists. The oldest, *St. Louis No. 1,* lies on the fringes of the Quarter; the largest, and most photographed, is *Metairie Cemetery.* Many of these Cities of the Dead are in high-crime areas; visitors should not venture into them alone. For a group tour, contact Save Our Cemeteries (tel. 504/525–3377) or Magic Walking Tours (tel. 504/588–9693).

City Park. Home of the *New Orleans Museum of Art* (1 Collins Diboll Circle, tel. 504/488–2631), this is one of the nation's largest city parks. Within its 1,500 acres are golf courses, tennis courts, baseball and softball diamonds, lagoons and boat rentals, botanical gardens, and, for the little ones, Storyland and an amusement park with a delightful antique carousel.

Foot of Canal Street. If you keep on going toward the river on Canal Street, you'll drive right off dry land and onto the commuter ferry (free outgoing, $1 returning) that sidles across the Mississippi to the neighborhood of Algiers on the West Bank. Smack at the river and the CBD, there are several diversions. The *Aquarium of the Americas* (Canal St. and the river, tel. 504/861–2537)—with four major exhibits, an IMAX theater, and a plethora of sea creatures—sits in the handsomely landscaped Woldenberg Riverfront Park. Riverwalk, sprawling upriver from the ferry landing, comprises Spanish Plaza—a broad, open expanse with mosaic pavement and a huge fountain—and a marketplace with some 200 specialty shops and restaurants. Several of the sightseeing boats dock at Riverwalk.

The Great Outdoors. At the 8,000-acre *Jean Lafitte National Historical Park/Barataria Unit* (Rte. 45 near Jean Lafitte, Westbank, tel. 504/589–2330) 8 mi of paved nature trails wander through wetlands where alligators and other critters slither; you can take a free park-ranger tour or stroll on your own. And at the nearby *Bayou Barn* (Rtes. 31, 34, and 45, tel. 504/689–2663 or 800/862–2968), you can rent canoes and paddle off on the bayous, with or without a guide. On the North Shore, the *Tammany Trace* (tel. 504/892–0520 or 800/634–9443) is a 31-mi hiking and biking route that follows an abandoned Illinois Central railroad bed from Slidell through Lacombe and Mandeville to Abita Springs, then to Covington. And west of Covington, the *Global Wildlife Center* (Rte. 40, 11 mi north of the town of Robert, tel. 504/624–9453) is a 900-acre preserve where endangered species roam free and humans watch them from covered wagons or horseback.

House Museums. Several restored homes (almost all in the Quarter) provide a glimpse of old New Orleans. *Pitot House* (1440 Moss St., tel. 504/482–0312) is a West Indies–style house typical of those built by early planters. *Gallier House* (1118–32 Royal St., tel. 504/523–6722) was designed and built by noted 19th-century architect James Gallier Jr. as his family home. The *Hermann-Grima House* (820 St. Louis St., tel. 504/525–5661) is an 1831 mansion in whose outbuildings Creole cooking demonstrations (and tastings) are held on Thursdays, October–May. *Beauregard-Keyes House* (1113 Chartres St., tel. 504/523–7257), a Greek Revival raised cottage, was home to Confederate general P. G. T. Beauregard and, much later, to novelist Frances Parkinson Keyes. *Longue Vue House & Gardens* (7 Bamboo Rd., tel. 504/488–5488), on 8 acres of manicured gardens in Mid-City, resembles an English country estate and is filled with priceless French, American, and Asian antiques.

Nightlife. *Tipitina's* (501 Napoleon Ave., tel. 504/895–8477; 310 Howard Ave., tel. 504/568–1702; 233 N. Peters St., tel. 504/566–7062), laid back and with a loyal following, has long been one of the city's most popular clubs for live reggae, rock, rhythm and blues, and Cajun music. Tip's was forced to air-condition the uptown location and open clubs in the Warehouse District and the French Quarter in order to compete with Dan Aykroyd's wildly popular *House of Blues* (225 Decatur St., box office tel. 504/529–2583, concert line 504/529–1421), where local and nationally known artists perform. *Michaul's* (840 St. Charles Ave., tel. 504/522–5517) offers live Cajun music, Cajun food, and free Cajun dance lessons nightly. The *Maple Leaf Bar* (8316 Oak St., tel. 504/866–9359) features live music seven nights a week. The dance floor is the proverbial postage-stamp size, and the dancing often overflows out onto the street. For great traditional jazz sans dancing (and creature comforts), *Preservation Hall* (726 St. Peter St., tel. 504/522–2238 or 504/523–8939) is the place to hear the city's jazz legends. Next door, *Pat O'Brien's* (718 St. Peter St., tel. 504/525–4823)—perhaps the world's most famous bar and birthplace of the now ubiquitous Hurricane cocktail—features a raucous sing-along piano bar that roars long after the fat lady has sung. *Pete Fountain's Club* (Hilton Hotel, 2 Poydras St., tel. 504/523–4374) is home base for the world-famous New Orleans clarinetist. Many of the city's best jazz and rhythm-and-blues musicians perform regularly at the *Palm Court Jazz Café* (1204 Decatur St., tel. 504/525–0200). The popular *Napoleon House* (500 Chartres St., tel. 504/524–9752) and *Lafitte's Blacksmith Shop* (941 Bourbon St., tel. 504/523–0066) are marvelous, musty old bars in buildings that date from the 1700s.

Riverboats. Frilly riverboats kicking up froth on the mighty Mississippi offer a variety of excursions. Among the most popular are the *Steamboat Natchez* (tel. 504/586–8777) and the *Creole Queen* (tel. 504/524–0814), both of which operate evening dinner-jazz cruises as well as daytime outings. Floating casinos have joined the parade of riverboats. The *Belle of Orleans* (1 Stars & Stripes Blvd., tel. 504/248–3200 or 800/572–2559), on Lake Pontchartrain adjacent to Lakefront Airport; the *Boomtown Belle* (4132 Peters Rd., tel. 504/366–7711 or 800/366–7711) on the Harvey Canal, Westbank; and the *Treasure Chest* (5050 Williams Blvd., Kenner, tel. 504/443–8000 or 800/298–0711), on Lake Pontchartrain, across from the Pontchartrain Center, are all aslosh with gaming tables, video poker, and one-armed bandits.

RESTAURANTS

The city's justifiably most famous old-line French Creole restaurants are **Arnaud's** (813 Bienville St., tel. 504/523–5433) and **Galatoire's** (209 Bourbon St., tel. 504/525–2021). Antoine's, the most famous of them all, has recently slipped and cannot be recommended here. **Commander's Palace** (1403 Washington Ave., tel. 504/899–8221), in a splendid Victorian mansion in the Garden District, is a great favorite for its innovative French-American menu and weekend jazz brunches. For Cajun cooking, try **K-Paul's Louisiana Kitchen** (416 Chartres St., tel. 504/942–7500), bastion of celebrity chef Paul Prudhomme. Newer award-winners are celebrity chef Emeril Lagasse's **Emeril's** (800 Tchoupitoulas St., tel. 504/523–9393) and **Nola** (534 St. Louis St., tel. 504/522–6622), both of which serve Creole and new American cuisine in contemporary settings; **Bayona** (430 Dauphine St., tel. 504/525–4455), noted for spicy New World cuisine; and the **Grill Room** (300 Gravier St., tel. 504/522–1992), the posh restaurant of the Windsor Court Hotel.

On the north shore of Lake Pontchartrain, about an hour's drive from central New Orleans, **La Provence** (25020 U.W. 190 East, Lacombe, tel. 504/626–7662) serves French provincial cuisine in an atmosphere evocative of a fine tavern in the French countryside. The **Abita Brewpub** (100 Levenson St., Abita Springs, tel. 504/892–5837), in a former microbrewery, is a casual spot for seafood and sandwiches.

SHOPPING

In New Orleans's French Quarter, both **Royal Street** and **Chartres Street** are lined with pricey antiques stores and art galleries. In the Warehouse District, **Gallery Row** (Julia St. between St. Charles Ave. and Convention Center Blvd.) is the best place for contemporary artwork. **Magazine Street** has 6 mi of antiques shops and galleries. In Slidell, the **Slidell Factory Outlet** (Exit 263 off I–10, 1000 Caruso Blvd., tel. 504/646–0756; open Mon.–Sat. 8AM–9PM, Sun. noon–6) has discount outlets for Levi's, Pottery World, Wembley, the Book Factory, and others.

VISITOR INFORMATION

The New Orleans Metropolitan Convention & Visitors Bureau (1520 Sugar Bowl Dr., New Orleans 70112, tel. 504/566–5011 or 800/672–6124, fax 504/566–

5021, www.neworleanscvb.com). On the North Shore, **St. Tammany Parish Tourist & Convention Commission** (68099 U.S. 59, Mandeville 70471, tel. 504/892–0520 or 800/634–9443, fax 504/892–1441).

RESERVATION SERVICES

Bed & Breakfast, Inc. (1021 Moss St., Box 52257, New Orleans 70152–2257, tel. 504/488–4640 or 800/749–4640). **New Orleans Bed & Breakfast** (Box 8163, New Orleans 70182, tel. 504/838–0071, fax 504/838–0140).

Note: The rates quoted below do not apply during special events. Prices skyrocket for Mardi Gras, the Sugar Bowl, Jazz Fest, and the Super Bowl; also, in addition to having three- to five-day minimums, inns sometimes request full payment in advance. Increasingly, New Orleans hotels and B&Bs are requiring minimum stays for any "special event," which includes anytime a large convention hits town. On the other hand, when summertime temperatures soar, rates can plunge much lower than those quoted, and attractive packages are often available.

B&W COURTYARDS 🐾

2425 Chartres St., New Orleans 70117, tel. 504/945–9418 or 800/585–5731,
fax 504/949–3483, www.bandwcourtyards.com

Innkeepers Rob Boyd and Kevin Wu (the "B" and "W" of the B&B) are only the third owners of their house, which was built in 1854. A permanent plaque on the front of the house proclaims it the 1997 winner of the mayor's award for architectural restoration.

In the Faubourg Marigny, four blocks from the fringe of the French Quarter, the house is a collection of three 19th-century cottages joined by two courtyards, which are sweetly scented with jasmine and honeysuckle and decorated with sculpted fountains and statuary. (Rob proudly points out his collection of orchids.) The rear courtyard also has a whirlpool, and a courtyard fridge is stocked with beer and soft drinks for guests.

Furnishings and artwork are a blend of antiques and reproductions, and terracotta tile floors and beds adorned with mosquito netting add to a Caribbeanesque ambience—the owners happily confess to a fondness for Barbados. There are also some lovely stained-glass windows in the house. Each of the rooms has its own entrance, and most open onto a courtyard. Fresh flowers are in virtually every room.

There are two ladies-in-residence at B&W: the Baroness Marna Del Mar Bismark and Bayona, who, with Bayona's baby, Boris, are miniature schnauzers, claimed by their owners to be the most spoiled dogs in the United States.

Rob trained at the Culinary Institute of America in Hyde Park, New York, and prides himself on B&W breakfasts: a luscious fruit plate, homemade granola, and a different pastry each day. The hosts sit with their guests during breakfast, getting to know them and helping them get to know New Orleans. Guests are presented with a printed four-day itinerary that includes recommendations for restaurants and shops. △ *4 rooms with baths, 1 suite. Air-conditioning, phone and cable TV in rooms. $105–$125; Continental breakfast. AE, D, MC, V. No children under 12, 3-night minimum stay on weekends Sept.–July, 5-night minimum stay for Mardi Gras and 2nd week of Jazz Fest, 4-night minimum 1st weekend of Jazz Fest.*

THE CHIMES ℘
1146 Constantinople St., New Orleans 70115, tel. 504/488–4640 or 800/729–4640,
fax 504/488–4639

If you're wondering about the name, you have but to stand for a moment on the front porch of Charles and Jill Abbyad's home and listen to the soft tinkling of the wind chimes. The house, built in 1875, is on a quiet residential street just upriver from the Garden District, three blocks from the St. Charles streetcar.

Accommodations are in cottages built around the rear courtyard; rooms and baths vary in size and decor. There is a mix of four-posters, twins, and white-iron beds. One of the largest rooms has slate floors, an overstuffed sofa, and a spiral stair that leads to a loft with a big white-iron bed. One of the baths has an old-fashioned claw-foot tub, another a shower but no tub, and a modern tile bath has a skylight. Each room has a coffeemaker, teapot, tea and coffee makings, and spring water. Just off the courtyard, tucked into a closet, is a full-size refrigerator for guests' use, as well as an ironing board and iron. The Abbyads welcome children and well-behaved pets; however, they discourage drop-in guests. ♧ *5 double rooms with baths. Air-conditioning, TV, phone, and stereo in rooms. $71– $129; full breakfast. AE, D, MC, V. No smoking.*

CLAIBORNE MANSION ℘

2111 Dauphine St., New Orleans 70116, tel. 504/949–7327 or 800/449–7327,
fax 504/949–0388

Faubourg Marigny, adjacent to the French Quarter, was one of New Orleans's first suburbs (*faubourg* is French for "suburb"). In the 1850s, the son of William C. C. Claiborne, Louisiana's first American governor, built this Greek Revival mansion for his family. Claiborne's descendants lived here until 1905; it was an apartment house when Cleo Pelleteri bought and restored it.

Cleo has created an elegant, secluded haven favored by some celebrities. In contrast to those in the area's Victorian B&Bs, the Claiborne's furnishings and objets d'art are contemporary. Crystal chandeliers hang from high ceilings, shining on polished hardwood floors and vases of fresh flowers. The sun-filled rooms and marble baths are spacious.

There are three suites and a room in the main house. Each suite has a large parlor and bedroom. One has a huge four-poster, curtained in an elegant white fabric. The room in the rear, overlooking the courtyard, has a canopy bed in delicious rose and white colors. The ground-floor room of the slave quarters, near the pool in the landscaped courtyard, has a wheelchair ramp; its bedroom–sitting room has slate floors, and twin red leather armchairs flank a fireplace. The two rooms above it, with whitewashed brick walls and white slip-covered sofas and chairs, can be combined for a suite.

For breakfast, Cleo does anything from croissants to waffles, depending on guests' individual preferences. In pleasant weather, guests like to eat beside the pool, but she says they often perch on stools in the kitchen.

A fax machine is available for guests, and there's a rack of videos in the hall. Pets are welcome with advance notice. ♧ *1 double room with bath and 3 suites in main house; 1 double with bath and 1 suite in slave quarters. Air-conditioning, phone with voice mail and cable TV/VCR in rooms, afternoon cocktails; pool, off-street parking. $150–$350; full breakfast. AE, D, MC, V. No smoking.*

DEGAS HOUSE 🐚

2306 Esplanade Ave., New Orleans 70119, tel. 504/821–5009, 800/755–6730, fax 504/821–0870, www.degashouse.com

On an 1872 visit to New Orleans, French Impressionist painter Edgar Degas stayed with relatives in this double-galleried Greek Revival house near City Park. Here, in a sun-filled studio, he produced 17 paintings. It is now operated by the Degas Foundation as an art gallery–cum–B&B.

This historic home, built in 1852, has been carefully restored, following original floor plans and original, gorgeous colors, which include pale peach, celadon, and golden mustard. Second-floor rooms are spacious and have floor-length windows with white lace curtains, antique claw-foot tubs, and chandeliers that hang from 14-ft ceilings: one room has a whirlpool bath; another, which has both a four-poster and a white-iron daybed, has exclusive use of an upper gallery, complete with rocking chairs, that stretches across the front of the house. Fresh flowers, antique hand-painted porcelain washbasins, and heavy wooden wardrobes commingle in rooms with modern-day conveniences such as TVs, clock radios, and individual temperature controls.

Third-floor garret rooms are small, have sloping ceilings and no windows, but are decorated with Degas's works and are less expensive. Parlors on the first floor have the artist's prints (more than 60 can be seen in the house) and can be visited by nonguests (call for specific dates and times). Overnighters may enjoy breakfast on a small private rear courtyard, where there is a garden with period flora. ♨ *7 rooms with baths. Air-conditioning, clock radio, phone, and cable TV in rooms. Rooms $125–$200; Continental breakfast. AE, MC, V. No smoking, 2-night minimum stay on weekends, 4-night minimum for Jazz Fest and Mardi Gras.*

DUVIGNEAUD HOUSE

2857 Grand Route St. John, New Orleans 70119, tel. 504/821–5009 or 800/755–6730, fax 504/821–0870, www.degashouse.com

Behind a white picket fence, a broad, old-brick walk leads to the double-galleried house, with French doors, shutters, and porch swing. An exterior staircase leads to an upper gallery, lined with rocking chairs. Guests in this 1834 raised cottage have maximum privacy; each suite has a separate gallery entrance.

Ideal for families with children, these suites are large; with convertible sofas in the living room, each can comfortably sleep four. Some of the furnishings are 19th-century Louisiana antiques—for example, a handsome sleigh bed—but there is not a clutter of priceless breakables. The modern kitchens are fully equipped; baths are large, with footed tubs. Foods for a self-serve breakfast are supplied daily for each suite. This house is under the same management as the nearby Degas House (*see above*). ♨ *4 suites. Air-conditioning, clock radio, phone, and cable TV in rooms. Dishwashers, washer/dryers in 3 suites. $135; Continental breakfast. AE, MC, V. No smoking, 2-night minimum stay on weekends, 4-night minimum for Jazz Fest and Mardi Gras.*

HOUSE ON BAYOU ROAD 🐚

2275 Bayou Rd., New Orleans 70119, tel. 504/945–0992 or 800/882–2968, fax 504/945–0993, www.houseonbayouroad.com

In New Orleans, near City Park, Cynthia Reeve's 1798 West Indies–style home and its cottages provide a quiet, elegant retreat. At various times, Brad Pitt, Dan Aykroyd, Alfre Woodard, and Fran Drescher have been guests.

The property sits on 2 landscaped acres; in pleasant weather, guests can enjoy the gourmet breakfast beside the pool and large hot tub, which sits in a tin-roofed gazebo.

The house and cottages are furnished with early Louisiana antiques; family heirlooms and oil portraits are displayed throughout. The house has hardwood floors, Oriental rugs, old brick fireplaces, screened porches, and large windows that afford a light, airy ambience.

Rooms and suites, each with a feather bed and a private entrance, are in the main house as well as in the cottages. The Kumquat, a large Victorian cottage to the rear, has four suites, one with a handsome antique sleigh bed, another with a big four-poster and a double whirlpool tub. A real treasure is the private Creole cottage, with a skylight over its four-poster, a wet bar, and stained-glass window in the bathroom, which has a hot tub. Both cottages have porches with rocking chairs and tinkling wind chimes. Among the main house suites, one has a fireplace, shelves filled with books, and a polo motif, reflected in framed prints.

Guests may use the fax machine; a modem is also available. A year-round cooking school is conducted here (ask about packages). Limousine service from the airport is provided at an extra charge.

A full breakfast is served every morning, but on Saturday and Sunday, Cynthia prepares a champagne mimosa breakfast that may include eggs Benedict or a soufflé Florentine. ⌂ *4 double rooms with baths in main house, 4 suites in cottage, 1 private cottage. Air-conditioning, cable TV, minibars, robes, complimentary sherry, and phones in rooms. $145–$250; full breakfast. AE, D, DC, MC, V. No smoking, 5-night minimum for Mardi Gras and Jazz Fest.*

JOSEPHINE GUEST HOUSE ☙
1450 Josephine St., New Orleans 70130, tel. 504/524–6361 or 800/779–6361, fax 504/523–6484

A block from St. Charles Avenue is the home of Jude Daniel Fuselier and his wife, Mary Ann Weilbaecher. The large Italianate mansion dates from 1870, and Mary Ann calls the furnishings "Creole baroque"; indeed, cherubs and angels decorate virtually everything. The most elaborate piece is a massive ebony bed inlaid with ivory and bone. Dutch marquetry daybeds are a focal point of the downstairs guest room. The couple's passion for collecting antiques is everywhere apparent; French Empire and English Gothic are among the periods represented. There is a Gothic refectory table in the cluttered country-style kitchen and an 18th-century mahogany banquet table in the formal dining room.

Dan and Mary Ann are eager to acquaint their guests with the "real New Orleans." Mary Ann, a former home economics teacher, makes the fresh breads that accompany morning café au lait and juice. Breakfast is served on Wedgwood china. ⌂ *6 double rooms with baths. Air-conditioning, cable TV, and phones in rooms. $95–$145; Continental breakfast. AE, D, DC, MC, V. No smoking, 4-night minimum during Sugar Bowl, 5-night minimum for Mardi Gras and Jazz Fest.*

LANAUX MANSION ☙
547 Esplanade Ave., New Orleans 70116, tel. 504/488–4640 or 800/729–4640, fax 504/488–4639

The stately Italianate Lanaux Mansion, built in 1879, stands on a quiet corner of Esplanade Avenue, between the French Quarter and Faubourg Marigny. Owner Ruth Bodenheimer, who is director of charters and incentives for the New Orleans

Steamboat Company, says she fell in love with the house when she was 17; in 1989, she became its proud owner.

The mansion boasts 14-ft ceilings both upstairs and down, as well as some of the original wallpaper, cornices, ceiling medallions, and mantels. A large oil portrait gazes over a formal parlor, with its grand piano, objets d'art, and Renaissance-revival furnishings.

There is one suite in the main house, two in a wing, and a cottage in the rear courtyard. The Lanaux Suite, upstairs in the main house, and the "Enchanted Cottage," as Ruth calls it, are awash with Victoriana, right down to displays of high-button shoes and old-fashioned clothes. The Lanaux Suite has a four-piece rosewood bedroom set made by 19th-century cabinetmaker Prudent Mallard. In the wing, the Library Suite, with its plethora of books, and the Weiland Suite, with its huge open fireplace, were the original library and kitchen, respectively.

Each of the accommodations has a kitchenette, with coffeemaker, fridge, microwave, and supplies for a do-it-yourself Continental breakfast; all have an iron, ironing board, hair dryer, TV, and phone with private answering machine. Guests have maximum privacy; those in the wing and the cottage have private entrances, while those in the mansion are given a key to the front door. ♨ *3 suites, 1 cottage. Air-conditioning, cable TV, phone with answering machine in rooms. $102–$252; Continental breakfast. AE, D, MC, V. No smoking.*

MCKENDRICK-BREAUX HOUSE ☙
1474 Magazine St., New Orleans 70130, tel. 504/586–1700 or 888/570–1700, fax 504/522–7138, mckenbro@cmq.com

Eddie Breaux's three-story Greek Revival home in New Orleans's Lower Garden District was built in 1865 for Daniel McKendrick, a Scottish immigrant. The ornate cornices and ceiling medallions in the double parlors are originals; a large brass chandelier in the front parlor shines over highly polished hardwood floors, Oriental rugs, and Victorian furnishings upholstered in velvet and brocade. The baby grand player piano was once used for practice in Radio City Music Hall.

In the rear of the house is a large kitchen-den, with an open fireplace, old-brick walls, and big windows. In the "current events room," where there are a huge stained-glass window and framed Mardi Gras mementos, area goings-on are noted on a bulletin board, and the day's high and low temperatures are posted on a gilt-framed blackboard. There is a wine basket for guests, a fridge stocked with beer and soft drinks, and a library. The fresh flowers throughout the house come from the courtyard garden.

Rooms are on the top two floors of the main house (the stairs are very steep), and in a two-story frame cottage across the courtyard. The high-ceiling rooms are large, with spacious closets, framed contemporary artwork, and custom-made fabrics. Modern baths have claw-foot tub with showers, big thirsty towels, terry robes, and Lord & Mayfair toiletries. Phones have modems; guests may borrow a VCR.

Breakfast (which includes pastries, fruit, and cereal, served in the dining room between 8 and 10), is casual; guests eat at the table, in their rooms, or on the deck overlooking the courtyard. ♨ *7 double rooms with baths. Air-conditioning, cable TV and phones with voice mail and modems in rooms. $95–$130. AE, MC, V. No smoking, 2-night minimum on weekends, 5-night minimum for Mardi Gras, 4-night minimum for Jazz Fest.*

MELROSE MANSION ☜

937 Esplanade Ave., New Orleans 70116, tel. 504/944–2255, fax 504/945–1795,
www.melrosemansion.com

This splendid Victorian Gothic on the fringe of the French Quarter was built in 1884. It has a turret, dormers, stained-glass windows, a steeply pitched roof, Corinthian columns, and a guest list that includes Lady Bird Johnson. The former first lady attended the grand opening of the bed-and-breakfast in 1990 and was the first person to sign the register.

Each of the large, high-ceiling rooms is furnished differently, but all have handsome 19th-century Louisiana antiques, including four-posters. Amenities include fresh flowers, down pillows, fine-milled soaps, monogrammed robes and towels, and small refrigerators stocked with mineral water and soft drinks. A decanter of Courvoisier is placed in each suite, where there are also wet bars and whirlpool baths.

The star is the Donecio Suite, in the turret, with its 14-ft ceiling, chandelier of brass and etched glass, and ecru and ivory lace touches. All the mansion's baths are sumptuous affairs, but in this suite the whirlpool bubbles in the turret and a huge window overlooks the French Quarter.

Melrose's owners, Melvin Jones and Sidney Torres, bought the building in 1976 from New Orleans entertainer Chris Owens. It was an apartment house then and remained so for more than 10 years. Melvin, a general contractor, spent more than two years in extensive renovations, and his wife, Rosemary, did the interior decoration.

Guests can take breakfast in their room, around the pool, or in the formal dining room. An astonishing array of hors d'oeuvres is served with afternoon cocktails. △ *4 double rooms with baths, 4 suites. Air-conditioning, library, meeting room, $225–$425; Continental breakfast, afternoon refreshments. AE, D, MC, V. 3-night minimum on weekends, varied minimum stay for special events.*

RIVERSIDE HILLS FARM ☜

96 Gardenia Dr., Covington 70433, tel. 504/892–1794, fax 504/626–5849

If you had a mind to—and a boat—you could arrive at the 14-acre Riverside Hills Farm via the Tchefuncte River, on which this farm sits, meticulously landscaped with year-round blooms. Sans boat, you approach it via a long driveway that runs between sky-high pines and lush shrubbery in the countryside near Covington.

The three-bedroom B&B cottage was once the caretaker's quarters. The pine-paneled living room has hardwood floors, furnishings redolent of the 1940s and 1950s, and displays of colorful patchwork quilts, as well as plenty of books. The large Early American kitchen comes with dishwasher, coffeemaker, full-size refrigerator, and owner Sandra Moore's collection of basketry, cookbooks, and Italian dishware. The side porch has rocking chairs, a swing, and a splendid view of the river. One of the bedrooms has twin beds, another a white-iron queen bed, and the other an interesting four-poster made of mimosa painted to look like white birch. With only a bath and a half, the cottage is let solely to people traveling together. △ *1 cottage. Air-conditioning, cable TV and phone in cottage; boat launch, fishing rods, nature trails. $95; Continental breakfast. No credit cards. No smoking.*

SALMEN-FRITCHIE HOUSE 🍍

127 Cleveland Ave., Slidell 70458, tel. 504/643–1405 or 800/235–4168,
fax 504/643–2251, www.salmenfritchiehouse.com

The little town of Slidell, on the Pearl River, about 35 minutes from downtown New Orleans, is home to one of the state's showplace B&Bs. Owners Sharon and Homer Fritchie live upstairs, and all 12 rooms on the main floor, as well as the restored carriage house, are for overnighters. The 1895 white mansion, which has a high-pitched roof, broad front porch, porte cochere, and beveled-glass door, basks on a spacious lawn. Immediately upon stepping inside the central hall, you'll notice a white Italian-marble sculpture on a table and an elaborate burgundy jardiniere, both original to the house. Nearby stands an 18th-century Chippendale long-case clock. A tour of the mansion and its priceless antiques is included.

The mansion has 12-ft ceilings, wood-burning fireplaces with ornate mantelpieces, cypress paneling, and a central hall that measures 85 ft by 25 ft. Within that ample space are a sitting area (with a TV/VCR) and a grand piano, which displays miniature family photographs. The twin Queen Anne sofas flanking the fireplace in the library came from Linden in Natchez, Mississippi; the bookcase holds contemporary novels and volumes of the *Encyclopaedia Britannica*.

Each of the guest rooms is furnished in period style. The Mallard Bedroom, for example, features the hand-carved work of Prudent Mallard, a well-known 19th-century New Orleans furniture maker. Three of the guest rooms have wood-burning fireplaces, and two can be combined to create a suite. Baths are spacious and modern. The carriage house, with contemporary furnishings, full kitchen, huge four-poster, and double whirlpool bath, has a large screened porch surrounded by greenery.

Breakfast, served at a long table in a many-windowed breakfast room, may take the form of pecan waffles, French toast stuffed with fruit, or cheese, chive, and mushroom omelets with bacon. △ *5 double rooms with baths, 1 cottage. Air-conditioning, clock radios, Corell toiletries, phones and cable TV in rooms, VCR in 1 room. $85–$150; full breakfast. AE, D, MC, V. No smoking.*

SULLY MANSION 🍍
2631 Prytania St., New Orleans 70130, tel. 504/891–0457, fax 504/899–7237

Most of the Garden District's fine mansions are private houses, but this one—a huge Queen Anne with wraparound veranda, dormers, turrets, and frilly trim—is a B&B. New Orleans architect Thomas Sully built it, and it's now Maralee Prigmore's home. In the spacious foyer, sunlight filters through original stained-glass windows and falls on a grand piano. An ornate carved staircase spirals up to the second floor. The house has 14-ft coved ceilings, 10-ft cypress doors, and heart-of-pine floors covered with Oriental rugs. Swagged, floor-length draperies hang from tall windows, and porcelain figurines are displayed on the fireplace mantels. An upstairs room has 1950s French provincial–style furnishings, while the downstairs bedroom–sitting room has a handsome four-poster, damask draperies, and upholstered sofa and chairs. There are scores of books and magazines to browse through, and a gathering room is the place to chat, watch TV, or play board games.

At 8:30 each morning, guests gather in the dining room to breakfast and chat over eggs Benedict, Spanish omelets, or quiche; the menu changes daily. △ *5 double rooms with baths. Air-conditioning, cable TV and phone in rooms. $109–$195; full breakfast. AE, D, MC, V. 5-night minimum for Jazz Fest, Mardi Gras, and special events.*

WOODS HOLE INN ☞

78253 Woods Hole La., Folsom 70437, tel. 504/796–9077,
www.quikpage.com/W/woods-hole

Seven miles from downtown Covington on the north side of Lake Pontchartrain, a long tree-shaded drive takes you to the home of Mike and Bea Connick. (He's the uncle of crooner Harry Connick Jr.) Their rustic B&B cottages and 120-year-old cabin are in a veritable forest of tall trees and greenery.

The cabin and each of the cottages are completely private, each with its own entrance. The cottages adjoin, with a connecting door that can be opened to create a two-bedroom, two-bath suite. All three accommodations have wood-burning fireplaces, cathedral ceilings with exposed wooden beams, stained-glass windows, and a blend of antique and contemporary furnishings. Windows are dressed with café curtains. One cottage has an antique white-iron bed, the other a large four-poster; the larger of the baths has a stained-glass window and a claw-foot tub, as well as a modern shower stall. Both cottages have kitchenettes, while the cabin has a full kitchen. There are plenty of books and magazines to read, lending an even more homey ambience.

Kitchens have coffeemakers, microwaves, and mini-refrigerators and are supplied daily with fresh juices and pastries for a self-serve breakfast. △ *2 cottages, 1 cabin. Air-conditioning, cable TV and phone in rooms. $95–$110; Continental breakfast. No credit cards. No smoking.*

PLANTATION COUNTRY

From north to south, the state of Louisiana is graced with fine old plantation homes, but the area officially designated Plantation Country begins with a reservoir of grand houses north of Baton Rouge and stretches all the way down the Mississippi River to New Orleans.

As the crow flies (or I–10 runs), Plantation Country is more than 100 mi long, though wherever you go you won't be far from the bright lights of a big city. As the river flows—and twists and curves—the going is much slower. The Great River Road (U.S. 61) follows its serpentine meanderings between Baton Rouge and New Orleans, but unfortunately, it is less scenic than the interstate—huge industrial and chemical plants line the road and the river. The stretch of Route 1 between Baton Rouge and Donaldsonville on the west bank is an alternative.

This is proverbial moonlight-and-magnolias country; there are more mint juleps sipped on sweeping verandas than you can shake a swizzle stick at. Homes with sky-high ceilings are filled with such 19th-century necessities as petticoat mirrors, hoopskirt chairs, courtship settees, and fire screens. The hostesses and docents tell tales of Union gunboats, Yankee soldiers, the valorous men and women of the Confederacy, and the tons of silver that were buried to keep the Bluebellies from stealing it. Ghosts are also favorite topics; it seems that almost every mansion is haunted—by a tiny child, an entire massacred family, or a wild-eyed murderer dragging around chains.

The terrain north of Baton Rouge—rolling hills, high bluffs, deep valleys, and piney woods—is much more akin to North Louisiana than to South Louisiana. So, too, is the culture: The East and West Feliciana parishes, which compose the instep of this boot-shape state, roll eastward from the Mississippi (the river) to Mississippi (the state). The Felicianas were settled by the English, many of whom came from Virginia, and the people of this area, which includes the towns of St. Francisville, Jackson, and Clinton, proudly cling to their English heritage.

St. Francisville, less than a half hour north of Baton Rouge, has been described as "2 miles long and 2 yards wide." Much of the long, skinny little city is listed on the National Register of Historic Places. In the early 19th century, West Feliciana Parish, in which it lies, was the seat of government for the short-lived Republic of West Florida. Antiques-seeking is popular here; the Feliciana towns are loaded with wonderful old poke-around places.

But a ferry ride across the Mississippi puts you in a pocket of South Louisiana that has a definite Gallic flair. Not yet Cajun Country, which is farther west, this area was settled by French Creoles. Though it is cloaked in a southern disguise of white columns and Spanish moss, Pointe Coupee Parish preserves the culture of the Creoles who settled here in the 18th century. The parish "capital" is the tiny town of New Roads, which snoozes on the banks of False River—an oxbow lake left behind long ago when the Mississippi changed its course. The large number of fishing cabins attests to the quality of False River's fishing and boating.

As the Mississippi nears New Orleans, the land flattens out and becomes marshy. Stark cypress trees poke up through the swamplands, and pirogues bob lazily on sluggish bayous. You can almost hear Cajun fiddles tuning up to the west and Dixieland bands stomping off to the east, but much of the charm of Plantation Country is in, well, sipping mint juleps on the veranda and listening to tales of carpetbaggers, scalawags, and Yankees.

PLACES TO GO, SIGHTS TO SEE

Audubon State Commemorative Area (Rte. 956 near St. Francisville, tel. 504/635–3739). In 100 wooded acres, you can tour Oakley Plantation, where John James Audubon created many of the paintings for his Birds of America series.

Catalpa Plantation (3½ mi north of St. Francisville, tel. 504/635–3372), reached by an elliptical oak alley, has been in the same family since the 18th century and contains fine antiques, silver, and family heirlooms.

Houmas House (40136 Rte. 942, Darrow, tel. 504/473–7841), a large white Greek Revival house, was the setting for the Gothic thriller *Hush . . . Hush, Sweet Charlotte,* starring Bette Davis and Olivia de Havilland.

Oak Alley Plantation (3645 Rte. 18, near Vacherie, tel. 504/265–2151) is a Greek Revival mansion on whose splendid grounds scenes from the Tom Cruise film *Interview with the Vampire* were shot.

Laura Plantation (2247 Rte 18, Vacherie, tel. 504/265–7690), unlike the white mansions built by Americans, is a Creole plantation home painted in vibrant colors; the 1805 house, with its 12 outbuildings, is a restoration-in-progress.

Parlange Plantation (8211 False River Rd., just north of Rte. 78, New Roads, tel. 504/638–8410) is a working plantation built in 1750 and operated by the eighth generation of the founding family. It's open by appointment only.

Plaquemine Lock (downtown at the Mississippi River, tel. 504/687–0641), built in 1909 and no longer in use, has the original lock house and an interpretive center with displays and exhibits that examine the history of the river and its boat traffic.

The Port Hudson State Commemorative Area (756 W. Plains–Port Hudson Rd., south of St. Francisville, tel. 504/654–3775) encompasses part of the Port Hudson battlefield, a Civil War site that saw the longest siege in American military history. There is an interpretive center and a picnic area, as well as 6 mi of hiking trails on the 650 acres.

Republic of West Florida Historical Museum (E. College St., Jackson, tel. 504/634–7155) is a sprawling indoor-outdoor facility whose displays include an antique, computerized Wurlitzer organ; antique cars, including a replica of Henry Ford's first auto, built in 1896; a working cotton gin; a general store; a blacksmith's forge; a Civil War room; and a diorama of the Port Hudson battlefield.

Rosedown Plantation House and Gardens (12501 U.S. 61 at Rte. 10, St. Francisville, tel. 504/635–3332), a restored 1835 mansion with original furnishings on 28 acres of landscaped gardens, is one of the state's most impressive houses.

RESTAURANTS

Lafitte's Landing (10275 Sunshine Bridge Access Rd., Donaldsonville, tel. 504/473–1232) serves south Louisiana specialties in a quaint raised Acadian plantation house. **Joe's "Dreyfus Store"** (2731 Maringouin Rd. W, Rte. 77, Livonia, tel. 504/637–2625) is a rustic old-time general store transformed into one of the state's best restaurants, serving creative seafood concoctions, steaks, charbroiled pork tenderloin, stuffed quail in port wine sauce, plus burgers, soups, and sandwiches. For hungry boaters, there is a marina smack on False River at **Satterfield's** (108 E. Main St., New Roads, tel. 504/638–5027), as well as seafood, steaks, and raft tours by reservation. Boaters also often dock at **Morel's on the River** (210 Morrison Pkwy., New Roads, tel. 504/638–4057), a casual eatery on False River, to partake of the fried catfish, sandwiches, and such.

SHOPPING

About 25 minutes east of Baton Rouge on I–10, the **Tanger Factory Outlet** (exit 177, 2200 Tanger Blvd., Gonzales, tel. 504/647–0521 or 800/482–6437) has 56 brand-name stores, including Levi's, Liz Claiborne, Fieldcrest, Jantzen, and Nine West, at savings of 40% to 65%.

VISITOR INFORMATION

Baton Rouge Area Convention & Visitors Bureau (Drawer 4149, Baton Rouge 70821, tel. 504/383–1825 or 800/527–6843, fax 504/346–1253, www.bracvb.com). **New Orleans Metropolitan Convention & Visitors Bureau** (1520 Sugar Bowl Dr., New Orleans 70112, tel. 504/566–5011 or 800/672–6124, fax 504/566–5021, www.neworleanscvb.com). **Pointe Coupee Parish Tourist Commission** (Box 733, New Roads 70760, tel. 504/638–9858). **West Feliciana Tourist Commission** (Box 1548, St. Francisville 70775, tel. 504/635–6330).

RESERVATION SERVICE

Bed & Breakfast Travel (8211 Goodwood Blvd., Suite F, Baton Rouge 70806, tel. 504/923–2337 or 800/926–4320, fax 504/923–2374, www.bnbtravel.com) has B&B listings for Louisiana and other Southern states.

BUTLER GREENWOOD 🕊

8345 U.S. 61, St. Francisville 70775, tel. 504/635–6312, fax 504/635–6370,
www.butlergreenwood.com

Shaded by huge live oaks dripping tangled tendrils of Spanish moss, Anne Butler's home—a two-story frame house with a wraparound veranda, dormers, and gables—was built in the early 1800s. The 12-piece set of rosewood Victorian furniture in the parlor is original to the house. Still a working plantation, the property, about 2 mi north of St. Francisville, has been in her family since 1796. A tour of the house is included with an overnight stay.

The bed-and-breakfast accommodations are in six cottages sprinkled around the grounds. Each cottage has either a full kitchen or kitchenette—stocked with a coffeemaker, toaster oven, fresh juice and croissants in the refrigerator, cereal, and fruit—so you can prepare breakfast at your leisure, as well as remote-control cable TV, plenty of books and magazines, and good lamps for reading.

Anne found three 9-ft stained-glass church windows in an antiques shop and designed the Gazebo cottage around them. It has a king-size metal four-poster, wicker furnishings, and a kitchenette. The Cook's Cottage, which dates from the 1800s, has a working fireplace, brick walls, a porch with rocking chairs, and an old-fashioned bath with claw-foot tub. It's a small shoe box with a high-pitched roof and a front porch with round, white columns. Another charmer is the Old Kitchen, built in 1796, which has exposed beams, old brick walls, skylights, and a bath with a 115-ft floodlit well covered with heavy glass. The three-level windmill-shape Dovecote has bedrooms on the first and third levels, with a parlor and full kitchen in between. Sunny and airy Treehouse has a wood-burning fireplace and a three-level rear deck overlooking lush bluffs. In each cottage is a copy of Anne's *Tourist Guide to West Feliciana Parish*. A writer and journalist for more than 25 years, Anne has written children's books, books on the criminal justice system, and a cookbook that includes vintage Feliciana photographs and anecdotes. ▲ *6 cottages. Air-conditioning, cable TV and clock radio in cottages; pool, guided nature/bird-watching walks. $100–$110; Continental breakfast. AE, MC, V. No smoking.*

COTTAGE PLANTATION 🕊

10528 Cottage La., St. Francisville 70775, tel. 504/635–3674, www.virtualcities.com

The country road to Cottage Plantation ambles across a wooden bridge and through a splendid wooded area thick with moss-covered live oaks, as well as dogwood, mimosa, and crepe myrtle trees. The plantation nestles in 400 such idyllic acres, far from traffic noises and other 20th-century distractions.

Built between 1795 and 1850, Cottage is one of only a handful of antebellum plantations that still have their original outbuildings. The office and one-room schoolhouse, kitchen, tiny milk house, barns, slave quarters, and other dependencies that made up the working plantation are intact, though weathered. One outbuilding is now a rustic restaurant called Mattie's House (open for dinner only); another is an antiques shop.

The well-maintained main building is a long, low yellow-frame structure; green shutters outline the gallery and dormer windows. The sloping roof is punctuated with chimneys and dormers from which window air-conditioning units jut anachronistically. A variety of dogs and cats nap or amble around the grounds.

Angling off from the main house is a similar structure—also original to the plantation—which houses the guest rooms. Downstairs rooms open onto the porch and get more light than those upstairs. All have four-posters and baths with modern plumbing and fixtures.

A tap on the door in the morning signals the arrival of a demitasse of coffee, accompanied by a flower. A serious breakfast is later served in the formal dining room, which, like the rest of the house (including guest rooms), is furnished with antebellum Louisiana pieces that might have been in the house when General Andrew Jackson called on the original owners after the 1815 Battle of New Orleans.

The plantation has been in the Brown family since 1951; Harvey and Mary Brown, the present owners, moved to St. Francisville from Miami to take charge in 1984. One of Mary's hobbies is apparent when you see the flower gardens that decorate the grounds near the main building. ♙ *5 double rooms with baths. Restaurant, air-conditioning, TV in rooms; pool. $95; full breakfast. MC, V. No smoking, closed Dec. 24–25.*

GARDEN GATE MANOR ☙
204 Poydras St., New Roads 70760, tel./fax 504/638–3890 or 800/487–3890

Feather beds and bubble baths are among the luxe touches in Ivonne Cuendet's romantic hideaway. A veteran of B&Bs in Oregon and Minnesota, the Natchez native lives now in a 1903 gingerbread-trimmed Creole cottage on a quiet street.

It has a porch with wicker rockers, an etched-glass door, lace curtains, and a lovely rear garden (with, of course, a gate); a floral motif is carried out with wreaths of dried flowers. Guests gather in the antiques-filled formal parlor, with its baby grand, vintage books, and wet bar. Guest rooms vary in size; Dogwood, which has a skylight in the bath, was the house's original formal dining room, and Camellia, with a queen and white-iron daybed, sleeps three. The upstairs suite has an antique bed and two baths, one with shower and the other an oversize tub.

During afternoon tea, Ivonne gives her guests pointers about the area; by prior arrangement, she will prepare a private candlelit supper. Breakfasts are recipes from vintage cookbooks, such as apple pancakes with homemade applesauce found in a 1910 Union Pacific Railroad cookbook. ♙ *4 double rooms with baths, 1 suite. Air-conditioning, cable TV in parlor, cable TV/VCR in suite; off-street parking. $90–$140; full breakfast, afternoon tea. AE, MC, V. No smoking indoors.*

GREEN SPRINGS PLANTATION ☙
7463 Tunica Trace, St. Francisville 70775, tel. 504/635–4232 or 800/457–4978, fax 504/635–3355, www.virtualcities.com

When Madeline Nevill and her late husband, Ivan, opened their bed-and-breakfast in 1991, they had three average-size guest rooms in the new home they had modeled after an 1800s cottage. Those rooms are still in use, but Madeline has expanded her facility and now has six freestanding cottages for overnighters.

Moved from other locations to her property, the frame cottages are painted in ice-cream colors and sit beneath shade trees. The decor differs from cottage to cottage. Rustic Woodrose, done in safari style, has a huge iron four-poster with leopard-print comforter, cypress armoire, and CD player; Marigold is redolent of the 1950s, with blond furniture and framed abstract paintings. In another there is a white iron bed, walnut armoire, and upholstered wicker furnishings.

In each, a fine eye was given to detail, as with fabrics picking up colors in the wallpaper. Some cottages have open fireplaces; most have hot tubs as well as showers, and all have kitchenettes with microwave, toaster, and coffeemaker. There are even umbrellas in a stand by each front door. Cable TVs are available on request.

The guest rooms in the main house are decorated with a mix of contemporary and antique furnishings. One has a queen bed tucked under a sloping ceiling; the Iris room, with its big four-poster, and an adjacent "lagniappe room," as Madeline calls it, can be rented as a suite. The modern tile baths are large.

You can be assured of a superb breakfast. A fine cook, Madeline is well known for her Spinach Madeleine, which appears in *River Road Recipes*, a cookbook of the Baton Rouge Junior League, as well as many other regional cookbooks.

From the back gallery there is a splendid view of rolling hills, trees, and the natural spring for which the house is named. ♨ *3 double rooms with baths, 6 cottages. Air-conditioning, clock radios; kitchenettes, microwaves, refrigerators, toasters in cottages. $95–$150; full breakfast. MC, V. No smoking.*

MADEWOOD PLANTATION ☙
4250 Rte. 308, Napoleonville 70390, tel. 504/369–7151 or 800/375–7151, fax 504/369–9848

In a lush country setting about equidistant from New Orleans and Baton Rouge, this handsome 21-room Greek Revival mansion offers a nostalgic glimpse of 19th-century life. Built in 1846 for Colonel Thomas Pugh, the house was bought and restored in 1964 by the Harold K. Marshall family of New Orleans. It is now owned by the Marshalls' son Keith and his wife, Millie. The Marshalls sometimes spend weekends at Madewood, but the resident managers are Janet Ledet and Michael Hawkins, who preside at the informal wine-and-cheese gatherings and candlelit southern dinners served to guests in the main mansion. Thelma Parker, the cook and housekeeper, who's been at Madewood for more than 25 years, makes a mean pumpkin casserole.

Madewood has spacious rooms with high ceilings, hardwood floors, handsome carved moldings, Oriental rugs, and sparkling crystal chandeliers. In addition to 18th- and 19th-century Louisiana antiques in the mansion and in Charlet House, there are English antiques collected by Keith when he was a Rhodes scholar.

There are four bedrooms upstairs and one downstairs; the latter has a handsome half-tester bed. Though all baths are private, those for the two back bedrooms upstairs can only be reached through the hall. Originally dressing rooms, these baths are much more spacious than those that were squeezed in when indoor plumbing became all the rage. The master bedroom, upstairs, has a large canopied four-poster; across the hall is a guest room decorated with antique children's toys. In addition, there are three suites in Charlet House, an outbuilding on the property. Its Honeymoon Suite has a working fireplace and a large screened porch. The house has served as a set for films, among them *A Woman Called Moses*, starring Cicely Tyson. ♨ *5 double rooms with baths, 3 suites. Air-conditioning, turndown service, free tour of house and grounds. $215; MAP. AE, D, MC, V. No smoking, closed Thanksgiving Eve and Day, Dec. 24–25, Dec. 31–Jan. 1; rooms must be vacated for tours 10 AM–5 PM in the main mansion and noon–3 PM in Charlet House.*

NOTTOWAY 🐚

*Rte. 1 (Box 160), White Castle 70788, tel. 504/545–2730 or 504/346–8263
in Baton Rouge, fax 504/545–8632*

This three-story Greek Revival/Italianate mansion built in 1859 is a knockout. In a lush country setting, across a quiet road from the Mississippi River levee, it has 22 white columns, 200 windows, and 53,000 square ft of living space.

Guest rooms are in the main mansion (the best are those facing the river) and the overseer's cottage, which overlooks sculpted gardens and a duck pond. Four-posters, testers, brass beds, and armoires are among the 19th-century furnishings; the master bedroom's Rococo-revival furniture, made in New Orleans by Mc-Crackin, is original to the house. ♿ *10 double rooms with baths, 3 suites. Restaurant, air-conditioning, phones in rooms, free home tour; pool. $125–$250; Continental breakfast in rooms and full breakfast, sherry at check-in. AE, D, MC, V. No smoking, closed Christmas Day, Randolph Suite and Master Bedroom must be vacated for tours 9–5.*

TEZCUCO PLANTATION 🐚

3138 Rte. 44, Darrow 70725, tel. 504/562–3929, fax 504/562–3923

While vacationing in Louisiana, Annette Harland fell in love with the area—and with this historic 1855 plantation. (Tezcuco is an Aztec word meaning "place of rest.") She eventually purchased it and made it her home. On the River Road between New Orleans and Baton Rouge, it's an ideal base for sightseeing in this section of Plantation Country.

The extensive grounds are decorated with gazebos, flowering plants, a honey-suckle-covered wishing well, and a tiered cast-iron fountain, all shaded by moss-draped oaks. One of the outbuildings houses the African-American Museum, which traces the history of blacks on the River Road.

There are three rooms for overnighters in the main mansion; all other guest rooms are in 19th-century cottages. Of brick-between-post construction, with exposed beams and hardwood floor, each cottage has a kitchen; all but two have wood-burning fireplaces. Most have front porches with rocking chairs. Rooms are furnished in period antiques: brass or white-iron beds, four-posters, or sunburst testers. Shelves are filled with books, and there are plenty of magazines to read.

Breakfast—sausage, scrambled eggs, biscuits, and grits—is brought to each cottage on a silver tray. Guests who stay in the main mansion have breakfast in the full-service restaurant on the property. ♿ *3 rooms in mansion, 17 cottages. Restaurant, air-conditioning, TV, clock radio, kitchen, tea- and coffeemakers in cottages, free home tour; free parking, antiques-gift shop, Civil War museum. $65–$165; full breakfast, welcome glass of wine. AE, D, MC, V. No smoking in main mansion, closed Thanksgiving Day, Dec. 25, and Jan. 1.*

CAJUN COUNTRY

The Cajun craze of recent years has had the whole world two-stepping and tasting such hot-peppery dishes as Cajun chef Paul Prudhomme's blackened redfish. For the residents of South Louisiana, "Cajun" denotes not a passing fad but a way of life that spans almost 400 years. This way of life involves hard work, a strong Catholic faith, devotion to family and friends, plenty of good food, and an exuberant joie de vivre. In these parts, the Cajun motto is Laissez les bons temps rouler (Let the good times roll). And roll they do; though for the rest of the world fads may come and go, there is still plenty of big fun down on the bayous.

The Cajuns are descendants of the French who settled in what is now Nova Scotia and New Brunswick, Canada; they called their colony l'Acadie. The Acadians ("Cajun" is a corruption of the word) were expelled by the British in the mid-18th century, and a few thousand of them came to South Louisiana. Henry Wadsworth Longfellow's epic poem "Evangeline" is based on the true story of Emmeline Labiche and Louis Arceneaux (Evangeline and Gabriel in the poem), the real-life lovers who were separated during the arduous exile—called by the Cajuns Le Grand Dérangement.

Cajuns speak an antique 17th-century form of French, though they can understand and speak standard French (as well as English). Radio stations sometimes broadcast in French, and French-speaking disc jockeys spin Cajun music. Billboards touting a local fried-chicken chain proclaim, "J'aime cette poule!" (Love that chicken!), and at Evangeline Downs, races begin, "Ils sont partis!" (They're off!). Most shops have a sign in their window announcing, "Ici on parle français." Needless to say, this is a great place to brush up on your French.

Not surprisingly, given the Cajun exuberance, festivals pop up almost every 10 minutes in this neck of the bois. Events celebrate alligators, crawfish, strawberries, cotton, shrimp, tomatoes, and potatoes—and in between festivals, the Cajuns simply celebrate themselves.

The interstates that race through the region are the quickest routes from there to there, but the best way to savor the scenery is by taking the state and parish roads that follow twisting bottle-green bayous or amble by cane-brakes, rice paddies, exotic old plantations, and immense live oak trees whose gnarled boughs are draped with gray shawls of Spanish moss. South Louisiana is sprinkled with salt domes, called "islands," which have nudged up from under the flatlands over a few thousand millennia and look a bit like dry-land islands. There are several picturesque state parks that are ideal for hiking, picnicking, boating, or building castles in the air.

PLACES TO GO, SIGHTS TO SEE

Atchafalaya Basin, east of Breaux Bridge, is 800,000 watery acres, an eerily beautiful place where stark cypress trees dripping with Spanish moss rise from the murky waters. At *Henderson,* where the levee is lined with tour and fishing boats, a host of operators will take you gliding out beneath canopies of trees to find alligators, herons, egrets, beavers, and all other manner of critters. Try *McGee's Landing* (tel. 318/228–2384) for pontoon-boat tours or the *Atchafalaya Experience* (tel. 318/233–7816) for guided tours with a knowledgeable geologist.

Avery Island (on Rte. 329 south of New Iberia, tel. 318/369–6243) boasts both a 300-acre *Jungle Garden* (tel. 318/369–6243), thick with subtropical trees, plants, and flowers, and an aviary fluttering with egrets. Here you can also tour the *Tabasco Sauce factory* (tel. 318/365–8173 or 800/634–9599), where the McIlhenny family still makes the red-hot condiment created by Edmund McIlhenny in the 1800s.

Breaux Bridge, home of Mulate's (*see* Restaurants, *below*), draws some 100,000 visitors at its *Crawfish Festival,* held every year.

Chitimacha Indian Reservation (Rte. 326, Charenton, tel. 318/923–4830). Some 300 Chitimacha Indians live on a 280-acre reservation under the auspices of the Jean Lafitte National Historical Park. The Chitimacha are known for basket weaving, and their colorful crafts can be purchased on the reservation. The reservation has a museum and crafts shop, but far and away the biggest draw is the Cypress Bayou Casino (tel. 800/284–4386), with its plethora of gaming tables, slots, and restaurants.

Franklin, sitting smugly on Bayou Teche to the south, is unusual in that it was founded by English, not French, settlers. The lush little Main Street USA town has a half-dozen antebellum mansions open for tours, among them Oaklawn Manor (3296 E. Oaklawn Dr., tel. 318/282–0434), the estate of Louisiana governor Mike Foster.

Lafayette, a city of some 150,000 that proudly calls itself the capital of French Louisiana, lies less than two hours west of New Orleans. Lafayette's museums and music halls are good places in which to get acquainted with Acadian lore and life. The city is also a hub for exploring the smaller towns and villages in the area. *Cajun Mardi Gras* in Lafayette and environs is second only to its sister celebration in New Orleans. Picture a few hundred masked and costumed horsemen thundering around the countryside during the annual *Courir de Mardi Gras* (Mardi Gras Run). Lafayette is also home to the *Festival International de Louisiane,* which brings musicians, actors, dancers, jugglers, and all sorts of other performers and aficionados from all over the world. The *Lafayette Natural History Museum and Planetarium* (637 Girard Park Dr., tel. 318/268–5544) has an adjunct *Acadiana Park Nature Trail and Station* (E. Alexander St., tel. 318/235–6181), with an interpretive center. It organizes bird-watching walks, hikes, and other field trips. The *Jean Lafitte Acadian Cultural Center* (501 Fisher Rd., tel. 318/232–0789) is a large, modern facility with audiovisual exhibits that trace the Acadian heritage. *Acadian Village* (Greenleaf Rd., south of Lafayette, tel. 318/981–2364), a rural folk-life museum, re-creates a bayou village, with a cluster of authentic 19th-century houses, a church, a blacksmith shop, and a general store. *Vermilionville* (1600 Surrey St., tel. 318/233–4077 or 800/992–2968), a living-history museum of the Acadian culture, has a Cajun restaurant and performances of Cajun music.

New Iberia, proclaiming itself the Queen City of the Teche, is a picturesque town that was settled by Spaniards from the Iberian coast. One of the South's best-known antebellum homes—*Shadows on the Teche* (317 E. Main St., tel. 318/369–6446)—is a perfect example of what went with the wind. The *Conrad Rice Mill and Konriko Company Store* (307 Ann St., tel. 800/551–3245) is the country's oldest rice mill, and *Trappey's* (900 E. Main St., tel. 318/365–8281 or 800/365–8727) turns out red-hot spices. Both are open for tours.

St. Martinville was a major debarkation point for the Acadians. Here, on the banks of Bayou Teche, stands the *Evangeline Oak,* a giant tree that was the legendary last meeting place of the two lovers. It is one of the region's most photographed sights. In the late 18th century, St. Martinville was a haven for French aristocrats who fled from France during the revolution. The town was known then as Petit Paris because of the elaborate balls and operas staged there. St. Martinville is also home to *St. Martin de Tours,* the mother church of the Acadians. In the church square, the *Petit Paris Museum* (103 S. Main St., tel. 318/394–7334) has carnival costumes and historical displays pertaining to Cajun country. And behind the church, where Emmeline Labiche is buried, there is a statue of Evangeline. In 1929, *The Romance of Evangeline*, starring Delores del Rio, was filmed in the town; Ms. del Rio posed for the statue, and it was given to St. Martinville. The *Acadian Memorial* (120 N. Market St., tel. 318/394–2233) houses exhibits, including a 30-ft mural painted by Robert Dafford that depicts the arrival of the Acadians in Louisiana. Just north of town is the *Longfellow-Evangeline State Commemorative Area* (1200 N. Main St., tel. 318/394–3754), a 157-acre park with an interpretive center, an early 19th-century Creole home, an Acadian crafts shop housed in a Cajun cottage, picnic grounds, and a boat launch.

Washington, north of Lafayette, is a historic little town that flourished during the steamboating era. It's home to *Magnolia Ridge* (Prescott St., tel. 318/826–3027), one of the state's grand antebellum mansions; *Hinckley House* (405 E. DeJean St., tel. 318/826–3906), which is awash with steamboat memorabilia; and the *Nicholson House of History* (303 S. Main St., tel. 318/826–3670), built in the early 1800s and used as a Confederate hospital during the war.

RESTAURANTS

Standout Cajun restaurants include **Enola Prudhomme's Cajun Café** (4676 N.E. Evangeline Thruway, Carencro, tel. 318/896–7964) and **Prejean's** (3480 I–49 North, Lafayette, tel. 318/896–3247), both housed in cypress Cajun cottages; **Mulate's** (325 Mills Ave., Breaux Bridge, tel. 800/422–2586 or 800/634–9880 in LA), a wildly popular dance hall–cum–café with live Cajun music; and **Café Vermilionville** (1304 Pinhook Rd., Lafayette, tel. 318/237–0100), which serves Creole cuisine in a lovely restored 1799 inn. **Lagniappe Too** (204 E. Main St., New Iberia, tel. 318/365–9419) is a good lunch spot for salads, quiches, and sandwiches; the menu goes haute for dinner Friday and Saturday. The **Steamboat Warehouse Restaurant** (Main St., Washington, tel. 318/826–7227), a rustic, restored 19th-century structure, serves great seafood and steaks and has steamboat memorabilia and a dock overlooking Bayou Courtableau.

SHOPPING

Antiques-seeking is a favorite pastime in this part of the country. **Ruins & Relics** (900 Evangeline Dr., Lafayette, tel. 318/233–9163) is a freestanding, 7,000-square ft showroom filled with Victorian and Acadian furnishings, glassware, china, crystal, and stained glass. In **La Promenade Mall** (3601 Johnston St., Lafayette, tel. 318/981–9847) is a small antiques shop called Julia Martha, which carries French and American furnishings, art, and decorative pieces. **Cajun Flea Market and Auction** (1051 W. Laurel Ave., Eunice, tel. 318/457–7274) is a storefront operation that holds an auction every Saturday night. The **Opelousas Mall** (353 E. Landry St., Opelousas, tel. 318/942–5620) is a big, two-story, Acadian house that sells items including china, crystal, rugs, and paintings; it's closed Sunday and Monday. Dozens of vendors peddle their wares at **O'Conner's Antique School Mall & Ole School Café** (210 Church St., Washington, tel. 318/826–3580), in a 1940s schoolhouse.

VISITOR INFORMATION

Atchafalaya Delta Tourist Commission (Box 2332, Morgan City 70381, tel. 504/395–4905 or 800/256–2931). **Iberia Parish Tourist Commission** (2804 Rte 14 St., New Iberia 70560, tel. 318/365–1540 or 888/942–3742). **Lafayette Convention & Visitors Commission** (Evangeline Thruway and Willow St., Box 52006, Lafayette 70505, tel. 318/232–3808, 800/346–1958 in the U.S., or 800/543–5340 in Canada, www.lafayettetravel.com).

Throughout 1999 Louisiana will be highlighting its French influences in commemoration of the 300-year anniversary of the le Moyne brothers' landing at the mouth of the Mississippi River. For information about the more than 500 associated exhibits and events connected with **FrancoFête '99,** contact the **Louisiana Office of Tourism** (Box 94291, Baton Rouge 70804, tel. 800/934–3987).

RESERVATION SERVICE

Bed & Breakfast Travel (8211 Goodwood Blvd., Suite F, Baton Rouge 70806, tel. 504/923–2337 or (outside Louisiana) 800/926–4320, fax 504/923–2374, www.bnbtravel.com) has B&B listings for Louisiana and parts of East Texas, Mississippi, Alabama, and the Gulf Coast.

BOIS DES CHÊNES ❦

338 N. Sterling St., Lafayette 70501, tel./fax 318/233–7816

Beneath the branches of huge live oaks, Burmese jungle fowl preen in a thatched-roof aviary, while a Labrador and a miniature poodle greet visitors. The setting is so serenely bucolic that it seems to be deep in the woods rather than just off a busy thoroughfare.

This historic plantation is home to Marjorie and Coerte Voorhies, who have restored the mansion and carriage house. Marjorie is a former antiques dealer, and Coerte conducts guided tours of the Atchafalaya Basin. Three suites, each with private entrance, are in the carriage house; two are in the plantation home. Marjorie furnished them with 18th- and 19th-century American and Louisiana French pieces. Spacious, airy rooms have hardwood floors and Oriental rugs; the two-bedroom suite in the main house has four-posters, a sofa bed, and two wood-burning fireplaces. Four-posters have patchwork quilts and a crocheted canopy or a filmy mosquito net. Baths are especially well done: large and modern, with brass fittings and ample vanity space. △ *5 suites. Air-conditioning, cable TV, and mini-refrigerators in suites, wood-burning fireplace in 1 suite; fenced yard and kennel for small pets. $85–$185; full breakfast, wine. AE, MC, V. No smoking, closed Dec. 24–25.*

CAMELLIA COVE 🐚
211 W. Hill St., Washington 70589, tel. 318/826–7362

Herman and Annie Bidstrup's 1825 home sits on 2 acres on a peaceful residential street in the little town of Washington. The large, white, two-story house has double porches and lacy Victorian trim. Rocking chairs on the upstairs porch are great for relaxing and enjoying the peace and quiet.

After living in Scotland and England, where they enjoyed staying in B&Bs, the Bidstrups decided to run one themselves. The two have traveled extensively, and the house is filled with mementos and artifacts.

Camellia Cove has a wealth of wonderful memorabilia, in addition to its Louisiana antique furnishings. At the turn of the century, this was the home of Dr. Herbert Kilpatrick. His desk in the parlor remains much as it was when he lived in the house, and displayed on it is his license to dispense opium. In the central hallway, Herman's grandfather's handwritten marriage license, dated 1887, is pressed between the pages of the Bidstrup family Bible. (Herman is of Danish-German ancestry; Annie is French Acadian.)

Three of the spacious upstairs rooms are rented to overnight guests. A front room, just off the porch, has Victorian furnishings: a carved-wood bed, washstand, armoire, and dressing table. Its bath, almost as large as the bedroom, has a clawfoot tub with spray shower as well as a marble-topped dresser with a big mirror under a row of makeup lights. (Incidentally, part of the fun here is finding amenities, such as manicure scissors nestled in little porcelain potpourri-filled pots.) One of the guest rooms has two beds; its bath is across the hall. The third guest room does share that bath, but Annie only rents these two rooms to families or people traveling together.

Breakfast is served in the formal dining room. It always includes heaps of homemade biscuits and fig preserves. △ *1 double room with bath, 2 doubles share 1 bath. Air-conditioning. $65–$75; full breakfast. No credit cards. No smoking, closed Jan. 1, Thanksgiving, and Dec. 25.*

CHRÉTIEN POINT PLANTATION 🐚
665 Chrétien Point Rd., Sunset 70584, tel. 318/233–7050 or 800/880–7050, fax 318/662–5876, www.virtualcities.com

In the early 1930s, a local photographer took pictures of this house and sent them to Hollywood. As a result, the stairway and the window above it were used as a model for those in Scarlett O'Hara's Tara. Then, too, there's the tale of the long-ago lady of Chrétien Point who shot a man on the steps. Owners Jeanne and Louis Cornay will point out where the man was standing when he was killed.

Of solid brick construction, with six white columns and double front galleries, the two-story house was built in 1831 for Hypolite Chrétien II and his wife, Félicité. During the Civil War, the house figured in a major battle. There is still a bullet hole in one of the front doors. The last Chrétiens lost the house a few years after the war, and it began to fall into a sorry state.

Louis found the deteriorated mansion while looking for a barn in which to keep his son's horse. Hay was stored in it; chickens, cows, and pigs roamed through it. The Cornays bought the house and restored it to its former grandeur.

The colors used in the house are those of nature's sunsets. Silk wall coverings are in vivid scarlets and pinks; one of the ceilings is painted a cool blue. There are six working fireplaces with imported French Empire marble mantels. The 19th-century Louisiana antiques include a carved armoire and four-poster by Mallard.

Three rooms have full-tester beds, and the others have canopy and spread in rich fabrics and bold colors. A downstairs room, formerly the wine cellar, has redbrick floors, blue velvet chairs, a New Orleans armoire, and a hand-carved bed. The bins that once held wine are now filled with books.

Guests get acquainted over afternoon mint juleps, and the big plantation breakfast, served in the formal dining room. ♙ *5 double rooms with baths. Air-conditioning, free mansion tour, meeting room; pool, tennis court. $110–$225; full breakfast. AE, MC, V. No smoking.*

COOK'S COTTAGE AT RIP VAN WINKLE GARDENS ❦
5505 Rip Van Winkle Rd., New Iberia 70560, tel. 318/365–3332 or 800/375–3332, fax 318/365–3354

In the late 19th century, American actor Joseph Jefferson toured the country portraying Washington Irving's Rip Van Winkle. On a hunting trip to South Louisiana, Jefferson fell in love with the area, and purchased several thousand acres on which he built an elaborate winter home. Twenty-five acres of that property now comprise the Rip Van Winkle Gardens, a showcase of landscaped gardens that sit adjacent to Lake Peigneur.

Within the lovely gardens, the three-room former cook's cottage for the estate has been transformed into a modern and private guest house. It is furnished with a blend of antique and reproduction early French Louisiana pieces, including a handmade mahogany four-poster bed with down pillows. The bath is stunning, with a big whirlpool tub and shower, a large mirror, as well as a lighted magnified makeup mirror, a spacious vanity, and a lineup of aromatherapy soaps and sundry lotions, and a hair dryer. An ironing board and iron are tucked in the closet.

For entertainment, there is a stereo and a CD player, and TV/VCR. In the small kitchenette area, where there is a wet bar, microwave, toaster oven, and coffeemaker, the fridge is stocked with the makings of a do-it-yourself Continental breakfast, including fresh fruits and gourmet coffees. There are always fresh flowers from the gardens placed around the cottage.

Guests have unlimited access to the gardens, and are given a complementary tour of the Jefferson House, which is a wonderful Gothic house with Moorish flourishes. There is a restaurant overlooking the lake, and boat tours on the lake are conducted daily (at a reduced rate for B&B guests). ♙ *1 cottage. Restaurant, air-conditioning, cable TV/VCR, stereo, CD player, wet bar, microwave, refrigerator, phone, complimentary house tour. $145–$175; Continental breakfast. No smoking.*

ELTER HOUSE INN ❦
603 S. Main St., Washington 70589, tel. 318/826–7362

This 1850s two-story Acadian-style structure, painted a pale green with white trim, sits on 3 acres in a quiet residential neighborhood. There is a swing and rocking chairs on the broad front porch, as well as a lawn swing. The entire house is let to overnighters.

The living room has a wing chair, big upholstered sofa, rocking chair, and TV/VCR. There are plenty of videos and magazines. The downstairs bedroom has a four-poster with a dust ruffle and matching patchwork quilt, white lace curtains, and dark green walls hung with framed prints of English hunting scenes. A separate dressing area opens to a bath with a big marble tub. Up steep, uneven stairs are two other bedrooms, one with an antique sleigh bed and redbrick fireplace, the other a carved-wood bed and shower bath. The kitchen has modern, full-size appliances; breakfast is brought in daily. ♙ *3 double rooms with baths. Air-conditioning, kitchen, washer/dryer. $70–$80; Continental breakfast. MC, V. No smoking.*

ESTORGE HOUSE ☙
427 Market St., Opelousas 70570, tel. 318/942–8151

Double galleries and eight sets of French doors, each with its original transom, grace the front of this fine white-column house with double galleries on a residential street near the courthouse square. Built by French colonist Pierre Labyche in the early 1820s, it was occupied during the Civil War by Dr. Joseph Leonard Estorge, Mrs. Labyche's son by her first marriage to Frenchman Jean Estorge. The house was sold in the 1980s, but Judith Estorge, whose home it presently is, bought back in 1996, and opened it as a bed-and-breakfast the following year.

The high ceilings in the formal parlor and foyer have lovely trompe l'oeil paintings; an etched-glass chandelier shines over polished hardwood floors in the central hall, and a splendid crystal chandelier hangs over the dining room table. The parlor, with its ivory wall coverings and velvet Victorian settees, has a collection of nutcrackers lining the mantel, as well as a carved chess set and board game. Hutches contain fine china, cut-glass, and glistening crystal. Estorge family heirlooms are displayed in the wide upstairs center hall and throughout the house.

As is the case throughout the house, guest rooms are furnished with 19th-century French and Louisiana antiques. An upstairs room, with a handsome carved-wood bed and velvet-upholstered chairs, has a balcony; the downstairs room has a half-tester. Beds are dressed with top-quality Egyptian linens. Baths have the original claw-foot tubs, and are otherwise modern. There are plenty of magazines and books to browse through.

Guests are greeted with wine or tea, which is served in the parlor, or, if you prefer, in the outdoor hot tub.

Innkeeper Sherl Picchioni prepares the large breakfasts—which may include French toast or scrambled eggs and grits with homemade biscuits—which are served in a rear room that has large windows overlooking the garden and the hot tub. Sherl also bakes the chocolate-chip cookies for late-night snacks—or pops the popcorn, if you prefer. ♙ *2 double rooms with baths. Air-conditioning, turndown service, free mansion tour; outdoor hot tub. $75–$125; full breakfast. No credit cards. No smoking.*

LA MAISON DE CAMPAGNE ☙
825 Kidder Rd., Carencro 70520, tel. 318/896–6529 or 800/895–0235, fax 318/896–1494, www.virtualcities.com

Fred and Joeann McLemore's home is a gabled and galleried Acadian house, built in about 1871. It sits in a quiet country setting in a suburb about 15 minutes north of Lafayette. The drawing room is elegantly furnished with Victorian antiques: velvet and brocade-upholstered settees and chairs, marble-top tables, and white lace curtains. Frilly old-fashioned ladies hats are perched here and there on gilded mirrors.

The Magnolia room, downstairs, is the honeymoon suite: a spacious room with 13½-ft ceilings, heart of cedar floors, a reproduction canopy bed and armoire, and an 1890 marble-top dresser. Its bath has the original claw-foot tub and matching water closet, and a shower with a frilly white curtain. The Country Room, peopled with stuffed dolls, has turn-of-the-century Cajun furnishings, including a white-iron bed draped with a diaphanous canopy. A matching antique 1890 bedroom set is in the French Room, where German porcelain lamps are on the night stands. Attention to detail is evident in touches such as the wallpaper border that matches the golden oak finish of the furniture. Baths in this and the Country Room have walk-in closets.

In addition to rooms in the main house, there is the Sharecropper's Cottage, which was moved from a nearby plantation and restored with century-old cypress lumber—the same material used for the king-size bed and an entertainment center complete with TV/VCR and refrigerator. This cottage, suitable for families with children, has a full kitchen with microwave, dishwasher, and washer/dryer, rocking chairs, patchwork quilts, and a collection of German dolls.

The author of the cookbook *Lache Pas La Patate* (Don't Drop the Potato), Joeann takes pride in gourmet breakfasts that may include scrumptious seafood sauces, egg dishes, and homemade breads. ♣ *3 double rooms with baths, 1 cottage. Air-conditioning; pool. $95–$145; full breakfast. D, MC, V. No smoking, no alcoholic beverages on premises, 2-night minimum for Mardi Gras, Festival International, Festival Acadien, and Crawfish Festival.*

OLD CASTILLO HOTEL/PLACE D'EVANGELINE ☙
220 Evangeline Blvd., St. Martinville 70582, tel. 318/394–4010 or 800/621–3017, fax 318/394–7983, www.virtualcities.com

Hard by Bayou Teche, beneath the branches of the Evangeline Oak, this three-story brick building looks like a little red schoolhouse. In fact, in its more than 150-year history it has been a school, an inn (the Castillo Hotel), and a hall for operas and balls.

La Place d'Evangeline restaurant opened in 1987; two years later owners Peggy and Gerald Hulin began restoring the upstairs rooms for overnighters. The restoration is ongoing. Curtains, color-coordinated with the furnishings, have been added, as has a balcony on the front of the building. (Rooms 1 and 4 open onto the balcony.) Peggy plans to plant a rose garden and add fresh flowers in the rooms. The rooms themselves are enormous (ceilings are sky-high) and at present somewhat sparsely furnished with 19th-century Louisiana French antiques. Room 3 is of awesome size, with a four-poster and a book-filled breakfront. Its bath is also large, with double marble vanities. All baths are adjoining and have modern fixtures and vanities complemented by old-fashioned touches like porcelain washbowls and pitchers. ♣ *5 double rooms with baths. Restaurant, air-conditioning. $50–$80; full breakfast. AE, MC, V. No smoking.*

T' FRÈRE'S HOUSE ☙
1905 Verot School Rd., Lafayette 70508, tel. and fax 318/984–9347 or 800/984–9347

A trim white gazebo stands on the spacious lawn of T' Frère's House, a gabled Acadian cottage that was built about 1880 of cypress and brick. "Little Brother's

House" is now the home of retired restaurateurs Pat and Maugie Pastor. Their expertise is apparent in the sumptuous breakfasts and the Cajun canapés, served with a welcoming "T' Julep" on a glass-enclosed gallery.

A lead-glass door opens to a central hallway with a crystal chandelier and ornate gold-leaf mirror. Two guest rooms are downstairs, one with an 1840s full-tester bed, whirlpool bath, and working fireplace and the other with a sunburst half-tester and tiny bath with spray shower. Two charmers are upstairs. The green-and-white Garden Room has a sloping ceiling and patchwork quilts, and the delicious Victorian scarlet-and-green 1890 Room has double white-iron beds and a bath that was creatively fashioned from a wall of closets. In addition to rooms in the main house, there are two rooms, each with a fridge, in the garconnière, one with a big four-poster, the other with a canopy bed.

T' Frère's "Ooooh-la-la" breakfasts are showstoppers: Maugie, announcing "Showtime!," serves the big Cajun breakfasts in red-silk pajamas. **⌂** *6 double rooms with baths. Air-conditioning, cable TV, coffeemaker, alarm clock, phones with dataports, and terry-cloth robes in rooms, fireplace in 1 room, parlor, and kitchen. $95; full breakfast, afternoon cocktails. D, MC, V. No smoking.*

NORTH-CENTRAL LOUISIANA

Louisiana has always been a divided state. Natives invariably refer to North Louisiana and South Louisiana, and even in conversation you can detect a capitalized distinction. North Louisiana is southern, and South Louisiana is not. (New Orleans, though way down south, has neither a northern nor a southern flavor but is in a class by itself.)

Alexandria, in the middle of the state, is Louisiana's own unofficial but acknowledged Mason-Dixon line. North of "Alex," the terrain, accents, customs, and cuisine change. Flat marshlands, moss-draped cypress trees, and gray earth give way to rolling green hills, pine forests, and rich red clay. The area around Alexandria has several notable Civil War sites, including a cemetery and antebellum houses.

Natchitoches (pronounced nack-i-tish), about one hour northwest of Alexandria, is the oldest permanent European settlement in the entire Louisiana Purchase—four years older than the French Quarter of New Orleans. The town's restored historic district is a 33-block area containing fine old homes. Front Street, paved with old brick, stretches along the pretty Cane River Lake. Created when the Red River changed its course, Cane River Lake not only decorates Natchitoches but meanders on down through the region's plantation country.

Natchitoches gained fame as the town of Chinquapin in the film Steel Magnolias. *The film, which was shot here in 1988, has virtually transformed this sleepy little town. You can't walk 2 ft in any direction without encountering someone who wants to tell about the "part"—on camera or off—he or she played in the film.*

In this neck of the woods, Natchitoches has long been known for its Christmas Festival of Lights. The monthlong festival, which begins the first Saturday of December, draws about 150,000 people to town. The historic district, on which the festival centers, is a riot of twinkling lights, and the first weekend is a continuous festival of food and fun.

Another celebrated, though slightly smaller, event is the two-day Natchitoches Pilgrimage, held in October, which includes walking tours of the historic district, admission to some of the landmark homes and plantations, and candlelight tours.

Although I–49 makes the drive easy, you should take the state and parish roads to explore the backcountry of Louisiana and visit the house museums and plantations. State Route 1 slips diagonally from the northwest corner all the way to the Gulf of Mexico. Although the road is substandard along some stretches, the scenery is prettier, and you'll pick up more flavor than on the interstate. Routes 494, 119, and 493 are also picturesque, drifting alongside Cane River Lake between Natchitoches and Melrose. And the drive through the Kisatchie National Forest is spectacular.

PLACES TO GO, SIGHTS TO SEE

Cane River Cruises/Trolley Tours (Natchitoches, tel. 318/352–7093 or 318/352–2577) does narrated cruises and open tram tours that focus on *Steel Magnolias* locations and sundry dramatis personae.

Kate Chopin House (243 Rte 495, Cloutierville, tel. 318/379–2233 or 318/357–7907). In the late 1800s, Kate Chopin, who wrote the book *The Awakening*, lived in this region. Her home is now a museum containing costumes, furnishings, and memorabilia pertaining to her life and times.

Kent House (3601 Bayou Rapides Rd., Alexandria, tel. 318/487–5998), built around 1800, is the oldest known structure still standing in central Louisiana. Preserved structures include the milk house, carriage house, and kitchen; cooking and quilting demonstrations are among regular activities here.

Kisatchie National Forest. South of Natchitoches, a 100,000-acre Ranger District contains the 17-mi Longleaf Trail Scenic Byway and an 8,700-acre wilderness with biking and riding trails. For information, write to the District Ranger, Kisatchie Ranger District, Box 2128, Natchitoches 71457, tel. 318/352–2568.

At **Melrose Plantation** (Exit 119 of I–49, Melrose, tel. 318/379–0055), tours of the main mansion and outbuildings include the African House, which has murals by primitive artist Clementine Hunter, the "black Grandma Moses," who lived and painted here until her death in 1988, just short of her 102nd birthday.

RESTAURANTS

In the Natchitoches–Alexandria area, there are some standout restaurants. **Lea's Lunchroom** (U.S. 71, Lecompte, tel. 318/776–5178) is a down-home café that serves plate lunches, sandwiches, and mouthwatering homemade pies. Natchitoches is known for meat pies, and the best place to get them is **Lasyone's Meat Pie Kitchen & Restaurant** (622 2nd St., tel. 318/352–3353). The **Landing** (530 Front St., Natchitoches, tel. 318/352–1579) and the **Bentley Room** (Bentley Hotel, 200 Desoto St., Alexandria, tel. 800/356–6835) are more formal full-service restaurants.

VISITOR INFORMATION

Alexandria/Pineville Area Convention & Visitors Bureau (Box 8110, Alexandria 71306, tel. 318/443–7049 or 800/742–7049). **Natchitoches Parish Tourist Commission** (Box 411, Natchitoches 71458, tel. 318/352–8072 or 800/259–1714).

RESERVATION SERVICE

Bed & Breakfast Travel (8211 Goodwood Blvd., Suite F, Baton Rouge 70806, tel. 504/923–2337 or [outside Louisiana] 800/926–4320, fax 504/923–2374, www.bnbtravel.com) has B&B listings for Louisiana and parts of East Texas, Mississippi, Alabama, and the Gulf Coast.

BEAU FORT PLANTATION ☞

4078 Rte. 494, Bermuda (Box 2300, Natchitoches 71457), tel. 318/352–5340 or 318/352–9580

On the banks of the Cane River Lake, 10 mi south of Natchitoches, the home of Ann and Jack Brittain is a 265-acre working cotton and corn plantation. Built in 1790, the house, with its 84-ft gallery, is approached via a long alley of oaks. Louisiana Empire and European antiques, including stunning tester beds, sit among scores of other heirlooms and objets d'art that include Tsinge Dynasty lamp bases, original Audubon and Clementine Hunter paintings, and fascinating 19th-century artifacts. The house is famed in these parts for the punkah (pronounced *poon*-kah; or shoo-fly) fan that hangs over the dining-room table. Suites, each with a private entrance, are unusually large—the master suite is 28 by 26 ft—as are the modern tile baths, which were originally screened porches. Displays of antique clothing, patchwork quilts, dolls, and family pictures are abundant. ⌂ *3 suites. Air-conditioning, satellite TV in master suite, phone in 2 suites, free home tour. $125–$145; full breakfast. DC, MC. No smoking.*

CLOUTIER TOWNHOUSE AND PETIT TARN ☞

416 Jefferson St., Natchitoches 71457, tel./fax 318/352–5242 or 800/351–7666

In 1998 Conna Cloutier sold her town house on Front Street (also called the Cloutier Townhouse), and opened two bed-and-breakfasts in restored houses. Her present home is a 12-room turn-of-the-century house just a half block from Front Street's shops and restaurants. She is also the proprietor of the Petit Tarn, a restored 1950s cottage that sits in the hills on Natchitoches's east bank, a stroll across the downtown bridge away from Front Street attractions.

The high-ceilinged Townhouse is furnished with a collection of antiques, dating mostly from the Louisiana Empire and Victorian periods. Conna's purchase of two beds that had been in the old St. Mary's Convent in Natchitoches inspired her to create a convent suite. The four-posters, draped in mosquito netting, date from the early 19th century. Conna has decorated this suite with religious artifacts, including an old-fashioned nun's habit that hangs from a wooden peg. The master suite has a full tester bed, with embroidered spread, wing chairs, an upholstered settee, TV/VCR, and a whirlpool bath.

Conna's other bed-and-breakfast—the Petit Tarn—is named for the French town that was the ancestral home of Irma Sompayrac Willard, the noted Natchitoches artist and historian who built the house. In a garden setting, this house is filled with her artwork and family memorabilia. Each of the three stories is a suite: the top-floor Treehouse Suite, with two balconies, has a massive Empire bed; below it, the balconied Library Suite has an Eastlake Victorian half-tester. The ground floor River Suite has a water view, as well as a full kitchen. All three suites have whirlpool baths.

In the Townhouse, breakfasts that include homemade breads and mini–meat pies are served; in the Petit Tarn, the makings for a do-it-yourself Continental breakfast are provided. ⚔ *2 suites in Cloutier Townhouse, 3 suites in the Petit Tarn. Air-conditioning, 4 suites with whirlpool bath, 1 with TV/VCR, 1 with full kitchen, 2 with fridge, microwave, and coffeemakers. $95–$110. AE, MC, V. No smoking, 2-night minimum from Thanksgiving to Jan. 1.*

FLEUR-DE-LIS 🐚

336 2nd St., Natchitoches 71457, tel. 318/352–6621 or 800/489–6621, www.virtualcities.com

The Fleur-de-Lis, opened in 1983, is the granddaddy of Natchitoches bed-and-breakfasts. The turn-of-the-century house is now the home of Tom and Harriette Palmer, who operate the B&B with help from their friendly golden retriever, Ginger. The two-story house, which Tom and Harriette painted a lovely rose with Wedgwood blue trim, has a front porch with a swing and rocking chairs, shaded by a roof that juts out beneath a second-story bay window topped by a gable. Behind leaded-glass doors are a large foyer and stairway. Adjoining the foyer, a cozy family room has a sofa and chairs grouped around the TV. The Victorian motif is carried out in several elegant handmade beaded and fringed lamp shades. Knickknacks and framed family pictures are displayed throughout. Breakfast is served family-style at a long table in the dining room.

Guest rooms have four-poster, white-iron, or brass beds and patchwork quilts; some have white wicker furnishings and headboards. The quietest room is the Bird's Nest, an upstairs rear room with sloping ceiling. All the baths are tiny but have modern fixtures. ⚔ *5 double rooms with baths. Air-conditioning, cable TV/VCR in family room. $60–$80; full breakfast. AE, D, MC, V. No smoking, 2-night minimum during Christmas Festival.*

JEFFERSON HOUSE 🐚

229 Jefferson St., Natchitoches 71457, tel. 318/352–3957 or 318/352–5756

The back veranda of Gay and L. J. Melder's contemporary white-frame home affords a mesmerizing view of Cane River Lake. Although the house sits on a busy extension of Front Street, within walking distance of the historic district, the weeping willows, herb garden, rocking chairs on the veranda, and pier sneaking onto the lake create a bucolic ambience.

The house is a split-level whose lower floor is hidden from the street. The Melders live on the lower floor; guests occupy the entire street-level floor. The house is decorated with a blend of exquisite Asian objets d'art and traditional furnishings. The large, stately parlor has a high beamed ceiling, a brick fireplace, and doors opening to the veranda. Bedrooms have quilted spreads and matching draperies. The larger room has an adjoining tile bath that's big enough for a fair-size cocktail party. The rooms may be rented as a suite. ⚔ *1 double room with bath, 2 double rooms with shared bath (available as a suite). Air-conditioning, cable TV in living room. $65–$120; full breakfast. MC, V. No smoking.*

LEVY-EAST HOUSE ☙

358 Jefferson St., Natchitoches 71457, tel. 318/352–0662 or 800/840–0662,
www.virtualcities.com

The home of Avery and Judy East, a galleried 1838 house with lacy ironwork, gabled roof, and twin brick chimneys is just a block and a half from Front Street shops and restaurants. Furnished with Victorian antiques and heirlooms, the elegant house has heart-pine floors, six fireplaces, baths with beaded-wood wainscoting, and luscious mauve and green colors. Upstairs guest rooms, which flank a common room that opens onto a back porch with rocking chairs and a view of a century-old magnolia tree, have enlarged antique beds and armoires in which TVs and phones are tucked. Each room has a volume-control speaker that plays romantic CDs. Guests are given keys to a private entrance. A formal dining room, with handsome silver candelabra and fresh flowers, is the setting for a breakfast that may be a fruit-topped French toast sundae or baked eggs served in heart-shape dishes. ❧ *4 double rooms with whirlpool baths. Air-conditioning, coffeemaker, cable TV/VCR, phone, and terry-cloth robes in rooms, turndown service with candy; off-street free parking. $115–$195; full breakfast, sherry, complimentary champagne for guests celebrating their honeymoon or anniversary. MC, V. No smoking, 2-night minimum for Christmas Festival.*

LOYD HALL ☙

292 Loyd Bridge Rd., Cheneyville (5119 Masonic Dr., Alexandria 71301),
tel. 318/776–5641 or 800/240–8135, fax 318/776–5886

Loyd Hall is a 640-acre working plantation that grows cotton, corn, and soybeans. Frank Fitzgerald's father bought the land in 1949, unaware that a deteriorated 19th-century mansion was buried beneath a tangle of trees and bushes. Frank and his wife, Anne, now live in the restored house. Frank is a veterinarian, and in addition to sundry farm critters, a small army of cats and dogs calls Loyd Hall home.

Several of the plantation's original outbuildings have been restored, and contain modern guest accommodations. There are two suites in the 1800s carriage house; the others are in one- or two-bedroom cottages. All are furnished with 19th-century Louisiana, such as tester and four-poster beds, and some have woodburning fireplaces. Each has a kitchen with modern appliances, including microwave, toaster, and coffeemaker. Two cottages have washer/dryers, and one of them—the McCullough House—has a two-person hot tub in its garden. Kitchens are stocked with ingredients for a Continental breakfast, which guests prepare at their leisure and enjoy in privacy, wrapped in the cushy terry-cloth robes provided.

This is an excellent place for families; there is no charge for children under 6.

The plantation is in a quiet country setting, 16 mi south of Alexandria near the intersection of U.S. 167 and 71. ❧ *4 cottages, 2 suites. Air-conditioning, TV/VCR in cottage and suites, washer/dryer in 2 cottages; pool, bicycles, fishing rods, tour of mansion. $95–$145; Continental breakfast, complimentary wine on arrival. AE, MC, V. No smoking.*

MAGNOLIA PLANTATION ☙

5487 Rte. 119, Natchez 71456, tel. 318/379–2221

More than 20 cats, several peacocks, and a variety of other critters are at home on this 2,400-acre working plantation, the grounds of which are lavish with live oaks, greenery, and flowering plants. A barn houses the only cotton press in the country still in its original location.

With its broad porches, pitched roof, dormers, and chimneys, this raised cottage epitomizes early Louisiana plantation houses. One of only two National Bicentennial Farms west of the Mississippi River, Magnolia has been in the same family since a 1753 French land grant. The original Big House was severely damaged by fire during the Civil War. Restored in 1896, using the original brick foundation and 18-inch-thick brick walls, it is now the home of Mrs. Matthew Hertzog and her daughter Betty.

Upstairs and downstairs rooms open onto central hallways. The front door opens to a handsome crystal chandelier that shines over red velvet Victorian settees; every room in the 27-room house, except the hall, has an open, nonworking fireplace. Walls are lined with family portraits; glass cases display fine china and crystal. There is a marvelous back porch, with a punkah fan, wind chimes, and a big Victorian oak hat rack. In a wing off the back porch there is a chapel, in which services are still held.

Throughout the house are the Hertzog family's collection of Southern Empire furniture, such as a cherry early Louisiana bed and matching armoire in a guest room. One guest room has a sunburst tester, while another has an early Victorian mahogany bed and a cherry armoire. All three rooms are exceptionally large, and have antique washbasins as well as terry robes. The upstairs hall has a cable TV/VCR, a fridge, and coffeemaker, but a full breakfast is served in the formal dining room beneath a splendid brass chandelier. ♨ *3 double rooms with baths. Air-conditioning, cable TV/VCR, fridge, coffeemaker, complimentary tour of the house. D, MC, V; full breakfast. No smoking.*

TANTE HUPPÉ HOUSE ☙
424 Jefferson St., Natchitoches 71457, tel. 318/352–5342 or 800/482–4276

Robert "Bobby" DeBlieux (pronounced *dub*-you), a former mayor of Natchitoches, restored and lives in an 1830 Creole house in the town's historic district. Most of the furnishings and family heirlooms are original to the house; his library contains the state's oldest collection of 18th-century Creole books. A candlelit breakfast, made from recipes in a 1745 Creole cookbook, is served in the formal dining room.

Two suites are in the restored, detached former servants' quarters, each with bedroom, parlor, full kitchen, private entrance, and patio. Furnishings are contemporary, with a mix of wicker and upholstered sofa beds and chairs. Colors are rich burgundy and greens. There is plenty of closet space; modern tile baths have ample vanities and big, thirsty towels. A third suite in the main house, a former slave quarters, has exposed old brick walls, beamed ceilings, and a bedroom as well as a loft bed. ♨ *3 suites. Air-conditioning, kitchen, coffeemaker, phone with 2 private lines, 2 cable TVs/VCRs and videos of locally made movies in each suite, bottle of wine on check-in, free home tour. $95; full breakfast. AE, MC, V. No smoking.*

Tennessee

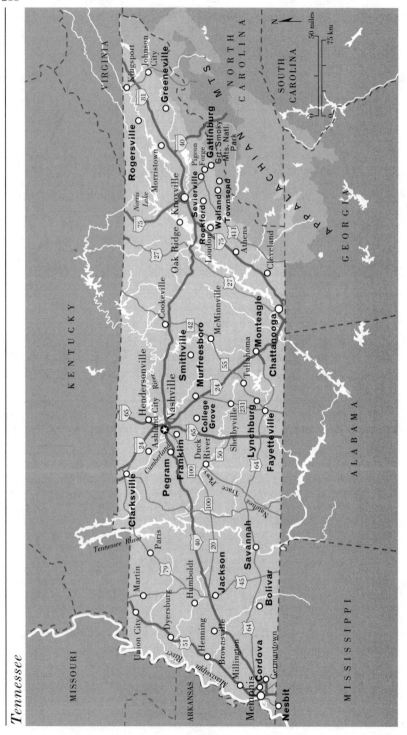

EAST TENNESSEE

High above a patchwork of rolling farmland and forests, the peaks of the Great Smoky Mountains dominate the landscape of East Tennessee. Covered with a dense carpet of wildflowers in spring and ablaze with foliage in autumn, the Smokies—named for the mantle of blue haze that so often blankets them—are a joy to hike or drive through.

The highest and most rugged elevations are in the Great Smoky Mountains National Park, the most-visited national park in the United States. The gateway city to the park is Gatlinburg, not too long ago a remote little place with a few hotels and some mountain crafts shops. Now hordes of visitors are attracted here for outdoor recreation. Neighboring Pigeon Forge—site of Dolly Parton's theme park, Dollywood, and numerous other tourist attractions—has become a favorite with family vacationers.

Less commercialized is the Great Smoky Mountains Arts and Crafts Community just outside Gatlinburg. Pretty byways into the national park take travelers far from the crowds to stunning vistas and roadside trailheads that mark the start of tranquil walks. Mountain folkways persist in smaller communities, preserved by artisans who practice age-old crafts and traditional cooks who conjure up hearty meals from surrounding streams, fields, and woodlands. Most bed-and-breakfast inns are off the beaten path but within a few miles of the major attractions. City lovers will find urban bustle and diversity at Knoxville and Chattanooga. The latter has become a favorite with tourists since the Tennessee Aquarium opened.

PLACES TO GO, SIGHTS TO SEE

Andrew Johnson National Historic Site (College and Depot Sts., Greeneville, tel. 423/638–3551). The 17th president's home, grave, and simple tailor shop are preserved here in the smallest national park in the country.

Chattanooga Choo-Choo and Terminal Station (1400 Market St., Chattanooga, tel. 423/266–5000). This renovated facility commemorating the heyday of railroads has several restaurants, shops, and train exhibits.

Dixie Stampede (3849 Parkway, Pigeon Forge, tel. 423/453–4400 or 800/356–1676). This live dinner show features barbecue and a musical Wild West rodeo.

Dollywood (700 Dollywood La., Pigeon Forge, tel. 423/428–9400 or 800/365–5996). Dolly Parton's popular theme park offers the food, music, and fun of the region in a re-created 1880s mountain village with modern rides and professional entertainment throughout the day.

The **Gatlinburg Sky Lift** (765 Parkway, tel. 423/436–4307) offers a bird's-eye view of the town. The **Ober Gatlinburg Tramway** (1001 Parkway, tel. 423/436–5423) goes to a ski area and mountaintop amusement park.

Great Smoky Mountains Arts and Crafts Community (take U.S. 321 east of Gatlinburg and turn left on Glades Rd., tel. 423/932–3532) is an enclave of 70 shops and galleries scattered along back roads only 10 minutes outside Gatlinburg.

At the **Great Smoky Mountains National Park** (tel. 423/436–1200), shared by North Carolina and Tennessee, the Southern Appalachians reach their ultimate grandeur as 16 peaks soar more than 6,000 ft. Highlights of the park include *Clingmans Dome*, which, at 6,643 ft, is the highest point in Tennessee; you can take a spiral pathway to the top of an observation tower here for panoramic views of the Smokies. *Cades Cove* (tel. 423/448–2472) gives a beautiful picture of mountain life more than a century ago. In an isolated valley within the park are farmhouses, barns, churches, and an old gristmill still in operation.

Knoxville Zoological Gardens (Chilhowee Park on Rutledge Pike S, Exit 392, tel. 423/637–5331). Home to more than 1,000 animals, this zoo is famous for breeding big African cats and elephants.

Museum of Appalachia (Rte. 61, 1 mi east of I–75, Exit 122, Norris, tel. 423/494–7680). Three dozen log buildings are preserved in a compound; historical displays and exhibitions are sometimes punctuated by musical hoedowns.

The **Tennessee Aquarium** (1 Broad St., Chattanooga, tel. 423/265–0695) is the largest freshwater facility of its kind. The fish range from 60-pound catfish, which prowl the Mississippi, to the small, mysterious fish that inhabit Japan's Shimanto River. The highlight of this world-class aquarium is a spectacular 60-ft canyon, comprising two living forests and 22 tanks. In the neighborhood are the **Creative Discovery Museum** (4th and Chestnut Sts., tel. 423/756–2738), a block from the Aquarium, and a **3-D IMAX Theater** (2nd and Chestnut Sts., tel. 423/265–0695). The **Hunter Museum of American Art** (10 Bluff View, tel. 423/267–0968) covers many periods in American visual arts, from the 19th-century Hudson River School and genre painting to abstract-expressionist painting and contemporary sculpture.

RESTAURANTS

The **Apple Tree Restaurant** (Parkway and Frances Rd., Pigeon Forge, tel. 423/453–4961) offers a traditional and inexpensive menu of mountain cuisine, including fried chicken and barbecue.

In Gatlinburg, the **Burning Bush Restaurant** (1151 Parkway, tel. 423/436–4669), decked out with Colonial-era antiques, is a favorite for its sumptuous breakfasts and Continental menu, and the **Smoky Mountain Trout House** (410 N. Parkway, tel. 423/436–5416), aptly named, serves eight trout dishes in a cozy restaurant also known for its country-fried chicken and prime rib.

The **Copper Cellar/Cumberland Grill** (1807 Cumberland Ave., Knoxville, tel. 423/673–3411), serving sandwiches and drinks, is a fun place to grab lunch or Sunday brunch.

Chattanooga's **212 Market Street** (212 Market St., tel. 423/265–1212), directly across from the Tennessee Aquarium, is a hip restaurant with a wide-ranging American menu.

SHOPPING

Among the amusement parks and tourist shops of bustling **Pigeon Forge** are the factory outlet malls that make this town a mecca for budget shoppers. **Belz**

Factory Outlet Mall (2655 Teaster La., tel. 423/453–3503), **Tanger Outlet Centers** (off Highway 441 at highway traffic light No. 3, and again in Sevierville, on Highway 441, tel. 800/482–6437), and **Pigeon Forge Factory Outlet Mall** (2850 Parkway, tel. 615/428–2828) are the three best known.

Among the as-yet-untrammeled hills outside Gatlinburg, the secluded **Great Smoky Mountains Arts and Crafts Community** offers some 70 shops, galleries, and eateries in an Appalachian-style village. One popular gallery is the Vern Hippensteal Gallery (452 Parkway, tel. 423/436–4372), which features the work of Hippensteal's Mountain View Inn's innkeeper. For more information on area stores, contact Gatlinburg's Chamber of Commerce (tel. 800/568–4748).

VISITOR INFORMATION

Chattanooga Area Convention and Visitors Bureau (2 Broad St., Chattanooga 37402, tel. 423/756–8687 or 800/322–3344). **Knoxville Area Convention and Visitors Bureau** (500 Henley St., Box 15012, Knoxville 37901, tel. 423/523–7263 or 800/727–8045). **Northeast Tennessee Tourism Association** (Box 415, Jonesborough 37659, tel. 423/753–4188 or 800/468–6882). **Smoky Mountain Visitors Bureau** (309 S. Washington St., Maryville 37801, tel. 423/983–2241 or 800/525–6834).

RESERVATION SERVICE

Tennessee Bed & Breakfast Innkeepers Association (Box 120428, Nashville 37212, tel. 615/321–5482 or 800/820–8144).

ADAMS EDGEWORTH INN ☞

Monteagle Assembly, Box 340, Monteagle 37356, tel. 931/924–4000, fax 931/924–3236, www.bbonline.com/tn/edgeworth/

Adams Edgeworth Inn is atop the Cumberland Plateau inside a Victorian community nicknamed the Chautauqua of the South. It is a southern hotel in the grand, old-fashioned sense, with a wraparound porch and screen doors. Every summer, the Monteagle Assembly, the 96-acre community surrounding the inn, hosts an eight-week program of events that range from literary seminars to classical music concerts. Guests are free to wander the paths among 160 Victorian houses. Originally a boardinghouse, the 1896 inn was renovated and reopened in 1977, losing none of its authenticity. The entire compound is listed on the National Register of Historic Places.

Proprietors David and Wendy Adams are outgoing and articulate, both retired from prominent jobs in Atlanta. Wendy was fund-raising director for the opera and ballet, and David headed the research department at a brokerage firm. The Edgeworth library boasts some 2,000 volumes, and its art collection ranges from old master paintings to contemporary art picked up during the Adamses' travels.

A gentle quiet pervades the Edgeworth, where guests read, talk, or play board games. Rooms have 12-ft ceilings and a country cottage decor, with lots of chintz in warm colors. Some rooms have fireplaces and four-poster beds; others have twin brass beds. In warm weather, the porch is the perfect place to spend an evening in a rocking chair; in the afternoon, the hammocks are irresistible. Breakfast is served in a cozy dining room, where Wendy, who graduated from the Culinary Institute of America, elegantly presents five-course, candlelit dinners by reservation.

Nearby attractions include the University of the South at Sewanee, a small, well-respected school, and the trails of South Cumberland State Recreation Area. The Monteagle Winery produces a nice selection of sweet German wines. ♣ *13 double rooms with baths, 1 suite. Air-conditioning, cable TV in 5 rooms, library, dining room, gift shop; pool, tennis courts on the Assembly grounds. $95–$195; full breakfast. AE, MC, V. No smoking, 2-night minimum weekends.*

ADAMS HILBORNE ☙

801 Vine St., Chattanooga 37403, tel. 423/265–5000, fax 423/265–5555, www.bbonline.com/tn/hilborne/

Calling Adams Edgeworth in Monteagle their "country house" and this their "city house," David and Wendy Adams have charted an ambitious course—giving two top properties their personal attention. With capable help in place at both inns, which are 45 minutes apart but in different time zones, the Adamses seem likely to pull it off.

Adams Hilborne is in an 1889 National Register Victorian Romanesque building that's the cornerstone of Chattanooga's Fort Wood Historic District. It was built for former mayor Edmond G. Watkins and for years was owned by businessman Edward G. Richmond. Inside are Tiffany windows, 16-ft coffered ceilings, arched doorways, and hand-carved moldings. A baby grand piano, marble fireplace, and English Sheridan and French Empire antiques contribute to the downstairs parlor's opulence. A ballroom, added by the Adamses, hosts large gatherings, while the Porch Cafe offers casual weekday dining and Sunday brunch.

Rooms have Old World charm, with a mix of English antiques and modern conveniences, such as private telephone lines with modem attachments, cable TV, and VCRs. The Adamses' sensitive restoration of the home involved borrowing space from the hallways to create private baths, without sacrificing room size. The Honeymoon, Anniversary, and Presidential suites are particularly luxurious. Guests eat breakfasts of quiche or French toast at a large common table under Tiffany windows in the formal dining room.

Downtown Chattanooga's many attractions, such as the Tennessee Aquarium and Hunter Museum, are a 5- to 10- minute drive away. ♣ *10 double rooms with baths. Restaurant. $100–$250; full breakfast. AE, MC, V. No smoking.*

BIG SPRING INN ☙

315 N. Main St., Greeneville 37745, tel. 423/638–2917

Walnut, maple, pecan, and magnolia trees shroud Big Spring Inn, a Greek Revival house built in 1905 as a wedding present. Since 1993, it has been owned by Oregonians Nancy and Marshall Ricker, who were a manager of a speech pathology department and an architect, respectively.

The expansive front porch has white wicker furniture. Inside are English and American antiques and good reproductions, purchased from one of many nearby antiques stores. The 1790 Hepplewhite dining table seats 12 for breakfast. The Rickers' taste runs to Laura Ashley prints and accessories, which complement the oak floors; beveled, leaded-glass windows; and original chandeliers. Six chimneys punctuate the unusual roof line, and metal shingles produce a soothing rhythm in the rain. A favorite bedroom is the Felice Noell Austin Room, light and airy with Victorian Rose wallpaper and a white wrought-iron bed. Its spacious bath has original black and white tiles and a large tub. The Hassie Hacker Doughty Room, the original master bedroom, has a fireplace with mantel, large bay window, king-size antique brass bed, and oversize bathroom.

The Rickers are gracious yet unobtrusive hosts and provide many special touches. At 7 AM a tea cart appears on the second-floor landing. Rooms have robes, Caswell-Massey toiletries, and homemade cookies, and croquet and other lawn games are played in the well-kept yard.

The inn is in historic Greeneville, a New England–style village settled in 1783, and is a short walk from the burial site and birthplace of President Andrew Johnson. The village is close to the brilliant fall colors of the Cherokee National Forest and the Great Smoky Mountains; white-water rafting; the Dixon-Williams Mansion, a pre–Civil War showplace that housed troops from both sides; and storytelling in Jonesborough—but it's far from the crowds and mini traffic jams that plague Gatlinburg. ♠ *2 double rooms and 2 singles with baths, 1 suite, 1 carriage house for long-term stays. Air-conditioning, cable TV, and phones in rooms; pool. $70–$86; full breakfast. AE, MC, V. No smoking. Closed Nov.–Mar.*

BLUE MOUNTAIN MIST COUNTRY INN ℘
1811 Pullen Rd., Sevierville 37862, tel. 423/428–2335 or 800/497–2335, fax 423/453–1720, www.bbonline.com/tn/bluemtnmist/

Blue Mountain Mist Country Inn sits high on a hill amid a 60-acre farm at the foot of the Great Smoky Mountains. A wraparound porch is well equipped with wicker furniture and rockers. In spring, flowers blossom in the yard; by summer, the pond, a short distance from the porch, is abloom with water lilies. Of course, fall, with its brilliant foliage, is the busiest season.

Owners Sarah and Norman Ball have deep roots in the area: Their parents grew up in the rugged terrain that is now Great Smoky Mountains National Park, so they know the history and geography of the area. Both were educators by profession—Sarah was an elementary school teacher, and Norm was principal at a vocational center.

Built in 1987, the inn is modeled after local, Victorian-style farmhouses. It's bright and airy, furnished with family heirlooms, quilts, and country crafts. Old photographs and paintings, by the Balls' daughter and a local artist, hang on the walls, and two rooms have claw-foot tubs. The Bridal Room's two-person whirlpool bath is in a turret, with windows on three sides. It shares a balcony with the Rainbow Falls Room, which has its own hot tub tucked behind a stained-glass partition, and with the LeConte Suite, the most spacious of the rooms. All bedrooms are carpeted.

Common areas upstairs and down have fireplaces and shiny hardwood floors. Each of the five small wooden cottages has a kitchen, fireplace, TV/VCR, porch, and large whirlpool tub.

The inn, near Little Pigeon River, is on a country road that serves as a back door into both the park and the Great Smoky Mountains Arts and Crafts Community, circumventing much of the local traffic. Pigeon Forge, known for its outlet shopping, is just 4 mi away. ♠ *12 double rooms with baths, 5 cottages. Meal service for groups, cable TV/VCR in parlor. $98–$140; full breakfast, evening dessert. MC, V. No smoking, 2-night minimum holidays and Oct., closed Dec. 23–25.*

BLUFF VIEW INN ℘
412 E. 2nd St., Chattanooga 37403, tel. 423/265–5033

Bluff View Inn consists of three striking, elegant homes that hug a bluff high above the Tennessee River. Owner Charles A. Portera, an oncologist, has spared no expense in restoring the 1927 Colonial-revival Mansion, or its two sister homes, the Victorian T. C. Thompson House and the Tudor-revival Maclellan House. Burgeoning among the narrow cobblestone streets are the lively restaurants, cafés, sculpture garden, and gallery of the Bluff View Arts District, developed by Charles and his wife, Mary.

Tastefully decorated bedrooms have whirlpool baths and fireplaces. Upstairs in the bustling, richly paneled Mansion, whose first two floors house the Back Inn Café, the Martin Room has a firm king-size bed and private balcony overlooking the river. The quieter Thompson House, built in 1908, has a wraparound porch with swings, perfect for people-watching. Rooms in the still quieter 1889 Maclellan House might feature a handcrafted African mahogany vanity, a pineapple post bed, or an antique secretary. In the parlor, large windows overlook a boccie ball court and the river below. Each home shares glossy hardwood floors and a mix of English, Queen Anne, and Chippendale antiques and fine reproductions. The art—glass, pottery and paintings—is switched often and is on sale at the River Gallery, down the street. Right outside the door lie a variety of dining options.

The Hunter Museum of American Art, one of Chattanooga's latest steps in its climb toward national recognition, is right next door. Within walking distance are the Tennessee Aquarium, IMAX theater, and the famed Walnut Street Bridge, one of the nation's oldest pedestrian bridges. ⚠ *13 double rooms with baths, 3 suites. Air-conditioning, cable TV, and phone in rooms. $100–$250; full breakfast. DC, MC, V. No smoking.*

BUCKHORN INN ❦

2140 Tudor Mtn. Rd., Gatlinburg 37738, tel. 423/436–4668, fax 423/436–5009, www.bbonline.com/tn/buckhorn/

The lobby of the Buckhorn Inn, on a wooded hillside at the edge of Great Smoky Mountains National Park, commands a good view of the local peaks, and several of the rooms have views as well. Designed to blend in with its surroundings, the 1938 inn has a rustic flavor. It sits in the middle of a lush, 35-acre estate surrounded by pine trees; comfortable fireside chairs in the sitting and dining rooms invite guests to relax with a glass of wine and look out on Mt. LeConte, one of the highest peaks in the Smokies. A Steinway grand piano rests in one niche of the lobby, and a library dubbed the "hikers' corner" is in another spot. With its well-loved, shabby decor, this inn appeals to the old-money crowd.

Rooms are small, carpeted, and furnished with simple, understated grace. With the feel of a tree house, the most interesting bedroom is in the inn's original water tower, where bath facilities are on one level and the bedroom is above. On all but the warmest days, the scent of wood smoke lingers in the air. In the dining room, breakfast and a six-course gourmet dinner are served by reservation on small tables. Four cottages and two relatively spacious guest houses are on the grounds, but the cottages are a cut below the inn rooms. Each has a fireplace, screened-in porch, and good view.

This secluded inn has its own ½-mi nature trail and fishing pond. It's 1 mi from the entrance to the national park and about 6 mi northeast of Gatlinburg and its myriad activities. It is in the midst of some 70 shops, galleries, and eateries of the Great Smoky Mountains Arts and Crafts Community. ⚠ *6 double rooms with baths, 4 cottages, 2 guest houses. Air-conditioning, cable TV in cottages. $105–$250; full breakfast. MC, V. Smoking in 2 cottages only, 2-night minimum holidays, weekends, and Oct.*

HALE SPRINGS INN 🐾
110 W. Main St., Rogersville 37857, tel. 423/272–5171

Overnighters here stay in the same rooms that hosted presidents James Polk, Andrew Jackson, and Andrew Johnson. Once an important stop in the nation's westward expansion, Rogersville is now off the beaten path, a Colonial-style burg known mostly for its tranquillity. The town is an hour from the Great Smoky Mountains National Park, and this Federal-style inn is right on its square.

Built of bricks between 1824 and 1825, this is the oldest continuously operated inn in the state. Bill Testerment is the quiet, solicitous manager. The lobby has a friendly, small-town quality about it, and rooms are decorated in the austere fashion of its frontier heyday. Original bent-pine floors and 12-ft ceilings remain, and every bedroom except one has a wood-burning fireplace. Central heating takes the chill off the spacious rooms, and the slight mustiness is overshadowed by the air of authenticity. There is a porch off the hallway on each of three levels; a small garden with a gazebo is next door.

In the restaurant on the first floor, waiters don Colonial-era outfits and some nights a fiddler serenades the room with renditions of the Tennessee Waltz and other folk tunes. The chef is a Culinary Institute of America graduate, and the menu contains inventive pesto variations, such as cranberry apple pesto on grilled pork. In the morning the restaurant becomes the breakfast room, where granola and breads are served.

Despite Rogersville's seclusion in the far corner of the state, the town comes alive with Civil War reenactments, historic walking tours, and an annual spring festival. The Smokies, about an hour away, are an easy day trip. ♤ *9 double rooms with baths. Restaurant, air-conditioning, cable TV in rooms. $40–$90; Continental breakfast. AE, MC, V. Closed Dec. 24–25.*

HIPPENSTEAL'S MOUNTAIN VIEW INN 🐾
Grassy Branch Rd. (Box 707), Gatlinburg 37738, tel. 423/436–5761 or 800/527–8110, fax 423/436–8917, www.hippensteal.com

This rambling, white, three-story New England–style inn is in the Great Smoky Mountains Arts and Crafts Community. From the broad-plank wraparound porch, which has rockers and ceiling fans, you can see Greenbriar Pinnacle, Mt. LeConte, and Mt. Harrison. The inn is owned by Lisa and Vern Hippensteal—he's one of the area's leading watercolorists, concentrating on local scenes.

Hairpin curves on a one-lane drive lead guests up to the secluded inn. The grand lobby has black and white tiles and hunter green walls; a fireplace blazes nearly all year. The great room is decorated with white wicker and English chintz. In the bedrooms, which have whirlpools and fireplaces, romance is on tap. The popular Victorian room has reading chairs and a private, spacious bath, whose whirlpool tub fits two. An upstairs library has an almost complete collection of *National Geographic* magazines.

The Hippensteals built the inn in 1990. They live on the property and divide their time between the inn's upkeep and Vern's art, which is showcased in two galleries in the Arts and Crafts Community.

Though the inn, off a gravel road, seems far from the madding crowds, Gatlinburg is still convenient. Between mid-November and the end of February, the spot provides an ideal vantage point for Gatlinburg's Million Dollar Smoky Mountain Lights, a popular display. Book well in advance for October, when Gatlinburg hosts a popular crafts fair. ♤ *9 double rooms with baths. Air-conditioning, ceil-*

ing fans, TV/VCR and phone jacks in rooms. $95–$130; full breakfast, evening dessert. AE, D, MC, V. No smoking, closed Dec. 24–25.

INN AT BLACKBERRY FARM
1471 W. Millers Cove Rd., Walland 37886, tel. 423/984–8166, www.blackberryhotel.com

What started as a private mountain estate, built in quiet Walland in the 1930s, has become a thriving inn that sets the standard for luxury among Tennessee B&Bs. Its 110 acres loll across the foothills of the Great Smokies, on green land full of blackberry brambles, two stocked ponds, trails, a fly-fishing stream, a cemetery, and a chapel, finally ending at the national park boundary.

A swarm of fresh-faced staff members in khaki uniforms attends each guest, whisking away cars, luggage, and every last care. Spacious common areas have an English country manor feel, thawed by American informality. Oriental rugs, English and French antiques, and handsome art are softened by overstuffed chairs in intimate groupings. Rooms continue the look, often with bright chintz or fireplaces, and always with feather beds and inspiring views. The Cotswold-style cottages are the crème de la crème, with wood-burning fireplaces, whirlpools, and loaded pantries. A flagstone veranda is a favorite place to breathe in the panorama.

But decor and land are only part of the story. Chef and inn director John Fleer, a Culinary Institute of America graduate, orchestrates a notable cuisine of such items as sweet tea-cured roast pork and mint-julep quail, served in a large dining room. Three gourmet meals a day are included in the room rate.

Owners Sandy and Kreis Beall bought the property in 1976 and reside in a renovated pre–Civil War farmhouse on the land. Sandy is CEO of Ruby Tuesday's; his wife, Kreis, devotes her time to Blackberry and is its chief decorator.

Should Adam or Eve deign to leave Paradise, Gatlinburg and Pigeon Forge are a half hour away, and the Great Smoky Mountains National Park is even closer.
♙ 23 double rooms with baths, 16 suites, 3-bedroom cottage, 2-bedroom gatehouse. Air-conditioning, terry-cloth robes, turndown service with chocolates; fireplaces, mini-refrigerators, whirlpools in some rooms; TV in game room; fly-fishing, trout and bass fishing, tennis, swimming, fitness facilities. $395–$1,745; full gourmet dinner and breakfast, picnic lunch, 24-hr access to snacks and beverages. AE, D, MC, V. No smoking, 2-night minimum (3-night minimum during Oct.).

RICHMONT INN
220 Winterberry La., Townsend 37882, tel. 423/448–6751

Designed for its mountain setting, this inn looks like a gray cantilevered barn. Opened in 1992 by Susan and Jim Hind, two former corporate executives eager to escape city life, this haven for couples is a short drive from postcard-perfect Cades Cove.

The architecture and decor combine the region's Appalachian culture with worldlier refinements: The main living room has beamed ceilings, broad-plank floors, and 18th-century English and American antiques; bookshelves flank the fireplace in the great room; and rustic twig furniture and rocking chairs on a stone patio provide a comfortable spot from which to take in the views.

One bedroom is paneled with old barn wood boards; others are bathed in light. Many have whirlpool tubs and private balconies. Old family photographs mingle with Impressionist paintings in the Stewart Room, and antiques throughout are a mix of formal and country. Most rooms are named after Appalachian pioneers and notables; a new floor honors Native American culture.

Guests are pampered here. Dessert is served at tables for two on china by the light of old-fashioned hurricane globes. Music is piped into rooms, or you can just enjoy the sound of gurgling water from the 40-ft cascade dropping into a pond. Stone paths meander through a replica Appalachian village, with a gift shop, chapel in the woods, frame house, and the Cove, a café made of 100-year-old barn wood, where guests can dine on light, healthy fare in the afternoon and early evening. ▲ *10 double rooms with baths. Air-conditioning, robes, coffeemakers, hair dryers; gift shop, café, chapel, nature trail. $95–$200; full breakfast, evening dessert. No credit cards. No smoking.*

TENNESSEE RIDGE INN ☙
507 Campbell Lead Rd., Gatlinburg 37738, tel. 423/436–4068, www.tn-ridge.com

On top of a mountain with a smashing view of 6,500-ft Mt. LeConte is this ultramodern chalet with walls of windows. Gatlinburg is only a five-minute, 1-mi drive below, but you feel far removed from its touristy kitsch. "Noise" here is the occasional drumming of a woodpecker getting breakfast. Nearby are trout fishing, hiking, rafting, and swimming.

Bob and Dar Hullander sampled inns around the world before opening their own. They've furnished it with a sleek mix of cool-colored modern pieces—primarily Asian—many picked up on their sojourns. Two spacious common areas have fireplaces and balconies; downstairs is a popular game room. Floor-to-ceiling windows seem to fill the rooms with the grand majesty of the mountains. Most rooms face south, the direction of the best views. Four bedrooms have stone wood-burning fireplaces, and all have private balconies, baths with two-person whirlpool tubs, and king-size beds. Honeymooners and anniversary celebrants seek out the inn because of the romance, privacy, and view of the mountains with the bright lights of the city glowing below.

Originally from Chattanooga, Bob is a retired navy pilot. The couple bought the home in 1991; they live in the house and devote their full-time energies to innkeeping. ▲ *7 double rooms with baths, 1 suite. Air-conditioning; pool. $98–$135; full deluxe breakfast. D, MC, V. No smoking, 2-night minimum weekends, 3-night minimum holidays.*

VON-BRYAN INN ☙
2402 Hatcher Mtn. Rd., Sevierville 37862, tel. 423/453–9832 or 800/633–1459, fax 423/428–8634, www.bbonline.com/tn/vonbryan/

The Von-Bryan Inn commands one of the best mountaintop views in the Smokies. A crooked road climbs to the inn, which is on a knoll with a 360-degree vista of the surrounding mountains. Morning mist blankets the patchwork farmlands in Wears Valley below and the wooded dales beyond.

Built in 1986, the home has wood surfaces and soaring, cathedral-like ceilings. Bright skylights filter in the sunshine, and big windows frame the view. Every room, furnished in a blend of traditional and country antiques, has a view. The honeymoon suite—one of two with a whirlpool—is appropriately decorated in passionate red hues. A tri-level suite has a canopy bed draped with silk wisteria on the second floor, a bath with a steam shower on the first, and a reading loft on the third. In winter a fireplace blazes in the downstairs living room. In summer, the pool and its nearby hot tub are good places to bask in the sun. The inn's telescope allows for a closer look at distant sights. The log-cabin chalet, designed for families, has a full kitchen and a television room as well as a living room with a fireplace, three bedrooms (one with a balcony), and two bathrooms.

Jo Ann and D. J. Vaughn opened the Von-Bryan after traveling extensively in surrounding states to research country inns. Jo Ann operated a telephone-answering service in Knoxville, and D. J. is a retired corporate accountant. They are quiet, amicable people who offer plentiful advice on the area. D. J., who enjoys woodworking, made many of the pendulum clocks in the house and some of the furniture.

Gatlinburg, Pigeon Forge, Dollywood, and the entrance to the national park are all within 30 minutes. ▲ *5 double rooms with baths, 1 suite, 1 chalet. Air-conditioning, TV in living room. $90–$200; full breakfast. AE, D, MC, V. No smoking, 2-night minimum on holidays and weekends and in chalet.*

WAYSIDE MANOR ☙

4009 Old Knoxville Hwy. 33, Rockford 37853, tel. 423/970–4823 or 800/675–4823, fax 423/981–1890, www.the-mid-west-web.com/wayside.htm

Mother-and-daughter team Becky and Abby Koella have made the most of their redbrick, tile-roofed, turn-of-the-century estate, on 8 acres just outside Knoxville. They cater to both the individual traveler and corporate and church groups with elaborate meals and attention to detail. Becky, who is retired from public relations, grew up in the Smokies. With a little encouragement, she charms guests with lively tales of mountain life.

Victorian lampposts and elaborate wrought-iron benches punctuate the grand lawn, where croquet is often played. A screened porch dominates the front of the house, while the side yard has lighted tennis, basketball, and volleyball courts. Badminton rackets, shuffleboard, bikes, a large pool, and a hot tub are available as well, and there's fishing, horseback riding, and golf nearby. Baby-sitting is also offered.

Inside, the plushly carpeted house has high ceilings and French doors. Flower arrangements—some fresh, some artificial—and old quilts are the centerpieces of an eclectic style mixing modern with antique. That nearly every couch opens to a bed shows Becky's great talent for accommodating crowds. The Presidential suite has kitchen facilities and its own private deck and entrance. Like two other rooms, it has an in-room double whirlpool.

Though Rockford is somewhat beyond the orbit of tourism surrounding Gatlinburg, the vacationer's mecca is accessible by car within an hour. Rockford is a good midway point between the dual destinations of Gatlinburg and Knoxville. ▲ *4 double rooms with baths, 1 2-bedroom cottage, 1 5-bedroom lodge. Air-conditioning, TV/VCR and phone in rooms, whirlpool in some rooms, business center; pool. $89–$199; full breakfast. AE, D, MC, V. No smoking.*

MIDDLE TENNESSEE

The sprawling city of Nashville (population more than 1 million) extends over eight counties in the middle Tennessee heartland, a pocket of rolling Cumberland Mountains foothills and bluegrass meadows that's one of the state's richest farming areas. Its impressive skyline, dotted with high-rise office towers, is a vivid reminder that it has been a long time indeed since Christmas Day 1779, when James Robertson and a small, shivering party of pioneers began to build a crude wooden fortress and palisades on the Cumberland River's west bank.

Heralded as the world's Country Music Capital and Music City USA, it also proudly calls itself the Athens of the South. The labels fit, and Nashville is one of the middle South's liveliest cities. Its role as a cultural leader is enhanced by an impressive performing arts center and the many colleges, universities, and medical and technical schools located here, most notably Vanderbilt University.

A rich southern heritage is evident in the surrounding countryside, where highways meander through farmland punctuated by small towns. Lynchburg, home of the Jack Daniel Distillery, is among the most famous of the outlying communities. Franklin, a restored 19th-century town that historian Shelby Foote calls one of the top three Civil War sites, has excellent antiques shops and art galleries. Columbia, site of the family home of President James K. Polk, is famous for its antebellum architecture. West of Nashville, Clarksville has its own vineyards and winery as well as several sites memorializing the colorful past of the Old South, from its frontier heyday to its Civil War pain.

PLACES TO GO, SIGHTS TO SEE

Belle Meade Plantation (5025 Harding Rd., Nashville, tel. 615/356–0501). One of the grand old houses of Nashville, this Greek Revival home is on a 5,300-acre estate near Centennial Park off West End Avenue. It is known for its Thoroughbred horse stables and a Victorian carriage museum.

Cheekwood (1200 Forest Park Dr., Nashville, tel. 615/356–8000). This verdant estate and Georgian-style mansion, built in the 1920s, is now a fine arts center. It's surrounded by the 55-acre *Tennessee Botanical Gardens*, a showcase picnic ground graced by roses, herbs, and southern wildflowers.

Country Music Hall of Fame (4 Music Square E, Nashville, tel. 615/256–1639). The definitive collection of country music memorabilia is housed here—from Elvis Presley's "solid gold" Cadillac to Kris Kristofferson's songwriting scribbles and Marty Robbins's six-string guitar. The museum ticket is also good for admission to nearby *Studio B*, where Dolly Parton, Elvis, and Roy Acuff—among many others—recorded classic hits.

The District (Nashville). Two blocks off the Cumberland River in the Church Street vicinity is one of the country's best-preserved rows of 19th-century commercial buildings, now transformed into some of the town's best restaurants, nightclubs, and boutiques.

The Hermitage (4580 Rachel's La., 12 mi east of Nashville, tel. 615/889–2941), built by President Andrew Jackson for his beloved wife, Rachel, is in a bucolic setting just beyond the urban sprawl of Nashville. It is the perfect place for a stroll beneath huge live oaks.

Jack Daniel Distillery (¼ mi northeast of Lynchburg on Rte. 55, tel. 931/759–4221). Demonstrations on the art of making Tennessee sour-mash whiskey are given on daily tours.

Opryland USA (2802 Opryland Dr., Nashville, tel. 615/889–6611). The musical-show park offers performances of 12 different musicals and two dozen rides as well as restaurants and shops. Opryland is also home to the Grand Ole Opry House.

The Parthenon (off West End Ave., Centennial Park, Nashville, tel. 615/862–8431). This exact replica of the Grecian original includes a gigantic statue of the goddess Athena and an art museum. Fans of Robert Altman's *Nashville* will recognize it as the site of the film's final scene.

RESTAURANTS

In Nashville, the **Wild Boar** (2014 Broadway, tel. 615/329–1313) offers fine Continental fare and wild game in a setting resembling an old English hunting lodge. The **Elliston Place Soda Shop** (21st Ave. and Elliston Pl., tel. 615/327–1090), an old-fashioned meat-and-three (so named because you choose one meat entrée and three vegetables from the menu) near Vanderbilt, serves wonderful diner-style lunches and malts big enough for two. The **Loveless Café** (8400 Rte. 100, tel. 615/646–9700) continues to draw lovers of southern food to its almost rural setting for a menu rich in local cuisine; reservations are advised. The **Bluebird Cafe** (4104 Hillsboro Rd., tel. 615/383–1461) is famed for its role in launching songwriters' careers (Garth Brooks was discovered here) and for good American fare.

At **Miss Mary Bobo's Boarding House** (Main St., tel. 931/759–7394), an 1867 white-frame home in Lynchburg, chatty hostesses serve a midday all-you-can-eat dinner of country fare every day but Sunday to a usually talkative crowd. Reservations are required, or you can wait and hope for a cancellation.

SHOPPING

There's no question that Nashville is the top destination for malls in Middle Tennessee. The **Mall at Green Hills** (2126 Abbott Martin Rd., Nashville, tel. 615/298–5478) houses all the stalwart favorites, such as Banana Republic and Body Shop. The **Outlet Village of Lebanon** (Hwy. 231, Lebanon, tel. 615/444–0433) is a long chain of designer and specialty stores that sprawl across the landscape 25 mi east of Nashville.

Historic Franklin has a well-deserved reputation as an antiques lover's candy store. Window-shoppers can't go wrong on Main Street, where stores such as **Strange Things** (418 Main St., Franklin, tel. 615/790–0720) and **Yarrow Acres** (434 Main St., Franklin, tel. 615/591–7090) are back to back with at least a dozen other antiques shops.

VISITOR INFORMATION

Nashville Convention & Visitors Bureau (161 4th Ave. N, Nashville 37219, tel. 615/259–4700). **Nashville Tourist Information Center** (I–40, Exit 209B, in the Nashville Arena Tower, Nashville 37203, tel. 615/259–4747). **Tennessee Department of Tourist Development** (Box 23170, Nashville 37202, tel. 615/ 741–2158) is good for information on outlying areas.

RESERVATION SERVICE

Tennessee Bed & Breakfast Innkeepers Association (Box 120428, Nashville 37212, tel. 615/321–5482 or 800/820–8144).

BLUEBERRY HILL BED AND BREAKFAST ☞

4591 Peytonsville Rd., Franklin 37064, tel. 615/791–9947, 800/400–4923 (PIN 7929), www.bbonline.com/tn/blueberry/

This Federal-style home just outside Franklin shares its steep hill perch with prolific blueberry bushes. Sweeping below are the soft valleys and hills that were 19th-century plantation country.

The white house, built in 1980 with a 1993 addition, clings unobtrusively to its hill. Small, intricate gardens shelter stone paths, wildflowers, and a goldfish pond. Two dogs keep a frisky vigil on the deck and screened-in porch. The house's decor mixes masculine Federalist antiques with comfortable couches that Joan and Art Reesmans' two fat cats lounge on. In the dining room, an L.L. Bean wall hanging depicts a bear; beneath it, stuffed bears throw a mock tea party at a child-size table. Blueberry print dishes and napkins also come from L.L. Bean. Baskets hang over a 7-ft, open-hearth decorative fireplace.

The two rooms have carpets and fireplaces and feel modern despite their craftsy touches. In the Blue Room, walls are patterned with heart-shape floral stencil and pastel Impressionist prints. Both rooms have four-poster beds with country quilts and cross-stitch canopies. They are close to the kitchen and the sounds of the Reesmans' industry.

In the morning, by candlelight, guests are sure to find their thrill over a veritable hill of blueberry pancakes; Art doctors his favorite recipe with twice the sugar. Add a plate of sausage, sticky coffee cake, and huge mugs of fresh coffee, and your arteries blissfully clog.

Joan and Art are a funny, forthcoming couple who stay out of guests' way. Joan, a retired nursing instructor, hails from Minneapolis, while Art, retired from a geology professorship at Vanderbilt, grew up in New Jersey.

Historic Franklin, with its Civil War landmarks and plantation tours, is within shouting distance. A half-hour drive, tops, and guests are in downtown Nashville. ♠ *2 double rooms with baths. Air-conditioning, TV/VCRs, terry-cloth robes. $70–$80; full breakfast. D, MC, V. No smoking.*

CHIGGER RIDGE ☜

1060 Hwy. 70 W (Box 349), Pegram 37143, tel. 615/952–4354,
www.bbonline.com/tn/chigger/

Don't be put off by the name. This secluded cedar-log home is as much a retreat as a bed-and-breakfast, sitting on 67 acres in woodsy Cheatham County, outside Nashville. Its 5 mi of trails meander through thick maples, hickories, and dogwoods, hidden valleys, and a 25-ft waterfall, which the wayfarer shares with wild turkey, deer, rabbits, and blackberry brambles.

Blond heart pine floors, hand-chiseled cedar log walls, and skylights lend the airy main house, built in 1989, a rustic western chic. The roomy and casual B&B has modern couches and chairs with chunky American primitive antiques, such as a pie safe from the early 1800s. In the tall vaulted dining room, guests eat robust breakfasts, featuring such fare as two-layer egg soufflés with cheese sauce or hash-brown casseroles, which proprietor Jane Crisp prepares on a reproduction wood-burning stove. A stone fireplace warms the two-story common room, whose balcony leads to two bedrooms.

The vaulted bedrooms have extra-plush carpets. One room's white iron bed frame is coupled with wicker furniture; another has a reproduction four-poster canopy brass bed. A three-bedroom, more sparsely furnished guest house sits on the hill and sleeps up to 10. Outside, there are wraparound decks and a large gazebo that holds 60.

Chigger Ridge is the name Jane Crisp and her husband, Doug O'Rear, affectionately gave the property after an ill-fated trek without insect repellent—which they now supply to guests. Jane is relaxed and unassuming, a semiretired attorney who had been on the hunt for a cabin in the woods after reading Thoreau's _Walden_. Doug works full time as a financial planner.

Nearby are Harpeth River with its fishing and canoeing excursions, the Narrows of Harpeth State Recreation Area, Natchez Trace Parkway, and Cheatham Wildlife Preserve. ⚐ _2 double rooms with baths, 1 3-bedroom guest house. Air-conditioning, phones in rooms, TV/VCRs in common rooms. $85–$250; full breakfast. MC, V. No smoking._

FALCON MANOR BED & BREAKFAST ☜

2645 Faulkner Springs Rd., McMinnville 37110, tel. 931/668–4444,
fax 931/815–4444, FalconManor.com

McMinnville offers an out-of-the-way base at the center of the Nashville-Chattanooga-Knoxville triangle. Twenty-five miles east of I–24's Manchester Exit 111 or 33 mi south of I–40's Smithville exit is Falcon Manor, an historic Victorian mansion lovingly cared for by George and Charlien McGlothin. For nature lovers, Rock Island State Park is 10 mi away; Fall Creek Falls, 35 mi; Old Stone Fort, 25 mi; and Savage Gulf State Natural Area, 15 mi away.

The house was built in 1896 by entrepreneur Clay Faulkner for his wife, Mary. Faulkner had a woolen mill nearby and produced "gorilla pants," so labeled because their strength kept even a gorilla from tearing them apart. Strength is evident here, too, as the house sits on a 17-ft concrete foundation with walls three bricks thick. From 1946 to 1968, the property was used as a hospital and nursing home. Attempts to demolish it in 1968 were unsuccessful. George McGlothin bought the house at auction in 1989 (sight unseen by Charlien), but by then, it required massive renovation. Charlien left her job at NASA and joined George in four years of restoration; they estimate they did most of the work themselves.

Guests will find rooms filled with massive Victoriana antiques. Red velvet settees and chairs, with marble-top tables, fill the common living room. Bedrooms have an almost overpowering amount of authenticity. What is called the Upstairs Suite has three bedrooms and one bathroom; two people can rent it for $105, four people for $170, and six people for $225. For group tours, George and Charlien dress in Victorian costumes.

Full breakfasts sometimes include New Orleans specialties like beignets. A Victorian Gift Shop offers stationery, potpourri, mugs, calendars, and a host of other items embellished with roses and other Victorian emblems. The carriage house has been converted into a restaurant with red walls, white medallion light fixtures, and a tile floor. ♨ *3 double rooms with baths, 1 3-bedroom suite. Restaurant, cable TV in common areas. $105; full breakfast. MC, V. No smoking.*

HACHLAND HILL DINING INN ☙
1601 Madison St., Clarksville 37043, tel. 931/647–4084, fax 931/552–3454,
www.eventsandmeetings.com/

This inn is a treat for the traveler in search of a rustic evening beside a fireplace. Forty-five minutes north of Nashville in rural Clarksville, it is surrounded by an 80-acre park full of raccoon and deer. Trails wander into the woods, and guests wake up to the sound of birds.

Phila Hach is a worldly woman who was a flight attendant before founding the inn in 1955 with her late husband, Adolph Hach. She appears on local television shows and is the author of 14 cookbooks. The dinner menu is laden with fried chicken, Tennessee country ham, surprises like Moroccan leg of lamb, and a decadent plantation breakfast. Phila's specialty is catering large events; the grand ballroom seats 300.

Phila designed the inn after Federal-style Cape Cod homes, and on winter nights, soup bubbles in a pot dangling on a fireplace crane. The bedrooms are neat and comfortable, with historic touches: One has a spool bed with a wedding-ring quilt, and many furnishings are Early American. Some have Germanic touches, heirlooms from Phila's North Sea ancestors. The mantel keystone over the main fireplace comes from the long-since-demolished local tobacco exchange (Adolph was a tobacconist). A 150-year-old, 2,000-piece "postage-stamp" quilt hangs from a wall. The Hachs traveled widely, and items from their sojourns are in evidence: a Japanese print here, a Swiss vase there.

The 1790 House is a log cabin transformed into a dormitory space for those taking part in a wedding or reunion. Out back sits a pair of cabins, perfect for either romantic solitude or family lodging. Each cabin offers modern bathrooms and tranquillity, with nonringing phones on which guests can make but not receive calls. The cabins are on a wide, shady terrace, where warm-weather cookouts are held, overlooking a wooded ravine. ♨ *7 double rooms with baths, 3 cabins. Air-conditioning, TV/VCR in 3 rooms, nonringing phones in rooms, office facilities. $75–$160. AE, MC, V. Pets by prior arrangement, closed Dec. 24–25.*

INN AT EVINS MILL ☙
1535 Evins Mill Rd. (Box 606), Smithville 37166, tel. 615/597–2088,
fax 615/597–2090

Smithville's 39-acre Evins Mill has a quiet, verdant setting for a warm and intimate hideaway. Originally a refuge for state senator Edgar Evins and his son, Congressman Joe L. Evins, the mountain getaway and its 4,600-square-ft lodge later became a retreat for the William Cochran family. It opened to the public in 1994, with innkeeper William Cochran Jr. at the helm.

Three four-bedroom cottages bring the inn's room count to 14. Request one of the top-floor rooms in the new lodges and you'll have a cantilevered deck that puts you in the treetops. Hand-hewn cedar log walls give the lodge a rustic, almost western style. A dramatic headboard made of twigs and branches in one room repeats this theme, as do the balcony's full log handrails and cedar rockers. Cottages are perfect solitary retreats, with loft beds and desks overlooking wooded views.

The working gristmill on the property can demonstrate corn grinding with advance request. Meeting rooms are in the mill and in the main house, which also has the Stone Room, where you can find premium cigars, darts, and a TV/VCR. A large pond and waterfall add to the pristine landscape.

Special theme weekends, usually coinciding with holidays, may include guest speakers, wine tastings, or special menus. Set-menu dinners are available at other times by reservation. ♨ *14 double rooms with baths. Air-conditioning, TV in lodge's living room. $120–$170 includes breakfast and dinner, $135–$200 includes 3 meals; holiday weekends $155–$410, including 2 nights and 5 meals. AE, D, MC, V.*

LYNCHBURG BED & BREAKFAST ☜
Mechanic St. (Box 34), Lynchburg 37352, tel. 931/759–7158

This cozy, centrally located inn is near the famous Jack Daniel Distillery in Lynchburg, a speck of a town (population 361) established in 1871 in the farmland of south-central Tennessee. The proprietors, Virginia and Mike Tipps, opened it in 1985 and welcome families with children. Longtime area residents—Virginia is a former mail clerk and Mike is in quality control at the distillery—they know what to see and do around Lynchburg.

The 1877 two-story house (built for Moore County's first sheriff) is decorated with country antiques and crafts. Both of its slightly cramped bedrooms, which have antique walnut washstands, are up a narrow staircase and can be combined as a suite. Rooms have sloped ceilings and old wide-paneled wood doors with porcelain knobs. Their simple decor is less picturesque than functional; they offer location as their primary attraction. Virginia sets a tray with a Continental breakfast by each guest's door in the morning. Meals typically include homemade muffins, such as her original country sausage muffins.

From a balcony on the landing is a clear view of the distillery's warehouses, where its famous whiskey is aged. The distillery has tours daily, and visitors won't want to miss midday dinner at nearby Miss Mary Bobo's Boarding House (*see* Restaurants, *above*). The tiny town square, a block away, has a handful of antiques and arts-and-crafts shops centered on a monument to Confederate soldiers. ♨ *2 double rooms with baths. Air-conditioning, cable TV in rooms. $60–$68; Continental breakfast. MC, V.*

OLD COWAN PLANTATION ☜
126 Old Boonshill Rd., Fayetteville 37334, tel. 931/433–0225

The Old Cowan Plantation captures some of the Old South in an 1886 Colonial home beside a country road. Hostess Betty Johnson's ambition was to open an antiques shop in the house, but after deciding there was a glut of such businesses in nearby Fayetteville, she turned the house into an inn. Though it was modernized in 1985, the place clings tenaciously to its farmhouse ambience.

Betty's hobbies show up around the house in various handicrafts, quilts, and cross-stitch items.

One upstairs room has a brass bed and a spacious bath and shower; the other, which has twin beds, uses a bath downstairs with a pedestal tub. The home's original staircase leads to a narrow landing with an antique pie safe that now serves as a linen closet. Breakfast is served at a lace-covered table with a view of the neighboring pasture.

The inn's rural setting is one of its biggest draws. In spring, the yard is full of wildflowers, and a rose garden blooms in June. Guests usually gravitate to the front-porch rocking chairs, particularly in the early evening, when deer graze across the road and sometimes even wander into the yard.

The Old Cowan Plantation is 2 mi from Fayetteville's town square and 15 mi from the Jack Daniel Distillery in Lynchburg. It is 30 mi from the Space and Rocket Center in Huntsville, Alabama, where you can tour NASA labs and space-shuttle test sites and roam through a park full of rockets, visit the center's hands-on museum, or view an Omnimax space film. Fifteen minutes away is Tims Ford Lake, with waterskiing in summer and fishing year-round. ♨ *2 double rooms with baths, 1 apartment. Air-conditioning, TV in common area. $48; Continental breakfast. No credit cards. No smoking, pets in fenced backyard only.*

PEACOCK HILL COUNTRY INN ☞

6994 Giles Hill Rd., College Grove 37046, tel. 615/368–7727 or 800/327–6663, www.bbonline.com/tn/peacock/

Thirty-five peacocks bob among these hills, neck and neck with cows and horses, on the 650-acre working farm and inn in sleepy College Grove, south of Franklin. The restored 1850s sprawling farmhouse bears little witness to its age. It rises pristine and white from a hilltop garden of hydrangeas and sunflowers, two neighboring log cabins—a renovated smokehouse and grainery—recalling its rustic origins.

Original hand-hewn cedar logs make an impressive entry in the main house. Stone fireplaces tower in the common rooms branching off on either side. Overstuffed couches and chairs, in bright florals and plaids, lend the rooms a cheerful air. Well-placed antiques, such as a vegetable bin turned coffee table, coexist with modern-day luxuries. Rooms have king-size beds, temperature controls, and possibly the finest bathrooms in the state, with massive whirlpools and separate European showers.

In the two-story Grainery Suite, a red toile armchair faces a fireplace; upstairs is a cozy sitting room with a stocked kitchenette. Down the road, the McCall House, another restored mid-1800s farmhouse, has large rooms with stupendous bathrooms. In the Grand Suite, the standing shower is of Italian tile, with rain-shower fixtures overhead and on the sides.

The sunny dining room's fireside tables host full—but healthy—breakfasts like German pancakes, as well as gourmet dinners at extra cost, with two days' notice.

Walter and Anita Ogilvie returned home to their family property in College Grove from Indiana, after Walter retired from a career in banking. Walter manages their working farm and cattle ranch. They live in the converted carriage house out back, with their outgoing sheepdog, Abby.

Murfreesboro, 30 minutes away, and picturesque Franklin are havens for both antiques lovers and Civil War buffs. Nashville is an hour away. ♨ *7 double rooms* *with baths, 1 suite, 2 cabins. Air-conditioning, terry-cloth robes; TV in suite, cabins, den; fitness facilities. $125–$225; full breakfast, serve-yourself snacks and beverages. Dinners $20, box lunches $10, with 48 hrs' notice. AE, D, MC, V. No smoking, pets by prior arrangement board in barn.*

SIMPLY SOUTHERN 🐚

211 North Tennessee Blvd., Murfreesboro 37130, tel. 615/896–4998, www.bbonline.com/tn/simplysouthern/

This stately, redbrick, 1907 four-square home rivals any in Murfreesboro's historic district. It sits on one of the town's main thoroughfares, right across from the endless lawn of Middle Tennessee State University's campus and the kindred architecture of the college president's house.

The myriad ways in which Simply Southern lives up to its name begin outside, on the wide, cushily furnished wraparound porch. A backyard patio has a slate tile path that leads to a small garden pond near flowering chives and other prolific herbs. Inside, 12-ft ceilings downstairs have thick poplar beams in the original extra-dark finish. Abundant East Lake Victorian antiques and burgundy and green fabrics give the rooms a lush though tasteful atmosphere. Magnolia blossoms are the dining table's centerpiece.

Rooms are carpeted, formal, and floral, many with original fireplaces (now purely decorative) and all with antiques and private baths. Deep tubs, some claw-foot, retain old fixtures. The upstairs suite feels like a one-bedroom apartment, with its own sitting room and kitchenette. There are several common areas: two spacious parlors downstairs, one cozier area upstairs, and a large basement rec room with a pool table, vintage Coke machine, 1910 player piano, and karaoke.

Georgia and Carl Buckner are gracious hosts. They even provide a trunk full of stuffed bears on the landing, should anyone need a sleeping companion. They had planned for 15 years to find an old home and open a B&B, before they retired from being, respectively, a retailer and high school principal.

Simply Southern is a perfect destination for those visiting MTSU. Murfreesboro has the Stones River National Battlefield and other Civil War sites. Downtown Nashville is a 30-minute drive, as is the airport. ♦ *4 double rooms with baths, 1 suite. Air-conditioning; cable TV/VCR in some rooms and rec room. $80–$140; full breakfast. D, MC, V. No smoking.*

WEST TENNESSEE

The mighty Mississippi River defines the western boundary of Tennessee, rolling through the fertile plain of the Delta and past the "cradle of the blues" on its way to the sea. Stretching east and north from Memphis, the western plains where cotton was king are interspersed with hardwood forests, wildlife refuges, and state parks. Outdoor types flock to the region's rivers and lakes, including Kentucky Lake, the second-largest artificial lake in the world, on the Kentucky border.

You can hear stories of folk heroes Davy Crockett and Casey Jones, explore the Civil War battlefield at Shiloh National Military Park, and visit the late Alex Haley's hometown of Henning.

The culture of the Mississippi Delta converges in Memphis, a city with a uniquely American music heritage that is well preserved today behind the gates of Elvis's beloved Graceland, on stage at the Beale Street nightclubs, and in the oft-told tales of rockers like Elvis Presley and Jerry Lee Lewis, whose careers were launched at tiny Sun Studio.

The city celebrates the mighty Mississippi with an entertainment park on Mud Island, and the Pyramid, beside the Hernando DeSoto Bridge, is actually the world's third-largest pyramid. The Memphis in May International Festival, scheduled before the arrival of summer's heat and humidity, pays tribute to the city's music and features the open-air World Championship Barbecue Cooking Contest. Memphis honors the civil rights movement and Martin Luther King Jr. at the National Civil Rights Museum.

 PLACES TO GO, SIGHTS TO SEE

Alex Haley State Historic Site Museum (Haley St., Henning, tel. 901/738–2240). The boyhood home and burial site of the Pulitzer Prize–winning author of *Roots* is in this charming little river town 50 mi north of Memphis via U.S. 51.
Beale Street Historic District. A restored row of nightclubs and shops pays homage to the Memphis blues. Highlights include the *W. C. Handy Memphis Home and Museum* (352 Beale St., tel. 901/396–3914); the *Old Daisy Theatre* (329 Beale St., tel. 901/525–1631), which was built in 1918 and shows silent short films and musical acts; and any of 10 nightclubs, whose acts are advertised in the *Memphis Commercial Appeal*. The *Rum Boogie Café* (182 Beale St., tel. 901/524–0150)

has one of the best house bands in the city, and *B. B. King's Blues Club* (147 Beale St., tel. 901/527–5464) features appearances by its famous eponym.

The **Casey Jones Home and Railroad Museum** (U.S. 45 Bypass and I–40, Jackson, tel. 901/668–1222), adjacent to an old-fashioned ice cream shop, houses an excellent collection of train memorabilia.

Chucalissa Archaeological Museum (1987 Indian Village Dr., Memphis, tel. 901/785–3160). At this peaceful, thought-provoking site about 10 mi southwest of downtown, a simple river culture that existed from 1000 to 1500 is immortalized. The 4-acre reconstruction is operated by the University of Memphis, and on-site archaeological excavations are often conducted during the summer. Outside, skilled Choctaw artisans fashion jewelry, weapons, and pottery. An annual August powwow is a highlight.

Dixon Gallery and Gardens (4339 Park Ave., Memphis, tel. 901/761–5250) blends art with nature, displaying French and post-Impressionist paintings and 18th-century Germanic porcelain in a museum surrounded by 17 acres of flowers.

Graceland (3717 Elvis Presley Blvd., Memphis, tel. 901/332–3322 or 800/238–2000), the city's most popular attraction, offers a glitzy and sometimes poignant look at Elvis Presley, who lived and is buried here and whose memory generates a sizable souvenir industry for a row of shops across the street.

The **Hunt-Phelan Home Foundation** (533 Beale St., Memphis, tel. 901/344–3166) is a restored antebellum home that offers guided tours. Its pre–Civil War opulence is strangely incongruent on the grittier end of Beale, where it's located. It offers a glimpse at the past well worth taking.

Mud Island. The 53-acre Memphis park is accessible by walkway, boat, or monorail (boat terminal, 125 Front St., tel. 901/576–7241). Attractions include a 5,000-seat amphitheater; the 18-gallery *Mississippi River Museum*; and the exceptional *River Walk*, a scale model of the great river five blocks long, tracing every bend of the Mississippi on its journey from Minnesota to the Gulf of Mexico.

National Civil Rights Museum (450 Mulberry St., Memphis, tel. 901/521–9699). The civil rights struggle of the 1950s and '60s is documented in the former Lorraine Motel, where the Rev. Martin Luther King Jr. was assassinated in 1968.

National Ornamental Metal Museum (374 Metal Museum Dr., Memphis, tel. 901/774–6380). This one-of-a-kind place is devoted to preserving the art of metalworking, from gold to iron. Exhibits include a working blacksmith's forge.

Peabody Hotel (149 Union Ave., Memphis, tel. 901/529–4175 or 800/732–2639). This Memphis treasure is worth a trip just to see the resplendent lobby, where the hotel's famous ducks spend the day.

The **Pyramid** (on the Mississippi River at I–40, Memphis, tel. 901/521–9675). The 32-story stainless-steel structure has a 20,000-seat sports arena. Tours are available between scheduled events.

Shiloh National Military Park (off U.S. 64 on Rte. 22, tel. 901/689–5696). A beautiful country setting 100 mi east of Memphis is a grim reminder of the horrific Civil War battle and of the 4,000 soldiers buried here.

Sun Studio (706 Union Ave., Memphis, tel. 901/521–0664), a working recording studio by night, offers daytime tours on the hour through the famous spot where Elvis Presley, Carl Perkins, Johnny Cash, and Jerry Lee Lewis made their first records. The adjacent *Sun Studio Café* sells burgers and chili.

RESTAURANTS

In Memphis, **Landry's Seafood House** (263 Wagner Pl., tel. 901/526–1966), on the riverfront, draws a loyal following for its seafood. In the Peabody Hotel (149 Union Ave.), **Chez Philippe** (tel. 901/529–4188) is worth the splurge, or for sandwiches and pastries made daily, try **Café Espresso** (tel. 901/529–4164). **Char-**

lie **Vergos' Rendezvous** (General Washburn Alley, tel. 901/523–2746), famous for its pork barbecue, is a real Memphis institution, as is **Corky's Bar-B-Q** (5259 Poplar Ave., tel. 901/685–9744), the place to do some down-and-dirty barbecue eating. **La Tourelle** (Overton Sq., 2146 Monroe Ave., tel. 901/726–5771), in an elegant turn-of-the-century bungalow, is one of the best French restaurants in the area. **Elvis Presley's Memphis** (126 Beale St., tel. 901/527–6900) has gained notoriety for its Sunday gospel brunch, fried peanut butter sandwiches, and other delights from the King's favorite recipes.

SHOPPING

West Tennessee's shopping revolves around Memphis. **Wolfchase Galleria** (2760 N. Germantown Pkwy., tel. 901/372–9409), 18 mi east of downtown Memphis, is one of the largest malls in the country. **Oak Court Mall** (4465 Poplar Ave., tel. 901/682–8928) has 70 specialty stores and two department stores. **Belz Factory Outlet Mall** (3536 Canada Rd., Lakeland, Exit 20 off I–40, tel. 901/386–3180), 20 mi east of downtown Memphis, has 50 stores including Van Heusen and Bugle Boy.

Memphis's midtown area, particularly along Central Avenue, is peppered with antiques stores. Two of note are **Palladio Antiques** (2169 Central Ave., tel. 901/276–3808), which also has a café, and **Antique Mall Inc.** (2151 Central Ave., tel. 901/274–8563), which represents about 100 dealers with bargains on jewelry, books, china, and furnishings.

VISITOR INFORMATION

Memphis Convention and Visitors Bureau (47 Union Ave., Memphis 38103, tel. 901/543–5333). **Memphis Visitors Information Center** (119 Riverside Dr., Memphis 38103, tel. 901/543–5333). **Tennessee Department of Tourist Development** (Box 23170, Nashville 37202, tel. 615/741–2158).

RESERVATION SERVICES

Bed & Breakfast Memphis Reservation Service (Box 41621, Memphis 38174, tel. 901/327–6129). **Tennessee Bed & Breakfast Innkeepers Association** (Box 120428, Nashville 37212, tel. 615/321–5482 or 800/820–8144).

BONNE TERRE COUNTRY INN & CAFE 🕊

*4715 Church Rd. W, Nesbit 38651, tel. 601/781–5100, fax 601/781–5466,
www.bonneterre.com*

Pecan groves, two lakes, cormorants, and wildflower gardens cover this country inn's 100 gently rolling acres 25 minutes from Memphis near the Mississippi state line.

White walls, green shutters, and wraparound porches give the 1996 Greek Revival inn the air of a small plantation. A conference center and café flank the building's sides and share a view of a 5-acre lake, decks, blue tile-trimmed pool, and organic gardens used in the inn's cuisine. Roses and wysteria climb the trellis-covered walkway that links inn and café. Bailey, a glossy Golden Retriever, lounges on the café's porch.

Red-oak floors and Colonial moldings with rosettes offer all the trappings of bygone embellishments. English, French, and German antiques span the centuries. Guests mingle in the study around Brie, fruit, and a decanter of sherry. Rooms have porches or balconies, marble jetted tubs beneath stained-glass windows, and feather beds; some have gas fireplaces behind hand-carved mantels. The café's dinners are superb, though pricey—rich with French cream sauces and fanciful presentation. In the morning, the cafe becomes the breakfast room, where guests gorge on waffles, spinach and cheese omelets, and melon.

Innkeepers Max and June Bonnin are discreet and courteous, devoting their full-time energies to the inn and café. They escaped fast-paced California, where Max ran a health-care business, after learning June had lymphoma. They live barely 20 yards away from the café, in a small house they share with their daughter.

Broad highways beyond the bend give easy access to all of Memphis, including Graceland, Beale Street, downtown, and several shopping malls. △ *14 double rooms with baths. Air-conditioning, robes, in-room masseuse; pool. $135–$185; full breakfast. AE, D, DC, MC, V. No smoking.*

BRIDGEWATER HOUSE 🐚
7015 Raleigh LaGrange Rd., Cordova 38018, tel. 901/384–0080,
www.bbonline.com/tn/bridgewater/

This Greek Revival, redbrick converted schoolhouse, circa 1890, sits on what used to be a country road on the outskirts of Memphis but has since become a path through subdivisions. Here and there a thick patch of trees recalls a more peaceful era, and within one of these patches sits an unobtrusive sign, easy to miss, identifying the small bed-and-breakfast hidden behind the trees.

Inside the 2-acre lot, the city falls away. A wide slope of land nurtures old oaks and a vineyard. In the massive common room, 10-ft leaded-glass windows rise to 15-ft vaulted ceilings with hand-marbleized beams and moldings. Narcissus blooms on the coffee table. Colors of terra-cotta and sand warm the homelike couches and armchairs. The Red Oak Room contains a fin-de-siècle French bed of glossy burled maple. In the Blue Silk Room an antique trunk houses a Victorian doll collection.

Katherine and Steve Mistilis, both talkative and hospitable, pull out all the stops in pampering their guests: gourmet snacks such as miniature tarts and fine cheeses, turndown service with chocolates, terry-cloth robes, Egyptian cotton linens, toiletries, and mineral water in the rooms. During candlelight breakfasts served on china, guests have the good fortune of sampling the Mistilises' creations, like Katherine's baked grapefruit meringue with Grand Marnier sauce or stuffed French toast with Cointreau.

Both Katherine and Steve are professional chefs. Katherine teaches culinary arts, caters, and does freelance food styling. Steve, who makes jams and preserves from the grapes and apples that grow on the property, is head chef at a well-regarded country club.

It takes about 20 minutes to get downtown, to Beale Street and other attractions. Shelby Farms, one of the largest city parks in the country, is practically next door. △ *2 double rooms with baths. Air-conditioning, terry-cloth robes, turndown service with chocolates. $100; full breakfast, evening snacks and beverages. D, MC, V. No smoking.*

HIGHLAND PLACE BED & BREAKFAST 🐚
519 N. Highland Ave., Jackson 38301, tel. 901/427–1472,
www.bbonline.com/tn/highlandplace/

Downtown Jackson's North Highland Historic District is home to this circa 1911 house. The stately home sits on a small hill behind an iron gate, its busy thoroughfare leading to downtown, five blocks away. Parking is in back, off a narrow, somewhat hard-to-negotiate alley.

The 10-ft ceilings seem taller than their height, and leaded-glass windows cast rainbows over the wide entry. Solid cherry paneling warms the library, while still-operational original plantation shutters cool the adjacent breezeway. The living room has a TV/VCR, a selection of videos, and a piano guests are welcome to use. In fact, owner-innkeeper Janice Wall enforced an hour-a-day practice schedule for one long-term corporate guest who was taking Saturday lessons.

Three double rooms upstairs are tastefully—if eclectically—furnished with antiques and reproductions. The Honeymoon Suite consists of two renovated basement rooms, with corkboard ceilings and a waterfall shower for two. Its table can be used for private dinners, by prior arrangement, prepared on Janice's six-burner Viking restaurant stove.

Janice and her husband, Glenn Wall, retired from jobs with Federal Express in Memphis in 1995 to occupy the B&B they had owned for four years and operated with the help of hired innkeepers. ♠ *3 double rooms with baths, 1 suite. Air-conditioning; TV/VCR in living room. $85–$135; full breakfast. MC, V. No smoking.*

MAGNOLIA MANOR 🕊
418 N. Main St., Bolivar 38008, tel. 901/658–6700, fax 901/658–6700

Well off the beaten path, Magnolia Manor creates an imposing presence along Main Street in tiny Bolivar, a historic burg whose claim to fame is the oldest courthouse in West Tennessee. The B&B is one of two dozen or so antebellum homes in the neighborhood spared from Union torches during the Civil War; tours of the area can be arranged.

The 1849 Georgian Colonial-style house has 13-inch thick walls, made of sun-dried red brick laid by slaves. It was constructed as a two-story symmetrical rectangle, with center halls upstairs and down separating the airy rooms.

Oil portraits of the four Union generals who occupied the house hang in the entry hall. Fourteen-foot ceilings, original sage-green silk wallpaper, heavy furnishings, and a lingering, musty scent bring the Old South to life. The downstairs suite is furnished opulently with early-Victorian, museum-quality pieces: a towering rosewood headboard, a rosewood gentleman's chair, and other pieces adorned with hand-carved roses. Upstairs are two double rooms and a spacious suite, which has a walnut-and-rosewood Victorian bed, shipped upriver by steamboat from New Orleans. Its shared bath has a claw-foot tub but no shower. All bedrooms have working fireplaces.

Elaine and Jim Cox, a reserved, polite couple, opened the inn in 1984 after visiting bed-and-breakfasts on a long trip through Europe. Elaine teaches cosmetology; Jim is a semiretired hospital administrator. The Coxes stay busy with travel, decorating, cooking, and floral-arranging classes.

For history buffs, Bolivar makes for a pleasant day trip from Memphis, 90 minutes away. An hour away is Shiloh National Military Park. Also of interest are the nearby Pinson Mounds, where there is a Native American museum. Historians believe Hernando de Soto passed through the area on his epic search for the Mississippi River, a journey noted by various markers. ♠ *2 double rooms, 1 suite shares 1½ baths; 1 full suite. Air-conditioning, cable TV on sunporch. $85–$95; full breakfast. No credit cards. No smoking.*

WHITE ELEPHANT B&B INN ☜

304 Church St., Savannah 38372, tel. 901/925–6410,
www.bbonline.com/tn/elephant/

There's no overlooking the White Elephant, which is 10 mi from Shiloh National Park, on a peaceful street in tiny Savannah's historic district. White and tall, the circa 1901 Queen Anne Victorian home is lent curves by a wraparound porch, circular tower with conical roof, and Palladian attic windows in gables. Two white elephant statues pose on the walkway.

The 1½-acre lot is simply landscaped, dominated by sugar maples and oaks. Columns and pediments distinguish the porch entrance. Two front parlors on either side of the entrance hall have curved-glass bay windows; fireplaces with original tiles, mirrors, and full carved mantels; and natural woodwork. Despite the 12-ft ceilings, the parlors feel surprisingly cozy, full of newspapers, magazines, and Civil War publications. Throughout, comfortable furnishings mix Victorian antiques and reproductions.

Upstairs are three airy bedrooms, with transoms, queen-size beds, and private baths. The cinnamon-toned Poppy Room has a towering carved Victorian oak suit; the whitewashed Ivy Room's walls and fabrics have crisp ivy patterns. Both these rooms have claw-foot tubs.

Quiet, unpretentious owners Sharon and Ken Hansgen have an unusual story. The Californians discovered Savannah in 1991 while on a hunt for ancestral records. Two other discoveries—a "white elephant" for sale and nearby Shiloh—kept them here. Ken is more than just a Civil War buff. His tours of Shiloh have earned him a substantial following. He even dons a uniform for school groups.

Needless to say, the key word for nearby activities is "Shiloh." Savannah's genealogical library is of note, as are many antebellum homes, such as Cherry Mansion, yet another stop on Grant's extensive march. ⚐ *3 double rooms with baths, 1 additional room may be rented in tandem with another double and share its bath, creating a suite. Air-conditioning, TV in parlor. $75–$95; full breakfast. No credit cards. No smoking.*

ALPHABETICAL DIRECTORY

A

Adams Edgeworth Inn *261*
Adams Hilborne *262*
Alexander House *185*
Amzi Love House *186*
Anchuca *197*
Annabelle *197*
Annie's Inn *111*
Arbor House *186*
Arrowhead Inn *67*
Ashby Inn & Restaurant *8*

B

B&W Courtyards *226*
Backstrom B&B *187*
Bailey House *198*
Bailiwick Inn *8*
Balfour House *198*
Ballastone Inn *142*
Balsam Mountain Inn *75*
Barksdale-Isom House *187*
Battery Carriage House Inn *98*
Bay Breeze *178*
Bay Town Inn *215*
The Beach House, A Bed & Breakfast by the Sea *179*
Beau Fort Plantation *252*
Beaufort Inn *98*
Bed and Breakfast Inn *143*
Beechwood Inn *123*
Belle Grae Inn *44*
Belle of the Bends *199*
Belmont Inn *111*
Big Spring Inn *262*
Bleu Rock Inn *9*
Blooming Garden Inn *67*
Blue Mountain Mist Country Inn *263*
Blueberry Hill Bed and Breakfast *271*
Bluff View Inn *263*

Bois des Chênes *244*
Bonne Terre Country Inn & Cafe *279*
Brasstown Valley Resort *124*
Bridgewater House *280*
Brodie Residence *112*
Buckhorn Inn *264*
The Burn *200*
Butler Greenwood *237*

C

Camellia Cove *245*
Canemount Plantation *200*
Cape Charles House *17*
Capps Cove *165*
Caragen House *188*
Carmichael House *135*
Carpenter Place *188*
Cartney-Hunt House *189*
Catherine's Inn *55*
Cedar Crest Inn *76*
Cedar Grove *201*
Cedar Grove Plantation *201*
Cedars by the Sea *55*
Cedars Plantation *202*
Channel Bass Inn *17*
Chesterfield Inn *89*
Chigger Ridge *272*
The Chimes *227*
Chrétien Point Plantation *245*
Church Street Inn *179*
Claiborne Mansion *227*
Clifton *33*
Cloutier Townhouse and Petit Tarn *252*
Coleman House Inn *143*
Colonial Capital *26*
Cook's Cottage at Rip Van Winkle Gardens *246*
The Corners *203*

Cottage Plantation *237*
Craven Street Inn *99*
Crockett House *135*
Cuthbert House Inn *99*
Cypress Inn *90*

D

Degas House *228*
Dunlap House *124*
Dunleith *203*
Duvigneaud House *228*

E

East Bay Bed & Breakfast *100*
Edgewood *26*
1884 Paxton House *156*
1842 Inn *136*
1870 Rothschild-Pound House *156*
1837 Bed & Breakfast and Tearoom *100*
Eliza Thompson House *144*
Elter House Inn *246*
Estorge House *247*
Evergreen-Bell-Capozzi House *44*

F

Fairview *204*
Falcon Manor Bed & Breakfast *272*
Farmhouse Inn *136*
Fassifern *45*
Father Ryan House *215*
Fearrington House *68*
First Colony Inn *56*
Fleur-de-Lis *253*
Foley House *144*
Four Chimneys *145*
French Camp Bed and Breakfast Inn *204*
Fulton Lane Inn *101*

G

The Garden and the Sea Inn *18*

Garden Gate Manor *238*

The Gastonian *146*

Glen-Ella Springs Country Inn & Conference Center *125*

Gordon-Lee Mansion *125*

Governor Holmes House *205*

Grace Hall *171*

Grand Hotel *137*

Granville Queen Inn *57*

Green Oaks *216*

Green Springs Plantation *238*

Greenleaf Inn *112*

Greyfield Inn *146*

Greystone Inn *77*

Guest House Historic Inn *205*

H

Hachland Hill Dining Inn *273*

Hale Springs Inn *265*

Harmony House Inn *57*

Hayne House Bed and Breakfast *101*

Henderson Village *138*

Henry F. Shaffner House *68*

High Meadows and Mountain Sunset *34*

Highland House *189*

Highland Place Bed & Breakfast *280*

Hippensteal's Mountain View Inn *265*

The Homeplace *69*

House on Bayou Road *228*

I

Inn at Blackberry Farm *266*

Inn at Celebrity Dairy *70*

Inn at Evins Mill *273*

Inn at Folkston *147*

Inn at Gristmill Square *45*

Inn at Little Washington *9*

Inn at Meander Plantation *35*

Inn at Monticello *35*

Inn at Narrow Passage *45*

Inn at Taylor House *78*

Inn at the Pass *216*

Island Inn *58*

Island Manor House *18*

J

Jasmine House Inn *102*

Jefferson House *253*

Jekyll Island Club Hotel *147*

Jemison Inn *172*

John Rutledge House Inn *102*

Jordan Hollow Farm Inn *46*

Josephine Guest House *229*

Joshua Wilton House *46*

K

Kehoe House *148*

Kendall Manor Inn *172*

Keswick Hall *36*

King's Arms Inn *59*

Kings Courtyard Inn *103*

King's Inn at Georgetown *90*

L

La Maison de Campagne *247*

Lanaux Mansion *229*

Langdon House *59*

Lattice Inn *173*

L'Auberge Provençale *10*

Laurel Hill Plantation *103*

Levy-East House *254*

Liberty Hall *189*

Liberty Rose *27*

Lincoln, Ltd. Bed & Breakfast Mississippi Reservation Service *217*

Linden *205*

Linden-on-the-Lake *206*

Litchfield Plantation *91*

Lodge on Gorham's Bluff *166*

Lodge on Lake Lure *78*

Lodging at Little St. Simons Island *149*

Loyd Hall *254*

Lynchburg Bed & Breakfast *274*

M

Madewood Plantation *239*

Magnolia Hall *157*

Magnolia Inn *71*

Magnolia Manor *281*

Magnolia Plantation *254*

Manor House *149*

Mansfield Plantation *91*

Maple Lodge Bed & Breakfast *79*

Mast Farm Inn *79*

McKendrick-Breaux House *230*

Melhana Plantation *158*

Melrose Mansion *231*

Mentone Inn *166*

Middleton Inn *104*

Millsaps Buie House *206*

Miss Molly's Inn *19*

Mistletoe Plantation *207*

Mockingbird Inn *190*
Molly's *207*
Monmouth *208*
Mountain Memories *126*

N
Nicholson House *127*
1906 Pathway Inn *158*
North Bend Plantation *28*
Nottoway *240*

O
Oak Square *209*
Old Castillo Hotel/Place d'Evangeline *248*
Old Cowan Plantation *274*
Open Gates *150*
Orangevale Plantation *174*
The Original Romar House *180*
The Owl and the Pussycat *29*

P
Peacock Hill Country Inn *275*
Pecan Tree Inn *60*
Perrin Guest House Inn *150*
Pickett's Harbor *20*
Pilot Knob Inn *71*
Presidents' Quarters *151*
Prospect Hill *36*
Puddin Place *191*

R
Rambling Rose *191*
Raven Haven *167*
Ravenna *209*
Red Bluff Cottage *174*

Redbud Inn *209*
Rhett House Inn *104*
Richard Johnston Inn *11*
Richmond Hill Inn *80*
Richmont Inn *266*
Riverside Hills Farm *231*
Roanoke Island Inn *61*
Rosemary Hall *113*

S
Salmen-Fritchie House *232*
Sassafras Inn *191*
Sea View Inn *92*
Serenbe *127*
Serendipity, An Inn *92*
Seven Hills Inn *47*
1790 House *93*
Shadowlawn *217*
The Shadows *37*
Shellmont Bed & Breakfast *128*
Silver Thatch Inn *37*
Silversmith Inn *47*
Simply Southern *276*
Skelton House *129*
Sleepy Hollow Farm *38*
Spahn House *192*
Spinning Wheel Bed and Breakfast *20*
St. James Hotel *175*
Stained Glass Manor *210*
Statesboro Inn *151*
Sully Mansion *232*
Sycamore Hill *11*

T
T' Frère's House *248*
Tally House *217*

Tante Huppé House *255*
Tennessee Ridge Inn *267*
Tezcuco Plantation *240*
Town & Country Inn *113*
Tranquil House Inn *61*
Trillium House *48*
Twenty-Seven State Street Bed & Breakfast *105*
Two Meeting Street *105*

V
Vintage Inn *114*
Von-Bryan Inn *267*

W
War Hill Inn *29*
Waverly Inn *80*
Wayside Manor *268*
Welbourne *11*
Wensel House *210*
Wentworth Mansion *106*
Weymouth Hall *211*
White Doe Inn *62*
White Elephant B&B Inn *282*
Whitlock Inn *130*
Whitworth House *130*
Who's Inn *218*
Willcox Inn *114*
William Thomas House Bed & Breakfast *72*
Windsor Hotel *159*
Winston Place: An Antebellum Mansion *167*
Wood Avenue Inn *168*
Woodbridge Inn *131*
Woods Hole Inn *233*
Worth House *62*

Fodor's Travel Publications

Available at bookstores everywhere. For descriptions of all our titles and a key to Fodor's guidebook series, visit www.fodors.com/books

Gold Guides

U.S.

Alaska

Arizona

Boston

California

Cape Cod, Martha's Vineyard, Nantucket

The Carolinas & Georgia

Chicago

Colorado

Florida

Hawai'i

Las Vegas, Reno, Tahoe

Los Angeles

Maine, Vermont, New Hampshire

Maui & Lāna'i

Miami & the Keys

New England

New Orleans

New York City

Oregon

Pacific North Coast

Philadelphia & the Pennsylvania Dutch Country

The Rockies

San Diego

San Francisco

Santa Fe, Taos, Albuquerque

Seattle & Vancouver

The South

U.S. & British Virgin Islands

USA

Virginia & Maryland

Washington, D.C.

Foreign

Australia

Austria

The Bahamas

Belize & Guatemala

Bermuda

Canada

Cancún, Cozumel, Yucatán Peninsula

Caribbean

China

Costa Rica

Cuba

The Czech Republic & Slovakia

Denmark

Eastern & Central Europe

Europe

Florence, Tuscany & Umbria

France

Germany

Great Britain

Greece

Hong Kong

India

Ireland

Israel

Italy

Japan

London

Madrid & Barcelona

Mexico

Montréal & Québec City

Moscow, St. Petersburg, Kiev

The Netherlands, Belgium & Luxembourg

New Zealand

Norway

Nova Scotia, New Brunswick, Prince Edward Island

Paris

Portugal

Provence & the Riviera

Scandinavia

Scotland

Singapore

South Africa

South America

Southeast Asia

Spain

Sweden

Switzerland

Thailand

Toronto

Turkey

Vienna & the Danube Valley

Vietnam

Special-Interest Guides

Adventures to Imagine

Alaska Ports of Call

Ballpark Vacations

The Best Cruises

Caribbean Ports of Call

The Complete Guide to America's National Parks

Europe Ports of Call

Family Adventures

Fodor's Gay Guide to the USA

Fodor's How to Pack

Great American Learning Vacations

Great American Sports & Adventure Vacations

Great American Vacations

Great American Vacations for Travelers with Disabilities

Halliday's New Orleans Food Explorer

Healthy Escapes

Kodak Guide to Shooting Great Travel Pictures

National Parks and Seashores of the East

National Parks of the West

Nights to Imagine

Orlando Like a Pro

Rock & Roll Traveler Great Britain and Ireland

Rock & Roll Traveler USA

Sunday in San Francisco

Walt Disney World for Adults

Weekends in New York

Wendy Perrin's Secrets Every Smart Traveler Should Know

Worlds to Imagine

Fodor's Special Series

Fodor's Best Bed & Breakfasts
America
California
The Mid-Atlantic
New England
The Pacific Northwest
The South
The Southwest
The Upper Great Lakes

Compass American Guides
Alaska
Arizona
Boston
Chicago
Coastal California
Colorado
Florida
Hawai'i
Hollywood
Idaho
Las Vegas
Maine
Manhattan
Minnesota
Montana
New Mexico
New Orleans
Oregon
Pacific Northwest
San Francisco
Santa Fe
South Carolina
South Dakota
Southwest
Texas
Underwater Wonders
of the National Parks
Utah
Virginia
Washington
Wine Country
Wisconsin
Wyoming

Citypacks
Amsterdam
Atlanta
Berlin
Boston
Chicago
Florence
Hong Kong
London
Los Angeles
Miami
Montréal
New York City
Paris

Prague
Rome
San Francisco
Sydney
Tokyo
Toronto
Venice
Washington, D.C.

Exploring Guides
Australia
Boston & New England
Britain
California
Canada
Caribbean
China
Costa Rica
Cuba
Egypt
Florence & Tuscany
Florida
France
Germany
Greek Islands
Hawai'i
India
Ireland
Israel
Italy
Japan
London
Mexico
Moscow &
St. Petersburg
New York City
Paris
Portugal
Prague
Provence
Rome
San Francisco
Scotland
Singapore & Malaysia
South Africa
Spain
Thailand
Turkey
Venice
Vietnam

Flashmaps
Boston
New York
San Francisco
Washington, D.C.

Fodor's Cityguides
Boston
New York
San Francisco

Fodor's Gay Guides
Amsterdam
Los Angeles & Southern
California
New York City
Pacific Northwest
San Francisco and
the Bay Area
South Florida
USA

Karen Brown Guides
Austria
California
England B&Bs
England, Wales &
Scotland
France B&Bs
France Inns
Germany
Ireland
Italy B&Bs
Italy Inns
Portugal
Spain
Switzerland

Languages for Travelers (Cassette & Phrasebook)
French
German
Italian
Spanish

Mobil Travel Guides
America's Best
Hotels & Restaurants
Arizona
California and the West
Florida
Great Lakes
Major Cities
Mid-Atlantic
Northeast
Northwest and
Great Plains
Southeast
Southern California
Southwest and
South Central

Pocket Guides
Acapulco
Aruba
Atlanta
Barbados
Beijing
Berlin
Budapest
Dublin
Honolulu

Jamaica
London
Mexico City
New York City
Paris
Prague
Puerto Rico
Rome
San Francisco
Savannah & Charleston
Shanghai
Sydney
Washington, D.C.

Rivages Guides
Bed and Breakfasts
of Character and Charm
in France
Hotels and Country Inns
of Character and Charm
in France
Hotels and Country Inns
of Character and Charm
in Italy
Hotels of Character
and Charm in Paris
Hotels of Character
and Charm in Portugal
Hotels of Character
and Charm in Spain
Wines & Vineyards
of Character and Charm
in France

Short Escapes
Britain
France
Near New York City
New England

Fodor's Sports
Golf Digest's
Places to Play (USA)
Golf Digest's Places to
Play in the Southeast
Golf Digest's Places to
Play in the Southwest
Skiing USA
USA Today
The Complete Four Sport
Stadium Guide

Fodor's upCLOSE Guides
California
Europe
France
Great Britain
Ireland
Italy
London
Los Angeles
Mexico
New York City
Paris
San Francisco

WHEREVER YOU TRAVEL, *H*ELP IS NEVER FAR AWAY.

From planning your trip to

providing travel assistance along

the way, American Express®

Travel Service Offices are

always there to help

you do more.